THE
BUDDHA AND HIS RELIGION

SIR JOHN LUBBOCK'S HUNDRED BOOK
94

THE
BUDDHA AND HIS RELIGION

BY

J. BARTHELEMY SAINT-HILAIRE

MEMBER OF THE INSTITUTE
(ACADEMY OF MORAL AND POLITICAL SCIENCES)

TRANSLATED BY

LAURA ENSOR

GYAN

Published by

GYAN

Gyan Publishing House
5, Ansari Road
Daryaganj, New Delhi-110002
Phone: 011-47034999, 9811692060
E-mail: books@gyanbooks.com

Distribution Network
gyanbooks.com
India, USA, Canada, UK, Australia, France

ISBN : 978-81-212-2602-8 (HB)
First Published, 1895

2nd Impression 2021

Printed at: Gyan Press, Delhi.

The
Buddha and his Religion
Author: J. Barthelemy Saint-Hilaire

SIR JOHN LUBBOCK'S HUNDRED BOOKS

94

THE BUDDHA

AND HIS RELIGION

BY

J. BARTHÉLEMY SAINT-HILAIRE

MEMBER OF THE INSTITUT

(ACADEMY OF MORAL AND POLITICAL SCIENCES)

TRANSLATED BY

LAURA ENSOR

LONDON

GEORGE ROUTLEDGE AND SONS, LIMITED

BROADWAY, LUDGATE HILL

MANCHESTER AND NEW YORK

1895

CONTENTS

INTRODUCTION.

THE AUTHENTICITY OF BUDDHISM.

PART I.

THE ORIGIN OF BUDDHISM.

CHAPTER I.

CHAPTER II.

CHAPTER III.

CHAPTER IV.

CHAPTER V.

PART II.

BUDDHISM IN INDIA IN THE SEVENTH CENTURY OF THE CHRISTIAN ERA.

CHAPTER I.

CHAPTER II.

CHAPTER III.

PART III.

BUDDHISM AT THE PRESENT TIME IN CEYLON.

CHAPTER I.

CHAPTER II.

APPENDIX.

INTRODUCTION

AUTHENTICITY OF BUDDHISM.

Purpose of this work: the knowledge of Buddhism enables us to judge some of our contemporary systems. General view of the Buddhist doctrine: the absence of God and belief in annihilation. Authenticity of Buddhism. The works of B. H. Hodgson, Csoma of Körös, Turnour, E. Burnouf, and A. Rémusat. Original Sanskrit and Pāli writings; Tibetan, Mongolian, Chinese, Burmese, and Siamese translations. Piyadasi's inscriptions. Evidence of the Greek historians of Alexander's expedition. Division of the work.

In publishing this work on Buddhism, I have but one purpose in view: that of bringing out in striking contrast the beneficial truths and the greatness of our spiritualistic beliefs. Nurtured in an admirable philosophy and religion, we do not seek to know their value, and we remain ignorant of the great debt we owe to them. We are satisfied to possess them, while, at the same time, we are often indifferent and even ungrateful towards them. Although civilization is incessant in its progress, and we reap its benefits, we never think of inquiring whence come the welfare, the security, and the comparative enlightenment which civilization brings with it; while we see around us a multitude of other races, which, from the beginning of time have remained in a semi-barbarous condition, incapable of forming any tolerable social conditions or governments. I believe that the study of Buddhism.

in its more general outlines, will give us the secret of this enigma. It will show how a religion which has at the present day more adherents than any other on the surface of the globe, has contributed so little to the happiness of mankind; and we shall find in the strange and deplorable doctrines which it professes, the explanation of its powerlessness for good. By an easy retrospect we shall be able more thoroughly to appreciate the moral inheritance which has been transmitted to us since the time of Socrates and Plato, and to guard it with all the more care and gratitude.

Buddhism, greatly modified and altered, it is true, dates from the seventh century before our own era; and prevails at the present day in Kashmir, Nepaul, Tibet, Tartary, Mongolia, Japan, a great part of China, the kingdom of Anam, Burmah, and the Island of Ceylon. The Buddha was born in the year 622 B.C., and died in 543 at eighty years of age, after having taught his doctrine in Magadha (actually Behar), a region of Central India, in the neighbourhood of Benāres, on the right bank of the Ganges. Buddhism was an attempt to reform the religion of Brahma, in the midst of which it arose, and by which it was finally expelled from India after centuries of somewhat contemptuous tolerance. But the doctrines which had but momentarily triumphed in the countries that had seen their birth, spread over the neighbouring countries, with a success that still continues and seems likely to last.

To reduce Buddhism to its essential elements, the following is a short summary of its aims, philosophical and religious.

Taking but a one-sided view of man's condition upon earth, looking chiefly at his miseries and sufferings, the Buddha does not try to revert to his origin, and to derive it from a higher source.

His beliefs carry him no further than to suppose that the

present life is a continuation of past existences, of which man is now bearing the fatal penalty. He believes in transmigration: herein lies his first dogma and his first error. It is necessary then that man should at any cost be delivered from the cycle of perpetual births to which he is condemned; and the Buddha takes upon himself to point out the path which leads to deliverance and frees him from this terrible bondage. Filled with mercy and compassion, he gives to mankind that he came to redeem, a moral code, and he promises eternal salvation to those who follow it. What then is eternal salvation, according to the Buddhist faith? and how can man be delivered from the law of transmigration? Only in one way—by attaining Nirvāna, that is annihilation.

When man, thanks to the practice of the austerities and virtues that the Buddha taught, has once reached annihilation, he is well assured that he will never, under any form, be reborn into the odious cycle of successive existences; and when all the elements of which he is composed, both material and spiritual, are completely destroyed, he need no longer fear transmigration; and the blind fatality which rules all things in the universe has power over him no more.

This seems indeed a hideous system; but it is a perfectly consistent one. In the whole of Buddhism, from beginning to end, there is not a trace of the idea of God. Man, completely isolated, is thrown upon his own resources. Cast into a world he does not understand, without Providence and without support, staggering under the weight of human infirmity, he has but one hope—that of escaping from his earthly suffering. Wandering in utter darkness, he yet does not seek for light by aspirations towards something higher. His horizon limited to what his senses bear witness, and his knowledge of self as limited and inaccurate as the phenomena amid which he drags out his existence, his intelligence is not sufficiently developed to attain the source from which he himself, as well as the world, has emanated.

Begun from nothing, it is natural that he should end in nothingness, and Buddhism must inevitably lead to this conclusion—a conclusion so terrible for us, but so consoling for the Buddhist. Born without God, living without God, what wonder that he should not find God after death?—that he returns willingly to the nothingness whence he came, which is the only refuge that he knows?

Such, in a few words, is Buddhism, and this is the system of faith which it presents, with the usual accompaniments of legend and superstition.

The religion of the Buddha, however irrational it may be in principle, is not without a certain grandeur, and, moreover, has not been without results. In India, from whence it sprang, it took no root. But, strange as it may seem, this doctrine, which seems calculated to shock the most natural and the strongest instincts of humanity, led to real progress in the races that accepted it; and, in submitting to it, they became less ignorant and less degraded. This is hardly, perhaps, a sufficient apology for Buddhism; but we are compelled to render it justice, and it contains so much that is erroneous, that it may well be credited with this secondary merit, which legitimately belongs to it.

I must unhesitatingly add, that with the sole exception of the Christ, there does not exist among all the founders of religions a purer and more touching figure than that of the Buddha. In his pure and spotless life he acts up to his convictions; and if the theory he propounds is false, the personal example which he gives is irreproachable. He is the perfect type of all the virtues he extols; his self-abnegation, his charity, his unalterable mildness are unfailing; at the age of twenty-nine he leaves his father's court to become a religious mendicant; he prepares himself to preach his doctrine during six years of retreat and meditation; he propagates it by the sole power of his word and persuasion for more than half a century; and when he dies in the arms of his disciples it is with the serenity of a sage who has practised good all his life and who is certain that he has found truth. The nations who have received his faith have not worshipped him as a God, for the idea of a God was as foreign to them as it was to him. But they have made of the Buddha an ideal they have striven to imitate; and Buddhism has formed, as we shall show, some great spirits well worthy to figure among those who are the most revered and admired by mankind.

Sad as it may be, it is a study worth making, and I shall not regret my task if I can attain the purpose I have set myself. The nobler sides of Buddhism may delude us, if we remain satisfied with imperfect information; those I shall set forth will, I believe, be sufficient to prevent any serious-minded reader from falling into such errors.

This work may possibly possess another advantage, for I regret to say it is to a certain degree opportune. For some time past the doctrines which form the basis of Buddhism have found favour amongst us, a favour of which they are most unworthy. We see systems arise in which metempsychosis and transmigration are lauded, and, after the manner of the Buddha, the world and mankind are explained without any reference to Providence or God; systems in which man is denied all hope of an immortal life, in which the immortality of the soul is replaced by the immortality of good works, and God is dethroned by man—the only being, it is averred, through whom the Infinite develops consciousness of itself. Sometimes it is in the name of science, sometimes in that of history or philology, or even metaphysics, that these theories are propounded—theories which are neither novel nor original, and which are calculated to be extremely hurtful to any weak or vacillating mind. This is not the place to examine these theories, and their authors are at once too sincere and too learned for them to be summarily discussed and condemned. But it is as well that they should be warned by the example of (Buddhism, of which hitherto so little has been known, what is the fate of man when he relies only on self; and when his meditations, led astray by a pride of which he is often unconscious, lead him to the abyss in which the Buddha has lost himself.)

Moreover, I am well aware of the great differences that exist: I do not indiscriminately confound their systems with Buddhism, although I condemn them also. I am ready to recognize that their merits have some value; but philosophical systems must always be judged by their conclusions, whatever road may have been pursued to attain them; and these conclusions, although they may have been reached by different paths, do not thereby become any the better. It is now two thousand five hundred years since the Buddha taught his doctrine: he proclaimed and practised it with an energy that has never been equalled nor surpassed; he displayed an ingenuous dauntlessness that will never be exceeded; and it is improbable that any of the systems of the present day will ever exercise such a powerful influence over the human mind. It might, however, be somewhat useful for the authors of these systems to cast a glance on the theory and destiny of Buddhism. It is not philosophy in the sense we give to that great word; neither is it religion as understood by ancient Paganism, or Christianity, or Mohammedanism; but it is something of all this, added to a perfectly independent doctrine which sees only man in the universe, and stubbornly refuses to see anything but man, who is confounded with the whole of Nature. Hence the aberrations and errors of Buddhism, which might act as a warning to us if only we had wisdom to understand it.

Unfortunately we seldom learn by our own mistakes, and still more rarely do we profit by those of others.

Now as the accusations I make against Buddhism are serious, it may be as well to set forth in order how the sources of the Buddhist religion have been discovered, and on what authentic basis our knowledge of the subject is founded.

It is hardly thirty years[1] since it has been properly studied, but circumstances have so favoured research, that at the present day our knowledge of the origins of Buddhism is more thorough than that of most religions, including our own. We are acquainted with the life of the Buddha down to the most trifling details, and we possess all the canonical writings which contain his doctrine, as collected and settled by the three successive councils. These books, primarily written in Sanskrit, or in a dialect of Sanskrit, have been translated into the ordinary language of all the races amongst whom the Buddhist faith has spread: Singalese, Tibetan, Tartar, Mongolian, Chinese, Japanese, Burman, &c. We possess these translations, and they are a perfectly reliable check on the original authorities, several of which have already been reproduced in different languages.

And besides these proofs there is other evidence no less unimpeachable: monuments of all kinds, the ruins of which still lie scattered all over India, numerous and conclusive inscriptions, journeyings of pious pilgrims who have at different periods visited the places made sacred by the memory of the Buddha. In one word, nothing is lacking at the present day to confirm our opinion; fresh discoveries may be made, but they will not change those which we already possess, and to which we owe so many curious revelations.

In order that no doubt may exist on this most important

[1] This work was published in 1860.

point, I will give a rapid sketch of the unprecedented success of these investigations, and recall once more the names of those whose labours have done so much to enlighten us, and who in the course of a few years have taught us much more about Buddhism than was known to William Jones or Colebrooke.

The earliest and most important witness is B. H. Hodgson, who in 1821 was appointed by the East India Company Political Resident in Nepaul. Hodgson soon heard that a number of books, supposed to contain the canonical laws of the Buddha, were piously preserved in the Buddhist monasteries of that country. The books were written in Sanskrit. Hodgson succeeded in obtaining a list of them through an old Buddhist priest of Pathan with whom he was acquainted, and by degrees he collected the books themselves. He found it easier to obtain them translated into the Tibetan language; for books are as plentiful in Tibet as in our own country, multiplied as they are by printing on wood, a process brought to Tibet by the Chinese, and which is now in general use there. The Sanskrit volumes, copies of which were handed over to Hodgson, had been, such was the tradition, imported into Nepaul in the second century of the Christian era, and were only understood by the priests. They had been brought from Magadha, the opposite side of the Ganges; and five or six centuries later, had passed from Nepaul into Tibet, where they were translated at the time Tibet adopted the Buddhist faith. B. H. Hodgson was able to announce this great discovery to the learned societies in 1824 and 1825. But he did more than this: he offered the Royal Asiatic Society of Bengal sixty Buddhist volumes in Sanskrit and two hundred and fifty in Tibetan. A few years later, he displayed the same liberality towards the Royal Asiatic Society of London and the Asiatic Society of Paris. He either gave them the manuscripts and printed matter he had collected, or had transcriptions made for them of the writings they desired. Thanks to him the Asiatic Society of Paris became the possessor of eighty-eight Buddhist works in Sanskrit, which it would have been unable to procure had it not been for the generosity and kindly energy of the English Resident at Kathmandu[1]. These labours and discoveries deserve the highest praise, and the name of B. H. Hodgson ought always to be remembered with gratitude.

It is to him we owe the original Sanskrit writings, which have since been consulted and translated by illustrious philologists, and it is he who first discovered the existence of the Tibetan translations.

Almost at the same time, Csoma, a young Hungarian doctor from Körös in Transylvania, had started on labours that were destined to prove hardly less interesting and fruitful than those of B. H. Hodgson.

Csoma, animated by an heroic enthusiasm which recalls that of Anquetil-Duperron, left Hungary, his native land, and, armed only with an indomitable courage, penetrated into Tibet, where, after enduring privations and sufferings that would have daunted any other man, he learned the language of the country, which no European before him had mastered, and thus he was able to read the two great works of Tibetan literature, called the *Kahgyur* and the *Bstangyur*. Now these two vast encyclopedias, the first composed of a hundred, and the second of two hundred and twenty-five volumes, printed in 1731 at the monastery of Snārthong in Tibet, were nothing else than a lengthy translation of books brought from India, referring, for the most part, to the Buddhist literature. Csoma, under the auspices of H. H. Wilson, the distinguished Indian linguist, and the Asiatic Society of

[1] In 1860 B. H. Hodgson again made a valuable present of Buddhist documents to the French Institute.

Calcutta, gave a full analysis of these two encyclopedias; and they were found to contain an exact reproduction of most of the Sanskrit books B. H. Hodgson had discovered in Nèpaul. Csoma died young, at the very outset of his labours, for the sake of which he had exhausted his strength; but he died consoled, doubtless, by the publications which, thanks to him, have enriched the 'Asiatic Researches,' and which will remain to perpetuate his memory.

About the time that B. H. Hodgson and Csoma were making their discoveries, L. J. Schmidt, of the Academy of St. Petersburg (1829), ascertained that the greater part of the Buddhist works translated from Sanskrit into Tibetan had also been translated from Tibetan into Mongol, and this under similar conditions. The Buddhist faith had been brought, with the books that contained its records, from Tibet into Mongolia, just as it had travelled from Nepaul to Tibet, and from the Indian Magadha into Nepaul. This happily confirmed all Hodgson's information, but it was not the only or the most important testimony to it.

While original Sanskrit works were being found in the north of India, George Turnour, whose name ought to be placed side by side with that of Hodgson, found in the south of the Peninsula, in Ceylon, an almost identical transcript of the canonical books. It is known that Buddhism had penetrated to Ceylon three centuries before the Christian era. George Turnour, who was a civil servant in Ceylon, had been able to devote some of his leisure time to literary research. He discovered that the Sinhalese priests possessed an exact and complete collection of Buddhist works in *Pāli*, a Sanskrit dialect, and that this collection had been taken over to Ceylon during the reign of an Indian king, who professed the Buddhist faith, in the year 316 B.C. The seventeen Sinhalese *Pāli* books reproduced almost identically the more important works of Magadha and Nepaul; they also contained the whole doctrine and life of the Buddha; and in the same manner that in the north the Sanskrit version in Magadha served as text for the Tibetan translations, so in the south the *Pāli* version in Ceylon served as text for the Burmese and Siamese translations; the island of Ceylon always having been in close religious communication with Siam and Burmah.

But there was again another source of information in Ceylon. Besides the sacred books, the priests had drawn up chronicles, in which they had noted down from age to age, up to the end of the last century, all the principal facts of their religion and their history. Turnour obtained these Sinhalese annals, and published the greater part of a valuable work, the *Mahāvansa*, as well as an analysis of several others. These historical books carry their narration back to the conversion of Ceylon to Buddhism, and retrace with the minutest details the whole life of the Buddha, just as tradition and religious writings had preserved them. The part of the *Mahāvansa* given by Turnour was composed in the fifth century of our era, by the aid of much more ancient writings which the author corrected and made use of.

The *Pāli* sacred books of Ceylon and the historical compilations must therefore rank among the most authentic of Buddhist documents.

But we ought to rank China as high and even higher than Nepaul, Tibet, Mongolia, Ceylon, Burmah, and Siam. The Chinese annals, which are kept with an exactitude which no nation in the world has equalled, testify that Buddhism was introduced into China 217 B.C. by some Indian monks. From the year 61 B.C. Buddhism became, under the Emperor Ming-Ti, the state religion of the Empire, where it seemed to satisfy all the religious requirements of that strange and little known people. It was also towards the end of the first century A.D. that the official translation of the Sanskrit

Buddhist books into Chinese was made. One of the most noted, the *Lalita-vistāra*, a kind of biography of the Buddha, has been translated four times into Chinese; the first of these translations dating from the year 76 A.D., and the last as much as eight centuries later. A large number of Buddhist works were thus reproduced from Sanskrit into Chinese; a learned man, M. Stanislas Julien, has given us the titles of about 1000 books, taken from the catalogues drawn up by order of the Government of the Celestial Empire.

As Buddhism still flourishes in that country, the translations of the canonical books, and of the most celebrated works—biographies of venerated monks, dictionaries, and vocabularies—have been diligently continued without interruption down to the present day. In China Buddhist literature fills the libraries with an almost incalculable number of volumes.

Another special source of information are the journeys of the Chinese pilgrims, who at different periods travelled to India to collect the sacred writings and bring them back to China, or to visit the places sanctified in former days by the presence of the Buddha. Two of these narratives, that of Fa-Hian and that of Hiouen-Thsang, have been translated into French by Abel Rémusat and Stanislas Julien, who deserve the highest praise for their studies in Buddhism.

But I will now pass to the evidence we gather in India itself, which reaches us in a more direct way, and is more ancient than that of the other countries I have mentioned. Within the last twenty-five years a most important discovery has been made in Central India of several inscriptions engraved on rocks, pillars, or stones. It was virtually the first time that India had ever furnished to European curiosity any monuments of this kind, of which it had generally been supposed to be destitute. Mr. James Prinsep, one of the secretaries of the Asiatic Society of Bengal, deciphered these inscriptions with a sagacity and erudition that have made him famous, although he likewise died young, before he had accomplished his career.

These inscriptions were in the dialect of the province of Magadha, where, according to all traditions, Buddhism had its origin. They recorded the edicts of a king called Piyadasi, which enjoined on all his subjects morality, justice, and tolerance of the new belief. Shortly after Mr. James Prinsep's explanations, Turnour, already well versed in the study of the *Pāli* monuments in Ceylon, showed that the King Piyadasi was identical with Aṣoka, the King of Magadha, who played a great part in the earlier centuries of Buddhist history, and whose conversion is related in the *Mahāvansa.* Another Sinhalese work—the *Dīpavansa*—quoted by Turnour, places the accession of Aṣoka 218 years after the death of Ṣākya-muni, that is about the year 325 B.C., in the days of Alexander the Great.

Later on similar discoveries confirmed these dates, and in three places: at Girnar in Guzerāt, at Dhauli in Orissa, and at Kapur da Giri (not to mention Delhi, Allahabad, Radhia, Mathiah, &c.), identical reproductions have been found of the religious edicts of Piyadasi, whose dominion extended over the whole of India. The dialects differ according to the provinces, but they are the same edicts, and the differences in expression are insignificant. Moreover, we know that one of the three formal councils which settled the rules of the Order and the doctrines of the Buddhist faith was held in the reign of Aṣoka, under his all-powerful protection. In 1840 Captain Burt discovered on a mountain near Babra, between Delhi and Jayapura, an inscription of this same King Piyadasi, which seems absolutely conclusive. This inscription, written in the same language, is, according to Burnouf, a kind of epistle addressed by the King Piyadasi to the Buddhist monks assembled together in Magadha. The king points out to the Council the principal questions on which they must deliberate, the spirit which should guide them, and the results they must strive to attain. And a detail that gives particular value to the inscription at Babra is the fact that the name of the blessed Buddha, whose faith Aṣoka upheld, is repeated several times, whereas it does not exist in the other inscriptions.

The grave importance of this inscription, with regard to the history of Buddhism and of India itself, has been accepted with all its consequences by Messrs. Prinsep, Turnour, Lassen, Burnouf, Weber, and Max Müller, and it would be idle to contest the authority of such competent judges. It appears therefore impossible to doubt that if Piyadasi was not the Aṣoka of Magadha, as Mr. H. H. Wilson contends, he was certainly a Buddhist king, who imposed Ṣākya-muni's doctrine on his subjects towards the end of the fourth century B.C.

We do not require any further evidence, and I would leave the Indian authorities and turn to the Greek authorities, if I did not wish to prove by a final example how the constant discoveries made in India confirm the great results I have indicated. On the walls of the fine grottoes hollowed out in a granite rock, near Buddha-Gāyā, in Magadha, inscriptions have been found in the same dialect as the larger inscriptions at Girnar and Dhauli, relating that these grottoes were intended for a habitation and retreat for the Buddhist mendicants, by order of the King Daṣaratha, second in succession to Aṣoka, and by Piyadasi himself, who is mentioned in several of the inscriptions, of which each contains but three or four lines. These inscriptions cannot be of later date than the year 226 B.C., and although they are far less important than the greater edicts of which I have just spoken, it will be seen that they recall and confirm them in a striking manner.

I shall quote only one of the facts stated by the companions of Alexander or their successors, which will show that the Greeks knew of the existence of the Buddhists, as they had known of that of the Brahmans. Nearchus and Aristobulus, who followed and survived Alexander, only mention the latter, and nothing demonstrates that they had heard of the former. Megasthenes, however, who about thirty years after penetrated as far as Pātaliputra, the Palibothra of the Greeks, to the court of Chandragupta, certainly meant to designate the Buddhists under the name of Sarmans or Garmans; he mentions them as a sect of philosophers opposed to the Brahmans, abstaining from wine, and living in the strictest celibacy. By his description and the spelling of the word, which is but little altered, we recognize the Buddhists, who called themselves more especially by the name of Sramans or ascetics. Another characteristic mentioned by Megasthenes is that 'the Sarmans,' he says, 'have with them women, believers in the same philosophy, and who lead the same life of celibacy.' He further adds that 'these philosophers live frugally on food which none refuse to give them.' This description applies most clearly to the way of life of the Buddhists, which was never practised by the Brahmans. Mendicancy and celibacy were the two conditions rigidly imposed by the Buddha on his disciples; and if Megasthenes is the only Greek historian of that period who distinctly alludes to the Buddhists, it is most probably because he was the only one who had seen any. In that part of the Panjāb where the Macedonian expedition penetrated, Buddhism had not yet spread, whereas it flourished in the country of which Pātaliputra was the capital, and where the third Council was held. Onesicritus, Nearchus, and Aristobulus did not find any Buddhists on the banks of the Indus and the Hyphasis; but Megasthenes must have met with many on the banks of the Ganges. We must also recognize as Buddhists the

Pramnes (a corruption of the word Sarmans), mentioned by Strabo as adversaries of the Brahmans, whom they derided and treated as charlatans.

I will add one last proof derived from the Greeks. The name of the Buddha is quoted for the first time by St. Clement of Alexandria[1], that is, in the third century A.D.; and as St. Clement drew from Megasthenes all he says about Indian philosophers, it is probable that he borrowed also from him the name of the reformer, for the ambassador of Seleucus-Nicator would have often heard it mentioned in the course of his journey, and in a city which from an early period has been the centre of reform.

It will thus be seen that the most authentic documents, Greek, Indian, Chinese, and others, agree in testifying in the most unimpeachable manner that Buddhism existed in India before Alexander's expedition. We can therefore accept the date of the Buddha's death that we borrow from the Sinhalese; and when we treat of the Buddhist doctrine we may feel certain that its teaching was really addressed to the Indian populations six centuries B.C.; that it strove to convert them to higher beliefs, and to overthrow the ancient teaching of the Vedas, henceforth considered insufficient to lead man in the right way of salvation.

Two of the sacred books containing this teaching have already been translated into French. One is the *Lotus of the Good Law* (*Saddharma-pundarīka*), by Eugène Burnouf, who, being the first Frenchman who perused the manuscripts sent to Paris by Mr. B. H. Hodgson, drew from it his admirable *Introduction à l'histoire du Bouddhisme Indien*. The other Buddhist Sūtra is the *Lalita-vistāra*, to which I have just alluded, and of which M. Ph. Ed. Foucaux has published a translation into French from a translation of this work into Tibetan, collated with the original Sanskrit.

[1] Stromates, i. p. 305, Sylburge's edition.

Lastly the Rev. Spence Hardy, a Wesleyan missionary, who resided twenty years in Ceylon, published in 1869 his *Manual of Buddhism*, based on various Ceylonese books.

It will be seen that we possess a great wealth of documents on the life and teaching of the Buddha. From all these sources the following work has been drawn, and every fact will be proved from competent authorities.

I shall take Buddhism at the three different periods of its existence. Beginning with its first appearance, I shall relate the life and legend of the Buddha, as they are told in the canonical works adopted by the three Councils, and I shall examine the doctrine taught, and judge it according to its merits and its defects.

Then I shall take up Buddhism as it existed in India twelve hundred years after the death of the Buddha, and as it is set forth in the *Travels* and *Memoirs* of Hiouen-Thsang, a poor Chinese monk, whose journeyings through the peninsula lasted sixteen years, from the year 629 to 645 A. D., and who carried back to China, after this wonderful pilgrimage, 657 volumes of Buddhist writings.

Lastly I shall study Buddhism in Ceylon, as it still exists under English rule.

There will therefore be about an equal lapse of time between these three epochs of the Buddhist religion. It is not a history of Buddhism that I presume to write. As I have shown, a general history of Buddhism would include a much wider range. From India and Ceylon we should have to follow it all over Asia, and that for a period of twenty-five centuries. Later on, no doubt, it will be possible to carry out such a stupendous undertaking, when learned and skilful labours have furnished a quantity of material which we still lack. At the present day, however, we can, without running the risk of premature enterprise, pass in review the most salient points of this vast subject. I have already noted them in giving to the *Journal des Savants* a summary of most of the works I refer to, and I shall republish in this volume the greater part of the articles I inserted in that important publication. It seems to me that by putting them together and giving them a less severe form, they might become interesting to readers whom a greater display of learning might alarm.

But I repeat, this study of Buddhism is principally a philosophical one. The Buddhist system, like many of the systems of the present day, is deficient in the knowledge of mankind. On all sides, it is an incomplete psychology that has always been the cause of so much error. It is easy to understand that in India, several centuries before the Christian era, this faulty method was but a natural continuation of all the fruitless efforts which had been made by former philosophers. In Greece, at about the same period, Socrates inaugurated the true knowledge of the human soul, whereas Indian philosophers took a mistaken view without hope of ever attaining truth, which was unfitted for their times and for their country. On the course that Indian philosophers pursued, two ways only were open, each as unfortunate as the other: either to stand still for ever in the immobility of Brahmanism, or to pursue with Buddhism the desperate course of self-ignoring atheism and of utter nihilism. The Buddha stopped at nothing, and his blind courage is one of the most striking qualities of his great spirit. In the present day, however, and after the teaching of Descartes, it seems difficult to understand and impossible to excuse such errors and such weaknesses. Philosophy has not changed its ancient precept. 'Know thyself' is its immortal motto. Its strength and its glory is to put this motto into practice; its weakness is to forget it. Whoever does not choose to be beguiled by empty words and hypotheses, as sterile as they are dangerous, must acknowledge that philosophy has one solid foundation, the observation of the workings of the human soul. If psychology does not form its basis, it runs a serious risk of becoming but a tissue of dreams,—dreams that will be bright or gloomy according to the imagination that gives them birth. The only method worthy of science and of our present time is to begin the study of man by the light of conscience and to rise upwards through man to the knowledge of the universe and of God. Every system that neglects to take this warrant, and to acquire this title to the confidence it claims, is ill prepared for seeking after truth, and must not be surprised if it falls into depths of error.

Here two excesses are equally to be feared: either exalting man beyond all measure as a God upon earth, or degrading him into a mere brute, a worshipper and victim of nihilism; for if the systems of the present day were likely to become a religion such as Buddhism, their disastrous consequences would soon show that they are equally unfitted to benefit social progress. In the teaching of the Buddha, and in the wretched governments it has contributed to form, there is no place for liberty or for God. The true idea ot humanity being absent, all liberty has perished with it, in practice as well as in theory; and the human image being defaced, man is unable to reassert himself or obtain the respect due to him. Many virtuous souls and noble hearts may yet exist amongst the Buddhists, but no man is free, and despotism is the infallible result of a doctrine that undertakes to save man at the cost of annihilation. It has only forged new fetters for him here below. I greatly fear that the present systems will serve the cause of liberty no better by going to the opposite extreme. Man, such as they conceive him, is not more real than as he is conceived by Buddhism. Though he would fain claim divinity, he is not therefore more divine, and his rights are none the more secure for being assimilated to those of a god. Liberty cannot exist in human societies unless it be first received and enshrined in the soul of man; it is of spiritual birth. This is a consideration that should be particularly noted by innovators. Asia can, as it appears, dispense with liberty, but to us liberty is life itself, and philosophers must beware of furnishing arguments, even unintentionally, to those who contend against liberty, and would be glad to destroy it by invoking in defence of their arguments what they believe to be the teachings of science. But leaving these preliminary reflections, and having sufficiently indicated the object I have in view, I will turn to the real subject of the book and to the life of the Buddha.

PART I

THE ORIGIN OF BUDDHISM.

CHAPTER I.

Birth of the Buddha; his education; his marriage; he chooses his wife Gopā. The Buddha's meditations; his vocation encouraged by the gods; the four visions; the young prince's determination; resistance of his father and family; he flies from Kapilavastu. His studies at Vaiṣāli and Rājagriha; his five companions; he renounces the world. His retreat of six years at Uruvela; his austerities and ecstasies; the attainment of Buddha-hood; Bodhimanda and Bodhidruma; Vajrāsanam. The Buddha leaves his retreat; he goes to Benāres to 'turn the wheel of the Law'; his teaching; his sojourn in Magadha and in Kosala; Bimbisāra, Ajātaṣatru, Prasenajit, Anātha Piṇḍika. The Buddha's interview with his father; his dissensions with the Brahmans; his triumph; popular enthusiasm. Death of the Buddha at eighty years of age at Kusi-nagara.

(TOWARDS the end of the seventh century B.C., in the city of Kapilavastu, the capital of a small kingdom of the same name situated in Central India at the foot of the mountains of Nepaul, north of the present kingdom of Oudh[1], the Buddha was born. His father Suddhodana, of the tribe of the Ṣākyas, a descendant of the great solar race of the Gautamides, ruled over the

[1] Towards the end of the fourth century of our era, Fa-Hian, a Chinese pilgrim, found Kapilavastu in ruins; see Rémusat, *Foe Koue Ki*, p. 198. Two centuries later, about the year 632 of the Christian era, Hiouen-Thsang also visited these ruins. He describes them as very considerable, the walls of the king's palace and garden, which were still apparent, being three miles in circumference; see *Life of Hiouen-Thsang* and *Memoirs of Hiouen-Thsang* by Julien. Among the ruins Hiouen-Thsang was shown traces of the bedroom of the Buddha's mother, and of the young prince's study.

country. His mother, Māyā Devi, was the daughter of the King Suprabuddha, and her beauty was so transcendent that the name of Māyā, or the Vision, had been given to her, her form seeming to be—as is related in the *Lalita-vistāra*—the creation of some enchanting dream. Māyā Devi's virtues and talents surpassed even her excessive beauty, for she was endowed with the highest and choicest gifts of intelligence and piety. Suddhodana was worthy of his consort, and 'King of the Law, he ruled according to the Law. No other prince among the Ṣākyas was more honoured and respected by all classes of his subjects, from his councillors and courtiers, down to the householders and merchants.'

Such was the noble family from which the Liberator was to arise. He thus belonged to the Kshatriya or warrior caste, and when he eventually embraced a religious life, he was called, in honour of his illustrious origin, Ṣākya-muni, that is to say the Ṣākya-sage, or the Sramana Gautama, the Gautamide ascetic. His father gave him the name of Siddhārtha or Sarvārthasiddha, and he retained this name as long as he lived as a Royal Prince (Kumārārāja). Later on he exchanged it for more glorious names.

His mother, the queen, had retired about the time of her expected delivery to a pleasure garden, called after her grandmother, the garden of Lumbini[1], and there overtaken by the pangs of childbirth, under the shade of a satin-tree she gave birth to Siddhārtha on the third day of the month of Utāraṣādha, or, according to another reckoning, the fifteenth day of the month of Vesākha. But weakened, no doubt, by the pious austerities she had practised during her pregnancy, perhaps also filled with anxiety on account of the predictions the Brahmans had uttered about the son who was to be born

[1] The Lumbini park was about twenty-four miles north-east of Kapilavastu. Hiouen-Thsang reverently visited it. See his *Memoirs*, vol. i. p. 322.

of her, Māyā Devi died seven days after his birth 'that she might not' says the legend 'have her heart broken, by seeing her son leave her to become a holy man, and to wander in beggary and in want.' The orphan child was confided to the care of his mother's sister, Prajāpatī Gotamī, another of his father's wives, who at a later period, in the days of the Buddha's teaching, became one of his most fervent adherents.

The child was as beautiful as his mother, and the Brahman Asita, whose duty it was in conformity with the ancient custom to present him in the temple of the gods, averred that he found on him the thirty-two principal signs, and the eighty secondary marks by which, according to popular belief in India, a great man may be recognized. Whatever may have been the truth of these prognostics Siddhārtha quickly justified the high repute in which he was held. When he was sent to the 'writing school' he displayed more talent even than his masters, and one of them, Visvamitra, under whose care he was more especially placed, soon declared that he had nothing more to teach him. In the midst of companions of his own age, the child took no part in their games; he seemed even then absorbed in higher thoughts; often did he remain aloof to meditate and one day when he had gone with his comrades to visit 'the agricultural village,' he wandered away alone in a great wood, where he remained for many hours while no one knew what had become of him. The king, his father, at length filled with anxiety, went in person to seek him in the forest, and found him there, under the shade of a djambu tree, plunged in deep meditation.

Now the time drew near, when the young prince should be married. The chief elders of the Sākyas remembered the Brahman's predictions, for they had foretold that Siddhārtha would very probably renounce the crown in order to become an ascetic. They therefore implored the king to marry his son as soon as possible, so as to assure the future of his race.

They hoped to bind the young man to the throne by an early marriage. The king, however, who doubtless was aware of the prince's intentions, did not dare to speak to him himself; he desired the elders to confer with him, and to make to him the proposal they deemed so important. Siddhārtha, who dreaded 'the evils of desire, more to be feared than poison, fire or sword,' desired to have seven days given him for reflection. After having well considered, feeling certain that marriage, having been already accepted by many sages, would neither deprive him of the calm necessary for reflection, nor of the leisure for meditation, he yielded to the request made to him, laying down, however, one condition: 'That the wife chosen for him was not to be a low-minded or immodest woman; otherwise it mattered little to him what might be her caste, he would take her from among the Veṣyas and the Sūdras, as willingly as from among the Brahman women and the Kshatriyas, if so be that she was endowed with the qualities which he required in his consort.' He then gave the elders, to guide them in their choice, a complete list which he had prepared of the qualities he desired his bride to possess.

The purohita or domestic priest of king Suddhodana was therefore instructed to go through all the houses at Kapilavastu, and after viewing the young maidens of every house, to choose her who best fulfilled the requirements of the prince, 'whose heart, undazzled by rank or birth took pleasure only in true virtue and morality.' The list of the virtues demanded was successively presented to a multitude of young maidens of all ranks and classes, none however seemed to fulfil the requirements. At last one of them told the priest that she possessed all the qualities demanded by the prince, and that if he would accept her, she would be his wife. Summoned to appear before the prince with several other beautiful girls of her own age, she was singled out by him, and the king gave his consent to the marriage. But the maiden's father Daṇḍāpāṇī, of the Ṣākya tribe, was not so easily satisfied, and as the young prince was supposed to be given up to indolence and effeminacy, he demanded that before bestowing on him his daughter, the beautiful Gopā, he should give proofs of the talents of all kinds, which he possessed. 'The noble youth,' said Daṇḍāpāṇī sternly, 'has lived in idleness within the palace, and it is a law of our race only to give our daughters to men skilled in the arts, never to those unacquainted with them. This youth has never practised fencing, nor boxing, nor bending a bow, neither does he know the rules of fighting; how can I bestow my daughter on one who is not skilful in these exercises?'

The noble Siddhārtha was therefore obliged, prince though he was, to display the talents his modesty had hitherto concealed. Five hundred of the most distinguished young Ṣākyas were assembled, and the beautiful Gopā was promised to the victor. The Royal prince easily proved himself superior to his rivals. But the contest was at first directed to different arts from those proposed by Daṇḍāpāṇī. Siddhārtha showed himself more skilful than his competitors or even his judges, in the art of writing, in arithmetic, in grammar, in syllogism, in the knowledge of the Vedas, of the philosophic systems, of ethics, &c. Then passing from mental to bodily exercises, he vanquished all his companions, in leaping, swimming, running, bending the bow, and a number of other games, in which he displayed as much strength as skill. Among his adversaries were his two cousins; Ānanda, who afterwards became one of his most faithful disciples, and Dewadatta, who, deeply irritated by his defeat, became from that day his implacable enemy. The beautiful Gopā was the reward of Siddhārtha's victory, and the young girl who had considered herself worthy of a king, was declared the first of his wives. From that moment she insisted, notwithstanding the opposition of her family, on never veiling her face in their presence, nor in that of the palace attendants. 'Those who are virtuous,' she said, 'whether sitting, standing or walking, are always fair to look upon. A precious, sparkling diamond glitters more brilliantly from the top of a banner. Women who control their thoughts and subdue their senses, are satisfied with their husbands, and never thinking of any other man, can show themselves unveiled, like the sun and moon. The supreme and magnanimous Rishi, as well as all the other gods, knows my thoughts, my behaviour, my discretion, and my modesty. Why therefore should I veil my face?'

Notwithstanding the happiness of a union contracted under such auspices, it had no power to change the designs Siddhārtha had already formed. In his splendid palace and surrounded by every luxury, in the midst even of the festivities and concerts that were perpetually going on, the young prince never relinquished the idea of his holy enterprise; and in the heroism and bitterness of his heart, he would often say,—'The three worlds, that of God, of the Asekhas, and of men, are consumed by the sufferings of disease and old age, they are devoured by the fire of death, and deprived of all guidance. The life of a human being is like a flash of lightning in the sky; as the torrent rushes down a mountain, so life flows on with an irresistible rapidity. By the fact of existence, by desire, and by ignorance, the creatures in the abode of men and gods are on the road to three evils. The ignorant but turn round and round, even as the potter's wheel turns on its axis. The nature of desire, ever attended by fear and misery, is the root of sorrow. It is more to be dreaded than the sharp edge of a sword or the leaf of a poisonous tree. Like a reflected image, an echo, a shimmer, or the dizziness of a dance, like a dream, an empty and idle speech, like magic or mirage it is full of deceit, and as empty as foam, or as a bubble on the water. Disease robs the human body of its beauty, weakens the senses, the faculties, and the strength, and puts an end to riches and welfare. It brings on the day of death, and of transmigration. Every creature, the fairest, the most beloved, disappears for ever; like a leaf or fruit fallen into the stream it is lost for ever to our eyes. Then man, solitary and unaided, wanders forth with but one possession, the fruit of his earthly labours.'

Then, he adds, after these melancholy but compassionate reflections:

'Decay is inherent in all component things; all that is composite is unstable; like a vessel of clay which the slightest blow will shatter, like wealth borrowed from another, or a city of sand which does not hold together, or the sandy bank of a river. All component things are in turn effect and cause. One contains the other as the seed contains the germ, although the germ is not the seed. But substance, though not durable, has no interruption; no being exists that does not emanate from another; and therein lies the apparent durability of substance. The wise man, however, is not deceived by these appearances. For instance, the wood that is rubbed, the wood with which it is rubbed, and the action of the hands, are three things which cause fire; but the fire soon dies out; and the sage, searching in vain for it, wonders: Whence it came, and whither it has gone? The sound of words is made by the movement of the tongue striking on the lips or the roof of the mouth or back of the palate, and language is formed with the help of the mind; but all speech is but an echo, and language does not exist in itself. It is the sound of a lute, of a flute, and again the sage wonders: Whence it comes and whither it has gone?

'Thence are all forms born of causes and effects, and the yogi, or sage, on reflection perceives that forms are but nothingness, which alone is immutable. The objects revealed to us by our senses do not exist in themselves, none of them possess fixity, which is the true characteristic of the Law.

'But this Law which is to save the world, I understand it, and I must make it known to both gods and men. Many a time have I thought, when I shall have attained supreme wisdom (Bodhi) I will assemble together all living beings, and I will show them how they may enter the gates of immortality. Withdrawing them from the wide ocean of Creation, I will establish them in the land of patience. Freed from the disturbing suggestions of the senses, I will establish them in peace. In showing the light of the Law to creatures duped by the darkness of profound ignorance, I will give them eyes to see things clearly as they are; I will endow them with the beautiful radiance of pure wisdom; the eye of the Law, without blemish or corruption.'

These grave thoughts haunted young Siddhārtha even in his dreams; and one night, one of the gods, Hrideva, the god of modesty, descending from Tushita the abode of gladness, appeared to him, and by the following gentle words, encouraged him to set forth on the mission, for which he had been preparing himself for so many years.

'The time and the hour have come,' said the god, 'for him who is resolved, to reveal himself to the world. He who is not liberated himself, cannot liberate others; the blind cannot show the way; but he who is freed, can free others; he who has eyes can show the path to those who know it not. To those, whoever they may be, consumed by earthly desires, clinging to their houses, their wealth, their children, their wives, impart due instruction, and inspire in them a desire to renounce the world, and to adopt the holy life of wandering monks.'

Meanwhile the king Suddhodana suspected the projects

that agitated the heart of his son; and his tenderness and care increased tenfold. He built him three new palaces; one for spring, one for summer, and another for winter; and fearful lest the young prince should take advantage of his excursions to escape from his family, he secretly gave the strictest orders that all his movements should be watched. However, all the precautions taken by his father were in vain. The most unforeseen and most extraordinary circumstances combined to give increasing strength to the prince's resolution.

One day, as he drove with a numerous escort through the eastern gate of the city, on his way to visit the garden of Lumbini, dear to him from the recollections of his childhood, he met a decrepit old man, seamed with wrinkles, and bald-headed, whose veins and muscles stood out like cords, while his chattering teeth hardly permitted the utterance of a few harsh and inarticulate sounds. His skinny hands clutched a rugged staff to support his tottering steps, and his bent body and limbs shook with palsy.

'Who is this man?' cried the prince to his charioteer. 'He is small of stature and devoid of strength, his flesh and blood are dried up, his muscles cleave to his skin, his hair is white, his teeth chatter, his body is emaciated; bent over his staff, he drags himself painfully along, stumbling at every step. Is this a condition peculiar to his family? or is this the law that governs all mankind?'

'Prince,' replied the charioteer, 'this man is overcome by age; all his senses are weakened, suffering has destroyed his strength, he is cast aside by his relations; and he has no protector; incompetent in business, he is abandoned like dead wood in a forest. But his is not a condition peculiar to his family. In all living beings, youth is conquered by age; your father and mother, all your relations and allies will end thus; it is the natural and fatal issue.'

'Since this is so,' replied the prince, 'an ignorant and weak man, lacking in discernment, takes pride in the youth that intoxicates him, and does not see old age awaiting him. As for me, I will go no further. Turn back quickly, charioteer. For I, too, am the future abode of old age; what have I to do with pleasure and joy?' And the young prince drove back into the town without going to Lumbini.

Another day, he was going with a large retinue through the southern gate to the pleasure garden, when he saw in the road a man who was stricken by disease, shaking with fever, a thin and mud-stained form, without friends or shelter, gasping for breath, and with all the appearance of intense terror at the approach of death. After interrogating his charioteer and receiving the expected answer:

'Health,' said the prince, 'is then like a deceptive dream, and the dread of evil is then an unbearable torture! Where is the wise man who, after having seen what it is, can henceforth enjoy happiness or pleasure?'

And the prince turned his chariot, and went back to the town, without going any further.

Again another time, he was going by the western gate to the pleasure garden, when he spied on the road a dead man stretched on a bier, covered over with a cloth. A band of wailing relations surrounded it, filling the air with their lamentations, tearing their hair, covering their heads with dust, and striking their breasts as they uttered loud cries.

The prince, calling again his charioteer to witness, exclaimed, 'Ah! woe unto youth that old age must destroy; ah! woe for the health so destroyed by sickness; ah! woe to life that gives man so short a time! If there were neither old age, nor sickness, nor death! Oh! if only old age, sickness and death were for ever destroyed!'

Then, for the first time betraying his secret thought, the

young prince added: 'Return home again, I must think over the accomplishment of this deliverance.'

A last meeting decided him, and put an end to all hesitation[1]. He was leaving the city by the northern gate to go to the pleasure garden, when he saw a Bhikshu or mendicant, who by his calm, chastened, and reserved demeanour, seemed dedicated to the calling of a Brahma-chari[2]; he stood with lowered eyes, fixing his gaze no further than the length of a yoke, in a befitting manner, wearing with dignity the garment of a monk and carrying an alms-bowl.

'Who is this man?' inquired the prince.

'Lord,' replied the charioteer, 'this man is one of those called Bhikshus; he has renounced all lustful desires, and leads a most austere life; he strives to subdue himself, and has become a mendicant. Without passion or envy, he wanders about subsisting on alms.'

'That is right and well said,' replied Siddhārtha, 'the choice of a religious life has ever been lauded by sages; it will be my resource, and the resource of others; it will become to us an efflorescence of life, happiness, and immortality.'

Then the young prince turned his chariot, and having come to a determination, went home without going to Lumbini.

His decision could not long be kept secret. The king was soon informed of it, and exercised still grea er vigilance. Guards were stationed at all the palace gates, and the king's servants anxiously watched day and night. The young prince would not at first make use of any stratagems as

[1] These different meetings are famous in Buddhistic legends. The king Aṣoka built stūpas and vihāras at all the spots where the Buddha made them. Hiouen-Thsang, in the seventh century of our era, saw these monuments and their ruins.

[2] Brahma-chari. or he who walks in the way of the Brahmans; this is the name given to the young Brahman all the time he is studying the Vedas, that is till he is about thirty-five years old. The principal condition of his noviciate is absolute chastity.

a means of escape, for they were repugnant to him, and he reserved them for cases of necessity. Gopā, his wife, was the first in whom he confided, and one night, when, startled by a dream, she asked him what such visions meant, he informed her of his scheme and was able to console her, for the time being, for the loss that threatened her. Then, in all respect and submission, he went the very same night to his father, and spoke as follows :

'Lord, the time is come when I must reveal myself to the world, do not I pray you oppose my wish, and be not too much grieved by it. Grant me leave, O king, together with your family and people, grant me leave to depart.'

The king, his eyes suffused with tears, replied: 'What can I do, my son, to make thee change thy purpose? Thou hast but to name the boon thou covetest and I will grant it. Myself, my servants, my palace, my kingdom, take all, all is thine.'

'Lord,' replied Siddhārtha, in a gentle voice, 'I desire but four things, which I beg you will grant me. If you can give them to me I will stay near you, and you will see me alway in your abode, which I shall never leave. Grant, Lord, that old age shall never overtake me; that I shall retain everlasting youth and freshness; grant that sickness shall have no power over me; and that my life shall neither decay nor end.'

On hearing these words, the king was overcome with grief. 'O my child,' he exclaimed, 'what thou askest is impossible, and I am helpless. The Rishis themselves, in the midst of Kalpa where they dwell, have never escaped the fear of old age and sickness, and death, and decay.'

'If I can neither escape the fear of old age, nor sickness, nor death, nor decay,' replied the young man; 'if you, Lord, cannot grant me these four chief things, bestow on me at least, O king, one thing that is not less important: grant that on disappearing from this earth I shall be for ever freed from the vicissitudes of transmigration.'

The king saw that it was no use trying to oppose so resolute a purpose, and at dawn he summoned the Ṣākyas to acquaint them with the sad news. They resolved to oppose the prince's flight by force. They took upon themselves the guard of the palace gates, and while the younger men were on sentry, the most venerable of the elders spread the alarm in all quarters of the city so that all the inhabitants should be on the alert.) The king Suddhodana himself, surrounded by five hundred young Ṣākyas, kept watch at the palace gate; while his three brothers, the young prince's uncles, stood at each of the city gates, and one of the chief Ṣākyas took his post in the centre of the city to see that all orders should be punctually executed. In the interior of the palace, Siddhārtha's aunt, Mahā Prajāpatī Gotamī, meanwhile directed the women's watch, and stimulated their vigilance, by saying: 'If after leaving the kingdom and the country the prince wanders far away as a monk, all the palace will be filled with sadness, and the kingly race, which is so ancient, will come to an end.'

All these efforts proved vain; on one of the following nights, when the sentries, worn out by long watching, were slumbering, the young prince ordered his charioteer Chandaka to saddle his horse Kanthaka, and succeeded in escaping unseen from the city. Before obeying his request, the faithful follower had for the last time tried to dissuade him from his purpose, and had implored him, with streaming eyes, not to sacrifice his splendid youth by going to lead the miserable life of a mendicant, and not to quit the magnificent palace, the abode of all happiness and pleasure. The prince, however, had not yielded to the supplications of the devoted servant, and had replied:

(' Earthly passions, I know too well, O Chandaka, are the

destruction of all virtue; I have known them and can no longer enjoy happiness; the sages avoid them like a serpent's head, and quit them for ever like an impure vessel. Rather would I be struck by a thunderbolt, or that showers of arrows and red-hot darts, like flashes of fire from the flaming heights of a mountain, should fall on my head, than that I should be born again to the cares and desires of a household.'

It was midnight when the prince left Kapilavastu, and the star Pushya, that had presided at his birth, was at that moment rising in the horizon. At the moment of quitting all that he had loved, the heart of the young man for an instant sank within him, and casting a last look at the palace and city he was forsaking:

'I shall not return to the city of Kapila,' he said in a low voice, 'till I have obtained the cessation of birth and death; I shall not return till I have attained the supreme abode exempt from age and death, and have found pure wisdom. When I return, the town of Kapila will stand upright, no longer weighed down by slumber.'

And, in fact, he did not see his father or Kapilavastu till twelve years later, when he converted them to the new religion.

Meanwhile Siddhārtha rode through the night; after leaving the country of the Ṣākyas, and that of the Kandyas, he passed through the country of the Mallas and the city of Mēnēya. By daybreak he had travelled a distance of six yodjanas, about thirty-six miles. Then he leapt from his horse, and handing the reins to Chandaka he gave him also his cap with the clasp of pearls which adorned it, an ornament he deemed no longer necessary, and dismissed him.

The *Lalita-vistāra*, from which most of these details are taken, adds, that at the spot where Chandaka left him, a chāitya, or sacred edifice, was raised; and 'to this day,' says the writer, 'this monument bears the name of Chandaka-

Nivartana, that is "the return of Chandaka."' Hiouen-Thsang saw this stūpa, which was, he says, built by the king Aṣoka on the edge of a great forest that Siddhārtha must have passed through, and which was on the road to Kusinagara, where he died fifty-one years later.

When the prince was alone he divested himself of the last vestiges of his caste and rank. First, he cut off his long hair with his sword blade, and cast it to the winds; a monk could not wear the flowing locks of a warrior. Then he exchanged his princely robes of Benāres silk (from Kāsi) with a hunter, whose clothing was of worn-out yellow deer-skin. The hunter, though embarrassed by the exchange, accepted it at once, for he saw that he had to deal with a person of high distinction.

No sooner was Siddhārtha's flight discovered than the king sent in pursuit of him, but the messengers failed to overtake him. In their rapid chase they soon, however, met the hunter dressed in the prince's attire, and would probably have ill-treated him but for the presence of Chandaka, who was able to calm them. He related Siddhārtha's escape, and when the messengers, in obedience to the king's orders, tried to continue the pursuit till they should reach the prince, the charioteer dissuaded them.

'You would not succeed in bringing him back,' he said; 'the young man is firm in his courage and resolve. He said "I will not return to the great city of Kapilavastu until I have attained perfect, complete, and supreme wisdom; I will not return except as the Buddha." He will not belie his words; as he has said, so it will be, the young man will not change.' Chandaka could offer the king no other consolation; he gave back to Mahā Prajāpatī Gotamī the jewels Siddhārtha had confided to his care, but the queen could not look at the ornaments that recalled such sad memories, and threw them into a pool, thenceforth called 'The pool of the

Jewels' (Abharanapushkari). But Gopā, Siddhārtha's young wife, knew too well the steadfastness of his purpose, to entertain any hope of his speedy return; and although she was to a certain extent prepared for the cruel separation, she remained inconsolable, notwithstanding the glorious future predicted by the faithful Chandaka.

After having accepted the hospitality of several Brahmans in succession, the young prince reached at last the large city of Vaiṣāli. He had now to prepare himself for the long conflict he had to undertake with the Brahmanical doctrines. He was too modest to believe himself sufficiently prepared for the contest, and wished to put himself to the test, and at the same time acquire a thorough knowledge of their doctrines. He sought out the Brahman Alāra Kālāma, who was renowned as the most learned of professors, and who had no less than 300 disciples, besides a throng of listeners. The beauty of the young man, when he appeared for the first time in this assembly, filled all present with admiration, and above all Kālāma himself; but before long he admired the learning of Siddhārtha still more than his beauty, and he besought him to share with him his work of teacher. But the young sage thought within himself:

'This doctrine of Alāra is not truly a deliverance. The practice of it will not completely free humanity from misery.'

Then he added in his heart: 'In rendering perfect this doctrine, which consists in poverty and the subduing of the senses, I shall attain true freedom, but I must still make further researches.'

He remained therefore some time at Vaiṣāli; on leaving that city he advanced into the country of Magadha, and reached its capital Rājāgriha. His reputation for beauty and wisdom had preceded him; and the people, struck with surprise at the sight of such self-abnegation in so handsome and youthful a man, flocked to meet him. The crowds that filled that day the streets of the city ceased, says the legend, both buying and selling, and even abstained from drinking wine and all liquors, in order to contemplate the noble mendicant who came begging alms. The king Bimbisāra himself, descrying him from the windows of his palace, in front of which he passed, borne forward by the popular enthusiasm, had him watched to his retreat on the slope of the Pandava mountain, and the next morning, to do him honour, went there in person, accompanied by a numerous retinue. Bimbisāra was about the same age as Siddhārtha, and deeply impressed by the strange condition in which he found the young prince, charmed by his discourse, at once so elevated and so simple, touched by his magnanimity and virtue, he embraced his cause from that moment and never ceased to protect him during the rest of his reign. His most seductive offers were, however, powerless to move the new ascetic; and after sojourning some time in the capital Siddhārtha retired far from the crowd and tumult to the banks of the river Nairanjanā, the Phalgu of modern geography.

If we are to believe the *Mahāvansa*, the Sinhalese chronicle, written in verse in the fifth century of our era by Mahānāma, who composed it from the most ancient Buddhist documents, the king Bimbisāra was converted to Buddhism, or to use the expression of the writer, 'joined the Congregation of the Conqueror,' in the sixteenth year of his reign. He had ascended the throne at the age of fifteen, and reigned no less than fifty-two years. His father was bound by the strongest ties of affection to Siddhārtha's father, and this was no doubt one of the reasons that had made Bimbisāra so favourable to him. His son Ajātaṣatru, who murdered him, did not at first share his kindly feeling towards the Buddha, and for some time persecuted the innovator before accepting his doctrine, as we shall see later.

Notwithstanding the enthusiastic welcome the Sramana

Gautama received, both from kings and peoples, he did not consider himself sufficiently prepared for his great mission. He determined to make a last and decisive test of the power of his arguments.

There lived at Rājagriha a Brahman even more celebrated than the Brahman of Vaiṣāli. His name was Udraka, son of Rama, and he enjoyed an unrivalled reputation among the common people and even among the learned. Siddhārtha went humbly to him, and asked to be his disciple. After some conversations Udraka raised his disciple to be his equal, and established him in a teacher's abode, saying, 'Thou and I together will teach our doctrine to this multitude.' His disciples numbered 700.

However, as at Vaiṣāli, the superiority of the young ascetic was soon apparent, and he was compelled to separate himself from Udraka: 'Friend,' he said to him, 'this path does not lead to indifference to things of this world, it does not lead to emancipation from passion, it does not lead to the prevention of the vicissitudes of mankind, it does not lead to calm, nor perfect wisdom, neither does it lead to the state of Sramana nor to Nirvāna.' Then, in the presence of all Udraka's disciples, he parted from him.

Five of the disciples, fascinated by the teaching of Siddhārtha and the lucidity of his precepts, left their former master to follow the reformer. They were all five men of high caste, says the legend. Siddhārtha first withdrew with them to Mount Gāyā, then he returned to the banks of the Nairanjanā, to a village called Uruvela, where he determined to settle with his companions before going forth to teach mankind. Henceforth he was decided with regard to the learning of the Brahmans, he knew its capacity, or rather its insufficiency; he felt himself stronger than they. Nevertheless he still had to gain strength against his own weaknesses, and although he disapproved of the excessive Brahmanic asceticism, he determined to submit for several years to a life of penance and self-mortification. It was perhaps by way of ensuring as popular a consideration as the Brahmans possessed, but it was also a means of subduing the senses.

Siddhārtha was twenty-nine years of age when he left the palace of Kapilavastu.

Uruvela is celebrated in the annals of Buddhism for this long retreat, which lasted six years, and during which Siddhārtha gave himself up, without a moment's wavering, to the most severe and rigorous mortifications, 'at which the gods themselves were filled with horror.' He withstood the most fearful attacks of his own passions, and we shall see later how the legend transforms these moral struggles into material conflicts with the demon Pāpiyān (the *most vicious*), who, notwithstanding his cunning, his violence, and his numerous army, was at last overthrown and vanquished, without being able to tempt or terrify the young ascetic, who, by his virtue destroyed the kingdom of Māra, the Spirit of Evil.

However, at the end of six years of privations, sufferings, and excessive fastings, Siddhārtha, persuaded that asceticism was not the path that led to perfect wisdom, determined to cease such excessive mortifications, and began again to take regular food, which a young village girl of the name of Sujātā brought to him. In a short space of time he recovered the strength and beauty which had been destroyed by his terrible macerations. His five disciples, who had hitherto remained faithful, and had imitated his acts of penance, were scandalized at his weakness; and losing all esteem for him, they forsook him and went away to Benāres, to the place called Rishi-patana, where he eventually rejoined them.

Alone, and abandoned by his followers, in his hermitage at Uruvela, Siddhārtha continued his meditations, although he diminished his austerities. It was no doubt in this solitude that he worked out the principles of his system, and laid down the rules of discipline for his followers. Henceforth he wore the garb and adopted the customs he intended to impose on them, and by the example he set he forestalled any resistance that his rigorous precepts might stir up even in the most ardent of his sectarians. The clothes the hunter had formerly ceded to him had fallen in tatters, they had been his only covering for the last six years—years spent in wandering from city to city, and jungle to jungle, often without shelter, with the bare soil as his only resting-place. It became necessary to renew those garments, and this is the way in which we are told that he replaced them. Sujātā, the daughter of the chieftain of Uruvela, who had been so devoted to him, and who, assisted by ten of her women, continued to bring him food, had a slave called Rādhā who had just died. The woman had been buried in a neighbouring cemetery, and her body had been wrapped in a coarse linen cloth (ṣana). A few days after her burial Siddhārtha opened the grave and took the shroud. Then, 'in order to show what a monk must do,' he washed in a pool the earth-stained shroud, and fashioned and sewed it with his own hands. The place where he sat at that time was afterwards called Pānsukūla-Sivana, that is 'the sewing of the shroud.' Hence the reason of the ordinance he made for his monks, that they were to be habited in clothes put together from cast-off rags picked up in the streets, by the roadside, or even in graveyards. Who indeed among them would have dared to complain or resist when the illustrious scion of a great royal family, the sole heir of the Ṣākyas, had abandoned all power and riches and robed his youth and beauty in such woful raiment?

However, the end of these long and painful trials was at hand. Siddhārtha had but one more step to take. He knew his future adversaries and he knew himself; he felt sure of their weakness and of his own strength, but his humility still gave him some lingering scruples. He debated with himself whether, entrusted with the salvation of mankind, he had indeed attained a sufficiently definitive and immutable knowledge of the truths he was to reveal.

'In all I have done and acquired, he thought, I have far surpassed human law, but I have not yet reached the point where I shall clearly distinguish supreme wisdom. I am not yet in the true path of knowledge, nor in that which will lead to the irrevocable end of old age, disease, and death.'

Then he would recall his childhood's memories, the brilliant early visions he had in his father's gardens under the djambu tree, and he anxiously inquired of himself whether his mind, matured by age and reflection, would indeed realize the marvellous promises that his youthful imagination had held out to him. Could he indeed be the Saviour of mankind? At last, after a meditation that appears to have lasted, without interruption, a whole week, during one of his frequent ecstasies, Siddhārtha found he could in all sincerity of heart answer the question affirmatively.

'Yes, he had at last found the true path of greatness. The path of sacrifice; the sure path which will not fail nor dishearten; the blessed path of virtue; the spotless path devoid of envy, ignorance, and passion; the path which leads to freedom and makes the power of evil be as no power; the path which overleaps the regions of transmigration and reduces them to nought; the path which outstrips Ṣakra, Brahma, Mahēṣvara, and the guardians of the world; the path which leads to the possession of universal knowledge; the path of experience and judgement; the path that softens old age and death; the calm, serene path, exempt from all fear of evil, which leads to the city of Nirvāna.'

In one word, Siddhārtha believed at this supreme moment that he could indeed call himself the true and perfect

Buddha, that is, the Wise One in all his purity and greatness, and in his power greater than gods or men.

The place where Siddhārtha became at last the perfect Buddha is as famous in the legends as Kapilavastu, the place of his birth; Uruvela, the place of his six years' retreat; or Kusi-nagara, the place of his death. The precise spot where the Buddha revealed himself is called Bodhimanda, that is to say the seat of wisdom, and tradition has preserved all the details of the solemn act.

On his way to the banks of the Nairanjanā at Bodhimanda, the Bodhisatwa[1] met, on the right-hand side of the road, a seller of grass, who was cutting 'a soft, pliable grass such as mats are made of, and of a very fragrant odour.' The Bodhisatwa turned aside, and going up to the man, whose name was Svastika, asked him for some of the grass he was mowing; then spreading it as a carpet, with the blades turned in and the roots outwards, he seated himself cross-legged, his body upright and turned to the east, at the foot of a tree which is called 'the tree of wisdom, Bodhidruma.'

Then, as he seated himself, he said, 'May my body waste away, my skin, bones, and flesh perish, if I raise myself from the grass I am seated on before I have attained supreme wisdom.'

He remained through the long hours of a day and night without moving, and it was at the last hour of watching, at the moment of dawn, when sleep most overcomes the senses, and as the Tibetans say at beat of drum, that, having assumed the rank of perfect Buddhahood, and of absolute wisdom, he attained the threefold knowledge.

'Yes,' he then exclaimed, 'yes, it is thus that I will put an end to the sorrows of mankind.' And striking the ground

[1] The Bodhisatwa is the future Buddha, that is, the being who has all the qualities requisite to become Buddha, but has not yet attained Buddhahood.

with his hand, 'May this earth,' he added, 'be my witness; it is the abode of all beings, it contains all that is moveable and immoveable, it is impartial, it will bear witness that I do not lie.'

If the human race was not saved, as Siddhārtha may at that moment have persuaded himself it was, a new religion was at all events instituted. The Buddha was then thirty-six years of age.

The tree under which he sat at Bodhimanda was a large fig-tree, of the species called *pippala* (*Ficus religiosa*); and the veneration of the faithful soon made it an object of fervent worship, which lasted for centuries. In the year 632 of our era, that is twelve hundred years after the death of the Buddha, Hiouen-Thsang, the Chinese pilgrim, saw the Bodhidruma, or at least the tree that passed as such. We are told in the *Lalita-vistāra* that it grew about forty-five miles from Rājagriha, the capital of Magadha, not far from the Nairanjanā. The tree was protected by huge walls of masonry, which extended to the east and west, and perceptibly narrowed towards the north and south. The principal gateway opened eastwards, facing the river Nairanjanā. The southern gate was in the vicinity of a large pool, no doubt the one in which Siddhārtha washed the shroud. To the west rose a belt of steep mountains, and the northern side communicated with a large monastery. The trunk of the tree was of a whitish-yellow colour, its leaves glossy green; and the traveller was told they did not fall either in autumn or in winter. Only, it was added, on the anniversary of the Buddha's Nirvàna they all suddenly fall off, and the following day grow again, finer and larger than before. Every year the kings, ministers, and magistrates assembled on that day beneath the tree, watered it with milk, lighted lamps, scattered flowers, and withdrew, bearing away the leaves that had fallen.

Near the 'tree of wisdom' Hiouen-Thsang saw a statue of the Buddha, before which he prostrated himself; its erection has been attributed to Maitreya, one of the Buddha's most famous disciples. All round the tree and the statue, in a very confined space, a number of sacred monuments, each recalling some pious memories, were to be seen.

The devout pilgrim tells us that he took eight or nine days to worship them, one after the other; there were stūpas and vihāras, or monasteries, of every size and shape. The Vajrāsanam or Diamond Throne was more particularly pointed out to the admiration of the faithful; it was the hillock on which the Buddha had sat, and which, according to popular superstition, was destined to disappear when men should become less virtuous.

It seems certain that, aided by the very exact information given in the *Lalita-vistāra*, and also by Fa-Hian and Hiouen-Thsang, Bodhimanda could be found, nor would it be surprising if one day some intelligent and courageous British officer were to announce to us that he had made this discovery, which would be well worth any trouble it might have cost. The features of the country have not altered, and if the trees have perished, the ruins of so many monuments must have left recognizable traces upon the soil[1].

The retreat of the Buddha under the sacred fig-tree at Bodhimanda was not, however, so secluded as to prevent his being visited. Besides Sujātā and her young companions, who supported the Buddha by their gifts of food, he saw at least two other persons, whom he converted to the new faith. These were two brothers, both merchants, who were passing

[1] See the reports of Sir Francis Buchanan (Hamilton) quoted by Montgomery Martin in his *History of Eastern India*, and that of Major Kittoe in volume xvi. of the *Journal of the Bengal Asiatic Society*. Sir Francis' exploration took place in 1810, and Major Kittoe's in 1847. See also the learned work of Vivien de Saint-Martin, volume ii. of the *Memoirs of Hiouen-Thsang*, 370 and following pages.

close to Bodhimanda on their journey from the south, whence they were bringing to the north, where they dwelt, a large quantity of merchandise. The caravan that followed them was numerous, as it was conveying several hundreds of waggons. Some of the vehicles having stuck fast in the mud, the two brothers, Trapusha and Bhallika by name, applied to the holy ascetic for help, and while they followed his advice, were touched by his virtue and superhuman wisdom. 'The two brothers, the *Lalita-vistāra* tells us, as well as all their companions, took refuge in the Law of the Buddha.'

Notwithstanding this first promising token of success, the Buddha still hesitated. Henceforth he was assured of being in complete possession of the truth. But how would men be disposed to receive it? He brought to mankind light and salvation, but would men consent to open their eyes? Would they enter the path they were bidden to pursue? The Buddha once more retired into solitude, and spending his days in contemplation, he thus meditated in his heart:

'The Law that emanates from me is profound, luminous, subtle, difficult of comprehension; it baffles analysis, and is beyond the powers of reasoning; accessible only to the learned and the wise; it is in opposition to all worldly wisdom. Having abandoned all individuality, extinguished all ideas, interrupted existence by absolute calm, it is invisible, being essentially immaterial; having destroyed desire and passion, and thus having put an end to any reproduction of entity, it leads to Nirvāna. But if I, the truly enlightened Buddha, teach this Law it will not be understood by others, and will expose me to their insults. No, I will not give way to my feelings of compassion.'

Three times was the Buddha on the point of yielding to this weakness, and perhaps he might have renounced his great enterprise for ever, and have kept for himself the secret of eternal deliverance; but a supreme thought decided him at last to put an end to his hesitation.

'All beings, he reflected, whether high or low, whether they are very good, very bad, or indifferent, can be divided into three classes: of which one-third is in error and will so remain, one-third possesses the truth, and one-third lives in uncertainty. Thus a man from the edge of a pond sees lotus-flowers that have not emerged from the water, others that are on a level with the surface, and again others that stand up out of the water. Whether I teach or whether I do not teach the Law, those who are in error will not be the wiser; whether I teach or do not teach the Law, those who possess the truth will still be wise; but those beings who live in uncertainty will, if I teach the Law, learn wisdom; if I teach it not, they will not learn it.'

The Buddha was seized 'with a great pity for the multitude of beings plunged in uncertainty,' and this thought, full of compassion, decided him. He was about to open the gates of Immortality to those who had so long been led astray by error, by revealing to them the four sublime truths that he at last comprehended, and the connecting links of causes.

Having once fixed the basis of his doctrine, and having determined to brave everything in order to scatter abroad its benefits, Siddhārtha asked himself to whom he should first communicate it. At first, it is said, he intended to address himself to his old teachers at Rājagriha and Vaiṣāli. Both had welcomed him in former days; he had found both pure, good, devoid of passion and envy, full of knowledge and sincerity. He owed it to them to share with them the new light that shone for himself, and which formerly they had sought together in vain. Before going to teach his doctrine at Varanaṣi, the holy city (Benāres), he wished to instruct Udraka, the son of Rama, and Alāra Kālāma, whom he gratefully remembered. In the interval, however, they had both died. When the Buddha heard this, he was seized with regret; he would have saved them both, and they would certainly not have scoffed at the teaching of the Law. His thoughts then reverted to the five disciples who had so long shared his solitude, and who, while he practised his mortifications and penances, surrounded him with tender care. It was true they had, in an excess of zeal, left his side; but 'those saintly personages of high caste were nevertheless very good, easy to discipline, instruct, and purify; they were accustomed to austere practices, evidently their faces were set towards the way of deliverance, and they were already freed from the obstacles which closed it to so many others.' Neither would they cast contempt upon the Buddha, and he resolved to seek them.

He therefore left Bodhimanda, and starting northwards crossed over the mount Gāyā, which was at a short distance, and where he broke his fast; then he stopped on his way at Rohitavastu, Uruvela-Kalpa, Anāla, and Sārathi, where the owners of the principal houses gave him hospitality. He thus reached the great river Gangā, the Ganges. At that season of the year the waters were high and extremely rapid. The Buddha was obliged to ask a ferryman to take him across, but as he had not wherewithal to pay the fare, it was with some difficulty that he managed to cross the river. As soon as the king Bimbisāra heard of the difficulty he had been placed in, he made the passage free of payment to all monks.

Directly he reached the great city of Benāres, the Buddha went straight to his former disciples, who were then living in a wood, called the Deer Park (Mrigadāwa), which was also called Rishi-patana. They saw Siddhārtha coming from afar, and all their grievances against him were stirred up; they had not forgotten what they called his weaknesses, when he had thought right to cease unnecessary mortification) and as he drew nigh they said to one another:

'We can have nothing in common with him: let us neither go to meet him, nor rise up with respect in his presence; let us neither take his religious garments nor his alms-bowl; let us neither prepare for him a beverage, nor a carpet, nor a place for his feet; if he asks for a seat, we will offer him what extends beyond the carpet, but we will keep our seats.'

(But their coldness and ill-will could not hold out long. By degrees, as the Master approached, they felt ill at ease on their seats, and a secret instinct made them wish to stand in his presence. Soon indeed, unable to bear the majesty and glory of the Buddha, they rose up simultaneously, unable to keep to their resolution. Some showed him marks of respect, others went forward to greet him, and they took from him his tunic, his religious garments, his alms-bowl; they spread out a carpet and prepared water for him to bathe his feet) saying:

'Ayushmat (Lord) Gautama, you are welcome; deign to seat yourself down on this carpet.'

Then, after having entertained him on subjects likely to gladden him, they all placed themselves at one side of him and said:

'The senses of Ayushmat Gautama are perfectly purified, his skin is perfectly pure, the oval of his face is perfectly pure. Ayushmat Gautama, do you possess within you the discernment of venerable wisdom, which is far above human law?'

The Buddha replied: 'Do not give me the title of Ayushmat. Full long have I been useless to you, and have procured you neither help nor comfort. Yes, I now see clearly what immortality is, and the path that leads to immortality. I am Buddha; I know all, see all, I have wiped out sin, and am master of the laws; come, that I may teach you the Law, hearken to me and lend an attentive ear; I will instruct you by advice, and your spirit delivered by the destruction of sin and the manifest knowledge of self, your new births will come to an end, you will become Brahma-charis, you will have done what is needful, and you will know no other existence after this—this is what you will learn from me.' Then he gently reminded them of the uncharitable manner in which they had spoken of him but a few minutes before.

His five disciples were abashed, and (throwing themselves at his feet, confessed their fault, and acknowledging the Buddha as the teacher of the world, accepted his new doctrine with all faith and respect. In this first conversation, and until the last watch of the night, the Buddha explained to them the fundamental truths of his system. These were the first conversions of any importance that he made.

Varanaṣi, or Benāres, is esteemed by the Buddhists even more than by the Brahmans as a most holy city. It was at Benāres that the Buddha preached for the first time, or, as is said in Buddhistic mysticism, 'for the first time he turned the Wheel of the Law,' symbolic and sacramental language that has been adopted by all sects of Buddhism, north, south, and east, from Tibet and Nepaul to Ceylon and China[1], Benāres, if we may judge of it by the descriptions given by Hiouen-Thsang in the seventh century of our era[2], had not in the days of the Buddha the same importance that it acquired at a later period. It must even then, however, have been

[1] See the curious details given by Biot on the praying wheels of the Tibetans, who have taken in a literal sense the figurative expression of the early Sūtras, and who pray to the Buddha by turning large wheels on which sacred formulas are inscribed. *Journal des Savants*, June, 1845.

[2] Hiouen-Thsang says that Benāres was six miles long by three wide; he saw among other monuments a stūpa a hundred feet high, and a stone column seventy feet high that had been built by Aṣoka on the identical spot where the Buddha had for the first time turned the Wheel of the Law. See *Histoire de la vie de Hiouen-Thsang*, pp. 132, 133, and *Mémoires de Hiouen-Thsang*, vol. i. p. 303, by Stanislas Julien.

a considerable town, and one of the principal centres of Brahmanism. No doubt this was the reason why the Buddha went there. And as at Vaiṣāli and Rājagriha the Brahman schools numbered respectively three and seven hundred disciples, it is probable that at Benāres they were even more numerous. The Buddha could not therefore have found a wider or more formidable field for the manifestation of his doctrine.

Unfortunately, we have few details of his sojourn at Benāres. The *Lalita-vistāra*, which up to this period has been our chief authority, ends with the Buddha's discourses to his five disciples. The other Sūtras, which are not, like the *Lalita-vistāra*, regular biographies of Ṣākya-muni, tell us little about the contests he must have sustained against the Brahmans at Varanaṣi. At this moment of his life, after having seen the slow elaboration of his ideas, it would have been interesting to know his first successes and rebuffs. We must, however, dispense with this information, interesting as it would necessarily be, till the publication of some other Sūtras may bring it to our knowledge. We do not find in any of those hitherto published, on the sequel of the Buddha's career, so complete an account as that contained in the *Lalita-vistāra*. Most of the Sūtras relate only one of the acts of his life, one of his sermons; not one of them gives an account of his life. It is, however, thanks to the materials they furnish, possible to reconstruct and complete it. The probability of its truth will be as great, the order in which the facts are related will alone be less certain. The principal events of the Buddha's life are somewhat confusedly told by them, and it will be difficult for us to state, with desirable exactness, the chronological order in which the events occurred.

It appears probable that Ṣākya-muni's sojourn in Varanaṣi was not of long duration, although he made there several other converts. The greater part of the Sūtras mention him as dwelling in Magadha at Rājagriha, or at Ṣrāvasti in Kosala, north of the Ganges. In those two kingdoms he spent nearly all the remainder of his life, which lasted forty years longer.) The kings of those two countries protected him, and both embraced the Buddhist faith. Bimbisāra was king of Magadha, and we have seen what favour he showed Siddhārtha, when the young prince was beginning his religious apostleship. This benevolence never failed during the whole of his long reign, and the Buddha took pleasure in residing at Rājagriha, which was situated nearly in the centre of the kingdom, and in visiting from thence the surrounding countries. All these places must have been beloved by him, as in later times they became sacred to his votaries. Bodhimanda and Uruvela were not far off; six or seven miles off rose the mountain called the Vulture's Peak (Gridhrakūta parvata); one of its summits, if we are to believe Hiouen-Thsang, recalled from a distance the shape of that bird. The Buddha found pleasure in wandering about this mountain, so rich in grand and picturesque scenery, shaded by magnificent trees, and fresh with sparkling springs. It was there that, surrounded by his disciples, he taught the *Lotus of the Good Law*, the *Mahāpradjna-Pāramitā Sūtra*, and many other Sūtras.

At the entrance of the city, on the north side, was a superb vihāra, where the Buddha often resided; it was called Kalantaka or Kalanta veḷuvana, that is the bamboo grove of Kalanta. According to Hiouen-Thsang's account, Kalanta was a rich merchant, who had first given his garden to the Brahmans, but after hearing the sublime Law regretted his gift, and took it away from them. He caused a magnificent house to be built there, and offered it to the Buddha. It was there that the Buddha converted several of his most distinguished disciples—Ṣariputra, Moggallāna and Katyāyana; it was also at this house that the first Council was held after his death.

A little further from Rājagriha there was another place, called Nālanda, where the Buddha appears to have made pleasant and prolonged sojourns, if we may judge by the costly number of monuments which have been erected there by the piety of Buddhist kings. Originally this place had been a garden of mango-trees (āmras), situated near a lake, and belonged to a rich man. Five hundred merchants had purchased it as a gift for the Buddha, who, during a period of three months, had taught them the Law at this spot; and the kings who succeeded Bimbisāra also tried to adorn it by the most costly edifices. They built there six monasteries called saṅghārāmas (places of assembly), each one larger than the other, and one of the kings had them enclosed by a new brick wall to unite them in one.

When Hiouen-Thsang saw them, he described them as the largest and most handsome buildings of that kind he had met with in the whole of India. He mentions as a fact that ten thousand monks or students were kept there by the king's liberality, provided for out of the revenues of several cities, designated for that purpose in turn. A hundred professors taught every day in the interior of these monasteries, and the pupils vied with their masters in zeal. With a forbearance no less surprising, the sectaries of eighteen different schools of the Little and Great Vehicles lived there together on good terms; and the Vedas as well as the Buddhist Sūtras were taught, besides physic and the occult sciences. It is just possible that the Chinese traveller may have given an exaggerated account, but it is certainly a fact that the ancient abode of the Buddha remained for many centuries an object of deep veneration. This pious institution was 700 years old when Hiouen-Thsang visited it, and he remained there several years, enjoying a generous and cordial hospitality.

We will not at present, however, indulge in any further descriptions of Nālanda; later on we shall be able to return to the subject, and we will now proceed with the history of the Buddha.

Bimbisāra, who had ascended the throne at an early age, reigned for no less than thirty years after his conversion to Buddhism, but his son and successor Ajātaṣatru, who had put his father to death, did not show himself at first so favourable to the new doctrine; instigated by Dewadatta, Siddhārtha's perfidious cousin, he laid many snares for him; but touched at last by the virtues and pious counsels of the Buddha, he became converted, and made a confession of the crime by which he had acquired the throne. One whole Sinhalese Sūtra, the *Sāmanna-phala Sūtra*, is devoted to the account of this conversion, which seems to have been one of the most difficult and important of the Reformer. Ajātaṣatru is represented as one of the eight personages who divided the Buddha's relics, and who, according to the Tibetan *Dulva*, had a rightful claim to them.

However great may have been the Buddha's attachment to Magadha, the scene of his severe novitiate and his glorious victory, he seems to have resided there less than in Kosala. This latter country, of which Benāres forms a part, lay north-west of Magadha; its capital was Ṣrāvasti, the residence of Prasenajit, the king of Kosala, and its site must have been near Fizabad, one of the richest cities of the kingdom of Oudh [1]. The Buddha had gone to Ṣrāvasti with the consent of Bimbisāra, and on a formal invitation from Prasenajit. The famous garden of Anātha Piṇḍika or Anātha Piṇḍadha, called Jetavana, was situated near Ṣrāvasti, and it was there that the Buddha delivered most of the discourses recorded

[1] Ṣrāvasti has been identified by General Cunningham in his *Ancient Geography of India* with the ruins of Sahet-Māhet in Oudh (translator's note).

in the Sūtras.) Hiouen-Thsang states that Anātha Piṇḍika, who owed his fame to his unbounded charity to the poor and orphaned, had given this magnificent garden to the Buddha. He was a minister of King Prasenajit, and had bought this property for a heavy sum of gold from Jeta, the eldest son of the king, hence the name of Jetavana, or Jeta's Wood. Anātha Piṇḍika had built a vihāra in the midst of it, under the shade of the finest trees, and there the Buddha dwelt twenty-three years. Prasenajit himself, when he was converted, built him a lecture-hall to the east of the city, and Hiouen-Thsang mentions having seen the ruins surmounted by a stūpa. At a short distance rose a tower, the remains of the ancient vihāra of Prajāpatī, the Buddha's aunt. This circumstance as well as several others would lead us to suppose that Siddhārtha's family, or at least some members of it, had joined him in this lovely spot, where he was so much beloved and in which he took so much pleasure. Māhā-Prajāpatī was the first woman whom, at the urgent solicitation of his cousin Ānanda, he permitted to adopt the religious life.

Eighteen or nineteen miles south of the city, the spot where the Buddha met his father, after twelve years' absence, was still shown in the days of Hiouen-Thsang. Suddhodana had been grievously distressed at being separated from his son, and had made continual efforts to bring him back. He had despatched eight messengers one after the other; and all, captivated by the prince's eloquence and superiority, had remained with him and had joined his community. At last he sent one of his ministers, called Charka, who was, like the others, converted; but who returned to the king and announced the coming of his son. It seems that his father forestalled this journey, and went himself to the Buddha. Nevertheless the Buddha returned the king's visit, and shortly afterwards went to Kapilavastu. If we are to believe the Tibetan writers, the Ṣākyas followed their king's example, and embraced Buddhism: most of them indeed adopted the religious habit, which was also assumed by the Buddha's three wives, Gopā, Yasodharā, and Utpalavarṇā, as well as many other women.

Notwithstanding the protection of kings and the enthusiasm of the populace, it appears that the Buddha had to contend with a most violent and stubborn opposition from the Brahmans. Their rivalry proved often dangerous to him. It is true that the Buddha was not sparing in his criticisms of his adversaries. Not only did he expose the ignorance and error of the very basis of their system, but he reproached them with being hypocrites, charlatans, and jugglers, censures which wounded them the more that they were not undeserved. His influence increased at the expense of theirs, and they neglected no means to arrest such a dangerous movement, their vanity being concerned as well as their authority. A legend, entitled *Prātihārya Sūtra*, is almost entirely devoted to the narration of a great defeat the Brahmans sustained at the hands of the Buddha in the presence of Prasenajit: it resembled a tournament, of which the king and people were umpires. In another, and even more curious legend, the Brahmans are said to have exacted a promise from the citizens of Bhadramkara, whom they ruled at their will, that they would not admit the Buddha who was then approaching. When, however, the Bhagavat entered the city, a Brahman woman of Kapilavastu, who had married in the country, disobeyed the order, got out at night, scaled the walls with a ladder, and threw herself at the Buddha's feet to be taught the Law; her example was soon followed by one of the richest inhabitants of the city, named Mendhaka, who harangued the people, and at once gained them over to the Liberator, whom the Brahmans wished to humiliate and to exile. Matters were sometimes carried still further, and if we may judge by the traditions quoted by Fa-Hian and

Hiouen-Thsang, the Buddha must often have been personally threatened and attempts made upon his life. This is not in itself astonishing, and the only wonder is that the Buddha escaped all the ambushes that were laid for him.

If there is a certain vagueness with regard to a part of his life, there is no doubt whatever as to the place of his death. All the legends, without exception, agree in saying that it took place at Kusi-nagara, in the kingdom of the same name, which no doubt in the days of Prasenajit formed part of Kosala. The Buddha, then eighty years of age, was returning from Rājagriha in Magadha, accompanied by Ānanda, his cousin, and a numerous crowd of monks and disciples. On reaching the southern bank of the Ganges, and before crossing the river, he stood on a large square stone, gazed tenderly at his companion, and said:

'This is the last time that I shall look from afar on the city of Rājagriha and the Diamond Throne (Vajrāsanam).'

After crossing the Ganges he went to the city of Vaiṣāli, to which he bade the same touching farewell, and he received several monks into his Order, the last of whom was the mendicant Subhadra. He was in the country of the Mallas, near the river Achiravatī, about half a mile north-west of the city of Kusi-nagara, when he was seized with a sudden faintness. He stopped in a grove of salas, under a tree of this species (*Shorea robusta*), and there died, or, as the Buddhist legends say, he entered into Nirvāna. Hiouen-Thsang saw the four sala trees, all of equal height, under which it was said the Buddha rested and drew his last breath. The Buddha died in the eighth year of the reign of Ajātaṣatru, if we may rely on Sinhalese chronology.

The Tibetan *Dulva* gives a detailed account of the funeral rites that were rendered him, which were as splendid and solemn as those reserved for the Chakrawarti kings (universal monarchs). The most illustrious of his disciples, Kāṣyapa, author of the Abhidharma, or Collection on Metaphysics, and who afterwards took such an important part in the first Council, was at that moment at Rājagriha, but instantly hurried back to Kusi-nagara. The Buddha's body was not buried until the eighth day after his death; and after much quarrelling, which almost ended in bloodshed, and was only allayed by an appeal to the concord and meekness inculcated by the Reformer, his relics were divided into eight portions, one of which was given to the Ṣākyas of Kapilavastu.

Such is, in its principal outlines, the life of Ṣākya-muni. All his actions, great though they were, seem so natural that we cannot hesitate to accept the account as true, since so much concording evidence has vouched for it. We have given it as it is related in the documents already known, and new documents can but complete it. The figure of the Buddha is shown under the most credible conditions, for if they reveal the originality of his genius, they also explain no less clearly the immense influence he exerted over others. But we must in all sincerity admit that we have in a slight degree transformed the Buddhist legends, while borrowing from them the probably true narrative which they furnish. We have made selections from them, but have never altered anything; (the record of events that has just been perused is, however, too simple to have satisfied the superstitious and extravagant imagination of Indian races. Legends have drowned realities in a mass of fabulous and excessive details, of which we think it necessary to give the general outline, in order that the exact value of the Buddhist canonical laws may be understood, and to show how they were able to create such an important revolution in the Asiatic world. The reader may smile as he glances over these legends; he may more probably feel impatient of their folly and absurdity. However, these extravagances form a part of the history of the human mind, and ought not to be contemptuously set aside, even when they stray into the wildest superstitions. Moreover, a careful study will enable us the better to appreciate the intelligence of the peoples to whom the Buddha addressed himself, and whom he was destined to reform.

CHAPTER II.

The legend of the Buddha. Analysis of the Lalita-vistāra. Prologue in the Tushita heaven. The four investigations. The Buddha's address. His departure and incarnation in Māyā-Devi's womb. The gods pay homage. Birth of the Buddha; his seven steps. The Brahman Asita's prophecy. The Buddha victoriously resists the attacks and temptations of Māra, god of love, sin, and death. Analysis of the Lotus of the Good Law. The Buddha's teachings. Parables: the children in the burning house; the blind man recovering sight; vision of the Prabhūtaratna Stūpa. The Buddha prophesies. Effects of the supernatural powers of the Tathāgata. Explanation of the Buddha's different names.

WE will begin with an analysis of the two Buddhistic Sūtras that have been translated into French: the *Lalita-vistāra* by M. P. Ed. Foucaux, and the *Lotus of the Good Law* (Lotus de la bonne Loi) by M. E. Burnouf. It is a very strange form of literature, but the doctrines they set forth are equally strange, and the style agrees with the matter.

The following is an exact analysis of the fabulous part of the *Lalita-vistāra*.

Ānanda, the Buddha's cousin, is the speaker, and is supposed to have been the author of this Sūtra, which is classed among the more developed Sūtras. Ānanda relates what he has personally heard, as is indicated by the customary opening sentence, which in the eyes of the orthodox imparts to the statements contained in the Sūtras the authority of infallible witnesses: 'The following discourse was one day heard by me.'

Bhagavat, the Buddha, was at Jetavana, in the garden of Anātha Piṇḍika, near Ṣrāvasti. He was surrounded by twelve thousand Bhikshus, amongst whom, in the first rank, were his five disciples, and by thirty-two thousand Bodhisatwas, 'all subject to one last birth, all having really attained the state of Bodhisatwa, all having reached the other shore,' &c. At the first watch of the night, Bhagavat was plunged in a deep meditation, called the Arrangement of the Buddha's Ornaments. No sooner was he completely absorbed than an excrescence[1] appeared on the top of his head, which caused him to remember exactly all the Buddhas who had formerly existed; and the light of pure knowledge being produced in him, it revealed to him the dwellings of the gods, and the sons of gods, in infinite number. All these divinities, summoned by stanzas of invitation, which emanate from the luminous sphere that envelops the Tathāgata, approach the Buddha, entreating him to teach them that part of the Law which is called *Lalita-vistāra.* Bhagavat, touched with compassion for the Bodhisatwas, Mahāsatwas, Mahāşcrāvakas, and the gods, men, Asekhas, and the world, silently consents to hear their prayer, and lifts up his voice to teach them himself the *Lalita-vistāra.*

Such is the first chapter, and it will suffice to give us an idea how much patience we shall require to examine these and similar extravagances of which we are only at the beginning.

We will then give the description from the Buddha's own narrative of his condition previous to his birth, and his incarnation on earth.

Worshipped by those who were adored as gods, receiving the homage of Şākra, Brahma, Mahēşvara, the guardians of the world and all the lesser deities, the Bodhisatwa leaves Tushita, the abode of joy, and goes to the great palace of Dharmochaya (nucleus of the Law). It is from thence that he has to instruct the immense multitude gathered to hear him, which amounts to sixty-eight kotis, that is to say six hundred and eighty million souls, all seated on sumptuous

[1] All the Buddha's statues bear on the top of the head this characteristic excrescence.

seats. Bhagavat first announces that twelve years must elapse before the Buddha will enter his mother's womb; and in order that this event may be properly accomplished with all the requisite conditions, it is necessary to make four important examinations. He has to examine, first time, secondly continents, thirdly countries, and fourthly families.)

Bodhisatwas, at the first development of the world, before the arrangement of beings in their order, do not enter a mother's womb. When, however, the world is entirely made manifest, and old age, sickness, and death have appeared in it, from that time the Bodhisatwas become born of a mother. For this reason Bhagavat makes an examination of time.

He examines the continents because a Bodhisatwa cannot be born on a frontier; neither can he be born in eastern Vidēha, nor in western Godani, nor in northern Kuru. He can only be born in the southern continent in Jambudvīpa (India). Neither can he be born in a frontier province 'among stupid men, of dull senses, and dumb dispositions like sheep, incapable of distinguishing good teaching from bad.' Therefore only in a central province can he be born.

Finally, the Bodhisatwa applies himself to the examination of families, because Bodhisatwas cannot be born in a family of low class, that of a chandāla, a flute-player, a wheelwright, or a servant. They are born in two castes only, that of the Brahmans or the Kshatriyas, according to whichever is held in greatest respect at the moment.

Nevertheless the throng of deities question among themselves 'in what choicest of families' the Bodhisatwa will be born. They pass in review the most illustrious races of the time, and, unable to come to any conclusion, they ask the question of the Bodhisatwa himself.

The Bodhisatwa answers them by enumerating the sixty-four signs with which the family he has chosen is endowed;

he names them one by one; they are so many virtues. The family is noble, of perfect descent; it is not ambitious; it is of pure morals, and is wise; it makes a magnificent use of its wealth; it is constant in friendship, knows its duties, is not led away by desire, passion, ignorance, or fear; it possesses firm heroism; honours the Rishis, honours the gods, the Chaītyas[1], the Manes; does not keep up enmity—in a word, the family is perfect in all things. The woman into whose womb the Bodhisatwa is to enter is no less perfect; for she possesses thirty-two kinds of virtues, and is free from all feminine defects.

The gods, whose curiosity was more excited than satisfied by these vague indications, wonder which can be this blessed family, and this still more blessed woman, and they can only think of the Ṣākya race, the king Suddhodana and the queen Māyā-Devi, who unite so many virtues and perfections. It is at Kapilavastu and of these two choicely-gifted beings that the Bodhisatwa will be born: 'for no other woman is capable of bearing the first among mankind.' When he is on the point of leaving the gods in Tushita to descend on earth, the Bodhisatwa addresses them once more from his throne, and recalls to them the precepts of the Law. He first points out the 'Visible Gates,' which number 108, the principal ones being: faith, purity, discretion, benevolence, pity, modesty, knowledge of self (*ātmajnatā*), respect, and the acquisition of magic formulae; then after a long and complete enumeration he adds, as he takes leave of the gods, these solemn words, which they listen to in respectful silence:

'Carefully avoid immodesty. All divine and pure pleasures born of the heart and mind are the fruit of a virtuous deed. Remember therefore your actions. As you have failed to

[1] The sacred monuments where the Buddha's relics and those of his principal votaries are placed.

amass virtues in a former life, you are now bound for a place, far from all comfort, where you will suffer all kinds of misfortunes and ills. Desire is not durable nor constant; it is like a dream, a mirage, an illusion, like lightning, like foam. Observe the practice of the Law; whosoever observes its holy practices will suffer no evil. Love tradition, morality, and almsgiving; be perfect in patience and purity. Act in a spirit of mutual benevolence, with a helpful spirit. Remember the Buddha, the Law, and the Assemblies of the faithful. All that you behold in me, of supernatural power, knowledge, and authority—all this is produced by the exercise of virtue, which is its cause, and comes from tradition, morality, and modesty. You also must act with the same perfect discretion. It is not by maxims, nor words, nor clamour that the doctrine of virtue can be attained. Acquire it by your deeds; as you speak, so act; strive therefore by unceasing efforts. There is no reward for all those who have done good deeds; but those who do them not will obtain nothing. Beware of pride, haughtiness, and arrogance; be ever gentle, and keep the straight road, diligently pursuing the path that leads to Nirvāna. Exercise yourselves to find the way of salvation, and dispel with the lamp of wisdom the darkness of ignorance. Disentangle yourselves from the meshes of sin, and let repentance accompany you. But what need is there to say more? The Law is full of wisdom and purity. When I shall have attained supreme wisdom, when the Law that leads to immortality shall have rained down upon spirits made perfectly pure, then return to hear anew the Law which I will teach you.'

Notwithstanding this exhortation, the gods were sorely distressed at the Buddha's departure; but in order to assuage their grief he left them as a substitute the Bodhisatwa Maitreya, whom he consecrated by placing on his head with his own hands his tiara and diadem. Maitreya is the Buddha who is to succeed him when the perversion of the world will have wiped out all recollection of the teaching of Ṣākya-muni

The Bodhisatwa then descends from Tushita into his mother's womb, and to accomplish the prediction contained in the Brahmānas and the Mantras of the Rigvēda, he assumes the form of a majestic elephant, armed with six tusks, covered with a network of gold, its superb head of a red colour, and its jaws wide open. Eight premonitory signs herald its arrival in Suddhodana's dwelling. The palace cleanses itself; all the birds of Himavanta fly to it, showing their gladness by their songs; the gardens are filled with flowers; the ponds are covered with lotus; viands of all kinds, spread upon the festive tables, renew themselves after being abundantly partaken of; musical instruments give out, without being touched, the most melodious sounds; caskets of precious jewels open of their own accord to display their treasures; lastly, the palace is illuminated by a supernatural splendour that outshines the sun and moon.

Such is the prologue, as it were, of the drama that is unfolded in the *Lalita-vistāra*; the scene is laid in heaven before opening on earth, The narrative would not be lacking in a certain grandeur if the manner and style corresponded to the majesty of the idea; but it is impossible not to feel that it is a pure fantastical invention, and that the author of the legend is only playing with his subject. In the original text the details are so lengthy that the first conception almost entirely disappears, to give place to endless repetitions and to the most tedious improbabilities.

All the time the Bodhisatwa was in Māyā-Devi's womb he remained in her right side, sitting cross-legged. These are the strange details which the sacred legend deems necessary to mention; but they are nothing in comparison to those that follow. Some of the sons of the deities are astonished that the Bodhisatwa, 'pure and unsoiled, far above all the worlds, the most sacred of all beings,' should dwell in the womb of an earthly mother, while the ordinary kings of the Gandharvas, Kumbhandas, Nāgas and Yākshas, inferior gods, always avoid the defilement of a human body. Suspecting the thought of the sons of the gods, the Buddha causes Ānanda his cousin to question him, and in reply he informs him of his occupation while in his mother's womb; this is called 'the sacred exercise of the Bodhisatwa.' The Buddha relates with the most prolix and confused details the visit that Brahma, the sovereign master, comes to pay him in Māyā-Devi's womb. Brahma, after having bowed his head at Bhagavat's feet, offers him a drop of dew that contains all the vital and generating essence of the three thousand great thousands of worlds. After Brahma, Ṣākra, the master of the gods, the four great kings of the inferior gods, four goddesses, and a multitude of divinities come to worship and serve the Bodhisatwa, and receive from him instruction in the Law.

We would not quote these absurdities were it not that they show the turn of mind of the Buddhists, and how they placed their Buddha far above all the gods of the Brahman Pantheon. Brahma, Indra, and all those hitherto considered the greatest and most venerated are hardly worthy to serve the Bodhisatwa, and even before his birth, according to the Buddhists, the most respected objects of popular superstition prostrated themselves before him. The *Lalita-vistāra* is not the work of the Buddha's own immediate disciples, and it is probable that in the days of their Master, and soon after his death, they did not hold such arrogant language. However, about three or four centuries later the new doctrine had made sufficient progress to permit the gods adored by the vulgar being treated with such insolent contempt. Sometimes the author himself seems conscious that he has gone too far, and the king Suddhodana, who is mentioned as a spectator of the evolutions of the gods before his unborn son, is overcome by certain scruples. However much he may rejoice at being the father of the future Buddha, he cannot conceal his astonishment, and says to himself: 'This is indeed the god of gods whom the four guardians of the world, whom Brahma, Indra, and the united deities surround with such deep respect; this will in truth be the Buddha. In the three worlds, not a god, nor a Nāga, nor Indra, nor Brahma, not a being in fact, would permit such worship without the others crushing him on the head and depriving him of life. But this one, because he is purer than the gods, can receive this worship without incurring any danger.'

We will not relate the precursory signs that announced the birth of the Buddha, nor the care that the gods bestowed on his mother Māyā-Devi in the Lumbini gardens, where her delivery took place, standing and leaning under the shade of a plaksa, clinging for support to a branch of the tree. Indra the king of the gods, and Brahma the lord of created beings, stand before her to receive the child. They bathe and wash it with their own hands—a needless precaution, as he has lain unsoiled in his mother's womb, the legend says, and that he was already clothed in a rich robe of Kāşi (Benāres) silk[1]. Directly he is born he stands on the ground and seats himself on a large white lotus, which has spontaneously sprung from the earth on the spot which his feet have touched. Then without any assistance he takes seven steps towards the east, seven to the south, seven to the west, seven to the north, and seven steps towards the lower regions, announcing in each direction the mission he had come to

[1] These details are reproduced on all the Buddhistic monuments that represent the birth of the Liberator. See the basrelief in the museum at Calcutta that M. Ed. Foucaux gives at the end of *Rgya tch'er rol pa*. Another and more decent legend, the Abinishkramma, supposes that Indra, to spare Māyā-Devi the shame of being delivered in his presence, assumed the form of an old woman. But in this disguise the child refuses his attentions, and repels him, not permitting him to touch him, although he recognizes him to be Indra.

fulfil on earth: 'I shall conquer the demon and the demon's army. I will pour forth rain from the clouds of the Law upon the beings plunged into hell and devoured by hell-fire, and they will be filled with joy and gladness.'

But the Buddha, who is supposed to relate all this to his disciples at Ṣrāvasti, interrupts his narration, and turning to his cousin Ānanda, predicts that many will not believe these miraculous deeds. 'In the time to come, certain Bhikshus, ignorant, incompetent, proud, haughty, of unbridled and unstable mind, sceptics and devoid of faith, the shame of the Sramanas,' will refuse to believe in the power of the Buddha, and will wonder at his having been born of a woman. 'They will not understand, foolish men! that if he had come in the condition of a god instead of coming into the world of man, he would not have been able to turn the Wheel of the Law, and all beings would have been plunged into despair. But those creatures who have denied the wisdom of the Buddha will at their death be cast into Avitchi, the great hell; whereas those who have believed in the Buddha will become the sons of the Tathāgata, and will be delivered from the three evils; they will eat of the food of the kingdom; they will tear asunder the chains of the demon; and will have left behind them the desert of a transmigatory life.'

The legend then recounts, with a multitude of details, how the child was brought from Lumbini to Kapilavastu after the death of his mother, and how he was, by the consent of the Ṣākyas and their wives, who contended for the care of him, confided to his aunt Mahā-Prajāpatī. The legend dwells at length on the prediction of the Brahman Asita (the black), who comes down expressly from the Himavanta (Himalaya) mountains, where he dwells, to verify on the body of the newborn infant the thirty-two signs of a great man, and the eighty secondary marks, which he most carefully enumerates one after the other, however extraordinary some of them may seem. The great Rishi, on ascertaining that the Buddha is born, mourns that his extreme age will prevent his ever hearing the teaching of the pure Law.

Then he retires, laden with presents from the king, who has been delighted at his prediction; and he returns to his hermitage as he had come, through the air, whence he had magically upraised himself in company with his nephew Naradatta. But it would seem that Asita's prophecy, important as it was, did not suffice, and after him a son of the gods, followed by twelve hundred thousand other gods, came also to verify the signs and marks, and once more assured Suddhodana that his son was in truth the Buddha. It will be remembered that the child was solemnly presented by his father at the temple of the gods; but the legend adds, that no sooner had the Bodhisatwa entered the temple than all the inanimate images of the gods, including Indra and Brahma, rose up and did obeisance to him. Then the gods, pointing to their own images, sang the following stanzas, or gāthas, which we quote, as they show a poetic inspiration that is generally lacking in Buddhism, although at least half the developed Sūtras are in verse.

'The greatest of the mountains, the Mēru, king of the hills, bows not down to the Sénevé. The ocean, the abode of Nāgas' king, bows not down before the water contained in the footprints of a cow. The sun, the moon that gives light, bow not down before the glowworm. He who has issued from a wise and virtuous family, who is himself full of virtue, bows not down before the most powerful gods. The deity or the man, whoever he may be, who persists in pride, is like the Sénevé, the water in the footprints of a cow, and the glowworm. But like Mēru, the ocean, the sun, and the moon, is Svayambhu, the self-existing, who fulfils the first need of the world; and whosoever renders him homage obtains heaven and Nirvāna.'

(The above will show with tolerable clearness the nature of the legend, and how it tries to transform and embellish—from its own point of view—the actual facts of Siddhārtha's life. To complete our information on the subject, we will relate one last episode that takes an important place, not only in *Lalita-vistāra*, but which figures in nearly every Sūtra; that is the conflict that Siddhārtha, at the moment of becoming Buddha, sustained with the demon called Māra, the Evil One, or Pāpiyān, the god of love, of sin, and of death.

Siddhārtha was at Uruvela, in the retreat we have already mentioned, where for six years he had given himself up to the severest penance. His mother Māyā-Devi, alarmed at her son's sufferings, and fearing lest he should die, had left Tushita and came to implore him to put a stop to these excessive mortifications. He comforted his mother, but did not yield to her entreaties. Māra in his turn came to tempt him, and in a gentle voice addressed him in the following flattering words: 'Dear one, thou must live; it is only by living that thou canst fulfil the Law. All that is done during life should be done without suffering. Thou art emaciated; thy colour has fled, thou drawest near to death. However great the merit, what can be the result of such renunciation? The path of renunciation is suffering, the victory over the mind is difficult to attain.'

Siddhārtha replied to him: 'Pāpiyān, friend of all folly and evil, art thou then come hither to tempt me? Although my merits are but small, the aim I have in view is not less worthy. The inevitable end of life being death, I seek not to avoid death. I possess resolution, courage, and wisdom; and I see no one on earth who can deter me. Demon, soon shall I triumph over thee. Thy first soldiers are desires, thy second in rank are weariness and vexation, thy third are hunger and thirst, passions are thy fourth, indolence and slumber thy fifth, fears are thy sixth, doubts are thy seventh, anger and hypocrisy thy eighth; ambition, flattery, homage, false reputations, self-praise, and the censure of others, these are thy dark allies, the soldiers of the fiery demon. Thy soldiers subjugate gods as well as men. But I will destroy them by wisdom; and then, Spirit of Evil, what wilt thou do?'

Māra, humbled and abashed, disappeared for a time. But the sons of the gods came in their turn to subject the ascetic to a temptation which was perhaps more dangerous still. They suggested that he should pretend to take no nourishment, and that they should impart to him through the pores of the skin all the vigour he lacked, and that he intended to get by ordinary food. However, the young Siddhārtha refused, saying: 'Assuredly, I might swear that I did not eat; and the neighbouring peasants who dwell in my vicinity would say that the Sramana Gautama did not eat, while the sons of the gods, respecting my weakness, would invigorate me through the pores of my skin; but I should be acting most deceitfully.' The Bodhisatwa, to avoid such a sin, would not listen to the words of the sons of the deities, and thus again he evaded a temptation more insidious than that of Māra.

However, before attaining Buddhahood he was obliged to conquer the demon; he therefore provoked him to the combat, while he was at Bodhimanda, by shooting forth from between his eyebrows—from the tuft of hair called Urnā, which is one of the thirty-two signs of a great man—a ray of light that illuminated all the dwellings of the demons and made them tremble with fear. Pāpiyān, terrified by the sudden brilliancy and the thirty-two horrible dreams he had had, at once summoned his servants and all his armies. His empire was threatened, and he wished to begin the fight. However, he first consulted his sons, some of whom advised him to yield and thus avoid a severe defeat; while the others urged him to engage in a strife in which victory appeared to them certain. The two parties, one black and the other white, spake in turn; and the thousand sons of the demon, some on his right and others on his left-hand side, gave their opinions in succession, and in a contrary sense. When the consultation was brought to a close, Pāpiyān decided in favour of giving battle, and his army, composed of four divisions, advanced against the Bodhisatwa. The army was strong and courageous, but was hideous beyond description. The demons who composed it could at will change their faces, and transform themselves in a hundred millions of ways; their hands and feet were encircled by a hundred thousand serpents; they were armed with swords, bows and arrows, pikes, javelins, hatchets, clubs, chains, stones, sticks, quoits, thunderbolts; their heads, eyes, and faces blazed like fire; their stomachs, feet, and hands were of a repulsive appearance; their faces glittered with sinister brilliancy; they had enormous teeth, terrible tusks, thick, big tongues that hung out of their mouths; their eyes were red and glowing like those of a black serpent full of venom, &c., &c. We abbreviate the lengthy description, which fills several pages of the *Lalita-vistāra*, in which the Indian imagination revels in the invention of the most monstrous and uncouth creations.

As may be supposed, all the attacks of the demon were powerless against the Buddha. The spears, pikes, javelins, projectiles of every description, even mountains, which they hurled down on him, were changed into flowers and hung in garlands over his head. Pāpiyān, seeing that violence was useless, had recourse to other means; he summoned his daughters, the beautiful Apsaras, and sent them to tempt the Bodhisatwa by showing him thirty-two kinds of feminine magic. They sang and danced before him, they deployed all their charms and seductions; they addressed to him the softest and most insinuating language. But their caresses proved as useless as their brothers' assaults, and filled with shame, they found themselves compelled to sing the praises of him whom they could neither vanquish nor seduce. They then returned to their father and informed him of this second defeat, more disastrous even than the first. Pāpiyān was astounded; but the sons of the Suddhāva-sakāyika gods filled the measure of his vexation by scoffing at him with the most poignant insults and the bitterest sarcasms. The demon, however, would not give in: 'I am the lord of desire,' he said to the Bodhisatwa, 'I am lord of the whole world; the gods, the throng of Dānāvas, all men and beasts overcome by me have fallen into my power. Like them, thou hast come into my kingdom; rise and speak as they do.'

The Bodhisatwa replied: 'If thou art the lord of desire, thou art not the lord of light. Behold me; I am truly the lord of the law; impotent as thou art, it is in thy sight that I shall obtain supreme wisdom.'

Pāpiyān tried another last assault, and called together again his armies. But again he succumbed. His army is scattered in disorder, and he has the grief of seeing those of his sons who had counselled him to yield go and prostrate themselves at the feet of the Bodhisatwa, and respectfully worship him. Fallen from his splendour, pale and colourless, the demon beats his breast and utters loud lamentations; then he stands aside with drooping head, and, tracing some signs with an arrow on the earth, he says in his despair: 'My kingdom is at an end.'

After this decisive victory, the Bodhisatwa attains supreme wisdom, Buddhahood; he becomes the perfectly enlightened Buddha, and goes to turn the Wheel of the Law at Benāres. Such is the mythological side of the *Lalita-vistāra*, without mentioning its other details, from which we have taken the life of the Buddha. Probably all this phantasmagoria was necessary for the people to whom it was addressed, but in our eyes it is a mere extravagance, calculated to throw discredit on the real historical facts which accompany it, and which it serves only to obscure.

We will pass on to analyze the *Lotus of the good Law.*

The *Lotus of the good Law* is nothing but a fabulous legend, devoid of any trace of historical facts, and infinitely less interesting than the *Lalita-vistāra*; to all appearance it was written somewhat later.

Bhagavat was at Rājagriha, on the mountain called the Vulture's Peak (Gridhrakūta, actually the Giddhar). He was surrounded by twelve hundred monks, all of whom were Arahats, or holy men, and attentive hearers (*Mahā-ṣrāvakas*) of Ānanda, his cousin, besides two thousand other monks, six thousand nuns, headed by Mahā-Prajāpatī, his aunt, and Yasodharā, one of his wives; eighty thousand Bodhisatwas, sixteen virtuous men, Ṣākra, the Indra of the Dēvas, with twenty thousand sons of the gods; Brahma, with twelve thousand sons of the gods, a crowd of other deities, and finally Ajātaṣatru, king of Magadha, son of Vaidehī.

Bhagavat, after having expounded the Sūtra called the Great Demonstration, remained silent, plunged in the meditation which is called the Place of Demonstration. A shower of divine flowers falls on him and on those who surround him, when suddenly a ray of light springs from the circle of hair that grows between his eyebrows, and illumines the eighteen thousand lands of the Buddha situated in the East, as far as the great hell, Avitchi, and to the very limits of existence. All the spectators were struck by this miracle, and one of them, the Bodhisatwa Mahāsatwa-Maitreya, inquired of Manju-ṣrī, who was next to him, the meaning of this marvellous appearance. Maitreya propounds his question in fifty-six stanzas of two verses each. Manju-ṣrī answers him in the same style, prose and verse, that this 'beam of light foretells that the Blessed One is about to explain the developed Sūtra, called the *Lotus of the good Law*.'

This is, in fact, an introduction somewhat similar to that of the *Lalita-vistāra*, of less grandeur, and, if possible, of less probability, as the scene is laid on this earth instead of being supposed to take place in heaven.

Bhagavat awakes from his meditation, and replying to Ṣariputra, who has not interrogated him, explains to him, first in prose and afterwards in verse, that are little more than a repetition, the difficulties which the teaching of the Law presents. At the same moment five thousand monks, who are incapable of understanding the Law, quit the meeting, and the Tathāgata congratulates himself on their departure. Then he informs his disciple that he makes use of a hundred thousand different manners of teaching the Law, although in reality there is but one way, one vehicle for attaining salvation. He repeats to him in one hundred and forty-four stanzas what he has already said in sufficiently wordy prose; and to give him an example of the means he employs for the instruction of human beings, he sets forth a parable.

The aged father of a family coming home one day finds his house in flames. His young children, shut up indoors, are unaware and heedless of their danger. In vain does their father call to them; the children, who do not see the conflagration, refuse to believe him, and will not listen to his entreaties. In order to persuade them he promises that if they will come out he will give them magnificent toys, and among others three kinds of chariots, which he assures them will delight and amuse them. As soon as the children have come out safe and sound, their father, instead of giving them three different kinds of chariots, presents them all three with the same kind of chariot. Nevertheless these chariots are superb and handsomely decorated. Has their father been guilty of a falsehood? Most certainly not. Well then, in the same way the Tathāgata, taking pity on the puerile levity of man, who, in the midst of all the miseries of life does nothing but seek for amusement and pleasure, adapts himself to his foibles. He offers him, to enable him to escape from the slavery of the three worlds, three different vehicles—that of the Ṣrāvakas, that of the Pratyīka Buddhas, and that of the Bodhisatwas. Man, tempted like the children in the burning house, quits the three worlds, and the Tathāgata then gives him only one vehicle, the great vehicle of the Buddha, which leads to complete Nirvāna.

To this parable four of the Buddha's principal disciples—Subhūti, Kātyāyana, Kāṣyapa and Moggallāna—reply by another, in order to excuse the miserable propensities which prevent men from hearing and following the Law. Man, they say, is like the son of a rich family who abandons his parents to lead a disorderly life, and who, after many errors and misfortunes, is restored to his father, whom he fails to recognize. The son, after cheerfully submitting to a long probation, at last returns to the right course and the possession of his inheritance, compromised by his misconduct.

Bhagavat propounds again several other parables, one of which is very remarkable.

There was a man blind from his birth, who used to say, 'There is neither colour nor form, whether beautiful or the reverse; there is no beholder to see it; there is neither sun, nor moon, nor stars, nor constellations.' In vain did those around him try to reason this blind man out of his gross incredulity. He continued to repeat his assertions until a skilful physician restored to him his sight. The blind man then passed to the other extreme, and said within himself: 'Assuredly I was mad, I who did not believe those who had eyes, and would not credit them. Now I see everything, I am delivered from my blindness, and nobody on earth can know more than I do.' But the wise Rishis, witnessing his present blindness, which was more to be feared than the first, strove to moderate his deplorable vanity. 'Thou hast only just recovered thy sight, O man,' they said, 'and as yet thou knowest nothing. Whence therefore all this pride? Thou hast no wisdom, and thou art uninstructed. When thou art seated in thy house thou seest not that which is outside; thou knowest not the thoughts of thy fellows; thou dost not hear at a distance of five yodjanas the sound of the coach and of the drum; thou canst not convey thyself the distance of one kroṣa without the use of thy feet. Thou hast been begotten and developed in thy mother's womb, and of that thou rememberest nothing! How therefore art thou learned? How canst thou say, I know all? How canst thou say, I see all? Recognize, O man, that light is darkness, and darkness light.' The blind man, ashamed of his presumption, desired the Rishis to instruct him in the mysteries of the Law; and soon his spiritual eyes were opened, as those of his body had been opened by the skilful physician, who was no other than the Tathāgata.

Then follow in the *Lotus of the good Law* several chapters devoted to the Buddha's prophecies. These prophecies commit him to nothing. The Buddha foretells that four of his listeners—Kāṣyapa and three others—will in their turn become Buddhas. He tells them the names under which they will be reborn in the universe they are to save. He even takes the trouble to describe to each of them, in prose and in verse, the beauty of the world over which they will reign, and even fixes the length of their reign, in figures which are fabulously enormous. He does the same for a less illustrious hearer than these four, Pūrna, who had formerly abandoned an immense fortune to follow the

Buddha. These splendid prophecies awake, as may be believed, the desire, if not the envy, of those who hear Bhagavat. Twelve hundred of his auditors are seized with the same thought: 'If only Bhagavat could predict to each of us our future destiny, as he has done for these great Ṣrāvakas!' Bhagavat guesses their thoughts, but he merely predicts that five hundred monks, all Arahats, will become Buddhas under the name of Samanta-Prabhasā, which will be common to all. Nevertheless Ānanda, the Tathāgata's cousin, Rāhula his son, and two thousand monks conceive the same desire; and Bhagavat is obliged to predict to each one the fate that awaits him; they will all be Buddhas under different names and in different worlds.

These are foolish and idle details, seeing that the explanation of the Law promised in the *Lotus* is not given; but the following accounts are still more absurd.

While Bhagavat 'unfolds these predictions, that fill with joy, satisfaction, pleasure, content and gladness' all those who are concerned, and even those who hear them without deriving any advantage from them, suddenly a marvellous stūpa[1] rises from the ground, in the midst of the assembly; it is made of seven precious substances, is five hundred yodjanas high and a circumference in proportion. It rises in the air and remains suspended in the sky, in full view of the assembly which gazes with admiration upon its thousands of balconies strewn with flowers, its thousands of porticos, banners, flags, garlands, bells, not to mention gold and silver, and pearls, diamonds, crystals, emeralds, &c. A voice proceeds from the stūpa and praises the explanation Bhagavat has made of the Law, or rather that he has promised to make. It is the voice of an ancient Tathāgata named

[1] Stūpas are buildings in the form of cones and cupolas, erected by the piety of believers to enshrine and cover relics. They are found throughout all India, particularly in the northern and central provinces.

Prabhūtaratna, who comes to pay homage to the Buddha, and to take his share of the teaching. After he had called together hundreds of thousands, millions, myriads of kotis of Bodhisatwas to honour the illustrious visitor, the Buddha, with the forefinger of his right hand, divides the stūpa in the middle; and the Tathāgata Prabhūtaratna is seen, seated cross-legged, his limbs dried up, without, however, his body being diminished in size. He seems plunged in deep meditation. He, however, rouses himself from his ecstasy and invites the Buddha, whom he loads with praises, to come and seat himself by his side in the stūpa. The Buddha consents, and both remain in the air, speaking to the Assembly, which has likewise risen into space, through the supernatural power of Bhagavat.

Then the predictions begin again, and this time they are addressed to women. The aunt of the Buddha, Mahā-Prajāpatī the Gautamide, will also, according to her wish, become a Buddha; Yasodharā, the mother of Rāhula is to enjoy the same happiness; and the thousands of nuns who follow them will become interpreters of the Law. It seems probable that, to accomplish this superhuman mission, the women will change their sex; for if the legend is silent in this case, it expressly announces it in that of the daughter of Sāgara, king of the Nāgas, who, gifted with perfect wisdom from the age of eight years, is, as a reward for her piety, transformed into a man so that she may become a Bodhisatwa.

We feel somewhat unwilling to expose such absurdities, which are as ungraceful as they are foolish, and we would fain spare our readers, were it not that we wish to give them an exact idea of these records which, monstrous and senseless as they are, have been venerated by so many nations. But before ending we must make a last quotation which, in the grossness of its folly, surpasses, we think, anything to be found in the Buddhist Sūtras. It is contained in the twentieth chapter of the *Lotus of the Good Law*, and is entitled *Effects of the supernatural power of the Tathāgata.*

Hundreds of thousands of myriads of kotis of Bodhisatwas, who equal in number the atoms contained in a thousand worlds, have risen from clefts in the earth created by a ray of light projected from the centre of Bhagavat's eyebrows. With joined hands they worship the Buddha, who has called them together, and promise him, after his entrance into perfect Nirvāna, to expound the Law in his stead. The master thanks them. Then the blessed Ṣākya-muni and the blessed Prabhūtaratna, still seated on the throne of the stūpa, smile to one another. Their tongues protrude from their mouths, and reach as far as the world of Brahma. At the same moment several hundreds of thousand myriads of kotis of rays issue from them. The innumerable Tathāgatas who surround these two personages imitate them; they put out their tongues in the same manner, and they continue to exhibit this supernatural power during a hundred thousand years. At the end of the hundred thousand years they draw in their tongues, making a sound like the noise produced on forcibly expelling the voice from the throat or in snapping the fingers.

In truth all this absurdity is revolting; and if it were not that all this wretched nonsense is in a canonical book, it would not be worth repeating; fortunately, however, our task is not always an ungrateful one, and we shall find later on, when we treat of Buddhist ethics, compensations for all this folly and rubbish.

The remainder of the *Lotus of the Good Law*, does not deserve any particular analysis. The twenty-first and following chapters are almost exclusively devoted to the enumeration of the advantages the faithful will derive from reading this Sūtra; and among other things they are promised magic formulas which will preserve them from all dangers. At last, in the twenty-seventh chapter, Bhagavat confides the charge of the Law to the assembly which has just listened to its explanation, and dismisses his gratified hearers.

Before taking leave of the legend of Ṣākya-muni, it is necessary, in order to complete it, to give an explanation of the principal names by which the Reformer has been called. They are many, and all have a certain importance, either from a dogmatic or a philosophical point of view. They may be divided into two classes: religious and secular. The secular names are already known to us. We know that the one the young prince received from his father at his birth was Siddhārtha, and the meaning of the two names Ṣākya-muni and Sramana Gautama will also be remembered.

The name of Buddha, which as it has given its name to a religion, is the most celebrated of all, means the Learned, the Enlightened, or the Intelligent One. It is derived from *Budh*, to know. It seems a modest title in comparison with the prodigious part played by him to whom it was given; but at the same time it shows what a high opinion Indian genius had of knowledge, which is thus held to be capable of saving man and assuring to him an immortality that the gods themselves could not attain to. As the word Buddha is not a proper name, it must never be used to designate Ṣākya-muni, without adding the article and saying: THE BUDDHA. It is merely a title added to or substituted for the name under which the prince of Kapilavastu was known to the world.

Tathāgata, one of the highest titles given to the Buddha, and which he appears to have given to himself, signifies: 'he who walks in the footsteps of his predecessors, he who has fulfilled his religious career in the same way as the Buddhas before him.' By this title Ṣākya-muni's mission is connected with that of all the sages who preceded him, and whose example he followed.

Sugaṭa, or the happy one, is a similar epithet, from an etymological point of view, to that of Tathāgata; but the historical and philosophical meaning is less important. It simply affirms that, according to Buddhist faith, Ṣākya-muni came to save the world and bring happiness to all beings.

Bhagavat, the blessed one or the fortunate one, is the Buddha's most usual name in the Nepaulese Sūtras. It was a title frequently applied in Brahmanical language to great personages; but in Buddhist language it was almost exclusively confined to the Buddha, or rather to the personage who was about to become the Buddha.

The name of Bodhisatwa is more complicated and contains more shades of meaning. Grammatically it means: 'He who has the essence of the Bodhi,' or the supreme wisdom of a Buddha. Now to acquire this supreme wisdom, it is necessary to have triumphantly endured the hardest and longest trials in a multitude of successive existences. The being is then ripe, as is said by Buddhists, for the state of a perfect Buddha. But the most energetic and determined will is not sufficient, virtue itself is ineffectual to enable a being to attain to this high state of sanctity; he must also gain the favour of one or several of the former Buddhas. When he has learned how to obtain it, he goes into one of the heavens suspended above the earth to await the moment of his appearance on earth. However, even after he has come to this world, he remains Bodhisatwa, and is not yet Buddha. He can only become Buddha after having shown by his austerities, and the practice of all virtue, by knowledge and study here below, that he is worthy of teaching mankind and saving the world into which he has entered. Under these conditions only can the Bodhisatwa become Buddha.

Another name is also given sometimes to the Buddha which is less exalted than the preceding ones; that of Arahat or Venerable, which is also used for monks of a superior rank. When, however, it is applied to the Buddha, it is completed and enhanced by adding, 'The Venerable One of the World,' or 'The Venerable One of the Age.')

The Buddhists are not satisfied by making the Buddha an ideal of virtue, knowledge, holiness, and supernatural power; they have also made him an ideal of physical beauty, and the same vivid imagination that has produced the extravagant descriptions in the great Sūtras has been called into play with as much puerile diffuseness in portraying the Tathāgata. (It seems probable that just as the legend contains real and historical facts, so the portrait of the Buddha has retained some of the particulars of the personal appearance of Siddhārtha. Here again, however, it is difficult to discriminate between truth and falsehood. In the thirty-two characteristics of a great man, and the eighty secondary marks, there are physical impossibilities, or rather exaggerations that verge on the impossible. Nevertheless these details cannot be thrust aside, for they show the taste of the people at that early date, and it forms part of their aesthetic ideas, and can furnish some information with regard to their ethnography. This exact nomenclature of thirty-two signs and eighty secondary marks dates from the earliest days of Buddhism, as it is already to be found in the *Lalita-vistāra*; moreover it is considered of as much consequence among the Southern as among the Northern Buddhists. It is therefore an important, although external part of Buddhist belief; and it forms a sort of beacon visible to the meanest intelligence to be verified before any profession of faith.)

Burnouf has devoted to this study one of the most voluminous appendixes of the *Lotus of the Good Law*. He has taken the trouble to study and compare seven different lists contained in Nepaulese and Sinhalese writings.

We will not enumerate one by one the thirty-two signs, still less the eighty secondary marks; but will be content with quoting a few of the most remarkable.

The first sign is a protuberance of the cranium on the top of the head. There is nothing to prevent our believing that Siddhārtha did possess this singular conformation. The second sign is to have hair curling towards the right side of a deep black, changing colour with the light. The hair turned to the right recalls doubtless the act of the young prince cutting off his hair with his sword; and the short curls, which have erroneously been taken for those of a negro, confirm this tradition, which still survived among the Sinhalese Buddhists when Colonel Mackenzie visited them in 1797. This second sign is probably as true as the first one. The third, which is a large smooth forehead, is no less likely. The fourth, on the contrary, seems a pure invention: that is, the famous tuft of hair, Ūrnā, growing between the eyebrows, and which must be white as snow or silver. Then follow the two signs relating to the eyes. The Buddha must have lashes like those of a heifer, and eyes of a deep black. His teeth must number forty, and must be even, close, and perfectly white. Then the description passes on to the voice, which must be like Brahma's; to the tongue, the jaw, the shoulders, the arms, which must reach down to the knees, a style of beauty we do not admire, but which the Indian poems never fail to give to their heroes; then to the figure, the hairs, each one of which must be separate and turn to the right side from the root; then to the most secret parts of the body; thence to the legs, fingers, hands, and finally to the feet which, among other things, must have a high instep, and be perfectly straight and firmly set.

The eighty secondary marks are simply supplementary and unimportant details added on to the thirty-two preceding ones. There are three for the nails, three for the fingers, five for the lines of the hand, ten for the limbs, five for the gait, three for the canine teeth, one for the nose, six for the eyes, five for the eyebrows, three for the cheeks, nine for the hair, &c., &c.

Too much importance must not be attached to all these minutiae, nevertheless they must not be entirely set aside. Some of them have given rise to superstitions that hold a great place in Buddhism. Thus the thirty-first sign of a great man is the mark of a wheel on the soles of the feet. Hence the Buddhists of Ceylon, Nepaul, Burmah, Siam, Laos, &c., have fancied they recognized in several places the impress of the Buddha's foot. It is the famous Prabhāt or Srīpāda, the blessed foot, of which one of the most celebrated traces is to be found on Adam's Peak in Ceylon, where Sinhalese superstition alleges that sixty-five auspicious signs are to be found.

We have given all the details of the real life of Ṣākya-muni and also of his legend, in order that the two sides of the Buddhist spirit should be clearly understood. On one side is a grandeur of mind seldom met with, a purity of morals almost perfect, a boundless charity, a life of heroism that never for a moment falters; and on the other hand an amount of superstition that shrinks at no extravagance, and that can only be palliated by the enthusiastic admiration for virtue and knowledge; on both sides the most noble sentiments allied with the most deplorable errors; the salvation of mankind sought for with indefatigable ardour and praiseworthy sincerity; and disastrous failures the just punishment of unconscious pride and a blind infatuation that nothing could enlighten. Such are the two general aspects of Buddhism. We shall find them again in its ethics and in its metaphysics.

CHAPTER III.

General character of Buddhist ethics derived from the canonical writings of the Councils. The Three Basketfuls, and the Three Pearls; the four noble truths; the ten precepts; the twelve observances specially applicable to monks on clothing, food, and residence; the six transcendent virtues and the secondary virtues; confession, family duties, preaching. Influence of Buddhist ethics on individuals and governments. The Buddha's ideal. Pūrna, Kunāla, Vāsavadattā and Upagupta. The kings Bimbisāra, Ajātaṣatru, and Aṣoka. Piyadasi's Edicts, spread all over India. Journeys of Chinese pilgrims in the fifth and seventh century of the Christian era. Fa Hian and Hiouen-Thsang.

ALTHOUGH Ṣākya-muni was a philosopher, and never pretended to any other title, it would be an error to expect of him a methodical and regular system. He preached all his life, but addressing himself to the people, he probably did not employ the rigid forms that science demands, which would not have been understood by his numerous hearers, and which the Brahmanic spirit has itself but imperfectly made use of. Entrusted by his self-imposed mission with the salvation of mankind and of all creatures, or better still with that of beings and the entire universe, the ascetic had to assume a language accessible to all, that is to say the simplest and most ordinary[1].

Thus the Buddha's ideas, although very clear and decided in his own mind, and all powerful in their sway over his disciples, were anything but precise in their form. The

[1] Burnouf remarks that this necessary condition of Buddhism explains its literary inferiority when compared with Brahmanism. Art, in every form, was almost unknown to Buddhism, and more particularly in literature; the style of the Sūtras is intolerable.

Buddha himself wrote nothing, and his principal adherents, assembled in Council directly after his death, settled in the Sūtras the words of the Master, and the doctrine which was about to become a dogma. Two other Councils after the first one made a definite code of the canonical writings, as they have been handed down to us, and as they were received through translations by all the nations professing Buddhism. This work of successive editions was finished at least two centuries before the Christian era. We know moreover that the first Council which met at Rājagriha in Magadha, under the protection of Ajātaṣatru divided the canonical books into three great classes, which remained unchanged in the subsequent editions. These were—the Sūtras or discourses of the Buddha, the Vinaya or Discipline, and the Abhidharma or Metaphysics. Ānanda was appointed to compile the Sūtras, Upali the Vinaya, and Kāṣyapa, who had regulated all the deliberations, reserved for himself the metaphysical part. The Sūtras, Vinaya, and Abhidharma formed what is called the Tripitaka, or Three Baskets, in the same way that the Buddha, the Law, and the Assembly formed the Triratna or the Three Pearls, the Three Gems. The Sūtras, which are also called Buddhavāchana or word of the Buddha, and Mūlagrantha, the textbook, are with good reason considered by the Northern Buddhists to be fundamental truths. It is evident that the remainder has been drawn from the Buddha's discourses.

The first theory that presents itself, and which, in due order must indeed precede all the others, is that of the four Noble Truths (āryāni satyāni). It was known to all Buddhists, and was adopted in the south and east, as well as in the north, in Ceylon, Burma, Pegu, Siam and China, exactly as it was in Nepaul and Tibet.

The following are the four truths:

First, the state of suffering which assails man under some

form or another, whatever may be the condition of his birth. This is unfortunately an undeniable fact, although it does not entail all the consequences that Buddhism ascribes to it; but it is given as an impregnable basis, sad but true, on which the whole building of the system reposes.

Secondly, the cause of suffering, which the Buddha attributes to the passions, to sinful lusts.

The third Noble Truth, a fitting consolation for the sad reality of the two first, is that sorrow will cease by Nirvāna, the supreme goal and reward of all man's efforts.

Finally, the fourth and last Truth, which forms the principal belief of Buddhism, the path leading to the cessation of sorrow, the method of salvation, the way that leads to Nirvāna (*marga*, in Pāli *magga*).

The way or method of salvation is called 'The Noble Eightfold Path.' It is summed up in eight principles or parts, which are so many conditions that man must fulfil in order to ensure his eternal deliverance.

The following are the eight divisions of the method.

The first, according to Buddhist phraseology, is Right Views, that is faith and orthodoxy; the second, Right Judgment, which dispels all doubt and uncertainty; the third, Right Words, that is perfect truthfulness, a horror of falsehood under whatever form, and a strict avoidance of it; the fourth condition of salvation, Right Aims, that is ever to pursue a pure and honest line of conduct; the fifth, a Right Mode of Livelihood, seeking for maintenance in an upright and sinless occupation, in other words by a religious profession; the sixth, a Right Application of the Mind to all the Precepts of the Law; the seventh, a Right Memory, which retains a clear and exact recollection of past actions; and the eighth and last, Right Meditation, which leads the intellect, even here below, to a quietude bordering on that of the Nirvāna.

These are the Four Noble Truths that Siddhārtha had attained to at Bodhimanda, under the Bodhi tree, after six years of meditation and penance; these did he first teach to his disciples, when he 'turned the Wheel of the Law' for the first time at Benāres. By the comprehension of these things did he become Buddha; and when he preached his doctrine to the world, he ever gave to these four Truths a preference over all other parts of his teaching. In his great struggle against the Tirthīyas or Brahmans of Kosala, in the presence of Prasenajit, when he defeated his adversaries, and the Brahmans fled, crying, 'We will fly for refuge to the mountain, we will seek a shelter amongst trees, waters, and hermitages,' Bhagavat addressed them in the following contemptuous words of farewell: 'Many men pursued by fear seek a refuge in the mountains and in the forests, in hermitages and under consecrated trees. But these are not the safest shelters, they are not the surest refuge. But he who seeks for a refuge in the Buddha, the Law, and the Assembly, when he beholds, with the eye of wisdom, the Four Noble Truths, which are the existence of Pain, the cause of Pain, the annihilation of Pain, and the way to the annihilation of Pain, and the Noble Eightfold Path that leads to Nirvāna, he of a surety knows the best shelter, the safest of all refuges. When he has attained this, he is freed from all suffering.'

If we are to believe the Mongol and Tibet traditions, the theory of the Four Truths took up the whole of the first Council, and their labour was confined to drawing up the Sūtras that explained it. It is, in a manner, the source and epitome of the whole Buddhist doctrine. It has, for the use of the faithful, been summed up in a stanza composed of two verses that all Buddhists know by heart, and which is for them a true article of faith. The monks constantly repeat it, and it is written on the pedestal of most of the images of the Buddha:

'Of all things proceeding from cause, the cause of their procession hath the Tathāgata explained. The great Sramana has likewise declared the cause of the extinction of all things[1].'

The things or effects are suffering and the present life, caused by past sins; the cause is the production of suffering; the extinction of all effects is Nirvāna; finally, the teaching of the Tathāgata, or the great Sramana, is the path that leads to Nirvāna.

Immediately following these Four Noble Truths are a certain number of moral precepts, very simple no doubt, but which the Buddha did not neglect any more than other reformers have done. The first five of these precepts are: not to kill, not to steal, not to commit adultery, not to lie, not to get drunk. To these commandments five others, which are less binding but still have their importance, are added: to abstain from food except at the appointed time; to abstain from the sight of dancing, singing, music, and stage plays; to abstain from wearing garlands or using perfumes; to abstain from sleeping on a luxurious bed; and, finally, not to accept gold or silver.

These are the ten aversions or repugnances (*vēramanīs*) that every novice must feel, or rather all men who believe in the Buddha. The first five commandments are binding on every Buddhist without exception. The others are more particularly applicable to monks, who moreover have a special code,

[1] Another stanza is sometimes added; Csoma de Körös found it in the Tibetan writings he consulted, and it is often quoted in the Sinhalese Sūtras: 'To cease from all wrong-doing, to get virtue, to cleanse one's own heart, this is the religion of the Buddha.' Two other stanzas of a similar character are found in the Nepalese Sūtras; they are attributed to Ṣākya-muni, and were written under his portrait, sent by Bimbisāra to Rudrāyana, king of Roruka: 'Begin, go out of the house, apply yourself to the Law of the Buddha; annihilate the army of death as an elephant upsets a hut of reeds. He who shall walk without distraction under the discipline of this Law, escaping renewed births, will put an end to sorrow.'

which we shall mention later. It will be easily understood that the most common rules assume a severity for them which they cannot have for the laity; thus, the monks must not only abstain from committing adultery, but must remain rigorously chaste.

Whole works, north and south, have been devoted to a methodical classification of sins and faults; but these works, written somewhat later than the days of the Buddha, are less an exact reproduction than a development of his doctrine, and we will not enter upon them, although their study might prove interesting; at present we are solely occupied by the theories of Ṣākya-muni.

It seems certain, however, that it was the Buddha himself who drew up for his monks and nuns the twelve following observances, which the Sinhalese and Chinese writings have handed down to us. They are extremely strict, but Siddhārtha had himself practised them for many years before imposing them on others, and when a young prince had given such an heroic example none of his believers could hesitate to follow it. Nor must we lose sight of the fact that these rules are addressed to the monks, that is men of superior piety, who had renounced the world, and were therefore bound to despise its interests and its pleasures.

The first observance signifies 'wearing rags found in the dust,' and refers to an injunction to wear garments made of rags picked up in graveyards, on dunghills, or by the roadside.

The second commands them to have no more than three of these wretched garments, which must be sewn together with their own hands in imitation of their Master. These rags are to be covered by a yellow woollen robe, procured by similar means.

So much for the clothing. The food is, if possible, still more simple.

The fourth, and one of the strictest rules, is to live by begging in utter silence from house to house; a wooden alms-bowl was allowed for this purpose.

Fifthly, the ascetic is allowed but one meal a day; and by the sixth observance he is not allowed any food whatever, even sweetmeats, after noon. It will be seen by a great many of the Sūtras that the Buddha, directly after he awoke, used to leave the vihāra or monastery to go and beg for his daily food, and his single meal was always made before noon, the remainder of the day being spent in teaching and meditation.

The rules about their residence were no less severe. The monks were to live in a forest[1]; that is the seventh observance. All the Sūtras tell us that the Buddha, and in general all monks, left the forests in which they had spent the night in order to beg in some neighbouring city. The eighth observance is the command to take shelter near a tree, and to seek no other shelter; the ninth order obliges them to sit on the ground, leaning against the trunk of the tree they had chosen as a shelter. They must sleep sitting and not reclining, this is the tenth observance; the eleventh is not to change the position of their mat when once laid down.

To these eleven observances is added a twelfth, of a totally different kind, which completes them, and clearly shows the object of all. The monks are to go from time to time at night, and at least once a month, into the cemeteries, and there meditate on the instability of human things.

From these details we are better able to comprehend the meaning of the names the Buddhists gave themselves: that of Bhikshu, a mendicant who subsists on the alms he receives; and Sramana, or ascetic, who overcomes the senses. The

[1] The rules prescribing a residence in the open air were applicable during the fine weather; in the rainy season they inhabited the vihāras or monasteries.

Buddha did not disdain to be known by either of these designations. Sometimes he calls himself 'the great mendicant,' Mahā Bhikshu, and at other times the Gautamide ascetic, Sramana Gautama. The state of mendicancy showed that the Buddhist had renounced the vanities and covetousness of the world; his chaste celibacy, which forbade him even the most innocent family affections, ensuring him, it is true, a control over the most formidable of human passions. Certainly this was not a way to make useful members of society, but it is thus that saints are made.

The rules devoted to clothing deserve particular attention, and in the Indian world they are perhaps more strikingly original than any other rule of the Buddhist ascetics. The Brahmans allowed their sages to remain in a state of complete nudity, and rightly described them as 'beings robed in space' (*digambaras*). The Greeks, who accompanied Alexander, and had seen them on the banks of the Indus, called them by analogy gymnosophists; and it was, so it seems, an admitted fashion for the highest caste to live, even in the cities, in a state of nakedness, a condition which the most degraded savages will hardly descend to. Though the Brahman ascetics doubtless took immodesty for piety, Indian society in general does not seem to have shown any want of regard for decency, for not only the women of a higher rank like Sumāgadhā, the daughter of Anātha Piṇḍika, were disgusted, but the courtesans themselves were indignant, as is shown by the one who mocked the Brahman Purāṇa Kāṣyapa when, in his anger at being conquered by Bhagavat, he tied a stone to his neck and drowned himself in a pond.

The religious life was an ideal that the Buddha alone carried out to its fullest extent; but if all men could not attain to it, all at least could, whatever their position in life, practise certain virtues that the Reformer considered, according to the 'precepts of his teaching,' as most important. These precepts were six in number: almsgiving or charity, purity, patience, courage, contemplation, and wisdom. These are the six transcendent virtues (*pāramitās*) 'which enable man to pass to the other shore,' as the etymology of the word used for them indicates. Man does not necessarily attain Nirvāna by the observance of them, he is but at the entrance to the path which leads to it; but he is on the road to faith, 'he has left the dark shores of the life of self-ignorance.' Henceforth he knows the goal he is to reach, and if he misses it, it is not through ignorance of the way.

Almsgiving, as Buddhism understands it, is not the ordinary liberality which gives to others a part of the goods we possess. It is an unlimited charity to all creatures without exception, entailing the most painful and excessive sacrifices. There is, for instance, a legend in which the Buddha gives up his body to feed a famished tigress that has no longer strength to suckle its young. In another, a neophyte casts himself into the sea to allay a storm evoked by the anger of the king of the Nāgas, and which threatens to wreck his companion's boat. The Buddha only came into this world to save mankind; all those who believe in him must follow his example, and shrink from no ordeal that may ensure the happiness of his fellow creatures. Charity must expel egotism from the heart of man, or, according to the Buddhist mode of expression, 'it leads to the perfect maturity of the egotistical being.'

Besides these six virtues, which may seem essential, are others of minor importance, which are also deemed beneficial, and of which the Buddha urges a strict observance. Thus, not only is falsehood forbidden, but in an almost equal degree slander, coarse language, and even idle and frivolous speech. Not to commit these faults is to acquire habits worthy of respect (ārīya vohārā); to give way to them is to contract habits which are contemptible.) A monk, who should be regarded as an example to men, hates slander; he will not repeat what he has heard so as to provoke enmity; on the contrary, he strives to reconcile those who have quarrelled; he does not separate those who are united; he takes pleasure in concord; and as he desires peace above all things, he holds the language calculated to promote it. He has also an aversion for any coarse word. 'A gentle language, pleasant to the ear, affectionate, appealing to the heart, polite and gracious to others,' is that which he employs. Finally, as he has renounced all frivolous speech, he only speaks to the purpose, in a sensible manner, according to the Law and the Order; his discourse is full of meaning, and always seemly.

Another virtue that the Buddha also impressed on his hearers, and that he himself practised unceasingly, is humility. Ṣākya-muni did not certainly fathom all the evil consequences of pride, but he nevertheless was too deeply impressed by the radical meekness and misery of mankind to let him glorify himself for any virtues he might acquire, and therefore he inculcated simplicity of heart and renunciation of all vanity. When the king Prasenajit, instigated by the Tirthīyas, urged the Buddha, whom he protected, to perform some miracles and so silence his enemies, the Buddha, while consenting to comply with the king's wishes, said to him: 'Great king, I do not teach the Law to my hearers by saying to them, Go, O mendicants, and perform in the sight of the Brahmans and the householders miracles by the aid of supernatural power—miracles greater than other men can do; but I say to them in teaching them the Law: Live, O mendicants, by hiding your good works and exposing your sins.'

It is evident that when the Buddha instituted confession among his monks, and even among all the faithful, he relied on this sentiment of humility. Twice a month, at the new moon and at the full moon, the monks confessed their faults out loud before the Buḍdha and the assembled Order. It was only by repentance and self-humiliation before others that they could redeem themselves. Mighty kings confessed to the Buddha the crimes they had committed, and it was at the cost of this painful confession that the culprits expiated the most infamous crimes. Although difficult to practise, this institution of the Buddha continued in force long after him, and in the Edicts of Piyadasi that pious monarch enjoined upon his subjects a general and public confession of their sins at least once in every five years. It appears that at these epochs the people were assembled together and reminded of the principles of the Law, and urged to make a confession of their sins. The ceremony could only last three days.

It is rather an astonishing fact that the Buddha, although preaching absolute renunciation and ascetic celibacy, not only respected family duties, but placed them in the very first rank. Personally, he always showed himself full of respect and tenderness for his mother's memory, although he had never known her, as she had died seven days after his birth; but the legends represent him as constantly anxious about her conversion, and he is said to have gone several times to the heaven of the Trāyastrimsats, where she dwelt, to teach her the Law that would save her.

In one of the simplest and most beautiful legends, Bhagavat thus addresses the monks who listen to him in the garden of Anātha Piṇḍika at Jetavana, near Ṣrāvasti: 'Brahma, O mendicants, dwells in families in which the father and mother are perfectly honoured, perfectly venerated, perfectly served. Wherefore is this? It is because, according to the Law, a father and mother are for their son, Brahma himself.

'The Teacher, O mendicants, dwells in the families where

the father and mother are perfectly honoured, perfectly venerated, perfectly served. Wherefore is this? It is because, according to the Law, a father and mother are for their son, the Teacher himself.

'The fire of sacrifice, O mendicants, dwells in those families where the father and mother are perfectly honoured, perfectly venerated, perfectly served. Wherefore is this? It is because, according to the Law, a father and mother are for their son, the fire of the sacrifice itself.

'The domestic fire, O mendicants, dwells in those families, &c. The Deva (Indra, no doubt) dwells in the families,' &c.

In another legend Bhagavạt explains the causes of filial piety: 'They perform, O mendicants, a most difficult thing for their child, the father and mother who feed him, bring him up, nourish him with their milk, and make him see the varied sights of the Jambudvīpa.'

There is but one way for the son to requite properly the kindness of his parents, and repay what they have done for him; that is, to establish them in the perfection of faith, if they do not possess it; to give them the perfection of morality, if they are unprincipled; the perfection of liberality if they are avaricious, and that of knowledge if they are ignorant. That is how a son who practises the Law can do good to his father and mother, besides all the tender care he should bestow on them; and this is how he can discharge the debt he owes to those who have given him life.

It might be thought that Buddhism, which has such a horror of life, has hardly the right to extol the duties and ties created by life; but this apparent contradiction does it honour, and may even be explained away. In order to attain perfection and reach Nirvāna, the Buddha was obliged to pass through the human state, and without culpable ingratitude he could not but cherish and venerate the beings who had opened to him the way to Nirvāna.

We shall confine ourselves to the above theories as regards the ethics of Buddhism, as, concise though they are, they certainly comprise the most important and profound part of it. These may be attributed to the Buddha, whereas the other parts, more subtle and less practical, belong only to the school and the casuistry founded by the Buddhist system.

We will conclude by a few observations upon the means employed by the Buddha to propagate his doctrine. (His only method, which has also a moral side, was by preaching. It does not appear that the Reformer ever thought he could employ any other means. Upheld and protected by kings, he might have had recourse to force and persecution, means that proselytism seldom fails to use. But all the legends, without exception, are unanimous on this point. The Buddha found his only weapons in persuasion. He called to him men of all castes and the mass of created beings; from the highest gods down to the most degraded creatures he exhorted them to embrace the Law which he declared to them; he charmed them by his discourses, astonished them sometimes by his supernatural power, but he never sought to constrain them. Often did he assist their backwardness by parables, of which some are most ingenious; he gave them examples to imitate; he drew from the history of his past existence a narration of his own faults, to instruct his hearers and awaken their fears by the punishments with which they were followed; he even delighted in these confessions if they were useful, and he related his faults in order that his listeners might be spared their consequences by learning how to avoid them.)

To rely on the power of truth and reason alone was indeed a just and noble idea of human dignity, so often disregarded, and we shall see how individuals, as well as nations, responded to the Buddha's appeal by virtues and refinements little to be expected at such a remote period.

In order to judge of the influence exercised by the moral teaching of Ṣākya-muni, it would be necessary to know in detail the state of public and private morality in the society to which it was addressed, and the exact history of the nations he tried to convert by preaching the new faith. Our information is, however, too incomplete on this point to enable us to gather sufficient knowledge. But in default of this, the Sūtras give us a number of facts which clearly show the influence the Reformer had on the minds of men. Some of the traits given are truly admirable, and it is but right to credit them to Buddhism, as it is Buddhism which called them into existence; for one fact stands out strikingly from the legends, and that is, the corrupt state of Indian society at the time of the Buddha's appearance. He does not pretend to correct by criticism, but he brings the remedy it needs and the ideal which is to guide it by making virtue the only means of salvation. We will choose some examples from these legends to show what the Buddha elicited from the hearts he had enlightened.

Pūrṇa was the son of an enfranchised slave whom, in return for her most diligent devotion in nursing him, her master had enfranchised by admitting her to his bed (at her most pressing request). Pūrna was brought up in the paternal house with his three elder brothers, and he soon distinguished himself by his activity and intelligence. Not only did he make his fortune in lucrative commerce, but, generous as well as clever, he made the fortunes of his family, who moreover had not always treated him very well. He went to sea on mercantile expeditions, and fortunate speculations soon placed him at the head of the Merchants' Corporation. During one of his voyages he had for companions some Buddhist merchants from Ṣrāvasti, and he was profoundly impressed by their religious demeanour. 'These merchants, at night and at dawn, read aloud the hymns, the prayers which lead to the other shore, the texts which disclose the Truth, the verses of the Sthaviras and those of the hermits.' These were the Sūtras and words of the Buddha.

Pūrna, struck by these things, of which he had never till now heard, on his return went straight to Ṣrāvasti, and having himself presented to Bhagavat by Anātha Piṇḍika, embraced the faith that had so touched his heart. He then received the investiture and tonsure from the Buddha, who remarked, 'that the most agreeable present he could have was a man to convert,' and the Buddha himself instructed him in the Law. He taught him in a few words that the whole Law consisted in renunciation; and Pūrna, henceforth dead to the world, chose as his abode the land of a neighbouring tribe, in order to convert them to the Buddhist faith. This tribe was noted for a cruelty and ferocity well calculated to deter any one less courageous. Bhagavat strove to dissuade him from such a dangerous enterprise.

'The men of Sronāparānta, among whom thou wishest to reside,' says Bhagavat, 'are violent, cruel, angry, furious, and insolent. When these men, O Pūrna, shall address thee to thy face in wicked, coarse, and insulting language, when they shall become enraged against thee and rail against thee, what wilt thou think of that?' 'If the men of Sronāparānta,' replied Pūrna, 'address me to my face in wicked, coarse, and insulting language, if they become enraged against me and rail at me, this is what I shall think of that: They are certainly good men, these Sronāparāntakas; they are gentle, mild men, they who neither strike me with the hand nor stone me.'

'But if the men of Sronāparānta do strike thee with the hand or stone thee, what wilt thou think of that?'

'I shall think them good and gentle for not striking me with swords or sticks.'

'But if they strike thee with swords and sticks, what wilt hou think of that?'

'I shall think them good and gentle for not depriving me entirely of life.'

'But if they deprive thee of life, what wilt thou think of that?'

'I shall think that the men of Sronāparānta are good and gentle, they who deliver me with so little pain from this body full of ordure.'

'Good, good, Pūrna!' said the Buddha; 'thou canst, with the perfection of patience with which thou art endowed, yes, thou canst take up thy abode in the land of the Sronāparāntakas. Go, O Pūrna! delivered thyself, deliver others; arrived thyself at the other shore, cause others to arrive there; consoled thyself, console others; having come thyself to complete Nirvāna, cause others to arrive there.'

Hereupon Pūrna took his way to the dreaded country, and by his imperturbable resignation he softened the cruel inhabitants, teaching them the precepts of the Law and the formulas of refuge.

The above example shows the courageous faith of the apostle, braving death in his dangerous mission. The following legends will show a heroism as difficult but of a different kind.

A son of King Aṣoka is sent by his father to Takshaṣita (Taxile) to govern that part of his states, and Kunāla (that is the name of the young prince) had made himself generally beloved there, when a royal order comes for both his eyes to be put out. This cruel order is sent by the queen Rishya-Rakshitā, one of Aṣoka's wives, who makes a false use of the seal of state, in order to wreak this terrible vengeance on the young prince, and punish him for having disdained her criminal advances. The inhabitants of Takshaṣita refuse to carry out the order, which seems to them iniquitous. In vain is an appeal made to the Chandalas, who answer, 'We have not the courage to be his executioners.'

The young prince, who has recognized his father's seal, submits to his sad fate; and when at last a deformed leper presents himself to do the cruel office, Kunāla, mindful of the lessons of his masters, the Sthaviras, says:

'Because they foresaw this calamity, the sages who knew the Truth did say to me in former days: "Look, the whole world is perishable, no one can remain in a stable condition." Yes, those magnanimous sages, exempt from passions, were indeed virtuous friends desiring my advantage and welfare, who taught me this law. When I consider the frailty of all things and reflect on the advice of my masters, I no longer tremble at my sentence; for I know that my eyes are perishable things. Let them therefore be put out or preserved, according as the king commands. I have received from my eyes the best they could give me, since, thanks to them, I have seen that all things are perishable here below.'

Then, turning to the man who had offered himself as executioner: 'Come,' he said, 'pluck out one eye first, and put it into my hand.'

Notwithstanding the lamentations and cries of the people, the man accomplished the hideous task; and the prince, taking hold of the eye lying in his hand, 'Wherefore dost thou no longer see things,' said he, 'as thou didst but a moment ago, vile globe of flesh? How self-abused and pitiful are the insensate beings who attach themselves to thee and say, "This is myself."'

The second eye was plucked out like the first. At this moment Kunāla, 'who had lost the eyes of the flesh, but in whom the eyes of knowledge were purified,' uttered the following stanza: 'The eyes of the flesh have been taken from me; but I have acquired the perfect and irreproachable eyes of wisdom. If I am abandoned by the king, I have become the son of the magnanimous king of the Law, and have been called his child. If I have fallen from supreme grandeur, which brings with it so much pain and grief, I have acquired the sovereignty of the Law, which destroys pain and grief.'

Kunāla crowns his resignation and energy by an unprecedented magnanimity; and when he shortly afterwards hears that he is the victim of Rishya-Rakshita's intrigues, he exclaims, 'Ah! may the queen Rishya-Rakshita long enjoy happiness, life, and power, for having employed these means, which have brought me such great benefits.' The remainder of the legend is no less touching. The blind prince wanders from place to place with his young wife, who guides his steps while singing of his misfortunes and his consolations. He thus arrives at the palace of his father, who in his just anger wishes to put the wicked queen to death. Kunāla intercedes for her, and declares that he alone is responsible for his misfortune, which he had no doubt deserved for some sin committed in a former life.

(Whether this legend be true or false, it is nevertheless of great value to us. It matters little whether it is a true story or simply the invention of the author of the Sūtra. It may have been only a lesson instead of a history; but the sentiments are no less noble and great, and they are inspired by the doctrine of the Buddha.)

In another legend we find a refined and striking example of chaste continence and of austere charity.

There was at Mathurā a celebrated courtesan called Vāsavadattā. Her maid went one day to a young merchant of the name of Upagupta to buy some perfumes. Vāsavadattā said to her on her return:

'It seems, my dear, that this young man pleases you, as you always buy from him.'

The maid answered her: 'Daughter of my master, Upagupta, the son of the merchant, who is gifted with beauty, with talent and with gentleness, spends his life in the observance of the Law.'

On hearing these words, Vāsavadattā conceived a passion for Upagupta, and a few days after she sent her maid to say to him: 'My intention is to go and find thee; I wish to enjoy myself with thee.' The maid delivered her message, but the young man told her thus to answer her mistress: 'My sister, it is not yet time for thee to see me.'

Now it was necessary in order to obtain the favours of Vāsavadattā to give her five hundred Purāṇas. Thus the courtesan imagined that, if he refused her, it was because he could not give the five hundred Purāṇas. For this reason she sent her maid to him again to say: 'I do not ask a single Kārchāpana from the son of my master; I only wish to enjoy myself with him.' The maid again delivered this message; and Upagupta answered her in the same way: 'My sister, it is not time yet for thee to see me.'

However, shortly after this Vāsavadattā assassinated one of her lovers, whose jealousy she feared, in order to sell herself to a very rich merchant who coveted her. The crime having been discovered, the king of Mathurā at once gave orders to the executioner to go and cut off the courtesan's hands, feet, ears, and nose, and to leave her thus mutilated in the cemetery.

Now Upagupta heard of the punishment that had been inflicted on Vāsavadattā, and he said to himself, 'When her body was covered with beautiful attire, and she shone with ornaments of different sorts, the best thing for those who aspired to deliverance and who wished to escape the law of renewed birth, was not to go and see this woman. To-day, when she has lost her pride, her love, and her joy, when she has been mutilated by the edge of the knife, it is time to see her.'

Then sheltered by a parasol carried by a young man who

accompanied him as a servant, Upagupta went to the cemetery with a measured step. Vāsavadattā's maid had stayed with her mistress out of gratitude for her past kindness, and seeing Upagupta's approach, warned her mistress, who, although racked by pain, by a lingering coquetry and desire to please, bid her maid pick up her scattered limbs and hide them under a piece of linen. Then Vāsavadattā, seeing Upagupta standing up before her, said to him:

'Son of my master, when my body was sweet like the lotus-flower, when it was adorned with ornaments and rich clothes, when it had all that could attract the eye, I was so unhappy as not to see thee. To-day why dost thou come to this place to contemplate a body, the sight of which the eyes cannot bear, from which amusements, pleasure, joy, and beauty have fled, which inspires nothing but horror, and is stained with blood and dirt?'

Upagupta replied to her: 'My sister, I did not come to thee formerly, attracted by the love of pleasure; but I am now come to see the real nature of the miserable objects of man's pleasures.'

Then he consoled Vāsavadattā by teaching her the Law; and his discourses bringing calm to the soul of the unhappy woman, she died professing faith in the Buddha, 'to be soon reborn among the gods.'

We will now quote a few legends treating of kings, beginning with Bimbisāra, the Buddha's constant protector, and the first prince among his contemporaries who was converted.

Before transferring the seat of government to Rājagriha, Bimbisāra resided at Kusāgāra; the city was densely populated, and the houses crowded together, and, doubtless built of wood, had often been destroyed by fire. In order to prevent such disasters, the king published an edict, saying that whoever, through carelessness or neglect, should let his house catch fire, should be turned out into the cold forest;

the name given in that country to the loathsome place where bodies were thrown—a burial ground. However, shortly after the palace caught fire, and the king then said:

'I am the master of all men; if I violate my own decrees I have no longer the right to repress the errors of my subjects.' The king therefore commanded the prince-royal to govern in his place, and went to dwell in the cold forest, in the cemetery.

Such is the tradition as related by Hiouen-Thsang, which he found still existing in the seventh century of our era, when he visited the ruins of Rājagriha, where Bimbisāra had raised fortifications, the remains of which lay scattered about. It would be difficult to affirm the exact truth of this tradition, but it tallies with all the legends tell us of Bimbisāra's character; at all events, it shows that in the opinion of the Buddhist peoples, kings were bound to be the first to obey the laws they promulgated.

It will be remembered that the whole of a Sinhalese Sūtra, already quoted, is devoted to a conversation between King Ajātaṣatru, son of Bimbisāra, and the Buddha, who at that time must have been seventy-two years old.

The king Ajātaṣatru, who assassinated his father and persecuted those who professed the new faith, was not yet converted. The Uposatha days had arrived; that is the four days in the lunar month when the moon is full or new (every fortnight , when a general confession took place among the Buddhists. It was a beautiful night, and the king on his terrace, surrounded by his ministers, enjoyed the cool of the evening and admired the grandeur of the spectacle before him. Moved by the sight, and remembering his crime, he wished—at the moment when so many guilty men were confessing their sins—to pay his respects to some Brahman, in order that the holy man should calm the agony of his remorse. His ministers proposed several Brahmans, but one of them mentioned the name of Bhagavat, and the king decided to go at once to him by torchlight. He found him in a wood of mango trees, surrounded by thirteen hundred and fifty monks; and requested an interview, which the Buddha granted.

The king did not at first tell him the real motive of his coming; and before making the confession he intended asked him a question which was closely connected with it, although indirectly, and the answer to which he had vainly sought from all the Brahmans he had hitherto consulted: 'Is it possible in this life to foretell to men, with absolute certainty, the general and foreseen result of their conduct?'

The king set forth the doubts which the answers of the most learned men had left in his mind; and he wished to have the Buddha's opinion. The Buddha, in a long and learned demonstration, which concluded his exposition of the Four Noble Truths, unhesitatingly affirmed that human actions have a foreseen and inevitable result. The king, enlightened by this revelation of the Law, understood the enormity of his crime, and, filled with remorse, said to the Buddha:

'I will take refuge in Bhagavat, in the Law, in the Order. Consent, O Bhagavat, to receive me as one of thy faithful, even this day that I have come before thee, that I have come to seek a shelter near thee. A crime has made me transgress the Law, O my Lord, like an ignorant man, like a madman, like a criminal. To obtain supreme power, I was capable of depriving my father, that just man, that just king, of life. Will Bhagavat deign to receive from my lips the confession I now make of this crime, and impose on me for the future the restraints of his Order?'

Bhagavat, in accordance with the Law, remitted his sin that he had expiated by confessing in public before a numerous assembly.

Another king, more powerful than Ajātaṣatru, Aṣoka, famous first for his cruelty and afterwards for his ostentatious piety, gives in a legend an example of humility, less difficult than the above, but of which few kings would be capable. He has just been converted, and he is possessed of all the fervour of a neophyte. Each time he meets any Buddhist ascetics, 'sons of Ṣākya,' whether in a crowd or alone, he touches their feet with his head, and worships them. One of his ministers, Yasa, although himself a convert, wonders at such condescension, and has the courage to tell his master that he ought not to prostrate himself before mendicants of a low caste. The king accepts his rebuke without demur, but a few days after he tells his counsellors that he wishes to know the value of the heads of different animals, and commands them each to sell the head of an animal. Yasa is to sell a human head. The other heads are sold at different prices; but nobody will purchase this one; and the minister is obliged to admit that, even gratuitously, he has not been able to get rid of it. 'Wherefore,' inquires the king, 'has nobody chosen to buy the human head?'

'Because it is a contemptible thing and valueless,' replies the minister.

'Is it only this particular head that is contemptible, or are all human heads equally so?'

'All human heads are despicable,' said Yasa.

'What!' said Aṣoka, 'is mine also contemptible?'

The minister, afraid to speak the truth, dared not reply; but the king commanded him to speak according to his conscience, and having obtained the expected answer:

'Yes,' he adds, 'it is by a feeling of pride and elation that thou seekest to prevent my prostrating myself at the feet of the mendicants. And if my head, that wretched thing which nobody will accept for nothing even, meets with an opportunity of being purified and acquires some degree of merit, what is there in that contrary to what is right? Thou lookest at the caste of Ṣākya's mendicants, and thou seest not their hidden virtues. When a marriage or an invitation is in question, then can we inquire about caste; but not when the Law is at stake, for virtue takes no heed of caste. If vice overcomes a man of high birth, it is said "He is a sinner," and he is despised. But the same is not said of a man born of poor parents, and if he is virtuous men will honour him by bowing down before him.'

Then appealing more directly to his minister, the king said:

'Dost thou not know the words of the compassionate hero of the Ṣākyas: "Wise men know how to find worth in things that have none." When I strive to obey his commandments, it is no proof of affection on thy part to try and dissuade me. When my body, abandoned like the fragments of a sugar-cane, will sleep on the earth, it will be incapable of rising, bowing, and joining hands as a sign of respect. What virtuous action shall I then be able to accomplish? Suffer me therefore now to bow down before the mendicants, for he who without inquiry says, "I am the most noble," is shrouded in the darkness of error. But he who examines the body by the light of the sage of the ten forces, he sees no difference between the body of a prince and that of a slave. The skin, flesh, bones, and head are the same in all men; the ornaments and attire alone lend a superiority to one body over another. But the essential in this world can be found in a vile body, and this is what the wise men deservedly honour and bow down to.'

Little can be added to such noble and stoical language, but whether the king Aṣoka really uttered these words, or whether he has falsely been credited with them, it is no less a remarkable fact that we find them recorded in writings dating two or three centuries before the Christian era.

We will now leave the legends, which are always of doubtful authority, and deal with the more reliable historical facts.

This king Aṣoka, whose elevated and sensible remarks on the equality of man we have just quoted, is the same who, under the name of Piyadasi, promulgated the Edicts engraved on stones, that we have already quoted in order to establish the real data of Buddhism. These inscriptions, which have only been mentioned for their chronological value, are even more interesting from the information they impart. Incredible as it may seem, they are really official lessons of morality given by Piyadasi to his subjects, which he caused to be engraved on stone in twenty different places in India, west, east, and north. They are Edicts of toleration, and such generous and advanced ideas can but be attributed to the influence of the Buddha's doctrines, Piyadasi having been his most powerful protector. The following is a proof. Let the reader judge.

We will begin by the Edict at Girnar, the eighth, which is repeated, with slight variations, at Dhauli and at Kapur-di-Giri. In this Edict the king announces to his people his conversion to the faith of the Buddha.

'In the days gone by,' says Piyadasi, 'the kings knew the path of pleasure; in those days they hunted and gave themselves up to amusements of that kind. But Piyadasi, the kindly king, "the delight of the gods," having reached the tenth year since his coronation, has attained the perfect knowledge taught by the Buddha; and the path of the Law is henceforth the only one that suits him. It consists in visiting and giving alms to the Brahmans and the Sramanas, in visiting the Theras, in distributing gold for their benefit, in inspecting the people and the country, in enforcing the execution of the Law, and inquiring into the Law. These are henceforth the only pleasures that can find favour in the eyes of Piyadasi, the king, the delight of the Devas, in this period of time, so different from any which preceded it[1].'

[1] See Prinsep, *Journal of the Asiatic Society of Bengal*, vols. vi. and

This first declaration, which marks a new era, a change of system in the government of King Piyadasi, is followed by another that completes it, and shows more thoroughly his magnanimous intentions. It is revealed in the tenth Edict, repeated like the former at Girnar, Dhauli, and at Kapur-di-Giri, in places distant several hundreds of leagues from one another.

'King Piyadasi, the "delight of the gods," believes that neither glory nor fame are of much value. The only glory he wishes for is to see his people practise obedience to the Law, and accomplish all the duties imposed by the Law. Such is the only glory and only fame desired by Piyadasi, "the delight of the Devas"; for all that the king Piyadasi, "the delight of the Devas," can display of heroism is done by him in view of another world. Who does not know that all glory is unprofitable, and often destructive of virtue? The salvation of an ordinary man as that of a man of high rank is a difficult thing, unless by a sublime merit he has abandoned all, and that makes the salvation of a man of high rank even more difficult.'

These solemn declarations preceded and followed the convocation of the third Council, which was held at Pataliputra, under the patronage of this same king, in the seventeenth year of his reign. We have already given the message he addressed to the monks in the Great Assembly. The Edict referred to, that of Babra, discovered by Captain Burt, runs as follows:—

'King Piyadasi of Magadha, greeting the Order, wishes it health and happiness.

'You know, reverend sirs, how great is my respect and reverence for the Buddha, the Law, and the Order. All

vii; Wilson, *Journal of the Royal Asiatic Society of Great Britain*, vol. xii. p. 199; Lassen, *Indische Alterthumskunde*, vol. ii. p. 227; and Burnouf, *Lotus de la bonne Loi*, p. 757.

those things, reverend sirs, which were spoken by the Blessed Buddha, were well spoken. By looking upon them, reverend sirs, as authority, the true Law will long endure, and this I think needful. I honour, reverend sirs, as such, the following Scriptures of the Law:—The substance of the Vinaya, or the discipline; the State of the Just; the Fears of the Future; the Poems of the Wise; the Questions of Upatissa; the Exhortations to Rāhula regarding Falsehood, spoken by the Blessed Buddha. These Scriptures of the Law, reverend sirs,—and it is the fame I most aspire to,—I hope that the honourable monks and nuns may constantly learn and reflect upon; and so also the laity of either sex. To that end, reverend sirs, I cause this to be written and have uttered my desire and my declaration.'

From the time of his conversion to the end of his life Aṣoka never ceased addressing useful exhortations to his people, and he was able to congratulate himself on the success of his efforts. The following are portions of an Edict dating from the twelfth year of his reign, which show that the restricted means then at the king's disposal had not proved useless:—

'In past time, during many centuries, mankind only practised the murder of human beings, cruelty towards the brute creation, disrespect towards parents, and want of reverence towards the Brahmans and Sramanas. Now, this day, because Piyadasi, "the delight of the Devas," practises the Law, the drum has sounded, and the voice of the Law is heard. That which has not been seen for many centuries is happily seen to-day, in consequence of the order given by Piyadasi, "the delight of the Devas," to practise the Law. The cessation of the murder of human beings, and of acts of cruelty to the brute creation, respect for parents, obedience to fathers and mothers, reverence towards the ancients—these virtues, as well as other practices recommended by the Law, have developed tenfold. And Piyadasi, "the delight of the Devas," will increase this observance of the Law; and the sons, grandsons, and great grandsons of King Piyadasi, "the delight of the Devas," will increase the observance of the Law till the Kalpa of destruction.'

This is the fourth Edict inscribed on the column at Girnar; and in the eleventh, which partly reproduces it, we find the confirmation and development of these precepts of morality.

During a reign that lasted thirty-seven years (263–226 B.C.) Aṣoka perseveringly carried on the moral reforms he had undertaken, and the following is the Edict issued in the twenty-sixth year of his reign. It is engraved on a pillar at Delhi, on the side facing the north, and is also written on the columns at Mathiah, Radhiah, and Allahabad. Piyadasi, 'the delight of the Devas,' speaks thus: 'In the twenty-sixth year since my coronation I have caused this Edict of the Law to be written. Happiness in this world and the next is difficult to attain except by an extreme love, an extreme attention, an extreme obedience, an extreme fear, and an extreme perseverance in the Law. Therefore do I command that the practice of the Law and the love of the Law shall in the future increase, as they have hitherto increased, in the heart of each of my subjects. All my people, whether the head men of the villages or those of inferior rank, must obey this order and execute it without negligence. It is also thus that the great ministers themselves must act, for this is my command, that the government shall be carried on through the Law, the commandment by the Law, public prosperity by the Law, the protection of all by the Law.'

These moral instructions could only bear fruit by constant repetition, and in one of his Edicts, the second of the two separate ones at Dhauli, Piyadasi enjoins that they shall be read to the people at least every four months by the assembly of monks, and in the intervals by a solitary monk. It was a kind of public sermon in which the very expressions the king had made use of were repeated, and it is easy to believe that in a short time the royal sermon, so often heard by the people, was pretty well known by heart. In the first of the two special Edicts at Dhauli the king also commands that a general confession of sins shall take place at least every five years, and he enjoins on the prince royal, who governed as Viceroy at Oudjdjayini, to have this important act fulfilled without disturbing the common people in their work.

In the Aṣoka *avadāna*, the legend of Aṣoka from which we have already quoted a few passages, it is affirmed that King Aṣoka, overcome with grief at one of his orders having been misunderstood and so costing his brother his life, abolished the penalty of death in his dominions, after having made a most excessive and barbarous use of it. It is not certain how far this tradition, transmitted by Nepalese Sūtras, is historically true; but the Aṣoka of the Edicts evinces great compassion towards those criminals condemned to death. He allows them three days' respite between their sentences and execution in order to give them time to prepare for death. They can by repentance, by alms and fasting, make atonement for their sins, and mitigate the punishments that await them in the next world.

It seems that in order to carry out all these moral and religious measures, so novel to Indian populations, Piyadasi founded a special body of officials whose duty it was to overlook and direct their application. These appointments were also recorded in the Edicts; the royal officials were considered guardians of public morality, and were called the king's men (*rājakas*).

Here are already many marvellous revelations which exhibit the Buddhist reformation in a new light, in its action on governments and nations; but the following disclosure is still more surprising. This king, the ardent promoter of faith, the religious teacher of his subjects, so vigilant in forming and preserving their morals, is at the same time most tolerant. He believes in the Buddha with all the strength of a conviction that betrays itself in the most decisive acts, and yet he never molests beliefs that differ from his own; on the contrary he protects and defends them against any attack. Not content with peacefully tolerating them in his own states, he insists that each one of his subjects, in his own narrow sphere, shall follow his example and respect his neighbour's conscience, however it may differ from his own. In the seventh Edict at Girnar, reproduced, like most of the others, at Dhauli and at Kapur-di-Giri, Piyadasi thus expresses himself:

'Piyadasi, "the delight of the gods," desires that the ascetics of all beliefs shall be permitted to dwell where they will. All these ascetics equally seek to gain an empire over self and purity of conscience. But the people hold divers opinions and attach themselves to divers faiths; the ascetics therefore sometimes obtain all they ask for, and sometimes only obtain part of what they require. But even he who does not receive alms liberally must retain a self-control, purity of conscience, gratitude, and a steady and lasting devotion.'

The idea, which is not very clearly expressed in this Edict, is set forth in a manner that leaves no doubt about the king's intentions, in the twelfth Edict at Girnar:

'King Piyadasi, "the delight of the Devas," honours every belief, and honours both mendicants and householders—he shows them respect by almsgiving and divers marks of honour; but the king, "the delight of the Devas," esteems less almsgiving and marks of respect than that which can essentially increase a consideration for all these beliefs and their good reputation. Now the increase of what is essential for all beliefs is of different kinds; but for each one the capital point is praise. Each man must only honour his own belief, but he must not cast blame on that of others; thus will no one be injured. There are even circumstances in which the belief of another should be honoured, and by acting in this manner our own belief is strengthened as well as that of others. Whoever acts differently lowers his personal belief and injures that of another. The man, whoever he may be, who by devotion to his own belief, exalts it and blames the belief of others, saying, "Let us display our faith," only wrongs the belief he professes. Thus good understanding and concord is alone useful. Moreover, let all men listen deferentially to one another and follow the Law; such is the desire of the king, "the delight of the Devas." May men of all beliefs abound in wisdom and prosper in virtue! And those who believe in a particular religion must repeat this to themselves: "The king, 'the delight of the Devas,' does not esteem almsgiving nor marks of respect as much as that which can essentially increase the good reputation and development of every belief." To this effect high officials, ministers of the Law, and ministers to supervise the women, and inspectors of secret things, and other agents have been appointed; to the end that a speedy development of religion may ensue and diffuse the Law.'

We fancy our readers will agree that these quotations suffice to show the immense and beneficial influence of Buddhist ethics on individuals and on peoples. It seemed necessary to establish this fact, which henceforth must rank in the history of humanity.

Before quitting, however, this class of considerations, one fact, more undeniable than any of the preceding, must be mentioned. This is the ardour of proselytism and of conviction that Buddhism imparted to the most distant nations. In the fifth and seventh century of the Christian era, Chinese pilgrims journeyed, in the midst of terrible dangers, across the countries that separate Northern China from Western India, in order to seek the holy writings and pious traditions at the cradle of Buddhism, and to worship the many monuments built in honour of the Buddha.

Fa-Hian left Tchhang'an (Si-'an-Fou), in the north of China, in the year 399 A.D., crossed the whole of Tartary, passed over the mountains of Tibet—the highest in the world—crossed the Indus several times, followed the banks of the Ganges down to its mouth, embarked for Ceylon, which he visited, made a short stay at Java, and returned to his native land, after an absence of fifteen years, having travelled a distance of three thousand six hundred miles by land, and at least six thousand by sea; solely for the purpose of taking back more exact versions of the sacred writings than those then existing in China. After many trials and much suffering he returned home alone, having started with several companions, and Fa-Hian speaks in the following modest and dignified terms of his heroic self-devotion :—

'In recapitulating all I underwent, my heart involuntarily fills with emotion. The sweat that ran from me in my dangers is not the cause of this emotion. My body was preserved by the sentiments that animated me. The end I had in view made me risk my life in countries full of dangers, to obtain at all costs the object of my hope[1].'

Hiouen-Thsang, who travelled two hundred and twenty years after Fa-Hian, is much better informed than he was, although not more courageous. He collected a great many more materials, and his narrative, which we know by his *Memoirs*, and an analysis of two of his disciples, is an invaluable mine of information of all kinds on Indian Buddhism of the seventh century. Nevertheless Hiouen-Thsang did not throw more energy or tenacity of purpose into his enterprise than did Fa-Hian. He remained absent sixteen years, taking

[1] Rémusat, *Foe Koue Ki*, p. 363.

his departure from Liang-Tcheou in the north-west of China in 629, and returning to Si-'an-Fou in 645. Reaching India by way of the country of Oïgus, Jungaria, and Transoxan, already in possession of the Turks, and by the Hindu-Kush, he began his holy researches in Attok and Udyāna. He visited the northern parts of the Panjāb, Kashmir, and returning south-east, reached Mathurā; he travelled over all the kingdoms situated between the Ganges, the Gandaki, and the Nepaul mountains; visited Ayodhyā, Prayāga, Kapilavastu, the birthplace of Ṣākya-muni, Kusi-nagara, where he died, Benāres, where he preached his first sermons, Magadha, where he spent his life, and the kingdoms situated north-east and east of the Ganges. Hence he returned south, went through the greater part of the southern peninsula without going as far as Ceylon; and directing his steps westwards he reached Guzerāt, turned northward to Multān, visited Magadha, the Panjāb, and the mountains of Hindu-Kush for the second time, and returned to the north-west of China, by the kingdoms of Kashgar, Yarkand, and Khokan, bringing back with him relics and images of the Buddha, as well as six hundred and fifty-seven works treating of all the different parts of Buddhist doctrine.

The work of these pilgrims did not end with their fatiguing journeys. Two fresh duties lay before them on their return home—writing a narrative of their enterprise, and translating the books they had secured at the price of so many dangers and fatigues. Thus Hiouen-Thsang devoted the last twenty years of his life to translating into Chinese the principal documents he had collected among the most eminent teachers of Buddhism. What noble lives! What heroism! What disinterestedness and faith! And in their actions what gentleness, resignation, simplicity, and uprightness. Moreover, what admirable testimony to a doctrine which, at a distance of twelve hundred years, can still inspire so much courage, confidence, and self-abnegation. Yet the principles on which these ethics are based are false; and the errors they contain are at least equal to the virtues they propagate.

We will return later to the journeyings of Hiouen-Thsang, but will now pass on to the metaphysical side of Buddhism.

CHAPTER IV.

Metaphysics of Buddhism, or Abhidharma. Transmigration, its unlimited compass from man to inert matter. Obscurity of the Buddhist doctrine on the origin of transmigration. Explanation of human destiny by the Connecting Chain of the twelve reciprocal Causes. Theory of Nirvāna, or Eternal Salvation by annihilation. The Dhyāna.

ALTHOUGH Ṣākya-muni devoted himself more to the practical side of religion, it is impossible to doubt that he had also a theory. He had been a pupil of the Brahmans, and the reflective tendency of his own genius led him to seek for the essential basis of his doctrines. He did not, it is true, positively separate metaphysics from ethics, but the latter naturally obliged him to seek for higher principles, and in his teaching he joins to the precepts he gives on the discipline of life, axioms which explain and justify these precepts. Hence, in the very first Council, his disciples made, under the name of *Abhidharma*, a collection of his metaphysical axioms, one of the Three Baskets (*Tripitaka*), in which the canonical books were divided.

The work that contains more particularly Buddhist metaphysics is called the *Pradjnā-Pāramitā*, that is the Perfection of Wisdom[1]. It is the first of the nine Dharmas or Nepalese

[1] The *Pradjnā-Pāramitā* was probably written three or four hundred years after Buddha. It was the text on which the Madhyamikas, a school founded by the famous Nagārdjuna, built their doctrines a hundred and fifty years before the Christian era. Burnouf gives a specimen of this compilation in eight thousand paragraphs, which he has almost all translated, and which he had compared with a hundred thousand articles. This comparison had betrayed no difference of

canonical books. There were three principal compilations: one in a hundred thousand, another in twenty-five thousand, and the last in eight thousand paragraphs; the most developed merely add words to the more concise explanation of the others. In fact, if these different compilations contain fresh deductions, they do not offer a single new principle, and in order to become acquainted with the real metaphysics of Ṣākya-muni, we must have recourse to the simple Sūtras, as they have much more affinity with his teaching.

We must expect to find in Ṣākya-muni's metaphysics, as in his ethics, more axioms than demonstrations; more dogmas than systematic and exact developments. But it is necessary that we should bear in mind that we are treating of India, and not of Greece or modern Europe. The doctrines are no less important, but the form in which they are expressed is thoroughly unscientific, even when we endeavour to classify them.

The first theory of Buddhist metaphysics, borrowed indeed from Brahmanism[1], is that of transmigration. Before his present existence here on earth, man has already gone through a multitude of varied existences; if he does not make the most strenuous efforts, he will probably be obliged to go through a still larger number of lives; and his constant and anxious attention must be devoted to escaping from the fatal law to which his birth has subjected him. Life is but a long series of pain and misery; salvation consists in avoiding existence. Such is, in the whole of the Indian world, from whatever side it is viewed and at whatever epoch it is taken, the universal belief professed by Brahmans and Buddhists of

doctrine. *Introd. à l'Hist. du Bouddh. Indien*, p. 465. According to Tibetan tradition the *Pradjnā-Pāramitā* was expounded by Ṣākya-muni himself sixteen years after he became Buddha, that is when he was fifty-one years of age.

[1] See in the *Laws of Manu* the complete theory of transmigration. Vol. xii. Slokas 39, &c.

every sect, every shade, and every period. The Buddha accepts this general opinion, no one indeed raising any possible objection to it; and the only originality he shows on this point consists in the new means of deliverance he offers to his adherents. But he accepts the principle itself; he accepts without discussion.

Further on we will examine the value of this principle, or rather the terrible consequences it has produced among the people who adopted it. At present we will simply point out its all-powerful and absolutely undisputed domination. We have shown how this monstrous doctrine was ignored in the Vedas[1], and seen in this silence a proof of the greater purity of Vedic faith. Transmigration is a doctrine invented by the Brahmans, and can be traced back to the origin of the society and religion they founded. Ṣākya-muni, therefore, merely conformed to the current idea in adopting it.

How far did this idea of transmigration extend? Can man, after losing his present form, take again a human form only? Can he equally assume a superior form, or receive at a lower grade that of an animal? Can he even descend lower than the animal, and according to his actions in this world become one of those forms in which life disappears, and nothing but mere existence remains, in its most rudimentary and vague condition? It would indeed, as far as orthodox Brahmans are concerned, be difficult to answer these questions, all that is known of their literature showing no precise limit set to their conception of transmigration[2].

As regards the Buddhists, the answer is decisive: the idea

[1] *Journal des Savants*, Feb., 1854, p. 113; April, 1854, p. 212.

[2] For transmigration according to the Kapila system, see B. St. Hilaire, *Premier Memoire sur le Sānkhya; Mémoires de l'Académie des Sciences Morales et Politiques*, tome viii. p. 455.

of transmigration extends to the uttermost limits; it embraces all, from the Bodhisatwa who becomes a perfect Buddha, from man to inert matter.

A being can transmigrate into any form whatever without exception, and according to his good or bad actions he will pass to the highest or the lowest state. The texts are so numerous and so positive that there can be no doubt on the subject, however extravagant this idea may appear to us.

It will be remembered that, according to the *Lalita-vistāra* legend, the Bodhisatwa entered his mother's right side in the form of a young white elephant armed with six tusks; and that when on the point of becoming a perfectly enlightened Buddha, all the innumerable births, the incalculable hundreds of thousands of kotis[1] of incarnations he has already gone through before attaining this one, which is to be his last, pass through his mind[2]. In other legends the Buddha relates the transformations he has undergone, or those that have been undergone by the personages whose good or ill fortune he desires to explain. Hiouen-Thsang saw at Benāres, many splendid stūpas built on the spots where the Buddha had in divers existences assumed the form of an elephant, a bird, a stag, &c.

The Sinhalese *Jātakas*, which number five hundred and fifty, contain as many accounts of the different births of the Bodhisatwa. The Sinhalese have even been very reasonable in limiting themselves to this number; for it is a general belief that the Buddha went through all the existences of the earth, sea, and air, as well as all the conditions of human life;

[1] A koti is equivalent to 10,000,000.

[2] A great difference exists between transmigration and metempsychosis as understood by the Pythagoreans; these latter confined it to the animal series. See H. Ritter, *History of Ancient Philosophy*; and Aristotle, *Traité de l'Âme*, vol. i. ch. iii. of Barthélemy St. Hilaire's translation.

he had even been a tree and a plant[1], if Chinese Buddhism is to be credited.

In a legend, which is interesting by the details it gives about the life of the monks in the vihāras, that of Samgha-Rakshita, transmigration takes place, it is said, in the shape of a wall, a column, a tree, a flower, a fruit, a rope, a broom, a vase, a mortar, a pot, &c.

'What actions have led to these metamorphoses?' asks Samgha-Rakshita.

Bhagavat replies:

'The beings thou hast seen under the form of a wall were the hearers of Kāṣyapa (a former Buddha); they defiled the walls of the Assembly Hall by spitting upon them, and the consequence of this action is that they are turned into walls. Those whom thou hast seen in the shape of columns have been transformed for the same reason. Those thou hast seen under the shape of trees, leaves, flowers, and fruit, have assumed that shape because they formerly enjoyed in a selfish manner the flowers and fruits of the Order. Another, who with equal selfishness used the rope belonging to the Order, has been changed into a rope; another, because he did not make better use of the Order's broom, has been metamorphosed into a broom; a novice, who cleaned the bowls of the Order, was hard-hearted enough to refuse drink to strange mendicants wearied by long travelling, he has been changed into a vase; he whom thou sawest under the form of a mortar is a Sthavira, who formerly in coarse language demanded of a novice an instrument of this kind, &c.'

Thus the Buddhists have so monstrously exaggerated the

[1] See Rémusat, *Foe Koue Ki*, and a curious notice of Landresse on the Sinhalese *Jātakas*. Upham gives a list of them in his *Sacred and Historical Books of Ceylon*, vol. iii. p. 269. Burnouf has translated some of the most important *Jātakas*.

idea of transmigration that the human personality is lost sight of and confounded with the lowest things on earth.

These transformations are regulated solely by conduct in a previous state of existence; man is rewarded or punished according to his virtues or vices. How this long series of trials had begun, why man had been compelled to submit to them, and what was the origin of this succession of endless causes and effects, was, as it appears, a fundamental question in the Buddhist system itself; but, strangely enough, Ṣākyamuni never seems to have raised this question, nor did any Buddhist after him even enter upon the subject. It is unlikely that this was an omission; it seems more probable that the Buddha considered it advisable to remain silent on such an obscure problem. Nevertheless, one thing is certain, nowhere in the Sūtras do we find even an attempt at an explanation, not a word—not a theory, not a discussion. All that can be inferred from a few rare passages is that the Buddha believed in the eternity of beings—we dare not say souls—and that he saw no beginning to the evils he came into the world to cure, namely, birth, old age, disease, and death, although they might come to an end in Nirvāna. The universe is created by the deeds of its inhabitants; this is the effect, and 'if by impossibility,' as Burnouf says, quoting from the Buddhist Sūtras, 'there were none guilty, there would be neither hell nor any place of punishment.'

The Buddha, notwithstanding the boundless knowledge he possesses, will not explain the things of this world by going back to the intricacies of their origin. He takes things as he finds them, without inquiring whence they come; and as life, from whatever aspect he looks at it, seems to him 'but a great mass of evils,' he comprehends it thus.

Twelve conditions, in turn effects and causes one of the other, act as connecting links in the production of life. Man must be born in order to grow old and die. Death is therefore an effect of which birth is the cause.

Birth (*Jāti*) is itself an effect, and could not exist without existence. This idea, curious as it may appear to us, is very consistent with the Buddhist system, which believes in the eternity of beings. Long before their birth they exist; and birth, under whatever form it presents itself (moisture, ova, matrix or metamorphosis, for Buddhists as well as Brahmans), is but the effect of the preceding existence, for without existence (*bhava*) birth would be impossible. However, the question at issue is not existence in its vague, general acceptance, but existence with all the modifications wrought by previous trials—the moral state of the being according to the actions he has successively accumulated, virtuous or vicious, in the infinite duration of ages. Thus existence causes birth, and conformably to what man has been, he is reborn into a different state, either higher or lower.

Existence is caused by attachment (*upādāna*). Without an attachment, a clinging to things, a being would not assume nor take a certain moral condition which compels him to a renewed birth. Attachment is a kind of falling off which makes him come under the fatal law of transmigration.

Attachment, the cause of existence, is itself only an effect, which has for cause desire (*trishnā*, thirst). Desire is an insatiable longing to seek for whatever is pleasant, to avoid whatever is disagreeable. It is caused by sensation (*vedanā*), which endows man with the perception and knowledge of things, showing him their qualities, which morally and physically affect him. Sensation caused by desire is itself caused by contact (*phassa*). Things must touch man either externally or internally for him to feel them, and thus it has been said that Buddhists made sensation the sole source of knowledge; but as among the senses they include also the inner sense or *manas*, their doctrine is not so materialistic as it at first appears. Contact, the cause of sensation, is in its turn the effect of the six places or seats of the sensitive qualities and the senses. These seats (*skandhas*) are sight, hearing, smell, taste, and touch, to which must be added the *manas* or the heart, which includes all we should call moral sentiments.

Here we have eight of the twelve conditions that produce life united together by the relation of causes to effects. Four more remain to finish the complete evolution, which, according to Buddha, embraces and explains the entire human destiny.

The six seats of the senses and of perceptible objects have for cause the name and form (*nāmarūpa*) expressed in one word, as the word *jāramarana* expresses old age and death. Without the name and form the objects would be indistinct; they would be non-existent to our senses, whether external or internal. They come into contact with us first by the material form they assume, and then by the name that designates them and recalls them to the mind, *manas*. (The name and the form which the Buddhists unite into a single idea are that which renders objects perceptible, and thus they are the cause of the senses.) But the name and the form are not only effects; they have also a cause, namely, knowledge or consciousness (*viññana*), which distinguishes objects one from another, and attributes to each one both the name that represents them and the qualities which belong to each. Consciousness or reason is the tenth cause. The tendencies or potentialities (literally, *confections*, *Sankhārās*) are the eleventh; they are the ideas composed by the imagination, the illusions which constitute the fictitious universe it creates for itself. The twelfth and last cause is ignorance (*avijjā*) or delusion, which consists exclusively in looking upon what is transitory as lasting, in believing that all that is passing and fugitive is permanent; in one word, in giving to this world a reality it does not possess. Such is the mutual connexion of causes, and this theory, added to that of the Four Noble Truths, forms the most ancient and most authentic basis of the Buddha's doctrine.)

We see in the *Lalita-vistāra* all the importance Ṣākya-muni attached to it. When he discovered it at Bodhimanda, he fancied he had at last discovered the secret of the world. He can save human beings by teaching it, and it is because he has understood this, after long meditations kept up by terrible austerities, that he believed himself to be, and that he became, the perfectly enlightened Buddha. As long as he had not grasped the mysterious chain that links this tissue of causes and effects, he was ignorant of the Law and the way of salvation. Once he had unravelled the thread, he is in possession of the truth which will enlighten and deliver all creatures. He knows the road to Nirvāna, which he can henceforth reach and can make other beings attain.

(We have now gone through the series of effects and causes, tracing backwards the progress of the being to his primitive condition. From old age and death we have, through twelve successive degrees, reached delusion, which, from a certain point of view, may be confused with non-existence; for error itself has no existence, if it had it would cease to be a delusion. However, if instead of working backwards we take ignorance as our starting-point, instead of our end and goal, we then reverse the connexion of causes and effects, which nevertheless remains closely bound together, and we begin at the point where we first ended. Thus from delusion, or nothingness, proceed the concepts, which are its effects; from the concepts come consciousness, and from consciousness name and form; from name and form, the six seats of the senses; from the six seats of the senses, contact; from contact, sensation; from sensation, desire; from desire, attachment; from attachment, existence; from existence, birth; and from birth, old age and death. This inverse order is the one adopted in the *Pradjnā-Pāramitā*, and also followed sometimes by the Sinhalese. It is not, it is true, the method recommended by the example given by the Buddha at Bodhimanda, but it is perhaps more in conformity with the general spirit of primitive Buddhism, which, without precisely denying the reality of things, as is done later in the *Pradjnā-Pāramitā*, does not, however, believe in the permanence of any of their elements, and considers that immutability is found only in void or nothingness.

It would be unjust to hold the Buddha responsible for the excess of scepticism which carried away most of his adherents, but to a certain degree he was responsible, for he himself sowed the seed of it in his principal doctrines. It is more than likely that he admitted axioms similar to those attributed to him by some of the Sūtras, and that he may, for instance, have upheld the following:—'Every phenomenon is void; no phenomenon has substance in itself. All substance is void. Internally and externally all is void. Personality itself is without substance. Decay is inherent in all component things, and, like a flash of lightning in the sky, does not last long.'

It is very probable that, wishing to condense his system in a single axiom, he may have said, 'It is transitory; it is miserable; it is void'; making this knowledge of the instability of things, of the evils of life, and of nothingness, the higher knowledge which contained and replaced all others, the threefold science (*trividyā*) which sufficed to enlighten and save mankind. Finally, we may even believe, without doing the Buddha an injustice, that he made sensation the sole and absolute source of all information for the mind; and the gross sensuality of his disciples, with its natural sceptical consequences, may be imputed to him without his having precisely taught it.

We now reach the last and most important of the Buddhist theories, namely, Nirvāna. Nirvāna is the supreme goal the Buddha sought to attain. It is the deliverance to which he invited all creatures; it is the reward he promised to knowledge and virtue—in one word, it is eternal salvation. What, then, is Nirvāna? Is it an immortality more or less disguised? Is it nothingness? Is it simply a change of existence? Is it absolute annihilation? It is a strange and remarkable fact that Ṣākya-muni leaves the idea of Nirvāna in a hazy obscurity, and that we cannot quote one Sūtra in which he has tried to define it, as he has defined so many other and less important ideas. The utmost he has done is to refute the false notions that were accepted by the Brahmans (Tirthakaras); but these negative explanations, if they do to a certain degree show what Nirvāna is not, never say what it is, and that is the important point.

If we turn to the etymology of the word, it teaches us but little. It is composed of *nir*, which expresses negation, and the root *vā*, which signifies to *blow out*. Nirvāna is therefore extinction, that is to say the condition of a thing that can no longer be blown out; hence the comparison so frequent in Buddhist writings of a lamp that is extinguished and cannot be relit. But this analysis, exact as it is, regards only the surface of things, and the expression of the Nirvāna thus understood, if sufficient to represent the image of death, tells us nothing of the succeeding state, according to Ṣākya-muni's system. When the Buddha dies at Kusi-nagara, his cousin Anuruddha, who as well as Ānanda accompanied him, uttered the following stanza, which has remained famous: 'With a spirit that did not fail he suffered the agony of death; as a lamp that goes out, even so was his intelligence set free.'

Burnouf, who is a great authority, has no hesitation; in his opinion Nirvāna means complete annihilation, not only of the material elements of existence, but also of the thinking principle. He has repeatedly asserted this in his *Introduction à l'histoire du Bouddhisme Indien* and in the *Lotus de la bonne Loi*, published eight years later. Clough, Turnour, Schmidt, Foucaux, Spence Hardy, Bigandet[1] take the same view. Colebrooke, although not having the latest discoveries to guide him, declares, however, that Nirvāna, as understood by the Buddhists, is the same as an eternal sleep.

If we examine the few and imperfect definitions to be found in the Sūtras, we arrive at the same conclusion. The word Nirvāna is almost always followed by an epithet meaning 'Where nothing remains of the aggregates, where nothing remains of existence, where absolutely nothing remains.' We must add that the Brahmans call the Buddhists Sarvavaināṣikas and Nāstikas, meaning those who believe in a complete destruction, and this they regard as a serious accusation, though the Buddhists themselves adopt those names instead of rejecting them.

Thus etymology, the most learned contemporary philologists, the texts themselves, and even the criticisms of the opponents of Buddhism, all agree in demonstrating that Nirvāna was in reality the definite and absolute annihilation of all the elements that make up life. Without dwelling further on these considerations, there is another which we think conclusive, and which has not been sufficiently taken into account; that is the theory of Dhyāna or contemplation, which may be called the method and practice of Nirvāna.

In a number of passages taken from all kinds of Sūtras there is a distinction made between complete Nirvāna—the great complete Nirvāna and simple Nirvāna. Complete

[1] Bishop Bigandet, author of *Life of Buddha*, translated from Burmese into English, published at Rangoon in 1858.

Nirvāna is that which follows death, when man has known how to prepare for it by faith, virtue, and knowledge; while simple Nirvāna may be acquired even during this life, by adopting a certain line of conduct that Buddhism teaches, and of which the Buddha himself sets an example. Thus, in the *Lotus of the Good Law* the Sthaviras approach Bhagavat and submit to him their doubts, they confess their weakness and their vanity in the following words: 'Worn out by age, we say to ourselves, we have obtained Nirvāna. We fancy we have reached Nirvāna because we are overwhelmed by age and disease.' In other passages, even more clear, it is said: 'Men who live in the knowledge of the Law, exempt from imperfection, have attained Nirvāna. He who makes use of the vehicle of the Ṣrāvakas has attained Nirvāna. The Ṣrāvakas imagine that they have attained Nirvāna; but the Djina says unto them: This is only a place of rest; this is not the true Nirvāna.'

Nirvāna is therefore to a certain degree compatible with life, according to Buddhist belief, and it may be obtained even before death, although that is not yet the true Nirvāna.

The process to attain this incomplete Nirvāna, the foretaste of the one that follows and remains eternal, is by Dhyāna or contemplation, and, to put it clearly, by a state of mystic ecstasy.) The Dhyāna has four stages, which succeed each other in regular order, and it plays a great part in the most important circumstances of the Buddha's life. In the village of Agriculture, under the shade of a djambu tree, when his family, alarmed at his absence, seek for him in vain, the young Siddhārtha is occupied in passing through the five meditations he already knows. At Bodhimanda, where Ṣākya-muni conquers the demon, he prepares himself to become Buddha and save the world by four meditations; at Kusi-nagara, where the Buddha is dying, he passes for the first time through the four different stages of Dhyāna, and expires in a fresh effort before attaining the fourth stage.

We will now describe the four stages of Dhyāna, as given in the Nepalese and Sinhalese Sūtras, which completely agree on this fundamental theory. It is almost needless to add that the monk who gives himself up to Dhyāna or contemplation lives in complete solitude, and, delivered from all earthly cares and troubles, thinks of nothing but eternal salvation, Nirvāna, on which all his thoughts are henceforth concentrated.

The first stage of Dhyāna is a state of joy and gladness born of seclusion, when the ascetic realizes that he can at last distinguish the nature of things. He has then divested himself of all desire except that of Nirvāna; he is full of reflection and investigation, but is freed from all sensuality and all sin; and the contemplation of Nirvāna, which he longs for and is approaching, throws him into an ecstasy which leads him to the second stage. In this second stage the purity of the ascetic remains the same, vice and sin no longer pollute him; moreover, he has put reasoning and argument aside, and his mind, which dwells no longer on external things, is fixed solely on Nirvāna, feeling only a deep satisfaction and tranquillity, without reflection or investigation of its cause.

In the third stage the joy of this satisfaction has vanished, the sage has become indifferent even to the happiness that his mind felt in the former stage. The only pleasure he feels is a vague sensation of physical comfort that fills his whole being. He has not, however, lost the recollection of the conditions through which he has just passed, and he still retains a confused notion of self, notwithstanding the almost complete indifference to which he has attained.

Finally, in the fourth stage, the ascetic no longer possesses the feeling of physical comfort, vague as it was; he has also lost all recollection; he has even lost the sensation of his indifference, and henceforth, without sorrow and without joy, whatever may be its object, either externally or internally, he has reached impassibility, that is a condition as near Nirvāna as is possible in this life. Moreover, this absolute impassibility does not prevent the ascetic acquiring at this same moment omniscience and magic power; but this is a flagrant contradiction, which does not, however, disturb the Buddhists any more than many others.

Such are the four stages of Dhyāna, as gathered from all Buddhist authorities. They will not astonish any one who has studied mysticism, as it is well known how, by successive eliminations, the mind reduces itself to that transitory vacancy which is called ecstasy. The mystics of Alexandria, those of the Middle Ages, and of the Renaissance, have known, like the Buddhists and the Brahmans, these workings of the mind, struggling against self in order to temporarily destroy all its mental power. Plotinus, Gerson, Saint Teresa, all think that they thereby unite themselves to God, and become one with him. The Buddhists do not claim this, as they do not know of a God, and in the whole of Ṣākya-muni's system the idea of an infinite being never presents itself; but they seek and practise ecstasy, which for them is an image of the annihilation which they take for eternal salvation.

We have now seen that for the Buddhists, Dhyāna is the road and preliminary conquest of Nirvāna; but, as though the idea were not sufficiently clear, Buddhism has added to the four stages of Dhyāna four other stages, superior, or rather corresponding; these are 'the four regions of the world devoid of form.' The ascetic who has courageously passed through the first four stages is rewarded by entering into the region of infinite space. Thence he goes up another degree to the region of infinite wisdom. Having reached this height he attains a third region, where nothing exists. However, as in this void and this darkness it might be supposed that an idea could subsist and represent to the ascetic the void in which he is plunged, a last and supreme effort must be made, and he then enters into the fourth region of the world devoid of form, where there are neither ideas nor even an idea of their absence. The doctrine of Dhyāna may therefore be considered a decisive commentary on that of Nirvāna; for as by this transitory ecstatic state a transitory annihilation is already sought for, then an eternal and definite annihilation may be sought for in Nirvāna.

Buddhism has no God, it has not even the vague and confused notion of a Universal Spirit, in which, according to orthodox Brahmanism and the Sānkhya, the human soul is absorbed. Neither does it admit nature properly so called, and it does not make that great distinction between the spirit and the material world which is the system and glory of Kapila; lastly, it confuses man with his earthly surroundings, even while it preaches virtue to him. It cannot, therefore, unite the human soul, which it never even mentions, either to a God whom it does not know, or to nature which it ignores. One course therefore remains for Buddhism, that is to annihilate the soul, and in order to be certain that it will not reappear under any form in this world, which it considers accursed as the abode of illusion and pain, all the elements are destroyed. This is repeated over and over again. What, then, is Nirvāna if not total annihilation?

No doubt this is a most serious statement, especially when we reflect that Buddhism at the present day counts so many followers all over the surface of the globe, that it is the belief of one-third of humanity, and that such an explanation of Nirvāna implies that a third of our fellow-creatures worship annihilation, and place in it all their hopes of the future.

Doubtless it is a hideous faith, but it is no calumny to impute it to Buddhism, and history would be faithless to itself, if it shrunk from this deplorable truth, which, moreover, sheds such light on the destinies of the Asiatic world.

It has therefore been shown, that Ṣākya-muni's ethics and metaphysics are summed up in a few simple but erroneous theories: The Four Noble Truths, Transmigration, the Mutual Connecting Links of Causes, and Nirvāna, explained by Dhyāna which precedes it and prepares man for it. We have only now to judge the value of these theories; rendering justice to the partial truth they contain, and pitilessly condemning the monstrous errors hidden under an apparent sublimity.

CHAPTER V.

Critical study of Buddhism. Its merits: practical tenaency, contempt of wealth, charity, sentiment of equality, meekness, austerity, resignation, horror of falsehood, respect for family ties. Its faults: social impotence, egotism, no idea of duty, ignorance of justice and liberty, scepticism, incurable despair, error as regards life and human personality, atheism. General condemnation of Buddhism. Opinions of Bayle and Voltaire on the atheism of China.

THERE is so much to be said against Buddhism, that it may be as well to begin by the good that can be justly attributed to it, for, limited as our praise must be, it will at least mitigate in some degree the severity of the judgment that must follow.

We will now, therefore, state the good points, without either exaggerating or unjustly curtailing them.

The most striking feature of Buddhism, that is as founded by the Buddha, is its practical tendency. The Buddha sets himself a great problem, which is no less than that of the salvation of mankind and even of the whole universe; and he seeks its solution by the most direct and practical method. It is true that, considering himself a philosopher, he might have indulged in speculative analysis, but the Brahmans had made such an abuse of this process that the Reformer deemed it better to abstain from it. For in seeking to penetrate into the origin of things, it is necessary to avoid sinking into needless obscurity, and speak only to a school instead of addressing the masses. Philosophy, even when it does not aim at founding a religion, should never lose sight of its first duty, which is to serve humanity; and the philosopher who is satisfied to understand and to save himself alone, by the truth he has discovered, is little worthy of his name. If these truths were to be solely for the advantage of one individual, they would lose their value; and as for the mass of humanity, the practice of morality is of more importance than the principle on which it is grounded; it is a credit to philosophers that they induce men to live according to what is right, rather than to think according to the principles of philosophy. All reforms must be preceded and strengthened by the long study which science demands; but when the Reformer at last appears upon the scene, his teaching should be as clear and simple as possible. He speaks to the people and not to the learned. He must lead minds rather than enlighten them; promulgate precepts rather than expound theories.

Moreover, although his aim was to convert and guide the masses, Ṣākya-muni does not endeavour to attract them by gross allurements, he does not flatter their passions; and the joys he promises them are neither earthly nor material. Contrary to most religious legislators, he does not predict to his followers either conquests, power, or riches; he calls them to eternal salvation or rather annihilation, which he confounds with salvation, by the narrow path of virtue, knowledge, and austerity[1]. It is a great deal to expect of man, but evidently not too much; and it is well for us to hear such a noble appeal to the human heart, in times so remote and in countries which our civilization has been accustomed to dis-

[1] We do not mention magic power and supernatural gifts, which, according to Buddhist doctrine, science and virtue confer on those who have attained the highest degree of sanctity. The legends are full of these superstitions, which the Brahmans indulged in long before Buddhism adopted them. See *Memoire sur le Sānkhya* in the *Memoirs de l'Academie des Sciences Morales et Politiques*, tome viii. pp. 198, 389. The Buddha himself never made any such fallacious promises, but left such tricks of charlatanry to the adversaries he despised.

dain. We too willingly fancy that these noble aspirations belong only to ourselves, and we are surprised at discovering the same in others. It was not in the Vedas or the religion that emanated from them that the Reformer found these lessons of self-renunciation. But the Brahmanic philosophy was not that base and selfish kind of worship, which consists in a mutual interchange between man and the gods—of homage and assistance. It had soared into the higher regions of thought, and the system of Kapila alone suffices to show that Ṣākya-muni has made no innovation in preaching eternal deliverance. The whole of Brahmanic India had the same solemn turn of thought, Ṣākya-muni shared it, but did not originate it.

His true glory, which no one can dispute, is the boundless charity that filled his soul. The Buddha does not think of his own personal salvation; he seeks above all to save others, and it is in order to show them the infallible road to Nirvāna that he leaves the Abode of Joy, the Tushita, and that he comes back to endure the risk and ordeal of a last incarnation. He does not redeem mankind by offering himself as a sublime victim; he only proposes to instruct them by his teaching and example. He leads them in the path from which there is no straying, and he guides them to the haven from which there is no return. No doubt the spirit of Christianity has inspired more beautiful and elevated sentiments, but six or seven centuries before its appearance it is wonderful to find this admirable conception, associating all men in a common faith, and uniting them in the same esteem and the same love.

This is how the Buddha was able to say, without presumption or error, that 'his law was a law of grace for all[1],' and

[1] These are the Buddha's own words in answer to the jeers of the Brahmans, who mocked him when he converted Svāgata, the son of a poverty-stricken merchant. *Svāgata Avadāna* in the Divya Avadāna,

how, although he did not attack the odious and degrading system of caste, he destroyed that fundamental basis of Brahmanic society. He never saw, it is true, the real principle of human equality, because he never rightly understood moral equality; but if he did not comprehend the real nature of man, he at least knew that if all men are equal in suffering, they ought also to be equal in deliverance. He endeavours to teach them to free themselves from disease, old age, and death; and as all beings are exposed to these necessary evils, they all have a right to the teaching, which by enlightening them is to free them. In the presence of the same amount of misery, he perceives no social distinction; the slave is for him as great as a king's son. He is struck, not so much by the abuses and the evils of the society in which he lives, as by those which are inseparable from humanity itself, and it is to the suppression of these that he devotes himself, the others appearing to him very insignificant in comparison. The Buddha did not limit himself to curing Indian society, his aim was to cure mankind.

This great elevation and large-mindedness is certainly to be admired, for although man is not entirely as the Buddha saw him, the victim of suffering, yet he is so more or less, and it was a generous enterprise to have sought to deliver him from its bondage.

The means employed by the Buddha to convert and purify the human heart are not less noble, and they are characterized by an unfailing gentleness, both in the Master and the least of his disciples. He never seeks to compel, but only to persuade men. He even makes allowance for their weakness, varying in a thousand ways the means of impressing them; and when a too inflexible and austere language might repel them, he has recourse to the more persuasive

quoted by Burnouf in his *Introduction à l'histoire du Bouddhisme Indien*, p. 198.

teaching of parables. He chooses the most familiar examples, and by the simplicity of his expressions suits his lessons to the capacity of his hearers. He teaches them to lighten the weight of their sins by confession, and to atone for them by repentance.

He even goes further. As it is already a great evil to have to expiate sin, the essential point is therefore to teach man not to commit it; for if he never falls, he will not have to retrieve himself. Hence, in the doctrine of Ṣākya-muni, such wise and well-defined precepts, such just and delicate prohibition of certain actions. He undertakes and advises an incessant struggle against the body and its passions and desires; the body is in his eyes the sole enemy of man, and although the Buddha does not use this precise expression, it is in truth the aim of his asceticism. Man must overcome the body, he must extinguish the burning lusts that consume him. If the Buddha strenuously enforces absolute celibacy on his monks, he also enjoins chastity and decency on all the faithful, virtues that the Brahmans constantly violated, but which a secret instinct reveals to all men.

To these virtues, he adds others still more difficult and no less useful, namely: patience and resignation, including the necessary energy to suffer courageously inevitable evil; fortitude and even indifference under all adversities and sufferings; above all humility, that other form of renunciation of worldly goods and greatness, which was not only practised by poor mendicants, 'sons of Ṣākya,' but also by the most powerful kings. From humility to forgiveness of injuries is but a step; and although the Buddha does not lay this down as a precept, his whole doctrine tends to this mutual forbearance, so indispensable to all human societies. The very belief in transmigration helped him; the first sentiment of a Buddhist under an insult or an outrage or violence, is not anger; he is not angry, because he does not believe in injustice. He simply thinks that in some former existence he has committed a sin which in this one deserves the punishment he receives. He only blames himself for the misfortune that befalls him, and instead of accusing his enemy or his oppressor, he accuses himself. Far from thinking of revenge, he only sees a lesson in the adversity he endures, and his sole idea is how he can henceforth avoid the sin that has rendered it necessary, and which if renewed, would also renew the punishment that has already followed it. When the young prince Kunāla, whose touching history is related in the legends, undergoes a painful and iniquitous torture, he forgives the cruel stepmother who persecutes him, he forgives his deluded father, and he thinks only of his past sins, by which he must have deservedly called down upon himself such an affliction.

This resignation, which may easily become fear and cowardice in the weak, no doubt leads to the domination and despotism of the strong and wicked; doubtless it also encourages tyranny in those countries which have only known despotism. But, in intelligent hands, what an element of order and social peace! What a healing of all the passions which too often destroy concord, and lead to relentless wars!

Add to this, the horror of falsehood, the respect for truth, the sanctity of the bond that unites intelligences; add the reprobation of slandering or even idle speech; add also the respect for family ties, pious veneration of parents, consideration and esteem for women, who are considered equally with men to be worthy of all religious honours—and we must feel astonished, that with so many social virtues Buddhism was not able to found, even in Asia, a tolerable social state or government. First it failed in India itself where it arose; and in all the countries where it was received, its influence, excellent as it was in some respects, never prevailed sufficiently to reform the political morals of the people, who remained, in spite of it, under the most degrading and arbitrary yoke. The feeble germs left by the Buddhist doctrine, which certain kings, like Piyadasi, had developed, remained fruitless; and even now our civilization has no power to give them life in the countries it has penetrated and where Buddhism is still in vigour. Our most benevolent and liberal efforts must remain ineffectual against these deplorable institutions, which have been sanctioned not only by time, but also by the inveterate habits of the people, their indifference, and their incurable superstition. Certainly Buddhism ought not to be judged solely on this one proof, and it should not be condemned only because the societies that have practised it are badly organized: but yet, the worth of religions can in some degree be valued by the social institutions which they have inspired or tolerated, and it is one of the glories of Christianity, that it has produced free societies and governments, which under the admiring eyes of history, advance each day to new progress and new perfection. Nothing of the kind is to be seen in Buddhist societies, and as regards politics and legislation, the religion of the Buddha has remained very inferior even to Brahmanism. It has instructed and sanctified certain individuals, who chose to follow the noble example of Ṣākya-muni; but as regards nations it has remained even more powerless than its adversaries, and it has hardly done anything either to organize them or to govern them equitably.

It is, therefore, probable that Buddhism contains in its core certain errors which have made it sterile; and having now shown the good it contains, we will proceed to examine the evil, the share of which is much greater.

In vain does Buddhism profess self-renunciation and self-sacrifice, it is in reality narrow and self-interested. It rests upon a single idea, which is neither the highest nor the truest, that of eternal salvation, understood in the sense of annihilation or Nirvāna. This is the reward offered to the highest efforts of man; the supreme end of his faith, the ineffable prize promised to his virtues. His life is framed to this end, according to the precepts and examples of the teacher. But he never acts but in view of the reward he hopes for. He extinguishes all other desires, but he retains this one, and exalts it by all those he has sacrificed to it. To this egotistical pre-occupation of reward, and the idea of Nirvāna, are attributable all the faults of Buddhism, for they are sufficient to falsify all morality.

Doubtless it is good for man to look forward to a future life; and to meditate upon eternity, which can alone explain to him whence he comes and whither he returns; face to face with this grand idea, he feels all his weakness and also all his worth; it gives him the key of his destiny, if he knows how to interrogate it discreetly and wisely. But he must beware of lowering or destroying it, by looking to nothing but a reward, as the price of his good actions. The thought of eternal salvation becomes then no longer a virtue; it is but a mercantile transaction; and as nothing is more fluctuating than calculation and self-interest, man could not but find his upward path beset with obstacles. In a truer and more saintly religion, he can rely on God's justice to reward or punish him eternally; but in a religion that knows no God—the irreparable error of Buddhist faith—man remains his own judge; it is he, who of his own authority decides that which merits or does not merit salvation; he is judge in his own case, and that is hardly the way to be equitable and infallible. He fancies he practises virtue, while in reality he only practises an unceasing egotism, which is hidden and strengthened by the harshest austerities and the haughtiest exclusiveness.

Man only works out his own salvation; he cannot save

others; the most he can do is, like the Buddha, to show others the road. But each one must walk in it himself, one cannot do it for another. Salvation is therefore exclusively individual, and places man in complete isolation. If a man is absorbed in this idea, he will become estranged from his fellow-creatures, and neglect them, if indeed he does not despise and avoid them. Thus the monks, who are the strength of the new religion and its most faithful and enlightened champions, remain virtually strangers in the society which maintains them. They spend their useless existences living on alms gained by the work of others, and wear rags that their humility does not disdain, but which their hands have not woven. The ascetic is taken out of the world where he dwells, by the world he aspires to, and admitting that this pretended sanctity has not become mere indolence, who it may be asked reaps the benefit of this sanctity, if not the ascetic himself? What would become of society, including the anchorites it liberally maintains, if every one chose to imitate such pious examples? Renunciation is sublime no doubt, but as Ṣākya-muni aimed at saving the whole world, all mankind without exception must be considered, and not only a few privileged persons. To abolish caste, and the unjust limits it prescribed, was well, but if another is created, wider only in appearance, and in reality narrower than the former, where is the benefit? By the very nature of things, the idea of salvation, unless kept within just limits, becomes as dangerous as it is false; if it pervades all the actions of man it destroys their merit; and without mentioning the evil it can do to society, it corrupts the soul of the individual, who thinks only of self, and who, notwithstanding his vanity as an initiated and an adept, is profoundly ignorant of what ought to be the true and sole motive of his life here below.

There is, indeed, no other motive to offer to conscience—

especially from a philosophical point of view—than the love of goodness. It is not only the most disinterested and noble idea, but it is also the truest and most practical. It is found naturally in the hearts of men, and often unconsciously directs their conduct. If we go back to its origin it leads us to God, revealing to us his true nature; if we follow it in its consequences, it explains and makes us comprehend the world. All other ideas proceed from this, the highest, which sheds light upon all. Now, this idea which is the essential part of our soul, our reason, and our intelligence, as it is the essential part of the Universe and of God, does not exist in Buddhism. Ṣākya-muni does not seem to know that it existed. In Greek philosophy, Socrates and Plato have won imperishable glory by giving to the conception of goodness its real place in the soul of man, in the world, and in God; and the fire they kindled has continued to burn and throw more and more light among us. In Buddhism, on the contrary, not a gleam of this divine flame has shown itself; not a single spark has flashed out; and the sun of intelligences, as Plato calls it, has never enlightened those of the Buddhist world. Hearts, souls, and minds have remained plunged in the deepest gloom, and time, instead of dispelling the darkness, has only made it thicker. The idea of recompense, substituted for the idea of right, has perverted everything. An impenetrable and dark veil is thrown over all things, and man henceforth can understand neither himself nor the nature amid which he lives, nor God, who has made both. From this first and greatest error a mass of others have spread.

One of the most certain and fatal consequences is that this idea of right being misunderstood, Buddhism at the same time ignored the idea of duty. It seems a strange fact that in a system where the word duty (*dharma*) is repeated at every line of the numberless writings it produced, the actual notion of duty has completely escaped it. We see, it is true, obedience to the law of the Buddha, a blind submission to his teaching, and a sincere veneration for his virtues, which each tries to imitate. But an order, a word of advice, does not morally constrain; all it can do is to exercise an external compulsion, and as long as conscience and reason do not speak, duty does not make itself felt. Man is not bound because he obeys, nor is he compelled because he bends under a yoke, be that yoke as reasonable and beneficial as possible. It is therefore to the conscience and its decrees that the legislator of morality must address himself, more especially when he has elected, like Ṣākya-muni, to do without God, the supreme source of all good and all duty. Otherwise he will perhaps make fervent adepts, and even very faithful subjects, but he will not make men. He neither teaches nor inspires virtue; at most does he inculcate prudence. When the young Upagupta resisted the allurements of a beautiful, wealthy courtesan, it was not by saying to himself that continence is a duty and that he does well to struggle against culpable desires; it was because he thought, 'that it is better for one who aspires after freedom and wishes to avoid re-incarnation not to go and see this woman.' Thus he calculates his salvation; and as he fears to risk it by giving way, he abstains, not from virtue, but from interest. He has therefore misunderstood duty, even while performing a praiseworthy action, and he is not morally virtuous, although he has conquered in this inward struggle. Doubtless it is a gain that what is right should be done, whatever the motive; but the moral merit is real and complete only on condition that the agent is guided solely by the idea of duty, which in reality is the same as the idea of right. Both of these are totally wanting in the Buddha's doctrine.

Another consequence, no less disastrous, is scepticism.

This is not, indeed, carried so far in the Sūtras which contain Ṣākya-muni's sermons, as it is later on in the Pradjnā-Pāramitā, which ends by denying both the known object and the conscious subject, the reality of things and the reality even of conscience. However, without falling into this excess, Ṣākya-muni nevertheless proclaims the vanity and emptiness of all things in the presence of Nirvāna, which alone in his eyes is immutable. 'All is void' is one of his favourite axioms, and on this he rests the renunciation he preaches to men. Assuredly among the phenomena amidst which we live, many are transitory and fleeting; few of them are permanent and bear 'the character of stability, true sign of the Law,' as the young Siddhārtha said in his first meditations. All beings are not, however, 'void externally, void internally,' as he thought, and if he had carried out his self-examination more attentively and accurately, he would have found a firmer standing. Man can deny all that surrounds him, he can doubt all external phenomena, and even a part of the phenomena he bears within himself. But do what he will, he cannot doubt his own conscience when it reproaches him for sins he has committed, or approves his good deeds. He does not perhaps ask himself—as a doctrine more subtle than true alleges—whether the precept which guides him can become a universal law; but he assuredly tells himself that he must act as he does, and that no reasonable being could act otherwise. When man thus recognizes duty in his own heart, it is easy for him to transfer it to the outside world; the good which he perceives in himself he will but see enlarged in the world around him, which goodness alone animates and governs. He therefore no longer believes in its being a void, and beings become substantial in his eyes in proportion as they participate in goodness; he doubts their reality only in proportion as they deviate from it, and on the firm basis on which he has placed himself all the conceptions of his intellect are strengthened and regulated. If some of these still waver, it is that they are scarcely worthy of being fixed.

Scepticism is therefore banished from the soul by the idea of goodness; not only does this idea enlighten man, but it also strengthens him. His conscience speaks so clearly to him, especially when it has to bear witness against him, that he is no longer tempted to believe, like Ṣākya-muni, in the sole testimony of his senses; and though he will not completely reject these, he knows the exact degree of confidence he must place in them. When the material universe alone is considered, it can no doubt be denied that good or evil exist, but when man considers himself he cannot sincerely reject the distinction of good and evil, unless in his perversity he is interested in so doing.

This seems to explain the most characteristic and painful point of Buddhism, that is, its deep and miserable melancholy. When man finds goodness neither in himself nor in the world, it is natural that he should hate both, and seek refuge only in annihilation. Hence the despairing view of life which under every form pervades all parts of this doctrine, surrounding it with gloom. It is like a sepulchre from which Buddhism would fain deliver us by Nirvāna, which it describes as definitely destroying what is for man 'only a great mass of evil.' With such an opinion it would seem that nothing remains but to be freed from a terrible burden, and suicide should logically be the resource left to man in his dire extremity. Many legends seem to show that adepts of Buddhism have drawn this conclusion, which is logical though absurd. But Ṣākya-muni, by an inconsistency which does him honour, insisted that man should employ his life in redeeming himself from that life by virtue. He wished man to live according to all the laws of reason, as he understood them, so as to attain cessation of life, and conquer an eternal death by the purest and most saintly existence. The high ideal he made of virtue, sole pledge of eternal salvation, should, it would seem, have enlightened the philosopher. Life is not then after all so poor a thing as he represents it, since it allows man such an admirable use of his faculties. But this light, bright as it is, does not suffice to dispel the darkness, and Ṣākya-muni sees in existence nothing but pain. In his compassion for his fellow-creatures he devotes all the efforts of his genius to deliver them from the fatal law of renewed birth.

According to the Buddha, life is a long tissue of grief and suffering. We must, no doubt, recognize the numerous evils inherent to it which disfigure it; indeed, it would be folly to deny them. But to say nothing of the salutary lessons that man can derive from the ills he endures, and which are chiefly caused by his own misguided will, is it so true that there is nothing but evil in life? Shall we not take into account the joys that life affords us, the simple joys of ignorant childhood, the austere joys of meditation matured by experience, and of conscience strengthened by wisdom, the pleasures of the senses, as well as those of the intellect, the incessant and resplendent spectacle of nature, and that of the soul sacrificing itself to duty, the joys of family ties, and those of the heroic passion of patriotism, which India itself has not ignored? Will any one venture to deny these? And if such importance is given to the ills of life is it fair to disdain its unquestionable benefits? Is it an equitable view of things to consider them only under one of the two contrary aspects they present? It would not indeed be any wiser to deny the ills of life as energetically as the Buddha asserts them. But if optimism is not essentially true, it is incomparably more so than despair. It has at least the advantage of sustaining courage, and if it slightly warps the mind it does not dishearten it; it elevates instead of degrading; it sheds more light than its opposite, for in human life and in the world the sum of good, in the eyes of impartial judges and of manly hearts, is greater than the sum of evil.

There is, moreover, a certain pusillanimity in dwelling so much upon outward evils, such as old age, disease, and death; and in forgetting the much greater and more formidable evils which attack the soul and are called vices. Buddhism has been at much pains to classify, with the most studied and refined casuistry all the differences of the *Kleṣa,* it is by hundreds that it has distinguished them; and why all this labour? In truth it is not vice that Buddhism detests and would avoid; it is Nirvāṇa which it ever seeks and must attain; and it only fears and rejects vice, because vice is an obstacle to salvation and deliverance. The one thing dreaded above all, is pain from which an effete sensibility makes man shrink; decay which fades the bright carnation of youth; old age which destroys vigour, death at last, which is only a passage from this life of pain to another more painful still. The thing to be avoided at any price, even at the cost of virtue, is not moral degradation consequent on vice, but the bodily degradation which, far from saddening the sage, should on the contrary strengthen him by the experience it affords. It would be unjust to pretend that Ṣākya-muni took no heed whatever of moral evil, but in reality he made it a secondary consideration, and physical evil was the principal object of his dread.

And here a strange contradiction is shown; while the Buddha apprehends beyond measure the ills of life, and seeks eternal deliverance from them in annihilation, the only means, or at least the most efficacious he finds to suppress existence, is to make it here below a torment to those who have to endure it, while loathing it. What a code Ṣākya-muni imposes upon his most faithful and beloved disciples! What observances he practises himself and prescribes to his monks! Rags and shrouds for clothing, forests for shelter, graveyards for meditation, to live by alms, to observe the most rigid abstinence, to abstain from all pleasures even the most innocent, to keep habitual silence, and refrain from all friendly intercourse! It is a living death. The very austerity of this doctrine, which is not limited to the cloister, but preached to the world, proves the ardent sincerity of the faith which commends it. It needs a truly energetic conviction to condemn oneself to such a life of sacrifice. But if life is so great an evil, why make it worse; why voluntarily add to inevitable suffering, mortifications under which the body must succumb? Would it not be more consistent with the Buddha's doctrine to make life a continual source of enjoyment, and pleasure the sole occupation of man; should not pain be alleviated instead of being increased? It is true that no one can reach the hearts of men by preaching pleasure to them: this base doctrine, which can only attract corrupt minds, does not appeal to the masses, however ignorant and sensual they may be. Ṣākya-muni was right not to preach a doctrine which his great soul could only reject with scorn; but ascetism was not the practice which his theories could logically prescribe.

Thus we find ignorance of the idea of right, blind egotism, entire misapprehension of duty, almost absolute scepticism, a fanatical hatred of life which is thus misconceived, a cowardly dread of its sufferings, inconsolable despondency in a world that is not understood. A long list this of errors; but more yet may be attributed to Buddhism.

It is sufficiently proved that Buddhism has not grasped man's true nature, and that while it prescribes an incessant and implacable warfare against the body it does not tend to the advantage of the soul. It distinguishes neither the body from the soul, nor the spirit from matter. Reducing all intelligence to external sensation, it does not appear to have suspected the existence in man of the two principles of which he is composed, and which explain his whole destiny. The Sānkhya system at least had made this essential distinction, and though it was mistaken as to its consequences it had conceded a large part to the spirit, although not as great a part as is due to it. In this respect Ṣākya-muni was far behind Kapila. Like him he remained an atheist; but he substituted for the decided, though spurious, spiritualism of Kapila a blind materialism, which he coupled with the most mystical asceticism.

Not only does the Buddha confuse the two opposing principles of which man is formed, but he confuses man himself with all that surrounds him. He first confuses him with the animals he makes use of, which often rend or fly from him; with the plants he nourishes himself with, which sometimes poison him; and, finally, with the inert matter in which there is no trace of organism or life, which man can fashion at will, when he chooses to employ his skilful hands upon it. Ṣākya-muni carries the idea of transmigration to this extreme, that is to a flagrant absurdity. It is true that we possess doctrines that degrade man to the level of a beast, and which refuse to recognize in him anything but a superior kind of animal; but what is this error—serious as it is—beside the one in which Buddhism has lost itself? Man, according to its doctrines, has nothing to distinguish him from ordinary matter. In the successive and infinite existences he passes through man can become all things without any exception, from the most exalted being down to the very lowest: from the most marvellous and complicated organization down to a state of complete absence of organization. If the texts were not so precise and so numerous, if this belief were not in perfect harmony with all the remainder of the system which infers it, and cannot be explained without it, we might really doubt that such a paradox could ever have deluded human intelligence.

Unfortunately it is impossible to doubt this. It is the idea of unity of substance pushed as far as possible, to the fullest and most absurd conclusions. Spinosa and modern pantheists, who believe themselves to be terribly audacious and thoroughly consistent, are far less so than Ṣākya-muni. He works out his ideas to their end, whereas they see but a part of theirs and stop half-way. By a kind of instinct that makes them feel the abyss before them they unwittingly draw back; and although they do not give man his rightful share in their systems, in which all beings are effaced and confounded in an obscure identity, they dare not avow the degrading blasphemies in which Buddhism delights. It is true, that in another respect they have done like it, by refusing to recognize any other God than man himself. But in our day such impious extravagances are less easy; the platonic philosophy and Descartes' method have taught us much about the soul of man, and moreover we live in the midst of Christian civilization. It is still possible to disregard all the teachings of psychology, and to strive if not to refute, at least to elude them by feigning to ignore them. But, however much one may try to follow out such deplorable reasoning, common sense will resist; the philosopher who thus goes astray vaguely feels the error into which he is falling; his own conscience, protesting against him, deprives his system of part of its strength, and his wavering conviction hardly suffices to dominate him, much less to influence others. But in the Indian world, where real science was unknown, and where pyschology was completely ignored, even by the Brahmans —speculative as they were—all aberrations, all follies became possible, and it only required an energetic and resolute spirit to carry them out. The Buddha went ahead—nothing stopping him—as far as logic would take him; and as psychological observation was more a closed book to him even than to his adversaries, he saw none of the errors, or rather follies, into which he was falling. The grandeur of his convictions is only surpassed by his blindness.

It will now be easily understood why Buddhism was necessarily atheistical. When the personality of man is so completely ignored it is absolutely impossible to have any idea of God. This last aspect of Ṣākya-muni's doctrine demands a few more reflections, for it is without comparison the most unfavourable of all.

We have already shown, as an undeniable fact, that in the whole Buddhist system there is not a vestige of the idea of God. It does not precisely deny, nor did it contest the idea of God; but it seems not to have known that such an idea existed in the human soul, nor that it was indispensable; in fact, it completely ignored it.

Brahmanism, at least from this point of view, was more elevated and more learned. If it did not understand the unity of God, it nevertheless constantly sought for it in the universal intelligence of Kosmos; and through this idea, which it never loses, it sometimes has a gleam of the true light. In certain hymns of the Vedas, and also of the Upanishads, this great discovery is very nearly being made by the genius of Brahmanism. It draws very near to it, and if one were to judge by the language alone, it would seem as though the truth had been really found. In any case, if it is not found, it may be hoped that with the light already acquired, the truth will not long remain hidden.

In Buddhism, on the contrary, even these gleams of light are extinguished, and not a spark remains to show that they could be revived. All is dark, and man, reduced to his own entity, finds himself so weak and abandoned that he throws himself with a sort of frenzy into death and annihilation, out of which he came and into which he longs to return.

Sad and depressing spectacle! We were accustomed to suppose that the notion of God is never completely wanting to human intelligence. 'This notion might be confused and obscure,' we thought, 'but cannot be totally absent,' and we imagined we should find it even amid the gross brutality of the lowest savages. Well, here is a great doctrine, the result of the deepest and most sincere meditations—a system of philosophy which, if not profound, is at least very consistent and extensive; a religion accepted and practised by innumerable nations, in which this essential idea, which seems to us indispensable, is utterly wanting; where man is so absorbed in his own selfishness and his puerile terrors that he can see absolutely nothing outside of himself. He believes in his misery with all the strength of a mind warped by fear, and he looks to no deliverer but himself, weak and miserable though he knows he is. It would be a marvel, indeed, if Buddhism were to reach the haven by such a road, and it suffices to remember its origin to be no longer surprised that it should have fallen into such depths.

Human personality has been misconceived by it in its exterior and manifest signs, and more outrageously still in its essence and inmost nature[1]. Free will, which is its pre-eminent characteristic, with all its accompaniment of faculties and consequences, is forgotten, suppressed, destroyed.

Man acts during the whole of this life under the weight, not precisely of fatality, but of an incalculable series of former existences. He is not punished or rewarded for the actions he commits during life, but he pays the penalty of his past lives, which he cannot reform, of which he has to endure the

[1] In a Pāli Sūtra especially devoted to an explanation of the theory of causes, *Mahā Nidāna Sutta*, it is said, 'It is the name of the individual that makes him know himself.' *Lotus de la bonne Loi*, E. Burnouf, p. 359.

necessary consequences, and which he cannot remember, although he can recognize their fatal results. Transmigration has placed him in his present life, and if he does not take heed it will again lay hold of him and throw him back into the cycle he has already passed, from which he has no power to escape. It is true that it seems to depend upon himself whether he will hear the Buddha and be saved, or turn a deaf ear and be lost. But even this option, the only point on which man seems to have any liberty, is barely granted him; his liberty is not complete in this decisive choice; it is clogged by a past of which he is not the master; and his rejection of the liberating law that is preached to him may be the punishment of faults committed in another existence, now followed by this new fault. Man is not then free in this life. Was he ever free? Was he free in the origin of all things to begin or not to begin this chain of successive existences? What was the first cause of his bondage to this terrible law?

All these questions Buddhism pretends to solve by its well-known but puerile theory of the Connective Chain of Converse Causes. Step by step it traces back from death, to which we are all doomed on earth, to nothingness out of which it believes all beings—or rather the shadows it recognizes in this world—to have originated. No doubt birth engenders old age and death, and ingenuous as the axiom must appear, it must be granted that if man was not born he would not be exposed to death. But it is a mere play upon words to say that life is the cause of death; it is but the occasion of it. If there was no birth, we repeat, there could be no death; but life is so little the cause of death, that death is in its turn recognized as the cause of life. Cause becomes effect, and the effect becomes its own cause; in reality it is a contradiction, and the true notion of cause escapes Buddhism as well as that of liberty. Buddhism seems here to acknowledge its own impotence, and in the chain which it follows it begins by nothingness or ignorance, and ends by the same. But if ignorance is the starting-point of its researches, and if it is also its term, we are at liberty to doubt its pretended knowledge. For to begin by nothingness, to finish by nothingness, is equivalent to acknowledging that it knows nothing and believes in nothing. This is the conclusion of the school of the *Pradjnā-Pāramitā*, more daring in its nihilism and also more consistent than the founder of Buddhism himself. Ṣākya-muni dared not admit this, or rather he deceives himself in deceiving others.

To sum up: absence of all idea of human personality, of liberty, of cause—such are the elements that Buddhism employs, and which it fancies it has deducted from an exact and attentive observation of reality. It is no wonder that with such materials Buddhism should not have attempted to construct a regular system of theology. When humanity is so imperfectly understood, it is natural also that the world and God should be equally misunderstood; for man has no other means of attaining to the idea of God than through himself and the surrounding world.

Moreover, the most surprising thing of all is that Buddhism should not have deified the Buddha. Destitute of the true idea of God, it might have attempted to impose upon that secret instinct in man—which reason never gets rid of—an idol in the place of the deity. Far from this, the Buddha remains man, and never seeks to overstep the limits of humanity, outside of which he conceives nothing. The enthusiasm of his disciples did not exceed the reserve of their master; for in the innocent worship they rendered him they bore witness only to the strengthening and consoling power of his example; never did they appeal to his power on their behalf. The Buddha had placed man, and himself personally, far above the absurd and cruel gods of the

Brahmanic pantheon; his followers maintained him in this supreme position, but they went no further. Neither the pride of Ṣākya-muni, nor the fanaticism of his votaries, ever conceived a sacrilege; and the Buddha, great as he thought himself, sought not the halo of apotheosis, nor did tradition in its piety and veneration ever attempt it. Temples and statues were raised to him; thousands of writings have related his life and celebrated his supernatural power; but no one ever dreamed of making him a god.

This reserve is not, however, a proof of the good sense of the Buddhists. Their moderation on this delicate point is dictated by motives which agree only too well with their general ignorance. According to their belief the Buddha, far from being God, had been preceded by other Buddhas as saintly as himself, and will have as successors still other Buddhas no less perfect and worthy of veneration. He saved the world by his doctrine, that world in which he appeared, as others had saved or will save the worlds of which they have been or are destined to be the saviours. The Tathāgata himself predicted to a number of his hearers destinies no less brilliant than his own; he assured them they would be Buddhas like himself. He described to them the glorious worlds in which they should reign; he even fixed the duration of their reign. Every man can therefore attain, like the Buddha himself, to this high dignity by the practice of virtue and holiness; and the least of his disciples can attain and equal the adorable and ineffable beauties of his master's nature. If Buddha were a god, then there would be as many gods possible as there are men capable of understanding 'the Four Noble Truths or the Connective Chain of Converse Causes, and of following the Noble Eight-fold Path that leads to Nirvāna.'

This is the first motive which prevented the Buddhists, notwithstanding their most constant and most sincere devotion, from making a god of the Buddha. There is a second one which, though as powerful, is not more creditable to their intelligence.

During the whole course of the Buddha's life, after his great triumph at Bodhimanda, he did not cease to perform miracles, and the most extraordinary and supernatural powers are ascribed to him. But the Brahmans, his adversaries, contended with him and vied with him in their miracles. It was therefore not a privilege exclusively belonging to Ṣākya-muni. He was more powerful than those he contended with, because his knowledge was greater than theirs. His powers surpassed theirs because he surpassed them in virtue. Moreover, it is well known that knowledge gives man superhuman powers. We know that the Yogi, when he has passed through all the stages of initiation, infallibly attains magic power, and is henceforth above all the ordinary conditions of nature. The most enlightened Brahmans have always held this belief; it has been propagated by the wisest systems of philosophy; all mankind in India has believed it; and Buddhism, had it repudiated this belief, would by that alone have placed itself far beneath its antagonists. The Buddha's miracles do not therefore specially distinguish him. All men can succeed in performing similar ones. On that account he is no more of a god than on any other.

It is therefore a mingled feeling of pride and senseless superstition that led Buddhism not to deify the Buddha, to say nothing of its absolute incapacity to conceive any idea of an infinite being.

From all that precedes it will be easy to understand the general enterprise of Buddhism. Through a radical incapacity of higher aspirations, or by a perversity of reason, it believed that only man himself was capable of understanding and saving man. It made him the greatest of beings, which in regard to this world was no error; but it made him a being subsisting by his own power, having no superior either for his origin or his end, placed alone in this universe which is yet filled with his personality, vague and scattered as it is, under an endless variety of forms; exclusively occupied with self, and without a thought either of nature—with which he is blended by his numerous metamorphoses—nor of God, whom he knows not. We admit that this idea has a certain appearance of grandeur; but it lacks truth, for man thus conceived is but a monster, who, notwithstanding his pretensions, would soon have a horror of himself, because he would be unable to understand himself.

However, it is scarcely fair to attack Buddhism with the weapons of Plato or Descartes—that is to say, to use against it the enlightenment of more favoured times and races. We will employ only its own weapons in opposing it; and since it sees in man only a suffering being, we must examine what part pain plays in his life and what it implies. By this road, as by every other, it is possible for man to reach God. The way is more laborious for our weakness, but it is no less sure, and God shines forth no less in the ills than in the benefits of humanity.

We have reproached Ṣākya-muni with having given too much importance to physical pain, but he also gave a certain part to moral sufferings. He wished to deliver man for ever from disease, old age, and death, by freeing him from the law of renewed birth, but he wished also to preserve him from vice. He does not therefore deny that if man suffers bodily he may not, and that still more keenly, suffer in another part of his being. *Klēṣa* includes both physical and moral evil; and when Ajātaṣatru confesses to the Buddha his parricidal crime, it is remorse that has urged him on. He confides his secret torment to the wise man who can comfort and heal him. Thus Buddhism recognizes suffering in its most poignant and real form, even when the most concealed. But he dwells too little on this great observation, which might have revealed to him the whole nature of man, and which at the same time would have raised him far above mankind.

We might inquire of Buddhism whether there is any other being except man who can experience the pangs that conscience sometimes inflicts on him and which the Buddhist system recognizes, as it undertakes to assuage them by its advice and by the solemn expiations it recommends. Does it believe that the creatures that surround man feel, like him, the inward anguish which the most powerful kings, assured as they are of impunity, cannot escape? We may concede, as the Buddhists claim, that man before assuming his actual form has passed by all the different stages of matter, from the most inert to the most highly organized; but in the present disposition of things can it be denied that man alone endures these torments—the consequences of his faults and of his crimes? Can it be believed that animals feel like man? Can inorganic matter, which the Buddhists themselves place lower than the beasts, can it feel remorse? This is indeed impossible, and notwithstanding its blindness Buddhism has not fallen into quite so deep an error. Man has therefore the privilege of this pain, which is exclusively his. This is an incontestable fact, and may be deplored as old age and death are deplored, but it cannot be said not to exist.

Whence does this suffering come to man, and what is its cause, when it agitates his whole being, embitters all his joys, and racks him with anguish in the midst of all the intoxications of power? Buddhism itself has answered the question. Man only experiences this terrible pain because he feels he is guilty in having transgressed the Law. If Ajātaṣatru had not known that he could have acted otherwise than he did, he would not have felt the remorse which brought him humbled and submissive to the feet of the Buddha, in spite of all his pride and power. But the Law he had violated and which punishes him had not been made for him; for this great criminal when he began to repent knew nothing of Buddhism, and was not aware that murder was forbidden. Still less was it the criminal himself who made the law against himself that chastised him. On the contrary, he would destroy it, abolish it if it were in his power. He would wipe out, if it rested with him, the very recollection of his sin, and heal at the same time the wounds this recollection constantly caused him. But this law is superior to man; it is not amenable to him; and notwithstanding his perversity, which sometimes defies it, he cannot silence in his own heart that persistent voice which will perhaps soon find echoes no less terrible in the heart of his fellow-creatures.

We know well that Buddhism would reply to all this, if not through Ṣākya-muni, at any rate through Nagārdjuna, author of the *Pradjnā-Pāramitā*, that if man experiences moral sufferings of this nature it is only because he is thus made; that it is his nature (*Svabhāva*); that it is not necessary to seek any other explanation; that beings are what they are by virtue of their own nature; that man has his, as animals, plants, and minerals have theirs; and, in short, it is useless to go beyond this. In reality this argument explains nothing, precisely because it refuses to explain anything whatever; it is a universal objection. Facts ought simply to be observed without ever striving to know their causes. Buddhism admits that the moral pain that follows crime is a fact, and through the medium of its greatest metaphysical school it declares that it is content with this, and has no mission to inquire whence this fact arises, nor what is its origin. But Buddhism cannot make use of this easy argument, which is forbidden to it by its own teaching. It may, indeed, be possible to the scepticism of those disciples who have but half learned their master's lessons, and who are satisfied with the driest logic; but the master cannot accept it. He did not pass with haughty indifference before moral suffering, and far from considering it a consequence of man's own nature, that is to say immutable, he gave his most attentive care and his noblest hope to the healing of those evils which he did not believe incurable. He therefore recognized not only that man violates a law superior to himself when he commits a fault, but also that he can, to a certain extent, repair the evil committed, and re-establish between himself and the law he has violated the affinity that his crime had destroyed. The Buddha had only one step more to take: this was to ascribe this law—which his virtue considered just—to a being more powerful than man, to a being propitious to order and goodness, who knows how to reveal and to uphold them by these secret and energetic means.

It would seem even that the Buddha might have gone still further on this track. He had but to question his heroic and virtuous soul, and compare the profound and unalterable peace of his own conscience with the tempest-torn souls of the guilty. This peace which the good enjoy in view of the law they fulfil, is a fact no less certain than the agitation of the wicked. Personally the Buddha offered an admirable example. He might therefore suppose that if the author of the moral law punishes evil, he also rewards good, and that his forbearance at least equals his severity.

These simple reflections upon moral suffering were certainly within the scope of Ṣākya-muni's intelligence, and had he made them they were of a nature to modify the whole course of his thoughts and to change all his system. By this means, not to mention others which the sight of external nature afforded him, he would have been able to understand men and calm the terror that blinded them and cast them into despair. In the presence of the all-powerful Being, who is just and who can at the same time be merciful, his spirit would have been reassured. Far from considering life a torture, he would have recognized it as a trial which it depends on ourselves to render less painful.

Man need not deplore his condition on earth, since he can improve and beautify it. He is not lost in this world, since he is under the yoke of reasonable and beneficent laws. It has been given to him to submit and to understand them. If he cannot overthrow them, he can, by obeying them, take a share in them; he can even, in a certain measure, unite himself to him who has made them, and who reveals them equally by virtue and by crime. It is not, therefore, a ruler or a tyrant that his heart appeals to—it is rather a father; and he can say to himself that far from being an orphan or a waif in this world, he may live in it, like one of a large family, where, since he has the second place, he occupies a noble position.

But this side of the question, which is not only the greatest, but also the truest, did not touch Ṣākya-muni. He looked only at the miserable side of man, and abandoned himself without measure to the painful sympathy this lamentable spectacle excited within him. Because man died here on earth after having lived more or less well, he condemned him to eternal death. The hope of annihilation seemed to him sufficient for this being, solely pre-occupied with the anxiety of avoiding pain. The moment man exists he suffers, and the only way not to suffer is not to exist. Nirvāna is the only safe refuge, and man is sure never to return on earth from the moment that he no longer exists.

But it is time to close these lengthy considerations on Buddhism. We will now summarize these criticisms by applying them to some fundamental theories.

Transmigration, which is the starting-point of all this doctrine, is but an indefensible hypothesis, which the Buddha doubtless did not invent, but which he accepted, and from which he drew the most deplorable conclusions.

His ethics are incomplete and fruitless, inasmuch as they repose on a thoroughly false idea of the nature of man, and of the life he leads here below.

Nirvāna, or annihilation, is a monstrous conception, repugnant to all the instincts of human nature, revolting to reason, and implying atheism.

Reduced to these terms, Buddhism ought to inspire more pity than contempt; yet it has reigned for many centuries, and it still reigns over a multitude of races, offering to their credulity the melancholy doctrines we have just reviewed as sole nourishment of their faith, which is all the more ardent the more absurd it is. By the idea of transmigration it plunges them into a fantastic world which prevents their understanding the real conditions of the one they live in. Moreover, his ethics, which were unable to save men, were even less fitted to constitute any equitable or intelligent societies. His doctrine of Nirvāna degraded man lower than the brutes, which have at least this advantage over him, that they do not deify annihilation, which they do not dream of. In one word. he has totally failed to recognize either nature. duty, or personal dignity. He aimed at delivering humanity, but only destroyed it; he wished to enlighten it, and has cast it into the deepest gloom. His intentions may have been noble, but his general action, with some few exceptions, has been fatal; and it may be justly doubted if the nations he has lost will ever find, or even accept, any remedy for the evil he has done them, and will continue to do for many a day.

At the close of the seventeenth and following centuries, when China began to be better known, a question was raised among some eminent thinkers. It had been wondered whether it were possible that a society of atheists could exist, and whether the accusation of atheism brought against that vast empire was reasonable or probable. Bayle made the discussion famous by pronouncing himself in the affirmative, and Voltaire contested the fact. Public opinion was divided, and the question, in the absence of any well-established facts, remained undecided. At the present day, and in view of the complete and clear revelations made in the Buddhist writings which have since then been discovered and explained, no doubt can exist. Buddhist nations may, without injustice, be considered nations of atheists. This does not imply that they profess atheism, and glory in their incredulity, in the boastful manner of those who profess it among ourselves; but it simply means that these nations have not attained, even in their highest meditations, to the idea of God, and that the societies formed by them have, to the great detriment of their organization, dignity, and happiness, lived without this idea.

However, these societies do exist, very numerous although powerless, very backward although very ancient, corrupt yet refined, and profoundly miserable, through the ignorance and vice that time has increased instead of amending. Bayle was therefore right in maintaining that such a social state was possible; we now know that it really exists. Perhaps, however, we ought to add with Voltaire, 'These nations neither deny nor affirm God; they have never heard of Him. To assert that they are atheists is the same as asserting that they are Anti-Cartesians; they are neither for nor against Descartes. They are, in fact, children, and a child is neither an atheist nor a deist; he is nothing[1].'

Voltaire's opinion is the most correct and the most consoling. Ṣākya-muni is no more an atheist than Kapila, only

[1] Voltaire, *Dictionnaire philosophique*, article on *Athéisme*.

he had the weakness and misfortune to be ignorant of God; if he had fought against him, then it would have been just to accuse him of atheism. The nations whom his doctrine suited were as blind as he was, and it has been proved by the learned men of our day that they did not know God even by name. Rémusat testifies that the Chinese, Tartars, and Mongolians, to whom might be added, we believe, the Tibetans, do not possess a word in their language to express the idea of God[1]. In presence of such a curious and deplorable phenomenon, confirmed moreover by their religion, it may be doubted if the intelligence of these nations is made of the same order as our own; and if in those climates, where life is held in abhorrence and where nothingness takes the place of God, human nature is the same as with us. Moreover, the faith of these peoples, senseless as it seems to us, has been so exclusive that they have devoted their whole thoughts to it; they have no other books than their sacred books; they have not permitted their imagination, disordered as it was, to be diverted to other subjects; and most of the Buddhist nations have no other literature than that of the Sūtras[2].

If we have dwelt at such length on the errors of Buddhism, it is, first, on account of its historical importance in the past, and even in the present state of humanity; but it is also in order to caution certain minds as much as possible against the illusions it may present. Doubtless it is little to be feared that its frightful asceticism should make proselytes amongst us; transmigration, annihilation, and atheism are little likely, we imagine, to attract many adherents. Nevertheless, Buddhism has its attractive side. The Reformer himself is a grand figure, we may even say a perfect one.

[1] A. Rémusat, *Foe Koue Ki*, p. 138.

[2] No doubt this is the reason why the Sūtras are so numerous and so extravagant, as they had to satisfy all the wants of Buddhist believers.

In his life there is not a fault, not a stain. The virtues he inspired were true and often splendid, even if his principles were false. A hero himself, he inspired heroism in others. His code of morality, erroneous as it is, redeems its errors by an austerity that nothing can discourage; its vices are neither low nor common. Self-renunciation carried to such a degree, even when it is misguided, is still worthy of esteem, for the folly of the ascetic may excite pity but never contempt. It is not, therefore, surprising that Buddhism, especially when it was less known, should have called forth admiration. Even its resemblance to Christianity has not failed to deceive believers as well as those hostile to the Christian faith. The latter chose to consider it the rival of the religion they opposed, while the former saw in it a reflection of the doctrines they venerated. Now, however, it would seem that all these misapprehensions, equally untenable, ought to be dispelled. Buddhism is perfectly original, in the sense that it has not borrowed from strange nations or higher civilizations precepts and theories that it has corrupted; it is exclusively Indian, and is an integral outcome of ancient India; without Brahmanism, which it pretended to reform, or the philosophical systems it perhaps unwittingly propagated, it could not have been possible, nor could it have been accounted for.

However, if Buddhism has learnt nothing from Christianity, it would be a still greater error to suppose that Christianity has taken lessons from Buddhism. The study of Buddhism is extremely interesting, and the works of Hodgson, Schmidt, Csoma, Turnour, Burnouf, Stanislas Julien, Lassen, Foucaux, &c., deserve all our gratitude. They reveal to us a page of the annals of humanity hitherto unknown or misunderstood; they make us fathom the moral and intellectual life of these nations, who after all are our brothers, little as they perhaps resemble us. But besides this, Buddhism can teach us nothing, and to follow its teaching would be disastrous to us. Notwithstanding its specious appearance, it is but a tissue of contradictions, and it is no calumny to say that, looked at closely, it is spiritualism without soul, virtue without duty, morality without liberty, charity without love, a world without nature and without God. What lesson can we draw from such teachings? And how much we should have to forget to become its disciples! How much lower we should have to descend in the scale of civilization!

PART II

BUDDHISM IN INDIA IN THE SEVENTH CENTURY OF THE CHRISTIAN ERA.

CHAPTER I.

Life of Hiouen-Thsang. The importance of his travels in India; his monastic education in China; his vocation as a missionary; his departure; first trials. The King of the Oïgurs, the Turkish Khan. Hiouen-Thsang's arrival in India; his superstitious piety; exploration on the banks of the Ganges; five years' sojourn in Magadha and the convent of Nālanda; travels throughout the peninsula; return to Nālanda; Sīlāditya; contest of the Master of the Law against the Little Vehicle. His return to China after sixteen years' absence; Hiouen-Thsang's retreat; translation of the sacred Buddhist books; death of Hiouen-Thsang; his character.

AFTER having studied the origin of Buddhism, we pass over a space of twelve centuries, and from the year 543 B.C., the date of the Buddha's death, we reach the 630th year of the Christian era, the date at which a Chinese monk, named Hiouen-Thsang (*the Master of the Law*)—a barbaric name which henceforth becomes familiar and even venerated—travelled through India. Hiouen-Thsang's travels are known by two works, which that excellent sinologist Stanislas Julien has translated from the Chinese into French: one is the *Histoire de sa vie et de ses voyages*, by two of his disciples, Hoeï-Li and Yen-Thsong; the other is a collection of Hiouen-

Thsang's own *Memoirs* on the western countries (*Si-yu-ki*) he travelled over for sixteen consecutive years. By western countries India is more especially understood, as it is in fact situated to the west of China.

By the help of these two authentic documents, we will study Buddhism as it existed in the Indian peninsula twelve hundred years after the Nirvāna of the Tathāgata, and about four hundred years before the invasion of the Moslem.

However, in order thoroughly to appreciate Hiouen-Thsang we must consider his position, not only among the five or six heads of missions whom he imitated and surpassed, or who followed him, but in the general effect of that great movement which, for so many centuries, incited all Buddhist China towards India. Facts and records of all kinds attest uninterruptedly and with undeniable authenticity that this movement, which still exists, was of national importance. Hiouen-Thsang, in the seventh century of the Christian era, assisted it as much as lay in his power; but he only followed it and took his part, after or before many others.

It appears certain that two hundred and seventeen years before Christ, a Sramana had first penetrated into the Chinese Empire, and had brought thither the germ of the new religion. This event, recorded in the Chinese Annals[1], proves that Buddhism, as might be supposed, had its apostles, and that the missionary spirit, of which the Buddha himself had given the example, was not wanting to this religion more than to any other. Proselytism is a duty when it is believed that men can be saved by a truth already in our possession; and this is one of the most noble if not the most justifiable pretentions of Buddhism.

However, China was not destined to receive Buddhism nor

[1] Rémusat, *Foe Koue Ki*, p. 41, and Landresse, preface to *Foe Koue Ki*, p. 38.

to see it propagated by the apostles who came from India This nation, which seems to do everything in an inverted order, far from waiting for the religious faith to be brought to it, went to seek for it in foreign lands. It was as it were proselytism reversed. The Chinese pilgrims, for they cannot be called missionaries, went to India, some thousand miles from their own country, to imbibe a purer dogma or to revive a failing faith. It was necessary to do this several times, and during six centuries there were constant pilgrimages carried on, with more or less success.

This is certainly a unique fact in the history of religions, and it would seem that no other example can be quoted in the annals of humanity; for if we take two of the best known, Christianity and Mohammedanism, we find that both have been propagated in the opposite manner. Christianity, which sprang from an obscure corner of Judea, was spread by missions and preaching over the Greco-Roman world, which it soon subjugated. Through its apostles it conquered by degrees the barbarians in different parts of Europe, and at the present day it is still through its missionaries that it seeks to carry its benefits to the uttermost parts of the globe, and more especially to China. But the nations were never converted, nor was their Christianity strengthened by returning to the spot from whence Christianity had issued; even the crusades, admirable as they were, did not attempt this object; and Europe did not free the Holy Sepulchre from the Saracens in order to learn more about the faith it professed. As for Mohammedanism, it was propagated like the Christian faith, far from the place of its birth. It spread rapidly and extensively, but the nations converted by force and by the sword never came, to receive its tenets, to the place where the prophet was born. The pilgrimage to Mecca was always an act of piety, never a religious teaching.

The Chinese, therefore, retain this kind of privilege, and the manner in which they appropriated Buddhism to themselves is not the least of their peculiarities.

The first Chinese pilgrim who wrote down his travels in India was Chi-tao-'an. He travelled at the beginning of the fourth century, that is about eighty years before Fa-Hian. His book, entitled *Description of the Western Countries*, is probably lost, or at least it has not yet been discovered in the convents, where it possibly remains concealed. It is only known by the very brief mention of it made in encyclopedias or biographies published some centuries later. The extent of the work is unknown, but Stanislas Julien seems to think its loss is much to be regretted.

The second journey recorded is that of Fa-Hian. His narrative, which has reached us, is famous under the name of *Foe Koue Ki*, or *Recollections of the Kingdoms of the Buddha*. It was a real revelation when, some fifty years ago, Abel Rémusat, aided by Klaproth and Landresse, brought out a translation which gave the first idea of this narrative. However limited this was, it threw a ray of light, and, thanks to the details it contained, it was at once seen, notwithstanding its omissions and defects, what resources such documents afforded. Fa-Hian had travelled fifteen years in India, from the year 399 to the year 414. But he had only travelled over thirty kingdoms, and his intelligence did not equal his courage. His short narrative is obscure by reason of its conciseness. The notes that Abel Rémusat, Klaproth, and Landresse added were not sufficient to render it perfectly intelligible. However, it was already a great work to have taken this glorious initiative, and this first discovery promised many others more fruitful and more complete.

About a hundred years after Fa-Hian, two pilgrims, Hoeï-Seng and Sung-Yun, sent to India by order of an empress, wrote a description of their journey, but with even fewer details than Fa-Hian. Ch. Fred. Neumann has translated this account into German in his *Recollections of the Pilgrimages of the Buddhist Monks*[1]. Hoeï-Seng and Sung-Yun seem more especially to have travelled through the northern parts of India, and they remained two whole years in the Udyāna country.

After these two narratives we come to Hiouen-Thsang's, which is of much greater compass, and in every point infinitely more instructive. This work is entitled *Si-yu-ki*, or *Memoirs on the Western Countries*. It consists of about 600 pages in quarto in the Chinese text, that is to say it is ten or twelve times longer than that of Fa-Hian. It was honoured by passing through several imperial editions.

To complete the *Memoirs* of Hiouen-Thsang must be mentioned the *History* of his life by his two disciples, who add a quantity of curious facts to the dry statistics of the *Memoirs*.

Between Hiouen-Thsang's journey and that of fifty-six monks a hundred years elapse, or at least it was in 730 that a learned man called I-tsing drew up, by virtue of an imperial decree, 'The History and itinerary of the monks of the dynasty of the Thangs, who travelled to the west of China in search of the Law.' This work is rather less extensive than that of Fa-Hian.

Finally, to complete the series of Chinese pilgrimages in India, there is the *Itinerary of Khi-Nie's journey through the Western Countries*. By the emperor's orders Khi-Nie had left China in 964 at the head of three hundred Samaneans, and remained absent from his country twelve years. It seems that there only exists a few memoranda of this long journey, not more that eight quarto pages, which a learned man has included in one of his works.

Such is the substance of the narratives by the Chinese

[1] Sung-Yun's short account will be found translated in Beal's *Fa-Hian*, pp. 174–208. (Translator's note.)

pilgrims; and in translating the *Biography* and *Memoirs* of Hiouen-Thsang, Stanislas Julien has given the most interesting portions of these narrations. These two works are far superior to all the others, and in comparing Hiouen-Thsang to his predecessors and his successors, his great superiority over them, both in the extent and in the exactness of his information, is strikingly shown. Hiouen-Thsang was gifted with a real aptitude for this kind of investigation, and had he lived at a different time, and amongst ourselves, he would certainly have been classed among the most learned and illustrious geographers and travellers.

It is true that the days in which he lived were peculiarly favourable to studies of this kind. From political and commercial, as much as from religious reasons, the Chinese emperors of the seventh century, either of the Souï or the Thang dynasties, appear to have taken great interest in the western countries, and more especially in India. Besides the missions of the Buddhist monks, there were a great number of missions composed of generals and magistrates, who all brought back from their travels very useful documents. The Chinese government, which in those days had, it would seem, much more intercourse with India than at present, did not fail to utilize all these documents and place them within reach of the public. Stanislas Julien mentions no less than eight large works of this kind which were published in the course of the seventh century.

With regard to pilgrims and famous men of learning their number was considerable, and the services they rendered were brilliant enough to excite public admiration—even in the most remote times—and to induce the ancients to preserve their history in special writings. The St. Petersburg library possesses eight Chinese miscellanies, some of which have twenty or two-and-twenty volumes in quarto on the biographies of the most celebrated Buddhists. The first of these biographies was composed from the year 502 to the year 556; and the last is almost of modern times, having been compiled in 1777. The others belong to the seventh, tenth, eleventh, thirteenth, fifteenth, and seventeenth centuries; for China, although often invaded by foreign nations, has known neither the intellectual cataclysm, called in western history the invasion of the barbarians, nor the darkness of the Middle Ages.

Even from the beginning of the eighth century, in 713, that is after six or seven hundred years of almost uninterrupted communication, the multitude of works brought back from India was sufficiently cumbersome to necessitate voluminous catalogues, in which the titles of the books were classed according to their dates, followed by the names of the translators and editors, with more or less detailed notices. One of these catalogues, printed in 1306 under the Yuens, comprised fourteen hundred and forty works, and was itself but the epitome of four others, successively published in 730, 788, 1011, and 1037. It was the collective work of twenty-nine learned men 'versed in the languages,' who were associated together for this long work, and of a Samanean especially appointed to verify the accuracy of the Indian words. Besides these catalogues, the Chinese had other collections that contained analyses of Buddhist writings, intended to take the place of this mass of unwieldy books. The *Tchin-i-tien*, which exists in the Public Library in Paris, and whence Stanislas Julien drew the most instructive information, is a compilation of this kind.[1]

[1] One of the most eminent services Stanislas Julien rendered to Buddhistical learning is having established methodical and unquestionable rules for the restitution of Sanskrit names mutilated by the Chinese transcripts. As there is no alphabet in the Chinese language, and several articulations are lacking, the foreign words of which it tried to represent the sound were often so altered as to be absolutely unrecognizable. To return to them their original form was a most difficult problem, which both Rémusat and Burnouf had, for lack of information, failed to solve.

With regard to the translation itself of the sacred books, it was the object of the most minute care, and surrounded with every possible guarantee. Colleges of translators, authorized by imperial decrees, were officially appointed. This work of translation necessitated the employment of whole convents; emperors themselves did not disdain to write prefaces for these books, intended for the religious and moral instruction of their subjects. Out of piety and respect for the traditions of their ancestors, the dynasty reigning at the present moment in China has had reprinted, in an oblong folio size, all the ancient Chinese, Tibetan, Manchou and Mongolian translations, and this immense collection fills no less than thirteen hundred and ninety-two volumes.

We will now study Hiouen-Thsang's share in this vast enterprise. When he followed his vocation as missionary, the Buddhist faith had been publicly adopted in his country for about five hundred years (the year 61 or 65 of our era). It had reaped great triumphs, and had sustained dismal eclipses. Hiouen-Thsang strove, like many others, to revive it during one of its periods of decline; but if he was one of its most useful and enlightened apostles, he was not the only one, and it would be showing little appreciation of his worth if a glory that he shares with many of his co-religionists were exclusively attributed to him. This point must not be lost sight of in studying his biography, which is calculated to excite the greatest curiosity; for it may be doubted whether in our western countries, in the midst of the seventh century, it would be possible to find a literary and religious personage more interesting than Hiouen-Thsang, notwithstanding his prejudices and his incredible superstition.

A native of Tchin-Lieou, in the district of Keou-Chi, Hiouen-Thsang belonged to an honourable family, who had held important posts in his province. His father, Hoeï, had refused, out of discretion and love of study, to follow the career of his ancestor, and had avoided public duties in times of civil disturbances. Having undertaken himself the education of his four sons, he soon noticed the precocious intelligence and earnestness of the youngest, Hiouen-Thsang, and he devoted himself to the culture of these remarkable dispositions. The child repaid him for his care, and at a tender age was confided to the management of his second brother, who had embraced a religious life in one of the monasteries of Lo-Yang, the eastern capital. He displayed the same diligence and prodigious aptitude at the convent as under his paternal roof, and by an exception, which the elevation and steadiness of his character more even than his knowledge justified, he was admitted without examination at the age of thirteen among the monks. The fact is that even at this early period his vocation had revealed itself, and 'his sole desire was to become a monk in order to propagate afar the glorious Law of the Buddha.' The books he studied most particularly, and with which he was thoroughly acquainted, were the sacred book of the *Nie-pan* (Nirvāna) and the *Che-ta-ching-lun* (*Māhāyāna Samparigraha Ṣāstra*, the complete summary of the Great Vehicle).

For seven years the youthful novice went with his brother to all the most renowned schools to finish his education, and in the midst of the sanguinary revolutions that were then agitating the empire, he underwent trials that prepared him for those he had to undergo in his future travels. He remained a few years in the Chou district, which was less disturbed than the others, and he there diligently followed the lectures of the best qualified masters. The two brothers vied with one another in learning and virtue, and in the Kong-hoeï-sse convent of the town of Tching-Tou they were both noticed for 'the brilliancy of their talents, the purity of their morals, and the nobility of their hearts.' At the age of twenty Hiouen-Thsang finished his novitiate and received full monastic orders; this took place in the fifth year of the Wou-te period, that is in 622. During the summer retreat that followed, he studied discipline, the *Vinaya*, and continued investigating the Sūtras and Ṣāstras. He still had some doubts about different points of doctrine that neither he nor his brother had been able to solve, and in order to decide these, he went from town to town during six years, to consult the professors who were considered the most learned. But even at that time he was himself a consummate master, and in the convents where he sojourned he was often requested to explain some of the most important works. Thus, in the convent of Thien-hoang-sse, at King-Tcheou, he expounded three times during the autumn season the two books of the *Māhāyāna Samparigraha Ṣāstra* and the *Abhidharma Ṣāstra*. Such was the fame of his teaching, that the king, Han-yang, accompanied by his officers and a multitude of monks, came to hear him, and were the admiring spectators of a brilliant victory the Master of the Law gained over those who had come to interrogate and discuss with him. At Tch'-ang'na his success was no less brilliant, and the oldest and most scholarly masters admitted that this young man's knowledge surpassed theirs. Nevertheless, Hiouen-Thsang felt that he still lacked many things, and far from being blinded by the praise that was lavished on him, he resolved to travel in the countries of the west, in order to consult wise men as to certain points of the Law on which his mind was still disturbed. Moreover, he recalled to mind the travels of Fa-Hian and of Tchi-Yun, the first scholars of their day, and 'the glory of seeking the Law which was to guide men and procure their happiness' seemed to him worthy of imitation.

In concert with several other monks, he presented a

petition for leave to travel in India; but having been refused by an imperial decree, he decided to start alone, notwithstanding the difficulties and perils which awaited him. He was still hesitating when the recollection of a dream of his mother's and one of his own settled his mind, together with the predictions of a skilful astrologer who had drawn his horoscope, and whose prophecy came true. Hiouen-Thsang was at this time twenty-six years of age.

He at once repaired to Liang-Tcheou, the general resort of inhabitants of the west bank of the Yellow River and of all the merchants of the neighbouring countries. He was preparing to leave this city, after having delivered there, as elsewhere, several well-attended lectures on the Law, when a first obstacle nearly overthrew all his plans. The governor of the city had received the strictest orders from the imperial administration to prevent anybody leaving the country. But, thanks to the secret assistance of some professors who approved his purpose, Hiouen-Thsang succeeded in escaping from the city, remaining hidden during the day and travelling all night. A little further on, at Koua-Tcheou, he would have been arrested on the denunciation of spies sent in pursuit of him, if the governor, touched by the frankness of the pilgrim, who confessed who he was, and by his magnanimous courage, had not saved him by destroying the official document containing his description.

Two novices who had followed him so far took fright at these first obstacles and abandoned him. Left alone and without a guide, Hiouen-Thsang bethought him that the best way to procure one was to go and prostrate himself at the feet of the *Mi-le's* (Maitreya Bodhisatwa) [1] statue and offer up fervent prayers. The next day he repeated them

[1] Maitreya was the future Buddha, whom Ṣākya-muni consecrated as his successor when he quitted the Tushita.

with equal faith, when he suddenly saw near him a man from the barbarian countries come in, who declared his wish to become a monk and receive his instructions, and who willingly consented to be his guide.

The flight was not easy. At the extreme frontier, about fifteen miles from the city, it was necessary to pass unperceived through a barrier, 'which was the key to the western frontier.' It was situated near the widest part of an extremely rapid river, and beyond this barrier five signal towers, guarded by vigilant sentinels, had also to be avoided. The barrier was cleverly evaded, thanks to the youthful guide; but he declined to go any further, and he left the Master of the Law to continue his perilous journey alone. The twenty-four long miles that separated the barrier and the towers was a desert of arid sand, where the road was only marked by heaps of bones and the marks of horses' feet. No sooner had Hiouen-Thsang entered it than he was assailed by visions caused by the mirage; he supposed them to be delusions, created by the demons who wished to oppose his undertaking; but he heard in the air a voice that cried to him to sustain his courage: 'Fear not! Fear not!'

Reaching by night the first tower, which he was obliged to approach in order to get water, he ran the risk of being killed by the arrows of the sentinels. Fortunately the commander of the guard-house, who was a zealous Buddhist, consented to let him pass, and moreover gave him letters of recommendation to the chief of another station, to whom he was nearly related. The traveller was obliged to make a long circuit to avoid the last station, where he would have found obdurate and violent men; but he lost his way in the second desert he had to cross. To crown his misfortunes, the goat-skin that contained his supply of water was empty. In utter despair, he was about to retrace his steps and return eastwards. But no sooner had he gone three miles in this new direction than, seized by remorse, he said to himself, 'Originally I swore if I did not reach Thien-tchou (India) I would never take one step to return to China. Why have I come here? I prefer to die going west than to return to the east and live.' He therefore resumed his way, and fervently praying to *Kouan-in* (Avalokiteṣvara), he again directed his steps towards the north-west. Four nights and five days he wandered in the desert without a drop of fresh water to refresh his parched throat. He kept up his drooping courage by reading in the midst of his prayers the *Pradjnā-Pāramitā* and Avalokiteṣvara's Sūtra. However, overcome by thirst, fatigue, and want of sleep, he was about to perish when a breeze that rose in the night revived him, as well as his horse, which was almost equally exhausted. They therefore managed to struggle on, and in a few moments they reached the bank of a pond surrounded by fresh pasture-land, towards which the animal's infallible instinct had led him.

After two more days of painful journeying he at last reached a convent in *I-gou* (the country of the Oïgurs), where he found some Chinese monks.

These first details, which bear an evident impress of truth, notwithstanding some exaggerations on the part of his biographers, give us an insight into the character of Hiouen-Thsang, as well as the terrible obstacles he had to overcome. Besides the knowledge which had already made him famous, he possessed an imperturbable faith, boundless courage, and an energy that nothing could dishearten; he was, in fact a perfect missionary.

Other trials of a different nature, but no less formidable, still awaited him. No sooner had he rested a few days at *I-gou* than the powerful king of *Kao-Tch'ang*, one of the tributaries of China, sent messengers to invite him to come to his kingdom. This was a command the poor pilgrim could not disobey. The reception which the king *Khio-wen-taï* gave him was no less cordial than it was magnificent, but when, ten days later, the Master of the Law wished to leave, the king declared his firm intention of keeping him to the end of his life, as teacher of his subjects and chief of the monks appointed to instruct them. In vain did Hiouen-Thsang protest, alleging the sacred purpose of his journey, the king remained inflexible. But the Master of the Law took on his side a no less extreme resolution, and knowing that 'the king, notwithstanding his great power, had no control over his mind and will,' he refused to eat, determining to die of hunger sooner than abandon his design. Three long days had already elapsed, when the king, ashamed and afraid of the consequences of his obduracy, respectfully offered him his apologies and set him at liberty. Feeling but little reassured after so much cruelty, Hiouen-Thsang made the king swear he would keep his word, first by taking to witness the sun, and then the Buddha, before whose statue they worshipped together. The king swore, in the presence of his mother the princess *Tch'ang*, that he would always treat the Master of the Law as a brother, on condition that on his return from India, he would come back to the country of *Kao-Tch'ang*, and spend three years there. Hiouen-Thsang consented to this, and sixteen years after fulfilled his promise. Moreover he consented to remain another month in the *Kao Tch'ang* country and he devoted all that time to the religious instruction of the court, which, with the king at its head, came every evening to listen to his pious lessons.

When the month had expired, the Master of the Law departed, loaded with rich presents and accompanied by a numerous escort he had himself chosen; he was provided with a quantity of provisions, besides twenty-four letters of recommendation to the sovereigns of the different countries he had to pass through. In an elegantly expressed letter, which his biographers have carefully given at full length and which was indeed worth preserving, he thanked the king for his great generosity.

The remainder of the journey, thanks to all these supplies, was somewhat less fatiguing, although interspersed with many hardships. On leaving the kingdom of Kutch, the first in which the pilgrim found Buddhism the established religion, the caravan had to cross a high mountain, *Ling-Chan* (*Musuraola*) covered with perpetual snows, which took seven days, and where they lost fourteen men and a quantity of oxen and horses. After having skirted the lake of Issikul and gone fifty miles beyond it, Hiouen-Thsang met, in the city of *Sou-che*, the Turkish Khan (*Tou-Kie*), who received him sumptuously in his tents of felt and, who, after a banquet, surrounded by his horde, listened to his pious instructions on the Ten Virtues and the Six Paramitas (*Po-lo-me*), dismissed him, loaded with magnificent presents, and gave him an interpreter to conduct him to Kapisa, in India. At Samarkand, Hiouen-Thsang tried to convert the king and the people, who were fire-worshippers, and by appointing monks, he was able to hope that he had re-established Buddhism, which had in former days been brought there, as the presence of two deserted convents attested. At Baktra (Balk, *Fo-ko-lo*), he first found Buddhism flourishing, with its monuments, relics, and legends of all sorts. There were no less than a hundred convents and three thousand monks,—all devoted to the study of the Little Vehicle. In a convent called the New Convent, an imposing edifice, richly decorated, situated north-west of the city, they showed the Buddha's water-jug, his broom, and one of his front teeth. On festivals, the three relics were exhibited, and the people and the monks worshipped them. It was said, in the city of *Poli*, situated about thirty miles from Baktra (Balk) that the Tathāgata had come to these places, and two stūpas had been raised as memorials of his presence and his benevolence.

In the kingdom of Bamian (*Fan-yen-na*) Hiouen-Thsang found no less ardent faith, with convents, stūpas, magnificent statues of the Buddha, and monks belonging to divers schools, devoted to the study of the Law. After having twice crossed the Black Mountains (Hindu Kush) and the kingdoms of Kapisa (*Kia-pi-che*) and Lampā (*Lan-po*) he entered the kingdom of Nagarahāra, where he saw the first monuments of the great monarch Aṣoka (*Wou-yeou*) whose dominion seems to have extended to these distant countries. A stūpa three hundred feet high, erected at the gates of the city, was attributed to him.

From this moment the pilgrim found everywhere traces of this potentate, whose empire appears to have comprised the greater part of the peninsula.

We have shown Hiouen-Thsang's courage and the knowledge he had acquired about the most difficult religious subjects; but his character would not be complete if we did not also mention some of his superstitions.

In the kingdom of Nagarahāra, he visited a city which bore the unknown name of City of the Top of Fo's Cranium. The following account gives the reason of this singular name. On the second story of a pavilion, in a small tower 'formed of seven precious things,' a famous relic called Uṣnisha was enshrined. This bone, enclosed in a casket, was more than a foot in circumference. It was of a yellowish-white colour, and the minute holes where the hair had grown were still distinctly visible. Those who wished to know the extent of their sins and their virtues used to pound perfumes, and with the powder make a soft paste which they deposited, well wrapped up in silk, on the sacred bone. The box was then closed, and according to the state of the paste when it was taken out again, each of the consulting parties knew what amount of happiness or misfortune they might expect. Hiouen-Thsang received for his share a moulded figure of the Tree of Wisdom (Bodhidruma), while a young Sramana who accompanied him only obtained the figure of a lotus. The custodian of the sacred bone, seeing this miracle, was delighted; he snapped his fingers and, scattering flowers, he said to Hiouen-Thsang: 'Master, what you have obtained is exceedingly rare, and clearly shows that you already possess a portion of the *Pou-ti* (Bodhi, Wisdom of the Buddha).' They also showed the pilgrim, who on his side was most generous, other relics no less saintly, and among others, the eyeball of the Buddha, which was so brilliant, the biographers say, that it was seen to shine through the box. They also showed him the Buddha's raiment (*sanghāti*) and his staff.

It might be supposed that in this first adventure Hiouen-Thsang was the dupe of some cunning trick; but the following is still more complicated and more extraordinary.

He heard that six miles distant from the city of Teng-Kouang-tch'ing (Pradīparasmipura) there was a cave where the Tathāgata, having conquered the king of Dragons who inhabited it, had left his shadow. He resolved to go and render him homage 'not wishing,' he said, 'to have come so near without worshipping him, and well aware that if he lived for a thousand kalpas, it would be difficult to find, even once, the real shadow of the Buddha.' In vain was it represented to him that the roads were dangerous and infested with robbers; in vain was it urged that for the last two or three years hardly any of those rare visitors who were so imprudent as to face this peril had returned; nothing could shake his purpose. After a great deal of difficulty he found, on a farm belonging to a convent, an old man who consented to act as his guide. No sooner had he started, than he was attacked by five ruffians, who rushed upon him sword in hand. Hiouen-Thsang calmly showed his religious habit and disarmed them by firm and kindly words.

The grotto he was bound for was situated near a river between two mountains, and the entrance was through a kind of door in a stone wall. On looking into it Hiouen-Thsang could discern nothing, but following the instructions of the old man, he found his way in the darkness and reached the spot where the shadow rested. Then, filled with deep faith, he made the hundred salutations prescribed; but still he saw nothing. He bitterly reproached himself for his sins, wept with loud sobs and gave way to his grief, devoutly reciting the *Ching-man-King* (the *Sri-mālādevī Sinhanāda Sūtra*) and the Gāthās of the Buddhas, prostrating himself at each strophe. He had scarcely finished the first hundred salutations, than he saw on the eastern wall of the grotto a slight glimmer which immediately vanished; it was as wide as a monk's jug. He recommenced his salutations, and a second light as wide as a bowl appeared and disappeared as rapidly. Filled with enthusiasm, he declared he would not leave the grotto till he had seen the shadow of the *Venerable of the Century*. At last, after two hundred more salutations, the cavern was suddenly flooded with light, and the shadow of the Tathāgata, of dazzling whiteness, stood out upon the wall, 'like when the clouds part, and suddenly reveal the marvellous image of the Golden Mountain.' A dazzling brilliancy lighted up the outline of his noble countenance, and his raiment was of a yellow-red colour. From his knees upwards, the beauty of his person shone in the full light. To the left, and to the right, and behind the Buddha, could be seen all the shadows of the Bodhisatwas and venerable Sramanas who form his retinue. Hiouen-Thsang, in an ecstasy of delight, gazed intently on the sublime and peerless object of his admiration. When he had sufficiently contemplated this miracle, he commanded from afar six men who waited outside, to bring fire and burn perfumes. As soon as the fire blazed, the shadow of the Buddha disappeared; and directly the fire went out, the image reappeared again. Five of the men saw it; but one of them did not see anything whatever. Hiouen-Thsang respectfully prostrated himself, proclaimed the praises of the Buddha, and scattered flowers and perfumes. The divine apparition having ceased, he took his leave and departed.

To all appearance, the pilgrim was once more deceived by some charlatan's trick; perhaps, however, he was his own dupe, and the old man who accompanied him gave him the true explanation: 'Master,' he said, 'without the sincerity of your faith, and the energy of your prayers, you would not have obtained such a miracle.' The history of superstitions is full of such hallucinations; and over-excited imaginations, like that of Hiouen-Thsang, are too ready to receive them, if circumstances permit. The countries the pilgrim travelled through have at all times been given up to the wildest dreams, and when he sees the traces of the Buddha's footsteps, on a large stone on the north bank of the Subhavastu that he crosses, he does not hesitate to say ingenuously: 'that these traces appear long or short, according to the degree of virtue possessed by those who look at them, and according to the energy of their prayers.'

It will at once be understood that being so easily satisfied with what he sees himself, he is still more so with what is related to him; for he is as credulous with regard to traditions as he is about his own supernatural visions. Near to the mountain *Hi-lo*, he visited the spot where *Jou-laï* (the Tathāgata), filled with gratitude towards the Yakshas, gave them his own body as alms; the place, not far from *Moung-Kie-li* (probably Manghelli or Manikiala), marked by a stūpa, where *Jou-laï* pierced his body with a knife; the spot near Takshasila where, as chief of a great kingdom, he made an offering of a thousand heads; in the same way as near Purushapura (actually Peshāwar) he saw the spot, marked by one of Aṣoka's stūpas, where during a thousand successive existences *Jou-laï* gave his eyes as alms; and not far distant from the river *Sin-tou* (the Indus) the spot where Siddhārtha, while only prince royal, gave his body to appease the hunger of seven tiger-cubs. Henceforth Hiouen-Thsang will for the remainder of his journey live in the midst of this world of marvels and delusions; and he mentions hundreds of such miracles with the most imperturbable composure.

After various journeyings in Udyāna, and the valley of upper Sindh and the Panjāb, he entered by the north-west into the kingdom of Kashmir (*Kia-chi-mi-lo*, Kasmīra). In its capital he found no less than a hundred convents, inhabited by five thousand monks. There also he saw four enormous stūpas, that had been built in former days by the king *Wou-yeou* (Aṣoka); each of these stūpas containing *Che-lis* (*sarīras*), that is personal relics of the Tathāgata.

As the report of Hiouen-Thsang's fame had preceded him in Kashmir, the king, to do him honour, sent one of his uncles to meet him, as far as the Stone Gate, on the western frontier of the country, and himself went to receive him at some distance from the capital. This respectful greeting was but the prelude to more substantial favours. The king, not satisfied with admitting at his table the foreign monk who came from Great China (*Mo-ho-tchi-na*, Mahā Tchīna), gave him twenty scribes to copy for him all the Sūtras and Ṣāstras he wished to have, and he moreover appointed five persons as his personal attendants, instructing them to furnish him, at the expense of the treasury, with all he might require. For centuries past, learning had been held in great honour in this kingdom, and the knowledge of the Law had been carried so far that in the four hundredth year after the *Nie-pan* of *Jou-laï* (the Tathāgata's Nirvāna) the king Kanishka (*Kia-ni-sse-kia*) held a council of five hundred learned monks, under the presidency of Vasubandhu, which drew up three Commentaries on the Pitakas. In the convent where the pilgrim resided, he followed the learned lessons of a professor of the Law, who explained to him all the difficult points of the principal Ṣāstras; and the lectures, at which the Chinese monk displayed the most lively and acute intelligence, became so interesting, that learned men came from all parts of the kingdom to hear them. The success and favour shown to a stranger soon excited the jealousy of the monks of Kashmir, but owing to the superiority of Hiouen-Thsang's intelligence, and his kindness of heart, he was able to overcome all enmity, and he spent two whole years in this kingdom in order to make a thorough study of the sacred books.

Wherever he found teachers capable of improving his knowledge he would stop to hear them and submissively follow their instructions. Thus in the kingdom of Chinapāti, he spent fourteen months under Vinītaprabha; in that of Djalandhara he passed four months under Chandravarma; in the kingdom of Srughna, he spent one winter and spring under Djayagupta; and in Matipura, half the spring and the whole summer under Mitrasena, all renowned professors, thoroughly acquainted with the Three Commentaries.

After having crossed the Ganges several times, in the course of his various wanderings, he reached the kingdom of Kanyākubja, governed at that time by a generous and devout prince called Ṣilāditya, with whom he was destined to become more intimately connected.

On going down the Ganges from Ayodhyā to the kingdom of Hayamukha, the pilgrim, who might have supposed himself secure from any further danger, nearly perished in a strange manner, and was saved only by a miracle. The boat that conveyed him and eighty other persons was surprised by a band of pirates. These robbers worshipped the goddess *To-kia* (Durgā), and every autumn they offered up in sacrifice to this divinity, 'to obtain good fortune,' the finest and handsomest man they could lay hands on. The Master of the Law was chosen as the victim, but not in the least dismayed he thus spoke to the ruffians: 'If this contemptible body were worthy of your sacrifice, I would certainly not grudge it to you. But as I have come from distant lands to honour the image of the Bodhi and the Vulture's Peak, to procure sacred writings, and to be instructed in the Law, my vow is not yet accomplished; and I fear, most generous men, that in taking my life you will call down upon yourselves the greatest calamities.' It could hardly be expected that robbers would be influenced by such pious arguments, and the chief pirate having ordered his men to prepare the altar, which was to be made of earth kneaded with water from the river, two of the robbers, drawing their swords, dragged off the poor monk to sacrifice him on the spot. Hiouen-Thsang betrayed no fear or emotion, but only asked for a few moments respite, to prepare to enter Nirvāna with the necessary joy and tranquillity of soul.

'Then,' his biographers add, 'the Master of the Law thought tenderly of *Ts'e-chi* (Maitreya) and turned all his thoughts to the palace of the Tushitas, offering up ardent prayer that he might be reborn there, so that he could pay his respects and do homage to that Bodhisatwa, and receive the *Yu-kia-sse-ti-lun* (*Yogāchārā Bhumi Ṣāstra*), and hear the explanation of the *Good Law* (*Saddharma*), and attain enlightened Intelligence, and then be reborn on earth to instruct and convert these men, to make them practise acts of superior virtue, and abandon their infamous profession, and finally to spread abroad the benefits of the Law, and give peace and happiness to all beings. Then he worshipped the Buddhas of the ten countries of the world, and seating himself in the attitude of meditation, energetically fixed his thoughts on *Ts'e-chi* (Maitreya Bodhisatwa), without allowing any other idea to distract him. Suddenly, it seemed to his enraptured mind that he was rising up to Mount Sumeru, and that after having passed through one, two, and three heavens, he saw the Venerable Maitreya in the palace of the Tushitas, seated on a bright throne, surrounded by a multitude of Devas. At this moment his body and soul were bathed in joy, unconscious that he was near the altar, unmindful of the pirates thirsting for his blood. But his companions burst out in tears and lamentations, when suddenly a hurricane arose on all sides, breaking down trees, scattering clouds of sand, raising great waves upon the river and sinking all the boats.'

The pirates, terror-struck and deprived of all means of retreat, exhorted one another to repentance, and threw themselves down at the knees of Hiouen-Thsang, who told them that those who give themselves up to murder, pillage, and impious sacrifices, suffer eternally in the future world.

'How dare you,' he said to them, 'for the satisfaction of this contemptible body, which vanishes in an instant, like a flash of lightning or the morning dew, bring upon yourselves tortures which will last throughout an infinite number of centuries?'

The robbers, touched by his courage, threw their weapons into the river, restored to each traveller his stolen goods, and respectfully listened to the Five Commandments.[1]

When he had reached the banks of the Ganges and the

[1] The Five Commandments are those prescribed by the Tathāgata: Not to kill, not to steal, &c.

Jumna, the pilgrim remained for several years in the places made famous by the presence and preaching of the Buddha, and he piously visited Ṣrāvásti (*Chi-lo-fa-si-ti*) the former residence of the king Prasenajit (*Po-lo-sse-na*) and the famous Anātha Piṇḍika; Kapilavastu, the city where the Buddha was born, amongst the ruins of which still lingered so many memories of his childhood and youth; Kusi-nagara, where the Buddha, resting under the shade of four sālas, entered for ever into Nirvāna; Benāres (Varānaṣī, in Chinese *Po-lo-ni-sse*), where he had 'for the first time turned the Wheel of the Law' in favour of his five disciples; Vaiṣāli (*Feï-che-li*), where he had studied under Arāta Kālāma before appearing in the world, &c.

In Magadha (*Mo-kie-to*) Hiouen-Thsang had still to visit places yet more sacred, if it were possible. After having spent seven days in visiting the monuments of Pātaliputra, and before going on to Rājagriha, he travelled thirty miles further south to worship the Bodhidruma, *the Tree of Wisdom*, still carefully tended, the Vajrāsanam, *the Diamond Throne*, seat of the Buddhas, contemporary it is said of heaven and earth, and a number of other monuments almost as venerable. It can be imagined with what ardour the devout pilgrim paid his homage. On beholding *the Tree of Wisdom* and the statue of the Tathāgata, which the Bodhisatwa Maitreya had erected near it, he contemplated them with an ardent faith, and prostrating himself before them, he gave vent to his grief in lamentations.

'Alas,' he said with a sigh, 'I know not what was the condition of my miserable existence at the time the Buddha attained perfect wisdom: and now that I have reached this spot, I can only meditate with shame on the immensity and depth of my sins.'

At these words, a flood of tears bathed his face, and all those who saw the Master of the Law in this afflicted condition, could not refrain from shedding tears likewise.

These places were full of monuments of all kinds: vihāras, saṅghāramas, pillars, and especially stūpas, most of them attributed to the great king Aṣoka, who, according to tradition had caused eighty-four thousand to be built all over India. Most of these were in ruins when Hiouen-Thsang visited them, as they had been already two hundred years before in the days of Fa-Hian; and this dilapidation made them doubtless still more venerable in the eyes of the courageous pilgrims who had come so far to worship them.

Hiouen-Thsang resided no less than five whole years in Magadha, not to speak of the second journey he took there, after having travelled over all the southern and western parts of the peninsula. But this first sojourn, which he spent entirely in the great monastery of Nālanda, inhabited at that time by ten thousand monks, is so full of interest that some details must be given about it. It is interesting to know something of the domestic life of one of these vast communities which, in the seventh century of our era, were so numerous in India. The saṅghārama of Nālanda, the largest of all, affords this opportunity; and the descriptions of this immense establishment, protected by kings and venerated by the faithful, will give us a very fair idea of the labours and customs of the Buddhist monks. It was in this sanctuary of knowledge and virtue that Hiouen-Thsang learnt the Sanskrit language, and acquired the higher knowledge which was to make his fortune among princes, and his fame among his fellow-countrymen.

The immense convent of Nālanda was situated in one of the most holy parts of Magadha, about thirty miles from the Bodhimanda, the renowned and sacred retreat, where after six years of continual austerities Ṣākya-muni had at last attained perfect Buddhahood. Tradition relates that the spot on which the convent was eventually built, was originally a wood of mango-trees, which rich merchants converted by the Tathāgata had offered to him. He had resided there some time, and in memory of his inexhaustible charity towards orphans and the poor, the place had been called Nālanda.[1] The piety of the kings of that country had not failed to strengthen popular belief by embellishing Nālanda with magnificent edifices. They had successively built six convents, at first separated from each other; but the last king had enclosed all these buildings by a single wall. He had divided the extensive space between the six convents into eight courts, and the monks' habitations were no less than four stories high. Towers, pavilions, and domes rose on all sides, and running streams and shady groves kept all cool and fresh.

In this splendid abode ten thousand monks and novices resided, maintained at the expense of the king and the neighbouring cities. Devoted to study, they were generally followers of the doctrine of the Great Vehicle. The votaries of eighteen schools gathered together there, and all the sciences were cultivated, from the vernacular writings and the Vedas, down to medicine and arithmetic. Moreover, there were halls assigned to lectures, where a hundred different professors discoursed every day to the students, who had nothing to disturb them from their pious tasks, and who, thanks to the generosity with which they were treated, could, without appealing to extraneous assistance, obtain from the convent the Four necessary things (that is to say, raiment, food, lodging and medicines). In fact their progress in knowledge was assured, and Nālanda was not only the finest vihāra in India, but it was the most learned and

[1] Nālanda, composed of three words, *Na alam da*, means in Sanskrit: *He who is never weary of giving*. The etymology of the word has certainly greatly assisted the legend.

the most famous for the zeal of its pupils and the talents of its masters. It reckoned about a thousand monks who could explain twenty works on the Sūtras and Ṣāstras; five hundred who knew thirty, and only ten who understood but fifty. The Master of the Law, Hiouen-Thsang, was in the last class, already deemed eminent. But the Superior of the convent, Sīlabhadra, had read and fathomed all the Sūtras and Ṣāstras without exception; and the high rank he occupied was due to his eminent virtue, his learning, and his venerable age.

Such was the holy sanctuary to which the Chinese pilgrim had been solemnly invited. Four monks, chosen from among the most distinguished, had come to Bodhimanda to bring him the invitation. He had accepted it, and when he went to Nālanda, two hundred monks, followed by a crowd of the faithful, came to meet him with parasols, banners, perfumes, and flowers; they walked round him singing his praises, and then led him to the convent. There, they made him sit on an armchair placed on the same platform as the president, and the sub-director (*Karmadāna*) striking a gong (*ghantā*), in a loud voice invited the Master of the Law to stay in the vihāra, and to make use of all the implements and goods belonging to the monks. He was then presented to the Superior by twenty men of mature age and dignified appearance, well versed in the knowledge of the Sūtras and Ṣāstras. When Hiouen-Thsang stood before Sīlabhadra, he did him homage as a disciple. In conformance with the rules of respect established among them, he advanced on his knees, and leaning on his elbows, beat his feet together, and struck the ground with his forehead. Sīlabhadra received this homage with kindness, and had seats brought for the Master of the Law and the monks who accompanied him; then after having questioned and highly praised him, he made his nephew, a very capable speaker, relate the history of a long illness from which he had suffered, and which had been miraculously cured, three years before, by a dream, in which three divine personages had come and announced to him the future arrival of Hiouen-Thsang.

'Since my journey is in accordance with your former dream,' replied the pilgrim, much affected, 'be kind enough to instruct and enlighten me, and complete my happiness, by allowing me to pay you the respect of an obedient and devoted disciple.'

On leaving the Superior, Hiouen-Thsang was established with his retinue, consisting of ten persons, in one of the best houses of the convent; every day, the necessary provisions were sent to him by the king, and two monks, one a Sramana and the other a Brahman, who served him, took him out in a chariot, or on an elephant, or in a palanquin.

When Hiouen-Thsang was settled at Nālanda, he only went out to visit the sacred places of the neighbourhood: Kusagarapura, the ancient capital of Magadha; the Vulture's Peak; the Bamboo grove at Kalanta; the places where the first orthodox Council, under the presidency of Kāṣyapa, and the dissident Council of the General Order had been held; Rājagrihapura; the stūpas and vihāras in the vicinity, &c. While he remained in the convent he diligently followed Sīlabhadra's instructions, making him explain several times the books he did not yet know, re-examining those he had formerly read, in order to dispel any doubts he might still retain; even perusing the books of the Brahmans, which were indispensable for his acquiring a perfect knowledge of Sanskrit grammar, among others the work of Pānini, a summary of all the previous works on the same subject.

The Master of the Law thus spent the five years of his residence at Nālanda, absorbed in these serious studies. At the end of that time he knew the language, and had so thoroughly sifted all the books of the Three Commentaries and those of the Brahmans that he no longer required the instructions of Sīlabhadra and his monks. He therefore gratefully took leave of his hosts, and continued the course of his pilgrimage. At this period, he had scarcely accomplished half his mission, as he had taken three years to get from China to Magadha, where he had resided five years. He had still to travel through the whole of the eastern side of the peninsula, the centre, the western part, and to return again to Magadha before retracing his steps homewards. He subsequently devoted eight years to these long peregrinations.

We will only mention the principal incidents of his journey.

On leaving Magadha, he travelled through the kingdoms of Hiranyaparvata, Champā, Kadjūgira, Karnasuvarna, Samatata and Tāmralipti. There for the first time he heard of the Island of Ceylon (*Seng-kia-lo,* Sinhala), where Buddhism was said to be perhaps even more flourishing than in India itself. He intended going there by sea, although the passage was no less than seven hundred yodjanas, when a southern monk advised him to avoid the dangers of such a long voyage by going down to the point of land at the extremity of the peninsula, whence, after a three days' voyage, he would reach the kingdom of the Lion (Sinhala): Hiouen-Thsang resolved to follow this prudent advice. He was not, however, destined to visit Ceylon: for when he reached the port of Kānchīpura, at the southern extremity of India, and was on the point of embarking, he heard that the island was a prey to civil war and famine. He therefore merely collected all the information he could obtain on the ancient history of Sinhala, on the introduction of Buddhism, which it was said had been imported there a hundred years after the Nirvāna of the Buddha by Mahinda, brother of king Aṣoka,[1] and on the chief monuments of the

[1] See Rhys Davids' *Buddhism*, p. 229, 'Mahinda was Aṣoka's own son.' (Translator's note.)

island, &c. But he did not cross the straits, and in company with seventy monks of Sinhala he continued exploring the continent. Leaving the kingdom of Dravida he went on to that of Kongkanapura, where the cap Siddhārtha had worn when prince royal was piously preserved. In Mahārāṭṭha (the country of the Mahrattas) he found the most martial and best disciplined population of these countries. The king was of the Kshatriya race; and when a general was defeated, he was punished by having a woman's dress sent to him. The Buddha's law was held in as high honour in this kingdom as in any of the others, and Hiouen-Thsang saw a number of monuments that tradition attributed to the great king Aṣoka.

Going up to the north-west he reached the kingdom of Malwah, which vied with Magadha itself for the gentleness and politeness of its inhabitants, the culture of letters, the esteem in which virtue was held, and the harmony of its language. Thence, passing through many extensive kingdoms, sometimes following the coast line, sometimes plunging across country, he reached the frontiers of Persia; but he did not penetrate any further, although he might, from what he had heard, have found there several Buddhist monuments. He therefore turned eastwards, and after many a long march he got back to the banks of the Indus that he had formerly crossed on his arrival from China, but this time he was much nearer its source. On the eastern bank of the river he passed through Multan, where the idolatrous inhabitants worshipped the Sun-god; and from the kingdom of Parvata he returned to Magadha, whence he had started on this fatiguing journey.

On his return to Nālanda he found fresh studies awaiting him, but this time he met with full compensation in the shape of divers brilliant successes. The aged Sīlabhadra still ruled over the convent, and Hiouen-Thsang was henceforth capable under his guidance of communicating to others the deep learning he had acquired. Sīlabhadra, who appreciated his worth, appointed him several times to expound the most difficult books to the multitude of monks; and Hiouen-Thsang acquitted himself of this duty to the general satisfaction of the community. He was, moreover, capable of writing Sanskrit, and he wrote several books, which excited the admiration of the whole Order, and in which he refuted the errors of the Sānkhya and the Vaiseshika systems, while striving to reconcile the different doctrines which at that time divided Buddhism. These studies pointed him out as a fit person for an important mission, which he fulfilled with great credit to himself.

Magadha was at that time ruled by King Ṣīlāditya, whose dominions, it appears, extended over a considerable part of India. Full of piety and veneration for the convent of Nālanda, he had built near it a magnificent vihāra, which excited the jealousy of the neighbouring states. The king, returning from a military expedition, was passing through the kingdom of Orissa, when the monks of the countries that followed the doctrine of the Little Vehicle came to complain to him of the advantages he had given their adversaries (the convent of Nālanda followed the doctrine of the Great Vehicle) by bestowing such a benefit upon them. In order to further their cause, they presented him with a book in which their principles, they said, were explained, and they defied the partisans of the Great Vehicle to refute a single word.

'I have heard,' replied the king, who belonged to the latter school, 'that a fox, finding himself one day in the midst of a troop of rats and mice, boasted that he was stronger than a lion. But no sooner did he see a lion than his heart failed him, and he disappeared in the twinkling of an eye. You have not yet, venerable masters, seen the eminent monks of the Great Vehicle; that is the reason why you so obstinately assert your foolish tenets. I greatly fear that when you perceive them you will resemble the fox I have just spoken of.'

'If you doubt our superiority,' they replied to the king, 'why not assemble the adherents of the two doctrines, and bring them face to face to decide on which side lies truth or error?'

The king gave his consent to this religious combat, and wrote at once to Sīlabhadra to send to the kingdom of Orissa four of the most eloquent of his monks, in order that they might solemnly confute the heretics. Sīlabhadra, who knew Hiouen-Thsang's abilities, and did not share the jealousy he had excited around him, appointed him as the fourth champion.

The four vindicators of the Great Vehicle and of the honour of Nālanda were getting ready to start, and only awaiting a fresh order from the king, when an unexpected circumstance gave a still greater authority to Hiouen-Thsang, and dispelled all the doubts that certain persons had of his capabilities.

A heretic of the Lokāyata sect came to Nālanda to argue on the most difficult questions with which the professors were at that time occupied. He wrote a summary of his system in forty articles, and hung up this document on the convent gates.

'If any one,' he said, 'can refute a single article, he may cut off my head to proclaim his victory.'

This was, it appears, the ordinary and somewhat dangerous formula employed for this sort of challenge. Some days elapsed before any one answered this insolent provocation, and the Lokāyata had already flattered himself that he had at least won a tacit triumph, when the Master of the Law sent from the interior of the convent 'a man without sin,' a monk, with the order to take down this writing. Then Hiouen-Thsang tore it to pieces and trampled it under foot. When the Brahman heard whom he had to deal with, he declined to contend with the Master of the

Law; but Hiouen-Thsang compelled him to appear before Sīlabhadra and the chief monks, and in their presence he refuted the opinions of all the heretical schools—Bhūtas, Nirgranthas, Kāpālikas, Sankhyīkas, Vaiseshikas, &c.—with such force and irony that the Brahman remained speechless, without power to utter a word. At last he arose and said:

'I am conquered; you are free to avail yourself of my first condition.'

'We, the children of Ṣākya,' replied the Master of the Law, 'never injure men. To-day I will do nothing more than take you into my service as the obedient slave of my will.'

The Brahman, delighted at getting off so easily, respectfully followed him, and enthusiastically praised all he had just heard. Hiouen-Thsang kept him some time with him, and then set him free, without uttering a word which could wound the pride that had beem so painfully humiliated.

However, all was being prepared for the great contest at which Ṣīlāditya was to preside in person. Hiouen-Thsang had prepared himself for his part by contesting point by point in a work called '*A Treatise in Refutation of Erroneous Doctrines*,' the book which had been presented to the king by the adherents of the Little Vehicle.

The appointed place of meeting was Ṣīlāditya's capital, Kanyākubja, situated at the confluence of the Ganges and the Kalini. The Master of the Law accompanied thither the king, who overwhelmed him with attentions. It was the last month of the year. Shortly after, eighteen kings of central India (all tributaries of Ṣīlāditya) arrived, at the same time as three thousand monks, learned in both the Great and Little Vehicles, two thousand Brahmans and heretics, and about a thousand monks from the convent of Nālanda. Two enormous thatched buildings had been constructed at the place of convocation to receive the statue of the

Buddha and contain this multitude of people. On the appointed day the sacred ceremonies began at dawn. First was carried round with great pomp a golden statue of the Buddha, which had been expressly cast for the occasion; it was carried under a splendid canopy placed on a great elephant. Ṣīlāditya, holding a white fly-fan and dressed as Indra, walked on the right; on the left walked a tributary king, Kumāra, another of Hiouen-Thsang's admirers, dressed to represent Brahma. Two elephants, loaded with choice flowers that were scattered at each step, followed the Buddha. The Master of the Law and officers of the palace, riding large elephants, had been invited to take their places behind the king; and lastly the tributary kings, the ministers, and most celebrated monks advanced on both sides of the road, singing praises—they were borne on three hundred elephants. The procession had about two miles to go after leaving the king's travelling tent. At the door of the enclosure every one alighted, and the statue was placed on a costly throne in the palace designed for it. Ṣīlāditya, together with Hiouen-Thsang, first did homage, and then the assembly was brought in. It must have been composed, besides the eighteen kings, of a thousand of the most illustrious and learned monks, of five hundred Brahmans and heretics, and finally of two hundred of the ministers and chief officers of state. The remainder of the crowd, who could not enter, were obliged to place themselves silently outside the enclosure. After a magnificent repast, served indiscriminately to everybody, and after rich presents had been distributed to Hiouen-Thsang and the monks, the king requested the Master of the Law to preside at the conference, to make a eulogy of the Great Vehicle, and to state the subject of the discussion.

Hiouen-Thsang first ordered a monk of the convent of Nālanda to make known his prolegomena to the multitude, and he had a copy written out that was hung at the door of the enclosure, in order that they might be examined by all the spectators. He added at the end, as the Brahman he vanquished had done:

'If any one finds a single erroneous word in this, and is capable of refuting it, I will let him cut off my head to show him my gratitude.'

Although this solemn challenge excited them, not one of the adversaries dared to address the meeting to contest the arguments of the Master of the Law. The next and following days the pomps and ceremonies of the previous day were repeated. Hiouen-Thsang vindicated and developed the theses he had laid down, which were again received in silence by the heretics. The fifth day, seeing that he had confuted the principles of the Little Vehicle, they conceived a deadly hatred for him, and, unable to attack him by fair means, they made a plot to assassinate him. Ṣīlāditya, discovering this, undertook his defence, and threatened the malcontents with severe punishment. Thenceforth the partisans of error slunk away and disappeared, and the contest announced with so much pomp did not take place. Eighteen days were spent in waiting, but no one dared to utter a word of discussion. The evening of the day the Assembly was to disperse, the Master of the Law once more recommended the doctrine of the Great Vehicle, and extolled the virtues of the Buddha with so much enthusiasm, that a multitude renounced the narrow views of the Little Vehicle and embraced the sublime principles of the Great Vehicle.

Hiouen-Thsang had gained the victory; Ṣīlāditya and the other kings wished to reward him by enormous gifts of gold and silver. He refused to receive them, and, modest as he was disinterested, he only accepted the triumph awarded to the victor in conformance with ancient custom.

Mounted on an elephant richly caparisoned, and escorted by the highest dignitaries, he rode through the multitude, while the king himself, holding up his vestment, proclaimed with a loud voice:

'The Chinese Master of the Law has brilliantly established the doctrine of the Great Vehicle, and has reduced to nought all the errors of the sectaries. In eighteen days no one has been found who dare discuss with him. This great triumph shall be known to all men.'

The people in their joy bestowed on him the title of God of the Great Vehicle (*Mahāyāna-Deva*), and the partisans of the Little Vehicle, humiliated by his greatness, gave him out of respect the name of the God of Deliverance (*Moksha-Deva*). In memory of this victory Ṣīlāditya had the golden statue of the Buddha placed in the convent of Nālanda, with a great quantity of vestments and precious coins, which he confided to the care of the monks. At the zenith of favour, glory, and learning, Hiouen-Thsang had now nothing further to do than to leave India and return to China, with all the sacred spoils he had collected in his long researches. He therefore took leave of the monks of Nālanda, and taking with him the books and statues he had gathered together, he closed the series of his lectures. Before his departure he was obliged, at the urgent request of Ṣīlāditya, to accompany him to the kingdom of Prayāga (*Po-lo-ye-Kia*), to be present at the great distribution of alms which the king made every five years, in the vast plains situated at the confluence of the Ganges and the Jumna. Here, as the biographers of Hiouen-Thsang tell us, were gathered together no less than five hundred thousand persons, who received the royal alms. We shall give later a description of this solemn festivity.

At last Ṣīlāditya allowed Hiouen-Thsang to set out on his return journey to China. One of the kings of Northern

India undertook to have his books and statues conveyed as far as the Indus. After having revisited Takshasila, the pilgrim crossed the river, where, by a vexatious accident, he lost about fifty manuscripts and a quantity of curious seeds he was taking back to plant in China. He was able, however, to have the works he had lost recopied in the kingdom of Udyāna; and the collection of sacred writings, which was the real object of his travels, was neither diminished nor injured. Hiouen-Thsang did not return through Kashmir; he went by the kingdom of Kapisa, and crossed for the second time the snow-clad mountains (Hindu Kush), braving the same dangers he had so happily escaped from fifteen years before. This time he again extricated himself from all perils, but his caravan had gradually diminished, and was now reduced to seven monks, twenty servants, one elephant, ten asses, and four horses. At the foot of the mountains he reached the kingdoms of Antarava (Anderab) and Kustana, which in former days had formed part of the kingdom of Tukhara. Thence he continued his march to the north-west, crossed the Oxus, and then, directing his steps to the east, he advanced in a straight line to the Chinese frontier, passing through the kingdoms of Munkan, Sighnak, the valley of the Pamirs (*Po-mi-lo*) across the Tsong-hing mountains, the kingdom of Khasgar and that of Tchakuka. In Kustana (actually Khotan) he found a population whose honest and gentle behaviour strongly contrasted with that of the neighbouring tribes. They were full of respect for the Law of the Buddha, which, it was said, had been brought there at an early date from Kashmir by the arhān Vairochana. The inhabitants of Kustana held learning in high esteem, and delighted in music; the characters they used in writing were very similar to those of India, although the language was a different one; they were also most industrious, and the stuffs they made were exported far and wide. Hiouen-Thsang remained several months in this country, awaiting an answer to a letter he had written to the king of *Kao-Tch'ang*, who at the outset of his travels had tried to detain him against his will, and who had only given way on extracting from him the promise of a visit on his return journey.

After having passed through the former kingdom of Tukhara (*Tou-ho-lo*) and made several circuits, he at last reached the Chinese frontier, and saw once more his native land.

No sooner had he arrived at Cha-Tcheou than he hastened to forward a letter to the emperor, who resided at Lo-Yang, fearing he might have excited his anger by proceeding on his journey without his permission. But the emperor, who had kept himself informed of Hiouen-Thsang's success, displayed great friendliness, and sent an order to Si-'an-fo, chief of the kingdom of Liang and governor of the western capital, to receive him with the honours due to his piety and merit.

The pilgrim's journey was ended, but the missionary's work still remained. He still had to bring to the knowledge of his countrymen the sacred books he had brought back from India, and this task, to all appearance much easier, was nevertheless extremely laborious. Hiouen-Thsang, in a journey that he himself estimated at fifteen thousand miles, and which had lasted seventeen years, had collected the most abundant and valuable materials. He had now to work them up, and he devoted the remainder of his strength and life to this labour.

When the commander of Liang heard that Hiouen-Thsang was approaching Tchang-'an, he despatched the general commanding the cavalry and the chief official of the district to greet him. The two functionaries were ordered to go forward to meet and conduct him from the great canal to the capital, and to install him in the mansion assigned to ambassadors. At the same time the city magistrates invited the monks of all the convents to prepare hangings, sedan-chairs, flowers, banners, &c., for the procession of the morrow, when the sacred books and the statues were to be officially placed in the Convent of the Great Happiness (*Hong-fo-sse*). The next day they all assembled in groups, marshalled in due order, and the convent treasury received all that the Master of the Law had brought back from the western countries.

The following is its curious enumeration:

First, one hundred and fifty particles of *che-li* (*sarīras*) or relics proceeding from *Jou-laï's* (the Tathāgata) body.

Secondly, a golden statue of the Buddha, whose shadow had remained in the Dragon's Grotto, on the Prāgbuddha-giri mountain, in the kingdom of Magadha, with a pedestal of a transparent substance three feet three inches high, similar to the statue of the Buddha that is seen in the kingdom of Varānaṣi (Benāres), which represents him turning for the first time the Wheel of the Law in the Deer Park (Mrigadāwa).

Thirdly, a sandal-wood statue of the Buddha three feet five inches high, exactly like the one the king of Kosāmbi, Udāyana, had caused to be modelled from life.

Fourthly, a sandal-wood statue two feet nine inches high, similar to the one in the kingdom of Kapitha, representing the Tathāgata at the moment when he descends from the palace of the Devas.

Fifthly, a silver statue four feet high, similar to the one representing the Buddha explaining *The Lotus of the Good Law*, and other sacred books, on the Vulture's Peak.

Sixthly, a golden statue of the Buddha three feet five inches in height, similar to his shadow that he left in the kingdom of Nagarahāra, and which represents him overcoming a venomous dragon.

Seventhly, a carved statue in sandal-wood one foot three inches high, similar to the one in the kingdom of Vaiṣāli, which represents the Buddha going round the city to convert mankind.

After the statues came the books, deemed even more precious. They were divided into ten classes, of which the first included the sacred books (Sūtras) of the Great Vehicle, and numbered 124; and the other classes, the sacred books and special treatises of several schools, both of the Little and Great Vehicle, of the Sarvāstivādas, the Sammitiyas, the Mahīsāsakas, the Kasyapiyas, the Dharmaguptas, &c. This collection, which consisted of no less than 657 works divided into 525 parts, was carried by twenty-two horses.

Having fulfilled this first duty, Hiouen-Thsang went in all haste to rejoin the emperor in the palace of the Phœnix at Lo-Yang. The sovereign received him with much consideration and kindness; he questioned him at length about the climate, produce, and customs of the different countries in India, and the sacred monuments he had worshipped there. He urged him to write the history of his travels; and, delighted at all the virtues he discovered in him, he offered him an important office under government. But Hiouen-Thsang was wise enough to refuse this brilliant offer. He only knew the Law of the Buddha, and understood nothing about the doctrine of Confucius, 'which is the soul of the administration.' The emperor wanted to take him with his retinue on a military expedition to punish some rebels in the east. But the monk again refused, urging that his principles, founded on the love of mankind, did not permit of his being present at battles and scenes of bloodshed, and the sole favour he craved was to be assisted in translating into the *Fan* language the six hundred books which he had brought back from the western countries, and of which not one word was yet known in the Chinese language. The emperor indicated the Convent of the Great Happiness at Tchang-'an, and Hiouen-Thsang hastened thither to complete his pious mission.

Twelve monks were allotted to him, well versed in the explanations of the holy books and the treatises of the Great and Little Vehicle, to revise the translations, correct the style, and write out fair copies under his dictation; these monks had been carefully chosen from amongst the most talented in the principal convents of the neighbourhood. Nine others of high merit were especially employed to revise and polish the translated texts, and among them was Hoeï-li, the author of the first drawing up of Hiouen-Thsang's biography. Then two Samaneans, men learned in the study of the characters and revision of Indian texts, were added to this learned society, not to mention a number of subordinate copyists.

With this assistance Hiouen-Thsang was able in less than three months to offer the emperor, with the abridged narrative of his travels which he had been asked for, the translation of five books. In presenting these works, Hiouen-Thsang begged the emperor 'to deign to take up his august brush and write, in praise of the Buddha, a preface, in which his sublime thoughts would shine like the sun and moon, and the writing, precious as silver and jade, would last as long as heaven and earth, and become for future generations an object of inexhaustible admiration.' The emperor, after making some objections, consented to write this preface, which contained seven hundred and eighty-one characters. The biographers carefully reproduce the whole of it, as well as the correspondence that took place on the subject between the sovereign and Hiouen-Thsang. Soon after the prince royal followed his father's example, and wrote, like him, an introduction to the newly-translated sacred texts. At the request of the superior of the Convent of the Great Happiness, the emperor allowed the two prefaces to be engraved on metal and stone slabs, which were desposited in the convent.

The favour Hiouen-Thsang enjoyed soon brought forth most important results. Following his advice, the emperor decreed that in every convent of the different districts five monks should be ordained, and fifty in the Convent of the Great Happiness. As at that time there were three thousand seven hundred and sixteen convents scattered all over the empire, over eighteen thousand and six hundred monks or nuns were ordained. It seems that before this epoch, and under the last years of the Souï dynasty (581–618), most of the convents and temples had been plundered, and almost all the monks exterminated. This immense increase to their numbers re-established them in a flourishing condition. Thus Hiouen-Thsang might flatter himself that he had not only revived Buddhist faith by his travels, but that he had restored it to its ancient splendour. Moreover, the reigning sovereign, Thien-wou-ching-hoang-ti, was himself a very fervent adept; he frequently argued on the sacred texts with the Master of the Law, whom he admitted into his intimacy, and whom he more than once disturbed in his pious labours in order to have him near him. This emperor died in 650; but his son who succeeded him was equally the friend of the Master of the Law.

Moreover, Hiouen-Thsang gained this extraordinary favour by shunning it as much as lay in his power. Living secluded in the Convent of the Great Benevolence that the prince royal had built, near the palace at Lo-Yang, to honour the memory of his mother, 'his sole occupation was translating the sacred books without wasting a moment.' Every morning he set himself a fresh task, and if any business had prevented his finishing this task in the daytime, he never failed to continue his work during the night. If he met with any difficulty, he would lay down his brush and book; then, after having worshipped the Buddha and continued his religious exercises till the third watch, he would snatch a little rest, and at the fifth watch he would rise, read out loud the Indian text, and note down in red ink the passages he had to translate at daybreak. Every day for four hours he explained a fresh Sūtra or Ṣāstra to the monks of his convent, or to those of the different provinces who thronged to him in order to consult him as to the meaning of some doubtful or difficult passage. The disciples who came to take his instructions about the interior management of the convent, with which he was entrusted, filled the galleries and halls adjoining his cell. To all he replied clearly, omitting nothing. He expounded aloud and spoke with animation, without appearing to feel fatigue, such was the strength of his body and the vigour of his mind. 'Often did princes and ministers come to pay him their respects. When they had heard his counsels, all opened their hearts to the faith; and, abjuring their natural pride, they never left him without giving him sincere proofs of admiration and respect.'

The Master of the Law was still to spend fourteen years at this laborious work. In 659 he obtained the emperor Kao-Tsong's permission to withdraw with his assistant translators and disciples to the palace of Yu-hoa-Kong, where he hoped to lead a more secluded life. There he undertook the difficult and lengthy translation of the *Pradjnā-Pāramitā*, the Indian manuscript of which contained no less than two hundred thousand ṣlokas[1]. The book of the *Pradjnā-Pāramitā*, or Perfection of Wisdom, which the Chinese called *Pan-jo*, was the Sūtra at that time held in

[1] We do not possess this long transcription, but only three others: of 100,000, 25,000, and 8,000 ṣlokas, the shorter ones being abridgements of the longer. See Burnouf, *Introduction à l'histoire du Bouddhisme Indien*, p. 662, &c., and the *Journal des Savants*, January, 1855, p. 44.

greatest repute. It had in former centuries been translated, but it was far from complete, and from all sides the Master of the Law was strongly urged to undertake a new translation. The Sūtra of the *Pradjnā-Pāramitā*, it was said, had been expounded four times by the Buddha himself in sixteen solemn conferences—on the Vulture's Peak, in Anātha Piṇḍika's garden, in the palace of the king of the Devas, and in the Convent of the Bamboos at Rājagriha. As the text was very lengthy, all Hiouen-Thsang's disciples begged him to abridge it, and, following the example of preceding translators, he might have curtailed the tedious passages and suppressed repetitions. But he had a terrible dream that deterred him from this sacrilegious project, and he resolved to translate the whole work conformably with the Indian text, as it was taken down from the very lips of the Tathāgata. He had obtained three copies in India, but when he began his translation he found many passages of doubtful authenticity. By dint of care and zeal he was able to re-establish the text in all its genuineness. 'When he had fathomed a deep thought, thrown light on an obscure point, or re-established a vitiated passage, it was as if a god had brought him the solution he sought for. Then his spirit was gladdened like that of a man plunged in darkness, who sees the sun break through the clouds and shine forth in all its splendour. But ever mistrustful of his own wisdom, he attributed the merits to the mysterious inspiration of the Buddhas and the Bodhisatwas.

Nevertheless these varied and lengthy labours had exhausted Hiouen-Thsang's strength, and he hurried on as much as possible the translation of the *Pradjnā-Pāramitā*, lest death should overtake him. When he had finished it he said to his disciples:

'I came, you know, to the palace of Yu-hoa-Kong by reason of the book of the *Pradjnā-Pāramitā*; now that this work is finished, I feel that my life is coming to an end. When, after my death, you carry me to my last abode, let it be done in a simple and humble manner. You will wrap my body in a mat, and lay it down in the midst of a valley, in a peaceful and lonely spot. Avoid the vicinity of a palace or convent, for a body as impure as mine must be placed far from such buildings.'

His disciples tearfully promised to obey him, and tried to encourage him by the hope that his death was not so near at hand. But the Master of the Law was not mistaken in his presentiments. After the *Pradjnā* he tried to translate another compilation almost as voluminous, the *Ratanakūta Sūtra*, which the monks of his convent were most desirous of knowing. He made a great effort to comply with their wishes; but he had scarcely translated a few lines when he was obliged to close the Indian book, his strength proving unequal to his courage. He went out, therefore, with his disciples to offer up his last homage to the statues of the Buddhas, in the *Lou-tchi* valley, in the vicinity of the convent. From that day he ceased translating and gave himself up to religious exercises.

A short time after this, as he was crossing the bridge of a canal situated at the back of his house, he fell and grazed his leg. In consequence of this accident he was unable to rise from his bed. Feeling his forces failing and the supreme moment drawing near, he commanded one of his monks to write down the titles of the sacred books and treatises he had translated, numbering all together seven hundred and forty works and thirteen hundred and thirty-five volumes. He noted down also the ten millions (a koti) of paintings of the Buddha and the thousand images of Maitreya Bodhisatwa that he had caused to be made. Besides, he had had an immense number of untinted statuettes cast, and a thousand copies written of various sacred books. He had provided food and shown compassion to over twenty thousand believers and heretics. He had lighted a hundred thousand lamps and ransomed several tens of thousands of beings. When the monk had finished writing down the list of his good works, Hiouen-Thsang ordered him to read it aloud; then he said to those present, who overwhelmed him with praises:

'The moment of my death is approaching; I feel already as though my mind were giving way and leaving me. You must immediately distribute my garments and riches to the poor, have statues made, and desire the monks to recite prayers.'

In order to comply with his wishes, a feast was spread for the poor and alms were distributed. The same day the Master of the Law directed that a moulder should cast a statue of Wisdom (Bodhi) for the palace of *Kia-cheou-tien*, and after that he invited the whole of the convent, his fellow-workers, and disciples, 'to come and joyfully bid farewell to the impure body of Hiouen-Thsang, who, having accomplished his work, deserved to live no longer. I wish,' he added, 'that any merit I have acquired by my good works may revert to other men, that I may be born with them in the heaven of the Tushitas, be admitted into the *Mi-le's* (Maitreya) family, and serve that Buddha full of tenderness and love. When I shall return on earth to pass through other existences, I desire, with each new birth, to fulfil with boundless zeal my duties towards the Buddha, and at last attain *superlative and perfectly enlightened Wisdom* (*Anuttara samyak sambodhi*).' Then he repeated, with his dying breath, two Gāthās in honour of Maitreya, which he made the persons around him repeat after him. He then raised his right hand to his chin, and placed the left on his breast, stretched out his legs, crossed them, and turned on his right side. He remained motionless in this position till the fifth day of the second moon. In the middle of the night, his disciples inquired of him:

'Master, have you at last obtained leave to be born in the midst of Maitreya's Assembly?'

'Yes,' he replied in a failing voice, and a few moments later his soul had passed away. This took place on the fifth day of the second moon in the year 664.

The Emperor, distressed at such a loss, commanded a general mourning, and resolved to give the Master of the Law a magnificent funeral. But his disciples, faithful to his last wishes, had brought back his body on coarse mats into the capital, and had deposited it to await its burial, in the Convent of the Great Benevolence, in the centre of the hall appropriated to the translation of the books. It was in these coarse wrappings that the body of Hiouen-Thsang was brought to the funereal ceremony, which was celebrated with the greatest pomp. The Master of the Law's grave was chosen, according to his wishes, in a plain north of the *Fan-tchouen* valley, where a tower was built in his honour.

It would be unjust to Hiouen-Thsang's memory if, before taking leave of him, we did not record all the feelings of reverence and esteem which his memory ought to inspire. However, much as we may differ from this poor pilgrim, he is not less worthy of our consideration and remembrance.

What first strikes us in Hiouen-Thsang's character, and wins all our sympathy, is the ardour and sincerity of his faith. It might doubtless have been more enlightened and more rational, but it could never have been more living, more thoughtful, and more persevering. Superstition obscures the mind, but it does not corrupt the heart, and it may be allied to the most sterling virtues. According to the sphere in which a man is born, the education he receives, the habits and customs he conforms to, he may have the most ignorant, indeed absurd, beliefs, without his soul being any the less pure. He may worship the most insensate idols, and accept the most extravagant traditions, without losing any of his moral worth. A hero may be as credulous as the lowest of men; in truth it is impossible to be more credulous than the good Chinese pilgrim, but this can be overlooked; and in the seventh century of our era, we need not look far to find in Christian customs, still imbued with the habits of barbarians, equally foolish beliefs and traditions. We must not be too severe on others, when our own history contains such recollections and dark memories.

But with this single exception, we can find nothing but what is admirable in the life of Hiouen-Thsang, from which ever side it is viewed.

The singleness of purpose that directs it is never departed from, and during fifty consecutive years one invincible idea inspires and guides it. At the age of thirteen, perhaps even earlier, his vocation revealed itself, and up to the moment of his death, that is to say, till he was sixty-eight years old, his whole exertions were devoted to following, strengthening, enlarging, and fulfilling it. His only desire, from childhood, had been to propagate afar the glorious Law bequeathed by the Buddha; and during more than half a century his life was spent in serving this Law, without permitting any obstacle to dismay or discourage him. First, and as an introduction to this rough career, he went through the arduous studies that disciplined his youth, and led him, in spite of civil wars, into the various provinces of the Empire; then, when his harvest of knowledge was gathered, and when at the age of thirty he felt capable of putting into execution the resolve he had patiently trained himself for, he undertook this formidable journey, which kept him sixteen years far from his own country, and exposed him to endless perils of all kinds, unknown barbarous countries, deserts where his only guides were the bones of the travellers who had vainly striven to cross them before him, inaccessible mountains where for whole weeks he had to march through perpetual snow, over precipices, across impetuous rivers; then, besides the dangers of nature, dangers still more certain created by men, attacks of covetous and pitiless robbers, a thousand pitfalls laid for a stranger, amid races of whose language he was yet ignorant; and, above all, the allurements of riches and power, so often exercised on the pilgrim, and always victoriously repelled. Nothing could make him lose sight, even for a day, of the object of his pursuit; and at the beginning and end of his journey we see him resisting the offers of the kings of Kao-Tch'ang and of Kanyākubja, as he had resisted the pirates of the Ganges, the hospitable monks of Nālanda, and later still the yet more seductive proposals of the Chinese Emperor. He gathered information, travelled, and translated in order to propagate the Law of the Buddha; this was his whole life, simple and grand, humble and painstaking, disinterested as well as energetic.

In no other civilization, at no other period, even among the nations enlightened by the purer light of Christianity, can a more thorough example of zeal, courage, and self-abnegation be met with. It would be easy to find greater intellect, but difficult indeed to find a more magnanimous spirit.

One trait is particularly striking in the inner life of this soul, such as his disciples and biographers describe it, and this is the total absence of that veiled egotism, of which the Buddhist faith may with good reason be accused. Hiouen-Thsang is not occupied with the thought of his own personal salvation; and he only dimly intimates once or twice, that he counts on the eternal reward of his labours. He never thinks of self; he thinks of the Buddha, whom he worships with all the strength of his mind and heart; above all he thinks of other men, whom he strives to enlighten and save; his life is a perpetual though apparently unconscious sacrifice; and in this absolute self-renunciation he does not seem aware that his actions are as sublime as they are ingenuous.

He never reflects on his own conduct. To disdain riches, honours, power, and all the enjoyments of life, is already a very rare merit; but not to think even about the eternal salvation which he firmly believed in, while doing all that was needful to be worthy of it, is a merit still more rare and refined; and there are very few, even amongst the most pious, who have carried self-denial to this extreme limit, where nothing remains but the unalloyed idea of right. Hiouen-Thsang was one of these choice beings, and it is only right and just to recognize it. The singular ideal he made for himself may provoke a smile, but the irreproachable conduct this ideal inspired ought to be reverenced. It is not only in his external actions that he ought to be admired, but also in the motives that dictated those actions, and impart to them their true value.

Studied from this point of view, Hiouen-Thsang's character is one of the most curious of problems. We are too ready to believe that the virtues we possess under our temperate climates, and which, thanks to our civilization, are the growth of three thousand years, are an exclusive right that belongs only to us; we too easily believe that other times, other races, and especially other religions have no share in them. We shall not be suspected of any partiality for Buddhism, for we have severely criticized the vices and errors that disgrace it. But it must be admitted that in the presence of such examples, we feel more indulgent towards it, and while detesting its dogmas, we cannot deny that its influence has sometimes been excellent, if not on races, at least on individuals. In the seventh century of our era, about twelve hundred years after the Buddha, amid a people for whom we have little esteem, we find one of these noble personages, one of these beautiful lives that may be held up as an example to humanity. Without holding anything in common with the strange belief that inspires it, we might earnestly desire that the majority of men who live under a better faith, should have this purity of heart, straightforwardness of intentions, gentleness, charity, unalterable faith, boundless generosity, and elevation of sentiments which never relax under the most perilous trials.

We have hitherto only studied the personality of Hiouen-Thsang and the principal incidents of his life. We have now to see all he can tell us about the countries he travelled through, the history of those remote times, and the condition of Buddhism in India in the seventh century of the Christian era. Of course, his testimony, sincere as it is, must be received with the greatest caution; the good pilgrim was exceedingly credulous, and it is extremely probable that he more than once played the part of a dupe. However, we may be certain of one thing, he never seeks to deceive, and when he speaks of what he has himself seen, he must be attentively listened to, only we must, if reason demands it, somewhat modify the narrative. In general, however, we may trust and be grateful to him for the valuable information he hands down to us. At the moment he visited India, before the Mussulman conquest, it was still exclusively Brahmanist and Buddhist. It is a very obscure period of its history, and Hiouen-Thsang is almost the only eye-witness who has given us any information about it.

We will now see what he has to say on that subject.

CHAPTER II.

Memoirs of Hiouen-Thsang. Sources from which the Si-yu-ki is derived. History in India and China. Descriptive method of Hiouen-Thsang. His general views on India; his itinerary in Magadha; a page from his Memoirs on the Convent of Nālanda. Testimony of Hiouen-Thsang as to the Buddha, the Nirvāna, the Councils, and the kings of his day. Hiouen-Thsang at the Court of Ṣīlāditya, king of Kanyākubja and part of Central India. The great Council of the Deliverance in the Field of Happiness. Distribution of royal alms. Surprising tolerance of the Hindus.

It is not for the purpose of verifying the exact geographical position of the places Hiouen-Thsang describes, that we purpose to follow him in his long and perilous pilgrimages. This would be too special and lengthy a task for us to undertake, and we must leave it to those better fitted and more familiar with such studies [1].

We shall now limit ourselves to the composition of the *Si-yu-ki*.

In the large catalogue in the library belonging to the Emperor Kien-Long, the authentic and complete title of Hiouen-Thsang's work reads as follows: 'Memoirs on the Western Countries (*Si-yu-ki*) published under the great Thangs, translated from the Sanskrit, by Imperial decree, by Hiouen-Thsang, Master of the Law of the Three Commentaries, and edited by Pien-ki, a monk of the convent of Ta-tsong-tchi.' We are to understand by translated from the Sanskrit, not a translation in the ordinary acceptation of the

[1] See the excellent *Mémoire* of Vivien de Saint-Martin, following Hiouen-Thsang's *Memoirs*, vol. ii. p. 254, &c., and *Nouvelles Annales des Voyages*, 5e Séries, 1853.

word, but a co-ordination of the Sanskrit works which Hiouen-Thsang made use of to compose his own book.

The most important point would be to know the real nature of the Sanskrit works that Hiouen-Thsang consulted, and of which he has transmitted the substance. But it is rather difficult to form any exact idea of these works, and it is worth much even to know of their existence. The Sanskrit literature, as far as it is known to us, shows us nothing like them, and judging from the frequent quotations that Hiouen-Thsang makes from the Sanskrit *Memoirs* he made use of and had under his eyes—for he often translates them word for word—it seems certain that these *Memoirs* bore little resemblance to the *Mahāvansa* written in Pāli, which Turnour has given us, nor to the *Rājatarangini*, which we owe to Troyer. We must therefore conclude, that in the seventh century after Christ, at the time when the Chinese pilgrim travelled over India, there were to be found in Sanskrit literature works which described more or less faithfully the history, statistics, and geography of the country; none of which have come down to us. This is doubtless a very unexpected and curious discovery, but it is no less a fact. As Hiouen-Thsang found writings of this kind all over India, from the northern kingdom of Kutch down to Magadha, where he remained many years, in order thoroughly to study them, it is evident that these works were very numerous and well known. The names Hiouen-Thsang gives them are various; sometimes he calls them *Ancient Descriptions*, sometimes *Historical Memoirs*, sometimes *Collections of Annals* and *Royal Edicts*; at other times *Secular Histories*, or simply *Indian Books* on such or such a country, or *Memoirs of India*, &c. Hiouen-Thsang did not confine himself to these indications, already very exact; he does not even confine himself to the quotations he gives from the Sanskrit books; he also tells us the source of these valuable books and their official origin. In a general description of India, which fills the best part of the second book of the *Si-yu-ki*, and which may be considered an excellent introduction to all that follows, Hiouen-Thsang is careful to tell us, in a chapter devoted to literature, that 'special functionaries were generally appointed in India to take down in writing any remarkable speech; and that others had the mission of writing down an account of any events that took place.' Then he adds: 'The collection of annals and royal edicts is called *Nilapita*. Good and evil are both recorded, as well as calamities or happy omens.'

It is therefore certain that India possessed in the days of Hiouen-Thsang, and even long before his time, a large number of historical works, full of details, analogous in a certain measure to those which, since the famous days of Greece, have continued to be drawn up by all the nations of civilized Europe. It must be admitted, while recognizing the value of these annals, that judging even from Hiouen-Thsang's quotations, the natives of India had a peculiar method of understanding and writing history. India has never had a Herodotus, a Thucydides, a Polybius, a Titus-Livy, a Tacitus, or a Machiavelli. It had, however, its original historians, whoever they may have been; and this fact can no longer be denied. It would therefore seem that it is a hasty assertion to say that Indian genius had no knowledge of history; and that in its constant preoccupation about the absolute and infinite, it had never thought of noting the lapse of time, nor of recording in any lasting manner the events that were taking place. India felt this need like the rest of humanity, and tried to satisfy it in the best way it could; and Hiouen-Thsang's testimony, although it stands almost alone, is perfectly undeniable on this subject. His proofs are too constantly repeated, and he relies on too many different authorities, for his credibility to be doubted for an instant.

After trying to make allowance for the parts Hiouen-Thsang borrowed from Sanskrit historians, it is necessary to see, in order to know his personal historical value, what he added of himself. But first and foremost, great forbearance for his superstition must be exercised; for it is often carried to the verge of the ridiculous, although it is allied, in his person, to the most noble qualities; and had he not possessed an enthusiasm that blinded him and made him accept the most foolish legends and believe the most absurd miracles, he would never have undertaken and accomplished his difficult and most useful journey.

The following opinion of the editor of the catalogue of the Emperor Kien-Long's library ought to be our guide: 'The *Si-yu-ki*,' he says, 'constantly quotes supernatural facts and miracles that do not deserve any serious attention; but all that relates to mountains, rivers, and distances to travel may be strictly relied on. For this reason,' adds the librarian very sensibly, 'we have placed the book in our catalogue, and we retain it there in the hope that it may be of use to complete the comparative studies of learned men [1].' We have no reason to be more severe than a Chinese writer of the eighteenth century, and as Hiouen-Thsang's countrymen find excuses for his credulity, we can also be lenient on the subject. The strange stories of the Buddhist pilgrim may be put aside, without affecting the very exact and varied information he gives when he speaks as an ordinary traveller [2].

[1] Stanislas Julien, *Mémoires sur les Contrées Occidentales*, by Hiouen-Thsang, preface, p. xxvii.

[2] It must be admitted that the singular assertions of Hiouen-Thsang are justified by the unquestionable evidence of travellers of our day. Thus in mentioning the Buddha's statnes, Hiouen-Thsang states them to be of such enormous dimensions, that they would indeed seem imaginary. In many cases he does not exaggerate, for in a recent account given by Mr. Robert Fortune, this traveller mentions statues of the Buddha that are 165 feet long. The statues Mr. Fortnne actually saw represented him lying down, like the one mentioned by the Buddhist pilgrim. However strange this kind of statue may be, Hiouen-

The following was Hiouen-Thsang's usual method, and the strict and dry manner in which he carries it out, shows that he followed, and to a certain degree copied, the works of his predecessors.

The narrative is carefully divided according to the different kingdoms; moreover it only concerns India and the north-western frontier countries.

Hiouen-Thsang begins by giving the length and breadth of each of the kingdoms he visited; and, whenever he is able, he makes special mention of the dimensions and circumference of the capitals.

The pilgrim seems to have obtained the information—which he carefully transmits—not so much from his own personal investigations, as from local traditions and Sanskrit works, to which he had access.

After giving the general dimensions of the kingdom and the capital, and mentioning the frontier countries, the author proceeds to describe the soil and its principal products, as well as the climate and its characteristic qualities. He neither forgets the fruits that are cultivated, nor the different kinds of minerals which the land contains. This more or less concise description of the country is followed by an account of the inhabitants; their habits are described, their garments are depicted, their customs are noted down, and he never omits mentioning the style of writing they made use of[1], or the money that was current in their com-

Thsang's veracity on this point cannot be called in question. See *Revue Britannique*, June, 1857, p. 328.

[1] Thus Hiouen-Thsang, in remarking that the inhabitants of the *Sou-li* country in the kingdom of Bālukā, in the north-west of India, have few *Historical Records*, adds that they read from top to bottom of the page, and that the alphabet of these people is composed of thirty-two letters (*Mémoires sur les Contrées Occidentales*, p. 13). Further on (ibid. p. 24), it is said that the inhabitants of the kingdom of Koṣanna have an alphabet of twenty-five letters, which are combined together to express everything—a system that was quite new to a Chinaman—and that their books, written across, are read from right to left, &c. &c. It is certain

mercial transactions. Then from the inhabitants, he passes on to the governments; and even pronounces an opinion on the merit of the kings they obey, who do not always possess the talents requisite for the high position they occupy. He carefully notes down the countries that possess and those that do not possess a code of laws; as well as those in which the law is all-powerful, and those where it is powerless.

After all these preliminary details, which are never omitted, he comes to the religious part of the narrative. First, the precise number of convents are mentioned, as well as the number of monks who frequent and live in them. The sect to which these monks belong is carefully recorded; for instance, if they belong to the school of the Great Vehicle or the Little Vehicle. Their customs and habits are even more minutely described than those of the inhabitants; and he also states the sources from which the monks have drawn the sacred instructions and the discipline which direct them. He mentions with admiration their austere charity and their meritorious exercises; if their conduct is disorderly, he does not hesitate to point out and blame their errors; and he even goes so far as to note the kind of food they live on, for this is an important point in Buddhist discipline, which only recognizes three kinds of food as pure, and strictly forbids all other.

After the convents and monks, he notices the works which have formed the different sects; he recalls the more or less famous titles of these works, and sometimes analyzes in a few words the doctrine they contain, approving or contesting it. With regard to these literary observations, Hiouen-Thsang's *Memoirs* are naturally less abundant than the biography edited by his two disciples; but the two works complete

that these two alphabets of twenty-five and thirty-two letters, and this writing which is read from top to bottom or from right to left, do not belong to India.

each other, and together contain plenty of information of this nature, no less instructive than the rest.

But the part of his narrative in which the traveller has given most details, is that concerning the Buddha, the recollections of his personal presence—more or less authentic—the monuments of all kinds raised in his honour or for his worship, the relics treasured up of his blessed body, the legends collected or invented about him by the more or less intelligent piety of his followers, the marvellous traditions about his principal disciples, about the most important events, the most illustrious princes, the most authorized learned men, &c., &c. This is the weak side of the excellent pilgrim's work. In order to have a thorough knowledge of Hiouen-Thsang's *Memoirs*, and a specimen of his style, we will deal more particularly with his general description of India.

Hiouen-Thsang, after having described thirty-four kingdoms in his first *Memoirs*, from the kingdom of Agni or Akni, to that of Kapisa, reaches at last the kingdom of Lampā, now Laghman. With the kingdom of Lampā—that is, beyond the Black Mountains or the Hindu Kush—India, properly speaking, begins. The pilgrim has now, after many accidents, entered the country he has come such a distance to visit: the land of the Holy Faith. It would seem as though the Master of the Law pauses before beginning the detailed narrative of his exploration, in order to take a general view of his subject, which he approaches with the greatest respect. Hence in the *Memoirs* his interesting notice on India, full of curious details which certainly make it the most valuable part of his work. It gives a very exact picture of India in the seventh century as it presented itself to the observation of pious travellers, and a very precise description of its general features.

Hiouen-Thsang first studies the name of the country, and discovers, after having discussed the various and confused forms given to its name, that the true one is that given by the natives themselves—*Intu* (Indu). Twelve hundred years before Hiouen-Thsang, the country was called by this name, and Herodotus, the first historian who mentions it, always refers to it under this denomination. As the word Indu in Sanskrit also signifies the *moon*, Hiouen-Thsang endeavours to find out by the local traditions what analogy could exist between India and the moon.

After an explanation, half philological and half historical, which we must take for what it is worth, Hiouen-Thsang next turns his attention to the approximative dimensions of India, or as he calls it the Five Indias. He makes out the whole circumference to be ninety thousand *li*. Now, as a *li* is about a quarter of a mile, by this account the total circumference would be about twenty-two thousand miles. This estimate deserves attention, coming from a man who for years had travelled over the greater part of India, and who on this point was in a position to obtain reliable information. However, from recent investigations, it is certain that Hiouen-Thsang's figures are exaggerated. But it would be important to know what he precisely meant by the Five Indias, and what countries he included in this vast circle. Even at the present day, the boundaries are somewhat uncertain, for India this side of the Ganges and India beyond the Ganges are terms still in use. Moreover Hiouen-Thsang is well acquainted with the geographical configuration of India. 'On three sides,' he says, 'India is bounded by a great sea; on the north it is protected by snowy mountains (Himalayas). It is broad at the north and narrow in the south; its shape is like that of a half-moon.' It would have been more correct had he said: 'the shape of a triangle.' All these indications, vague as they necessarily are, are nevertheless exact in the main, and the Chinese traveller speaks like a man who, having under his eyes a somewhat faithful geographical map, wishes to give a general idea of what it represents.

Hiouen-Thsang asserts positively that India was, in his day, divided into seventy kingdoms. It is difficult to know if this number is really exact, although the traveller visited and describes the greater part of the Indian kingdoms.

It seems, however, certain that in the seventh century of our era India must have been divided into a number of small dominions, more or less independent of one another. These territorial divisions necessarily varied a great deal according to the rapacity of the petty sovereigns. However, at the death of the conqueror, all the local sovereignties reappeared with the dissolution of the transient empire which had for a brief space absorbed them. The country then returned to a political partition, which would seem to have been as natural to it as it was to Greece.

At the present time, and notwithstanding the uniformity of a common submission to the English rule, the peninsula is hardly less divided. Races, languages, religions, sects, and customs are still very varied; small states remain still very numerous and very different one from another, even under the power they are all equally bound to obey. It would not be difficult to make out, in the vast possessions of the English Crown, and in the native states it has thought fit to preserve, the elements of the seventy states Hiouen-Thsang speaks of, which probably existed long before as well as long after his time.

In order to make what he has said of the size of India better understood, the author tries to give the names of the principal measures used in the country, and as a logical consequence he goes on to the divisions of time, the names of the seasons and months, which he carefully compares with the analogous divisions current in China.

After these general remarks, Hiouen-Thsang explains the constructions of the cities and villages, the public buildings, convents and private houses. Then he mentions the interior arrangements of the houses, the beds, seats, ornaments, &c. He attaches great importance to the clothing of the different classes in India; and after having mentioned in a cursory manner the garments worn by the heretics or Brahmans, he dwells with a certain complacency on all the details of those worn by the Sramanas, or Buddhists. He insists on the extreme cleanliness of the natives, and this trait of their national character which strikes him, is in reality so marked that no observer could fail to notice it. At the present time the Hindus are in this respect just as particular as Hiouen-Thsang and Alexander's companions found them; and in the last mutiny the motive or rather pretext of the mutineers was a personal defilement imposed on them, they said, by discipline, and which they refused to submit to.

These purely material details are followed by a description of the morals and literature of India; and the Chinese pilgrim, himself a learned man, gives to this part of his narrative all the importance it deserves. One remarkable fact is that, notwithstanding his Buddhistical fervour, he does thorough justice to the intelligence and labours of the Brahmans, and he begins by first mentioning them. He describes the admirable writing they make use of, taught them by the god *Fan* (Brahma) himself; the qualities of their harmonious language; the principal books they study, at the head of which he mentions the Vedas; the length of their studies, which they carry on till the age of thirty; the honours and fame which surround the learned and the sages, &c. If the Master of the Law mentions with such esteem the Brahmans, whom he considers as heretics, he is still less sparing in his eulogies of his brethren, the Buddhists. He recalls the eighteen sects which divide Buddhism and by their continual discussions keep up its vitality; the severe discipline the monks bind themselves down to; the sacred books of the Buddha, which are distributed in twelve different collections; the proportional honours bestowed on those whose knowledge of these books is more or less profound, and above all on those who eloquently defend the Law during the solemn discussions, as well as the shame attending the learned men who are vanquished in the controversy; and finally the excommunication that pitilessly falls on those whom neither remonstrance nor reproof have brought back to the right path.

Hiouen-Thsang devotes but a few lines to the difference of castes, and only describes the four principal ones, as it would take too long, he adds, to notice all the others. He briefly analyzes the marriage laws of the Indians, and particularly mentions the horror they have of a second marriage for women; their laws expressly forbidding a woman to have a second husband.

It is well known that this law, which is sanctioned by relentless custom, continues to the present day; and that recently an English newspaper in India gave as an unprecedented fact, and as a great victory of civilization over inveterate prejudice, the case of a young Hindu woman who had just married a second time. This immense progress was obtained by the English authorities after ceaseless efforts, and it may well be considered as great as the abolition of sutteeism.

Hiouen-Thsang then turns his attention to the royal families, which belong for the most part to the Kshatriya class; to the soldiers, who are divided into the four different forces of the army—infantry, cavalry, chariots, and elephants; to the generals commanding them; and the weapons which they have made use of from time immemorial, &c. After the war department, the author passes on to the administration of justice; he mentions the principal penalties, and describes with many details the judicial ordeals, which were practised in India long before they were renewed by our Middle Ages. The poor Buddhist pilgrim seems filled with admiration at this simple and infallible manner 'of closing the way to all crime.'

After some details on the nine ways of showing respect, from simple politeness of speech to the prostration of the whole body, Hiouen-Thsang treats of the funeral rites, and the different ways of paying respect to the dead. He does not forget the strange custom of suicide by immersion in the Ganges; and he considers that nine out of every ten old men end their days in this manner, by which superstition eternal life is said to be assured.

Finally, Hiouen-Thsang devotes the last three chapters of his book to some general but disconnected considerations on public administration, on agriculture, and on the precious metals of all kinds that India possesses in abundance. From the above analysis of his notice on India, the process of the Chinese author, and its merits, will be clearly seen. In reality, his way of understanding and presenting things is exactly the same as ours; and a traveller of the present day who would explore India in order to describe all its different aspects would not adopt a different line of conduct. Many doubtless might lack the clear and sure method of Hiouen-Thsang; and few would show so just and upright a spirit. It is true that the investigations of the Chinese pilgrim do not go very deep, but everything is noted, and all is classed in proper order. This in itself is a great deal, and although modern science may find much to criticize, the peculiar talent of exposition possessed by Chinese authors is a very curious phenomenon in the seventh century of our era. At this epoch no one in Europe would have been capable of writing such books, and it is well to call attention again to this singular quality of Chinese writers, which has hitherto generally been ignored.

Leaving aside Hiouen-Thsang's itinerary from his arrival in the north-west of India till his entry in Magadha, we will pause at this latter country, which may be called the Judea of Buddhism.

The devout pilgrim has thought it necessary to devote two whole books of the *Si-yu-ki*, that is, one-sixth of his work, to the description of this Holy Land. There is no need to complain of this, for the details he gives are so precise and comprehensive that they may prove extremely useful for any future exploration of the localities he has so well described. The following are the principal points of Hiouen-Thsang's itinerary in Magadha, and he can be followed step by step on a special map that has been drawn up by Mr. Vivien de Saint-Martin.

On leaving Nepaul and the kingdom of Vaiṣāli, Hiouen-Thsang crossed the Ganges at Pātaliputra[1], the Palibothra of the Greeks, actually Patna, and directed his steps to the south. He went across the Nairanjanā, and visited the ruins of the convents of Tilasākya, Gunamati and Sīlabhadra, &c. He then returned for the second time to the Nairanjanā, and crossing it in a south-westerly direction, reached the city of Gāyā, inhabited, at the moment of his visit, almost exclusively by Brahmans. It was in the neighbourhood of Gāyā and the mountains near it that two of the most venerated monuments of the Buddhist religion are to be found: the tree under which the young Siddhārtha attained, after six years of terrible austerities, the state of perfect Buddha (Bodhi-druma) and the Diamond Throne, the Platform of Wisdom (Vajrāsanam, Bodhimanda) so called, from the hillock on

[1] Hiouen-Thsang heard, and quotes at length, a popular legend which explains the origin of the name Pātaliputrapura. *Pātali* in Sanskriṭ is the name of a sweet-scented flowering tree (*Bignonia suaveolens*, Wilson's Dictionary). The legend relates that under a tree of this species, a young Brahman was married and lived for a long time. The tree was afterwards miraculously changed into a sumptuous building that the king inhabited with all his court. As the city had been built by the spirits in favour of the son born to the Brahman under this tree, the place was called 'The city of the son of the *Pātali*.' Pātaliputra acquired fresh importance when the great Aṣoka made it his capital instead of Rājagriha.

which the Tathāgata sat when he entered into the ecstasy called the Diamond Ecstasy (Vajrasamādhi). These places are so full of monuments that the pious traveller, after mentioning several of them, relinquishes the task in despair. Wherever the Buddha had passed, stūpas had been raised to perpetuate his great and precious memory.

From Gāyā he resumed his road towards the north-east, again crossing the Nairanjanā, and reaching the mountain called Kukkutapada, or Gurupada. He then went round to the eastern side of the high mountain, from which the Buddha gazed for the last time on Magadha, before going on to Kusi-nagara to die. He crossed another mountain called Buddhavana, and the great forest of Yashtivana, near which are two springs of mineral waters, and reached the city of Kusāgārapura, situated in the midst of high mountains in the very centre of Magadha. Continuing in a north-easterly direction he visited the city of Rājagriha, famous by the first Council held there under the great Kāṣyapa, after the death of the Buddha.

About ten miles further north he reached the celebrated convent of Nālanda, where he eventually sojourned for five years. Leaving Nālanda, the pilgrim continued to travel northwards in the direction of the Ganges, and quitting Magadha, he arrived at the kingdom of Hiranyaparvata.

Such is briefly Hiouen-Thsang's itinerary in Magadha, and it is certain that, aided by his *Biography* and *Memoirs*, any intelligent traveller, attracted to these places by a legitimate curiosity, would find all the landmarks noted by the Chinese pilgrim, and the ruins of most of the monuments he mentions as having seen himself[1].

[1] Most interesting explorations have already been made in Magadha by Sir Francis Buchanan (Hamilton) in 1810, at the expense of the East India Company, and by Major Kittoe in 1847; but, for several reasons, these expeditions failed to produce the desired results.

As might be expected, the *Memoirs* do not give the minute details contained in the *Biography* concerning the magnificent retreat of Nālanda, the most frequented Buddhist seminary of the peninsula; for the latter was edited by the talented and loving disciples of the Master of the Law. In mentioning Nālanda, the *Memoirs* retain their official laconism; however, the picture they give of this great school is striking, and the following passage may be deemed interesting. It is one of the most remarkable pages of the *Memoirs*, and confirms all the previous information.

'The monks, who were several thousands in number,' says Hiouen-Thsang, or the editor of the *Si-yu-ki*, whoever he may have been, 'were all men of distinguished talents and deep learning. Several hundreds of them were esteemed by their contemporaries for their virtue, and their fame had spread to other countries. Their conduct was pure, and they faithfully followed the precepts of their discipline. The rule of this convent was extremely severe; moreover the multitude of monks conducted themselves with irreproachable discretion. The kingdoms of the Five Indias admired them and took them as models. Those who followed their teaching and discussed profound questions with them thought the days too short. From morning to night they mutually admonished one another, old and young striving to improve one another. Those among them who were incapable of treating the abstract matters of the Three Commentaries were held of no account, and were covered with shame. For this reason, foreign students desirous of acquiring fame came to this convent to dispel their doubts, and soon obtained the fame they sought. Even those who in travelling usurped their name received high honours. If a man of another country wished to enter and take part in the conferences, the custodian would first put him some difficult questions. The majority were reduced to silence and went away; for it was necessary to have a thorough knowledge of ancient and modern writings in order to obtain admittance. Consequently students who travelled in search of information had to debate at length to show their capacity; and seven or eight in every ten of the candidates were generally eliminated. If the remaining two or three seemed to be well informed, they were interrogated in turn by the whole Order, and their learning was put to the severest test. Only those who possessed real talent and vast erudition, a powerful memory, great capacity, high virtue and superior intelligence, might associate their glory with that of their predecessors, and follow in their footsteps.'

Here the *Memoirs* mention the names of some of the most learned monks of Nālanda, and add:—

'These men of eminent merit were known to all; by their virtue they surpassed their predecessors, and their knowledge comprised all the rules of the ancients. Each one of them had written about ten treatises and commentaries which were universally made use of, and which in their day were held in the highest esteem. Around the convents, a hundred sacred edifices might be counted. To be brief, we will only mention two or three.'

We will not follow Hiouen-Thsang in this description, which he makes much more lengthy than he had intended: we will not even follow him during the remainder of his travels throughout the peninsula. In the last three books, from the Tenth to the Twelfth, the traveller continues his journey down the banks of the Ganges, till he reaches the mouth of the river; he follows, more or less, the coast-line till he arrives at Kānchīpura; he then crosses the peninsula from east to west, and goes up again north-west to the Indus, returning through Hindu Kush and the northern kingdoms to the Chinese frontiers, at the extremity of the kingdom of Kustana. This immense round from Magadha comprises no less than sixty kingdoms which are fully described in the *Memoirs*.

The following passage shows the simple and touching style in which, after furnishing so many curious details, these *Memoirs* are brought to a conclusion.

'We have made known,' they say, 'the mountains and rivers; described the lands, and portrayed the gentle or barbaric customs of the inhabitants, connecting them with the nature of the climate and soil. The behaviour of man is not everywhere uniform; his tastes and antipathies are not always the same. It has been a difficult matter to investigate thoroughly many of these facts, and it is impossible to write exactly about them from mere recollection. As the traveller went through the different countries he wrote down a summary; he collected evidence furnished by his ears and eyes; and he faithfully noted down the people who wished to come under the rule of the Emperor of China.

'In the countries that witnessed his noble conduct everyone admired his perfect virtue. Can he therefore be compared to those men who start on missions with a single chariot and who post over a distance of a thousand *li*?' Such is the ending of the *Si-yu-ki*, or *Memoirs on the Western Countries*.

It is evident, by this last passage, that Hiouen-Thsang cannot have written in this manner about himself. Such an eulogy of his own virtue does not come from his own pen, and his modesty, which is revealed in so many ways, would never have permitted his indulging in such an ingenuous panegyric.

It has been seen that the *Memoirs* are richer than the *Biography* with regard to statistics, to history and geography. But, what is still more astonishing, they are also much richer in all kinds of legends. It is indeed difficult to imagine such blind, or rather foolish, credulity, as that shown by the

Buddhists. As a general rule, in popular legends the extravagance of the matter is redeemed by a certain elegance of form and detail. Sometimes a delicate intention, vaguely hinted, atones for much that is trivial and foolish. But it is a peculiar and deplorable fact that in most of the Buddhist legends it seems impossible to discover any meaning; they appear to be mere aberrations of the mind, with nothing to compensate for their incomparable folly. It would be easy to quote a large number of these from Hiouen-Thsang's *Memoirs*; indeed they can be counted by hundreds.

The following specimens are taken at haphazard, or rather from among the first-mentioned at the beginning of his book. The grave historian had reached the kingdom of Kutch, not far from the mountains now called Musur-Dabaghan, and near the Lake Temurtu, or Issikul. He has given, with Chinese exactitude, the dimensions both of this kingdom and its capital. He has described the climate and the produce of the soil; fertile in fruit, wheat, and minerals of all kinds. He has depicted the customs of the inhabitants, who are neither lacking in gentleness nor virtue, and who have even a certain taste for the fine arts. He recalls a curious custom which exists to the present day among these people—that of flattening the heads of the new-born children by pressing them under a board. The historian even goes further, and severely criticizes the king of that country, who is deficient in prudence as well as capacity, and is ruled by powerful ministers. Finally, he praises the convents, which are about one hundred in number, and in which he finds the monks subjected to a most strict discipline, and absorbed in the exercise of meritorious works.

It would seem that a narrative written in such a serious manner, and treating of actual facts, would hardly lead to Buddhist reveries. Suddenly, however, history gives place to the following legend:—

'To the north of a town situated on the eastern frontiers of the kingdom, there was in former days a great lake of dragons (Nāgahrada) in front of a temple to the gods. The dragons metamorphosed themselves and united themselves with mares. These brought forth foals which partook of the nature of the dragon. They were vicious, violent, and difficult to tame; but the offspring of these foal-dragons became gentle and docile. This is the reason why this kingdom produces such a large number of excellent horses.'

It is easy to perceive, even in this absurd legend, a trace of some real fact; and it would seem probably that the Kutch country, famed for its breed of horses, had been at some recent period ravaged by a horde of Tartars. But what an absurd interpretation! Where is the charm of so foolish a story? What is its hidden meaning? What explanation does it give of a very simple and intelligible fact, which it pretends to supersede and embellish?

After this historical and national legend, we will quote a religious one.

Hiouen-Thsang finds a stūpa on the banks of a river. This stūpa had been built to commemorate a meritorious action of the Venerable of the Century. 'Formerly, in the days of the Buddha,' says Hiouen-Thsang, 'five hundred fishermen having formed an association, devoted themselves to netting the denizens of the river. One day, in the middle of the stream, they caught a large fish that had eighteen heads, each one of which had two eyes. As the fishermen were about to kill it, the Tathāgata, who was then in the kingdom of Vaiṣāli, with his divine sight perceived them. Filled with pity, he seized the opportunity to convert them, and open their hearts to the true belief. He therefore addressed the great multitude and said: 'In the kingdom of Vriji there is a large fish; I will lead it into the right path, in order to open the minds of the fishermen; you must learn all the circumstances.' Then the Tathāgata left the multitude at Vaiṣāli, raised himself into the air, and went to Vriji to the fishermen, whom he had seen from a distance of ninety miles. When he reached the banks of the river he urged the fishermen not to kill the fish, to whom he wished, he said, to open the path of happiness by revealing to it its former existence. The Buddha then interrogated the fish, giving it the power to reply in human speech, and inquired what crime it had committed in its former existence to have fallen so low and received such an ignoble body. The fish confessed his crimes with deep repentance. He had been a proud and insolent Brahman and had not respected the law of the Buddhas. But now he recognized his sin, and to reward him the Buddha caused him to be reborn in the palace of the gods. The fish, under this divine form, came to thank the Tathāgata, and, throwing himself at his feet, moved respectfully round him, offering him celestial flowers of a delicious perfume. 'The Venerable of the Century,' continues Hiouen-Thsang, the faithful echo of tradition, 'the Venerable of the Century, gave this example as a warning to the fishermen, and explained the Good Law to them. Then, their hearts being opened, they showed him sincere respect and deep repentance. They tore up their nets, burnt their boats, returned to truth, and received the faith. After having clothed themselves in coloured garments and heard the noble doctrine, they renounced the corruption of the world, and obtained all the fruits of sanctity.'

It would be easy to quote any number of similar stories, but we must add that many other legends of a very different character may be found in Hiouen-Thsang's *Memoirs*, some of which are not only more rational, but also convey an exact idea of the facts they perpetuate.

In quoting Hiouen-Thsang as an historian it will be necessary to make a distinction between the facts he himself observed, and those he derives from more or less authentic traditions.

Of all these, the most important relates to the date of the Buddha's death, or the Nirvāna. What date does the Chinese pilgrim give, whether derived from the populations amongst whom he dwelt, or from the monuments he visited, or from the teachers of the Law who instructed him, and whose lessons he followed for more than fifteen years? It is well known that almost all Indian philologists agree in placing the date of the Buddha's death at 543 years before the Christian era. Thus the Nirvāna took place about twelve hundred years before Hiouen-Thsang's time, as he travelled from the years 629 to 645 of our era. But what was Hiouen-Thsang's own opinion, or rather what traditions did he find still subsisting in the places where the Buddha had lived, and where he died?

Hiouen-Thsang touches on the subject of the Nirvāna on two occasions. The first time, he was in the kingdom of Kusi-nagara: he had crossed the Ajitavati river, at some distance from the capital, and on his way through a forest had come upon the four sāla trees of equal height, under which, it was said, the Tathāgata had drawn his last breath. In a neighbouring vihāra was a statue, representing *Jou-laï* at the moment he entered Nirvāna; he was represented lying down, with his head turned to the north. Near this rose a stūpa two hundred feet high, and a stone column attributed to King Aṣoka. But Hiouen-Thsang sought in vain for any record of the year or month in which this great event had taken place. The two monuments were silent on this point, and in his pious solicitude he strives to supplement their silence. After stating that the Buddha remained on earth till the age of eighty, and that he quitted it, according to some statements, on the fifteenth day of the second half of the month of Vaiṣakha (April–May), and, according to others, in the second half of the month of Kārtika (October–November), he adds:—

'From the Nirvāna to the present day some people reckon twelve hundred years; others fifteen hundred; while others again affirm that more than nine hundred years have elapsed, but that certainly one thousand years have not yet been accomplished.'

Hiouen-Thsang does not deem it his duty to decide between these different opinions; he merely quotes them, and it would seem that he took the average estimation. This at least is the one he appears to adopt on a less solemn occasion, when he mentions for the second time the date of the Nirvāna. He was then in one of the kingdoms of Southern India (*T'o-na-kie-tse-kia,* Dhanakacheka?), and on the western side of the capital he visited a convent built on a mountain, by one of the former kings of the country, in honour of the Buddha. This convent, although a magnificent edifice, was deserted, and had remained uninhabited for a very long time. 'For a thousand years after the Nirvāna it had received a numerous throng of monks and laymen, but for the last hundred years (if we are to believe popular report) the spirits of the mountains had changed in their sentiments, and displayed so much violence and anger, that travellers, justly alarmed, no longer ventured near the convent, and this is the reason it no longer possesses either monks or novices.' Thus at the time Hiouen-Thsang visited this country, it was commonly believed that the Nirvāna had taken place eleven or twelve hundred years before.

It may therefore be considered that Hiouen-Thsang ascribes the same date as we do to the Buddha's death. This is an important fact, and if we recall all the uncertainty that still remains on this capital question, the information collected by Hiouen-Thsang is all the more valuable, as it concords with our own version.

Other evidence, no less important, is also forthcoming. There is not a detail in the well-known life of the Buddha that Hiouen-Thsang does not mention. From the most famous incidents of his childhood and youth, to the most decisive actions of his life, and to his death, the pious missionary has omitted nothing; for he found everywhere traces of these recollections in the stūpas and vihāras, on the columns and in the ruins of the cities, on the stones, on the hill-tops, and the trees of the forest. The birth and education of the Buddha at Kapilavastu, his visions at Lumbini, his flight from the paternal palace, his intimacy with Bimbisāra, his austerities at Bodhimanda, his first sermon at Benāres, his long sojourns in Magadha, Rājagriha, on the Vulture's Peak, and in the fertile domain of Anātha Piṇḍika; the contests he sustained, the dangers he incurred, the conversions he made, the charity he exercised, the influence he wielded, his endless journeyings in neighbouring provinces, the circumstances of his death and funeral, the division of his relics among eight kings—all this striking and simple story is brought back again before the traveller by the monuments he visits to pay him his homage.

For the learned world, the primitive history of Buddhism did not require this confirmation, but it may be said even now, without taking into account the discoveries which the future probably reserves, that there does not exist in the world another religion of which the origin has been better attested by undeniable evidence.

After the life of the Buddha and the date of the Nirvāna, the most important fact in the history of Buddhism is the meeting of the three Councils, who successively settled the canonical writings, and determined the orthodoxy of the official contents of the Three Commentaries, the *Tripitaka* (Three Baskets), which comprised the Sūtras, or the Discourses; the *Vinaya*, or the Discipline; and the *Abhidharma*, or the

Metaphysics. These three Councils have been brought to our knowledge, first by the Sinhalese *Mahāvansa*, of which Turnour has given both the text and a translation, and then by the Tibetan *Dulva*, of which Csoma Körösi made a learned analysis. Nepalese tradition agrees with that of Ceylon (which is much more ancient) in placing the three Councils under the same princes. The only serious differences are about the reign of Aṣoka and the date of the third Council, which the Sinhalese place one hundred and fifty years earlier. This point has not been cleared up, and the history of the Assemblies of the Law and the Buddhist Councils has yet to be written. However that may be, the following information has been transmitted to us by Hiouen-Thsang.

He knew of three Councils—one that was held immediately after the death of Ṣākya-muni; a second one under Aṣoka; and a third under Kanishka, king of Kashmir. On the first one he dwells at great length. According to tradition, which he repeats, it was not far from Rājagriha, two miles from the bamboo grove at Kalānta, in a large house situated in the midst of another wood, that the Arahats of the first Council assembled. Kāṣyapa, who had chosen them—they numbered nine hundred and ninety-nine—directed all the labours from which sprung the *Tripitaka*, and he presided over the learned assembly. Hiouen-Thsang shows him as exercising a kind of supervision, admitting some, excluding others as unworthy, and only receiving Ānanda himself on the condition of his performing a long penance. They had been in retreat for fifteen days, when Kāṣyapa made Ānanda take the chair, inviting him to read the *Sūtra-Pitaka*, or Commentary on the Sūtras. The assembly, who respected the profound knowledge of Ānanda, which had been recognized by the Tathāgata himself, received the Sūtras from his lips, and wrote them down under his dictation. Then

Kāṣyapa ordered Upali to read the *Vinaya-Pitaka*, or Commentary on the Discipline; after which he himself read the *Abhidharma-Pitaka*, or Commentary on Metaphysics. At the end of three months the work of the Council was finished. The writings of the three Commentaries were collected; Kāṣyapa had them transcribed on palm-leaves, and sent them out all over India. As he had presided over the monks, his school was called the School of the President (*Sthavīra-Nikāya*).

Those, however, who had been excluded from the Council by Kāṣyapa's severity, assembled at a place near there. They numbered several thousands, laymen as well as monks, and, basing themselves on the principle of equality that had always been inculcated by the Tathāgata among his disciples, they deemed themselves in a fit state to make their own Collection of Sacred Writings. This they composed of Five Commentaries, first the three first, then a collection of miscellanies, and a collection of Magic Formulas. This second school was called the School of the Great Council (*Mahā-Samgha-Nikāya*), and its partisans became celebrated under the name of Mahāsamghikas.

Hiouen-Thsang is much briefer about the second Council, which he only mentions in a cursory manner. It would seem from the somewhat confused details given, that it was not at Pātaliputra precisely, as is generally believed, that it was held, but near that city, in the convent of the Cock (Kukkutārama). It is all the more regrettable that Hiouen-Thsang should not give more particulars about this assembly, that he seems to have taken from some *Historical Memoirs* on Aṣoka the facts he does mention. This king, who probably ruled over the whole peninsula, had divided the Jambudvīpa into three parts and had given them to the Buddha, to the Law and the Order. He had also divided his riches in the same manner between the Three Gems. The *Historical*

Memoirs Hiouen-Thsang consulted vouch for this. Did they also mention the Council convoked by Aṣoka? This would seem probable, but Hiouen-Thsang does not mention it. Moreover, his statement agrees with the Nepalese tradition in placing Aṣoka's reign, and therefore the date of the second Council, about one hundred years after the Nirvāna; and he states that Aṣoka was the grandnephew of King Bimbisāra.

He is a little more explicit about the third Council. Agreeing again with Nepalese tradition, he dates the assembly as taking place in the four hundredth year after the Nirvāna of the Tathāgata. According to his version, it is also the king of Kashmir, Kanishka, who convoked it, at the request of the āchāryya, Pārṣvika. The assembly was composed of all the learned personages who had studied the Three Commentaries, besides the Five Luminous Treatises. They numbered five hundred, and were presided over by the famous Vasubandhu, the commentator of the *Abhidharmakoṣa*, the Treasure of Metaphysics. First, they collated the writings of the Three Commentaries, of which the canon had remained unaltered, and they proposed elucidating the real meaning of these works, which had apparently become obscure. They therefore composed a work in one hundred thousand ṣlokas called the *Upadesa-Ṣāstra*, to explain the Commentary on the Sūtras; then they composed one of a hundred thousand ṣlokas, called the *Vinaya-vibāshā-Ṣāstra*, to explain the Commentary on Discipline; and finally they composed a third work of another hundred thousand ṣlokas called the *Abhidharma-vibāshā-Ṣāstra*, to explain the Commentary on Metaphysics. These three hundred thousand ṣlokas contained nine hundred and sixty thousand words. The king Kanishka had these three works engraven on plates of copper, and sealed up in a stone box, over which he built a stūpa: 'If their deep meaning has been again brought to light,' adds Hiouen-Thsang, or rather his biographer, 'we owe it solely to the labours of this Council.' As Hiouen-Thsang remained two whole years in Kashmir, engaged in the most serious studies, and as 'for centuries learning had been held in high honour in this kingdom,' these traditions, which are moreover so precise, deserve particular attention.

As we have mentioned Aṣoka it may be as well to quote all the information Hiouen-Thsang gives us about him. Aṣoka, it would seem, was not born in the Buddhist faith, but as soon as his mind was opened to the belief, he resolved to build stūpas all over India, to display, at the same time as his power, the fervour of his munificent piety. It is difficult to believe, notwithstanding tradition, that these stūpas numbered eighty-eight thousand, but Hiouen-Thsang asserts that he saw with his own eyes monuments attributed to this potentate from the capital of Nagahāra, at the foot of the Black Mountains of the Hindu Kush, down to the kingdom of Malakūta, at the southern extremity of the peninsula; and from east to west, from the kingdom of Tāmralipti to the borders of Sindh and even the Persian frontiers. It is therefore extremely probable that Aṣoka, who convoked the second Council, reigned over almost the whole of India, and that his authority was recognized by the multitude of small States which before his time and after him were divided into separate kingdoms. This is an historical fact that has a certain importance in the annals of India, and which therefore admits of no doubt.

In another respect, this would lead us to believe that the Piyadasi of the religious and moral Inscriptions is, as Turnour maintains, one and the same as the great king Aṣoka. These pious Edicts, which commended to the people the observance of the Law of the Buddha, have been discovered, repeated in identical terms, on columns and rocks, in countries far distant from each other, and this circumstance alone would prove that the devout monarch who promulgated them ruled over almost all India. This is another point of resemblance between Hiouen-Thsang's Aṣoka, and the Aṣoka of the Inscriptions. Chronology, according to our present knowledge, opposes insurmountable difficulties in the identification of these two; but it is very possible that with fresh discoveries these difficulties will disappear.

It has therefore been seen, that in the days of Hiouen-Thsang the whole of India was divided into a multitude of small principalities, each distinct and independent of one another.

Nothing in the traveller's narrative reveals the cause of this political partition, which seems to have existed from a remote period. Sometimes it might be explained by differences of race, or natural obstacles that impose definite limits to provinces. But, generally, there is no such reason, and States are isolated from each other, although nothing exists in the nature of the soil, customs, language, beliefs, or races to divide them. Doubtless all these small local administrations had their reason for existence, but history does not give the reason, though it was powerful enough to have created agglomerations, if not nationalities, which time has not destroyed, and which have preserved their autonomy, notwithstanding all the convulsions that have agitated the peninsula.

The most powerful prince whom Hiouen-Thsang met with was Ṣīlāditya, the king of Kanyākubja. He had no less than eighteen tributary kings under his rule; and on solemn occasions, as, for instance, the contest between the Great and Little Vehicle, he made them accompany him. However, in spite of all his power, Ṣīlāditya, even with the help of his vassals, had not been able to conquer Mahāraṭṭha, that is, the country of the Mahrattas, situated in the centre of India. Even at that remote period, this warlike race, which was the last to submit to the English rule, knew how to defend its liberty, and protect its frontiers from all invaders. The picture Hiouen-Thsang gives of them conveys a high idea of the qualities of this people. 'Ṣīlāditya led his victorious armies from east to west,' says Hiouen-Thsang, 'and the most distant nations tremblingly obeyed him. But the men of this kingdom never submitted to his laws. Although he had placed himself at the head of all the troops of the five Indias, and called under his standard the bravest generals of the States he led into combat, he had not yet succeeded in overcoming their resistance; this will show their unyielding character and indomitable valour.'

A still more remarkable fact was that, notwithstanding their warlike temperament, the Mahrattas were passionately devoted to study; and this testimony the traveller readily gives them, although he is not lavish of it; in fact, he only bestows it upon three or four races: those of Kashmir, Magadha and Malwah. The Great and Little Vehicle were both followed in Mahāraṭṭha, where several hundreds of convents existed, containing about five thousand monks. The two sects lived there in harmony, and the heretical Brahmans were almost as numerous as the Buddhists. This happy country was particularly favoured: its fertile soil produced corn in immense quantities, the climate was mild and the heat moderate. The inhabitants were simple and gentle in their habits, lived in comfort, and were in general tall of stature and possessed of singular strength.

Ṣīlāditya, king of Kanyākubja (Central India), had succeeded his elder brother, who had perished a victim to the treachery of a neighbouring prince jealous of his military talents.

He devoted himself to the happiness of his people; like his ancestors he belonged to the caste of the Vaiṣyas; and doubtless this humble origin inspired him with greater sympathy towards the inferior classes. He forbade throughout his dominions the slaying of a single living being, and allowed no meat to be consumed. Full of zeal for the Buddhist faith, which his family had professed for many generations, he had founded convents at all the places where the saints had left traces of their passage; and had magnificently endowed the great vihāra of Nālanda.

Ṣīlāditya's generosity was as great as his piety, and once a year he fed this multitude of monks during three or seven days. Besides this, every five years he assembled the Great Order of the Deliverance (*Moksha mahā parishad*), and distributed in alms all the riches of the royal treasury. Hiouen-Thsang does not hesitate to compare his beneficence to that of the famous Sudāna (Sudatta), the Anātha Piṇḍika of the legends. This distribution of alms, not only to the monks but also to all the poorer classes of the population, is a characteristic institution of Buddhism, and one that has been retained.

The Buddha had not made this an absolute law for princes; but in recommending almsgiving as the chief virtue, he had strongly urged it upon them; and this singular custom partly replaced, in those remote days, the benefits of the poor-laws in the present time. As Hiouen-Thsang personally assisted at one of these solemn distributions, and as his biographers have retained his account of it, we are able to know how it was carried out, and it is certainly one of the most curious spectacles afforded by Buddhism at that period.

It will be remembered that the Buddha had instituted public confession as an atonement for sin, and that the monks were obliged to make these painful and salutary confessions twice a month; at the new moon and at the full moon. From the monks this pious custom had extended to the whole body of believers; but, as such frequent gatherings would have been prejudicial to the working-classes and the multitude who had to gain their daily subsistence, the force of circumstances had somewhat modified the primitive institution. The people were assembled every three years, or at least every five years, in order that all might confess, and settle, as it were, all their past offences. Piyadasi's religious edicts leave no doubt on this point, and Hiouen-Thsang's testimony, relating what he himself witnessed, thoroughly confirms them. These assemblies were the natural opportunity for royal liberalities; but, little by little, the real meaning of the institution died out, confession was first neglected, then forgotten; and the gathering became but the occasion for giving and receiving sumptuous alms. This was what the Chinese pilgrim saw, and what he relates.

He was at that time in the kingdom of Prayāga, in Central India, one of the principalities that acknowledged the suzerainty of Ṣīlāditya. Near the capital two rivers, the Ganges and the Jumna, united; to the west of their confluence rose a plateau, about four miles in circumference. From the days of antiquity, kings and high personages 'gifted with humane feelings' went to this place to bestow alms. It had therefore been called *the Great Plain of the Alms-giving*. According to tradition, it was more meritorious to give one coin at this place, than to give a hundred thousand coins elsewhere. At all times it had been held in singular esteem; and the king Ṣīlāditya, in this a scrupulous imitator of his predecessors, had gone thither to perform the generous and sacred ceremony.

He first had a square space enclosed by a hedge of reeds, measuring a thousand feet on each side. In the middle several thatched halls were erected, containing an abundance of precious things, ingots of gold and silver, pearls, red glass, and rare gems of every kind. Other houses contained also a quantity of silk and cotton garments, gold and silver coins, &c. Outside the hedge an immense refectory was built; and as the distribution was to last a long time, a hundred houses, each capable of sheltering a thousand individuals, had been built in a straight row, like stalls in a market. Some time previous to the event, the king had summoned by decree all the Sramanas and heretic Brahmans, orphans and men without families, and the poor, in order that they might have their share in the distributions. Since the beginning of his reign he had already held five similar assemblies, this one was the sixth; and Ṣīlāditya specially invited Hiouen-Thsang to this festival in order that he might witness the happiness it promoted. The king arrived in great state, followed by his eighteen tributary kings, amongst whom were his son-in-law Dhruvasena, king of Vallabhi in Southern India, and Kumāra, king of Eastern India. Each of these kings had pitched his tent in different places, one to the north of the Ganges, the other to the west of the confluence, and the third to the south of the Jumna, by the side of a flowering grove. The men who had come to receive the alms numbered several hundred thousands, and were placed at the west of Dhruvasena's tents. Military forces accompanied the kings, and took up the positions assigned to them, ready if necessary to maintain order. Moreover, everything was carried out in a methodical manner.

Religion necessarily presided over these acts of great beneficence. The first day a statue of the Buddha was installed in one of the thatched temples erected on the Place of the Almsgiving, and precious things and rich garments were distributed. Exquisite viands were served, and flowers were scattered around to the sound of sweet music. In the evening all retired to their tents. Thus the whole ceremony was placed under the protection of the Buddha, in whose name it was held. As at that epoch the people were as tolerant as they were pious, the second day they installed in another temple the statue of the Sun-god (Aditya) adored by the idolaters; but this time the distributions were only half of what they had been on the previous day. The third day the statue of the Supreme God (Iṣvara) was installed, and the same amount of alms were distributed as at the installation of the Sun-god. All the different religions practised by these nations were treated—except as to precedence—with the same respect; and as in ordinary life they co-existed without contest or persecution, the kings did not set them apart in their beneficence any more than they did in their protection.

On the fourth day the general distributions began, and they were first made to the monks, the fervent apostles of the Buddha's faith.

Then the distribution was extended to the Brahmans, and as they were much more numerous, it lasted twenty days. After them came the turn of the heretics, which took up ten days, and that of the naked mendicants (*nirgranthas*) from distant countries, which lasted another ten days, lastly alms were given to the orphans, the poor, and men without families, which distribution took up no less than a month.

The seventy-five days assigned to the distribution had now come to an end. All the wealth stored up during five years in the royal treasury was exhausted. The king had nothing left him but the elephants, horses, and weapons of war indispensable for the protection of his kingdom and the punishment of those who might cause disturbance. Personally, he had given away in alms all he wore, the best part of his garments, his necklaces, earrings, bracelets, the wreath round his diadem, the pearls that adorned his neck, and the carbuncle that glittered in the middle of his tuft of hair, in fact he had divested himself of everything he possessed. After having exhausted all his riches, he begged his sister to give him a common worn-out garment, and having clothed himself with it, he worshipped the Buddhas of the ten regions, and in a transport of ecstasy he joined his hands, exclaiming: 'In collecting all these riches and costly things, I constantly feared that I should not be able to conceal them in a safe and impenetrable place. Now that I have been able to deposit them in the *Field of Happiness*, I consider them safe for ever. I wish in all my future existences thus to collect wealth in order to give alms to men, and obtain the ten divine faculties in all their plenitude.' Some time after this, the eighteen tributary kings collected large sums of money from the people of their States and bought back the magnificent necklace, the carbuncle of his head-dress, the regal vestments, &c., that the king Ṣīlāditya had given in alms, and brought them back to him as an offering. But in a few days the king's raiment and the jewels of greater value were again bestowed in alms, like the first time.

This is Hiouen-Thsang's account; and he did not merely repeat what he had heard; he had seen what he relates, and it would be difficult to refute his assertions. He may have exaggerated certain details, and the distributions of alms may have been somewhat less abundant than he says, but the principal points of his narrative must be true; he most formally attests the existence of a custom created by religion, and maintained by the social condition of these enslaved and unhappy people not only in one part but over the whole of India. The Law of the Buddha enjoined almsgiving, and political reasons no less urgently dictated it. It would have been dangerous for the sovereigns not to have returned in gifts a part of the riches they extorted by taxation from their subjects, and it would have inevitably roused to despair and rebellion the impoverished masses who readily submitted to their rulers provided they were given a bare subsistence.

Prudence therefore came to the aid of piety, and the kings, while deeming that by almsgiving they were securing a place in the Tushita heaven, secured also for themselves a peaceful and durable authority.

What is still more astonishing is the general tolerance of both princes and people. Hiouen-Thsang only mentions one or two kings who had tried to overthrow Buddhism in their States. If Ṣaṣangka, king of Karnasuvarna in Eastern India, 'abolished the Law, and destroyed the Tree of Wisdom,' the majority of the sovereigns display on the contrary great forbearance, and it would not seem that any of them had ever thought of coercing their subjects in the matter of their religious beliefs.

This spirit of toleration cannot be ascribed either to reason or to indifference, for the Buddhist nations were too ignorant of justice and devoid of intelligence; while on the other hand it cannot be ascribed to indifference, as their religious fervour is shown by the quantity of monuments they have raised in honour of their faith. Cities lay in ruins, their walls recrumbled to pieces, while the stūpas and vihāras still remained standing; nothing, indeed, seemed to foreshadow the downfall of this religion, for new sacred edifices were constantly being built. They fervently believed the ancient dogmas; they sincerely respected tradition, however strange it might be; their hearts were warm, and nevertheless they remained tolerant towards other and even antagonistical beliefs. We can therefore only state this fact without explaining it; and the Indian mind in general, even more than the Buddhist, deserves all credit, for it must be remembered that the Brahmans were as kindly towards their adversaries as the latter were to them. In all the ancient history of Brahmanism there is not a single record of a religious persecution. The Buddha, although a reformer, had in this faithfully imitated Brahmanism, and he never, in the whole course of his long career, dreamt of turning the influence of the princes who protected him against his religious antagonists. He was satisfied with contending against them by doctrines which he considered superior to theirs; but he never tried to use compulsion, and the whole spirit of the new faith held violence in abhorrence.

In Hiouen-Thsang's time this happy state of things remained unaltered, and the struggle that was to lead to the expulsion of Buddhism had not yet begun. What was the condition of Buddhism in India in the middle of the seventh century of the Christian era, and what does the precise and devout pilgrim tell us on this subject? He will doubtless not give us all the information we should wish; but on the religious worship and the different sects he will furnish us with many details that will greatly interest us, although their ingenuous puerility may sometimes excite a feeling of contempt.

CHAPTER III.

Buddhist worship in India in the seventh century of the Christian era: its simplicity, worship of statues, the important part they play in Buddhism. Moving or flying statues, miraculous cures; relics of the Tathāgata and other saintly personages. Imprints of the Buddha's footsteps. The Maitreya Bodhisatwa. Absence of organization among the Indian Buddhist monks. Relation of Buddhism with Brahmanism in the seventh century. Buddhism divided into two sects: the Little and the Great Vehicle. Relation of the two principal sects; subordination of the Little Vehicle; its secondary sects. Course of Buddhist studies at the time of Hiouen-Thsang. His intercourse with illustrious learned men. Summary of Indian Buddhism.

At the time of Hiouen-Thsang's travels in India Buddhism had already existed for twelve hundred years, and during that long period the form of worship had not varied; for it had retained its simplicity, although superstition had increased with the legends. The images of the Buddha and his relics were still worshipped, as well as the monuments which contained them, or which had been erected on the spots sanctified by the presence of the Reformer. Flowers were scattered and perfumes burnt before the statues, offerings of silver and precious things were made to them, the stūpas were piously visited, and prayers, either mental or improvised for the occasion, were recited; prostrations and clasping of hands as tokens of respect were still made use of; and on solemn occasions, public worship was accompanied by music. The ceremonial, however, remained the same as at the outset, simple and inexpensive. Buddhism addressed itself exclusively to the hearts and minds of the faithful, and disdained external pomp; and sacrifices, which by all the minutiae of its exercises held such an important place in the Brahmanic religion, had completely disappeared in the religion of the Tathāgata.

As the Buddha had never claimed to be a god, it is evident that he never prescribed the form of worship that was to be rendered to him. A legend, however, attributes to him the institution of this form of worship, which it relates in the following manner.

'Rudrāyana, king of Roruka, had sent Bimbisāra, king of Rājagriha, a magnificent suit of armour endowed with miraculous virtues. Bimbisāra, not knowing how to requite such a valuable gift, consulted the Buddha, who at that time was at his court: "Let the image of the Tathāgata be drawn on a piece of cloth," replied Bhagavat, "and send it as a present to Rudrāyana."' It will be seen that this advice shows little humility on the part of the Buddha, and nothing in Ṣākya-muni's life authorizes a belief of such conceit. But the legend quietly ignores this; the Tathāgata therefore casts his shadow upon a cloth, and orders the painters to fill in the outline with colours, and to inscribe under the portrait the Formulas of Refuge and the Precepts of his teaching, not omitting to trace, both in its direct and inverse order, the Connective Chain of Converse Causes of existence. Rudrāyana respectfully receives this inestimable gift, and worships it with deep veneration, as Bimbisāra had instructed him to do in a previous letter announcing his present.

Such is, according to the legend, the origin of the form of worship. Only, in course of time, and by the very force of circumstances, statues were substituted for the less durable pictures, and they play an important part in Buddhism. They are extremely numerous, and often of an enormous size. The statues generally represent the Tathāgata in the attitude of meditation or rather of teaching: the right arm is uplifted and the gesture of the hand is that of a master speaking to his disciples. They bear all the marks that are visible of the thirty-two signs pertaining to a great man, and which tradition ascribed to the Buddha. These statues figured in great pomp on all occasions to which a solemn or religious character was attached.

This did not, however, constitute idolatry; but the merits these statues possessed, by preserving the image of the Buddha, and recalling his holy presence, were not the only qualities they were endowed with; superstition attributed to them many others better calculated to strike the imagination. Nothing is more common in the legends than statues that move or fly through space from far distant places. Near Purushapura in Gandhara (Peshāwar) Hiouen-Thsang saw a stūpa which, although in ruins, still measured 150 feet high, it had been built by King Kanishka. A hundred paces south-west of this stūpa, was a white stone statue of the Buddha, eighteen feet in height, with its face turned to the north. 'At this spot,' says Hiouen-Thsang, 'a great number of miracles take place; and the statue is often seen to move, during the night, round the great stūpa.'

Thus the pilgrim speaks of this prodigy, as if it could still be seen in his day. He does not, indeed, boast of having seen it himself, but it is probable that with a little more fanaticism he would have witnessed it, like so many other believers.

The miraculous appearance of two statues of the Buddha had formerly converted the kingdom of Kustana. One statue had come to Kashmir through the air, in answer to the prayers of a former king, who had gone to meet it at the head of his army. The statue had followed the monarch for some time, but when it reached the city of *Po-Kia-I* (Pogai?), it had stopped. In vain did the king unite his efforts to those of his soldiers to move it; no human power was able to dislodge it. They therefore erected a small chapel over the statue. The king had given his cap, enriched with precious stones, to adorn the head of the Buddha; and Hiouen-Thsang gazed at the ex-voto with an admiration that was shared by all those who were admitted to see it. The story of the second statue was no less extraordinary; it had come at the prayer of another king, and had placed itself in a convent, on a throne prepared to receive it; and it was—so the Chinese pilgrim was informed—the very same image that the Buddha had left to his disciples with the sacred writings.

Some of the Tathāgata's statues were endowed with miraculous powers. In the city of Pi-mo (Bhīma?) about sixty miles east of the capital of Khotan, Hiouen-Thsang saw a statue thirty feet high, representing the Buddha standing; it was remarkable for the beauty of its shape, and its serious and stern attitude. It was supposed to effect infallible cures in favour of those who invoked Bhagavat. When a man was ill, a leaf of gold was stuck on the statue at the spot corresponding to the seat of pain in the man, and he was immediately cured. Moreover, the vows and petitions made to this statue were nearly always crowned with success.

As the statues of the principal Buddhist personages also received the homage of the faithful, Hiouen-Thsang relates the visit he devoutly paid to Avalokiteṣvara's statue in the kingdom of Hiranyaparvata. It was placed in a vihāra on the summit of a mountain, and was made of sandal-wood. It was also the object of pious pilgrimages; at all times a numerous throng gathered around it to worship it, after severely fasting for a week or two. A balustrade kept the faithful at a proper distance, and as the statue could not be touched, the flowers offered it were thrown from afar. If the garlands that were respectfully thrown at it settled on the hands or arms of the statue it was considered a good omen.

'The Master of the Law bought therefore all kinds of flowers and wove them into garlands, then, when he got near the statue, he worshipped the Bodhisatwa in all the sincerity of his heart and celebrated his praise. After which, turning to his image, he bowed low before it, and addressed to it the three following petitions: 'After having studied in India I wish to return to my native land, and live there in perfect tranquillity, far from all danger. As an omen of success I ask that these flowers may settle on your venerable hands. Secondly, as a consequence of the virtue I cultivate and the wisdom I aspire to, I desire to be born one day in the heaven of the Tushitas and serve Bodhisatwa Maitreya. If this be granted, I pray that these flowers may settle on your venerable arms. Thirdly, the holy doctrine teaches us that in the multitude of men of this world, some are in no ways gifted with the nature of the Buddha; I, Hiouen-Thsang, have doubts about myself, and I do not know if I am one of these. If therefore I possess within me the nature of the Buddha, and if, by the practise of virtue, I can in my turn become Buddha, I beg that these garlands of flowers may settle on your venerable neck.' Saying this, he threw the garlands of flowers, and each one settled according to his wishes. Then, having obtained all he desired, he gave way to a transport of joy. At this sight, the persons near him, who like him had come to worship the statue, and the guardians of the vihāra, clapped their hands and beat the ground with their feet in token of their admiration. 'If at a future time,' they said, 'you attain the state of a Buddha, we ardently hope that you will remember this event, and make us pass among the first (to the other shore, that is to say, to Nirvāna)[1].'

The worship of relics was as widespread and almost as fervent as that of the statues. It will be remembered that

[1] See Stanislas Julien, *Histoire de la vie et des voyages de Hiouen-Thsang*, p. 172.

after the death of the Buddha, his relics had been divided in eight parts, amongst as many kings, who contended for them. As the body had been burnt, these relics could hardly consist of anything but ashes. But popular superstition easily transformed and multiplied them. In the days of Hiouen-Thsang, the *che-li*, as he calls them in Chinese (*sarīras*, body, in Sanskrit), were very numerous, and he found some in almost every part of India. He was able even to take back a collection of them to China, as well as statues.

It is easy to comprehend that *sarīras*, that is, fragments of the actual body of Ṣākya-muni, were the most holy relics; but they were not the only ones. In the kingdom of Nagarahāra, besides the eyeball of the Buddha, and the bone of his cranium (*uṣnisha*), his garment and staff were preserved; at Baktra, besides one of his teeth, his water-jug and broom were shown; at Kongkanapura, at the other extremity of the peninsula, the statue of Siddhārtha, prince royal (*Kumāra rāja*), and his cap were treasured up; doubtless it was the one he gave Chandaka, when he left the paternal palace; this cap was about two feet high. At each festival it was taken from the box where it was carefully locked up and placed on a high pedestal. 'Many of those who contemplate it,' adds Hiouen-Thsang, 'and worship it in perfect faith, have seen it surrounded by an extraordinary light.' It is the same with those who, gazing at the imprints which the Buddha's steps have left in many places, see these traces either long or short according to the virtue they themselves possess, and especially according to the fervour that animates them. At this rate miracles are easy, and the excited imaginations of believers can produce as many as they wish.

Amongst the personal relics, the teeth play the most important part. Hiouen-Thsang saw a dozen of them in the different parts of India he travelled over, and he asserts that his protector, King Ṣīlāditya, was on the point of undertaking a war against the king of Kashmir because he had refused to give him one of the Buddha's teeth. This one, although much shorter than many others, was an inch and a half long, it was of a yellowish white colour, 'and at all times emitted a bright light,' if we are to believe the devout missionary, who was allowed to contemplate it in the convent where the pious king had deposited it. There was another no less famous in the king's palace in Ceylon. We shall revert to this later, when treating of Singalese Buddhism.

The footprints of the Buddha are almost innumerable; as the Tathāgata, according to tradition, visited the greater part of the peninsula; and the credulity of the faithful as well as the trickery of the monks greatly assisted in making them visible. These marks were usually imprinted on stones, and the most famous were those on Adam's Peak in the island of Ceylon, where the Buddha had certainly never gone. It was called Ṣripada, or Prabhāt, that is, the Blessed foot.

The king Aṣoka was said to have raised stūpas at all the places where the Buddha had left traces of his footsteps, and it will therefore be easily understood how tradition had made these stūpas attain the number of eighty-four thousand; they were also called the eighty-four thousand Edicts of the Law.

At the side of the worship of the Buddha, by a deviation easy to understand, the worship of his principal disciples, and even that of personages famous by their virtue and knowledge, had followed that of the Buddha himself. Thus at Mathurā, in Central India, Hiouen-Thsang found stūpas in which had been deposited the relics of Rāhula, the son of Ṣākya-muni and of Ānanda, his cousin and faithful adherent, who compiled the Sūtras of the first Council; and those of Upali, who compiled the Vinaya at the same

Assembly, of Moggallāna, of Ṣariputra, of Pūrnamaitrāyanīpūtra, the first disciples of Tathāgata, and of Manjuṣri, a no less celebrated ascetic, though he lived some centuries later. Every year, on feast days, the monks assembled in great number, and each one made offerings to the saint who was more particularly the object of his devotion. The votaries of the Abhidharma made offerings to Ṣāriputra, and those who gave themselves up to meditation (the Dhyāna ecstasy) made them to Moggallāna. The partisans of the Sūtras paid homage to Pūrnamaitrāyanīpūtra; and those who studied the Vinaya honoured Upali. The nuns, the Bhikshunis, specially honoured Ānanda. The faithful who had not yet received all the rules of discipline honoured Rāhula. Lastly, those who studied the Great Vehicle honoured all the Bodhisatwas without distinction.

As for Hiouen-Thsang, he appears to have felt a special reverence for the Maitreya Bodhisatwa. When the boat in which he was descending the Ganges was surprised by pirates, and his life threatened by the ruffians, who dragged him to the altar on which they were about to sacrifice him, he addressed his prayers to Maitreya and not to the Buddha; on him alone does he energetically concentrate his thoughts; it is this Bodhisatwa whom he sees appear in the ecstasy into which his spirit is plunged at this supreme moment, and it is to the all-powerful intervention of this saint, that he attributes his deliverance. At the end of his career, when, at the point of death, he recalls to mind all the good deeds he has accomplished, and dictates a list of them to his sorrow-stricken disciples, he boasts that he has had a thousand images of the Maitreya Bodhisatwa painted; and his most ardent wish, at this moment when he is quitting life, 'is to be admitted into the family of Maitreya in Tushita, in order to serve this Buddha, so full of tenderness and affection.' The Gāthās he recites when dying are addressed to Maitreya; and at the very instant when his spirit is vanishing, he tells his disciples 'that he has at last obtained his wish to be born in the midst of Maitreya's Assembly.' Thus the simple Bodhisatwa Maitreya seems to hold as high a place as the Buddha himself in the worship of the learned missionary.

All these details clearly show the condition of Buddhist worship in the days of Hiouen-Thsang: it was a spiritual homage rendered in the first place to the holiness and virtue of the Tathāgata, and in the second to all those who had best followed his incomparable example. The worship was full of meekness and devoid of all costly state; it was accessible to the very humblest, since it only required prayers and flowers, and the faith that accompanied these modest offerings was deemed more precious than the offerings themselves.

No privileged class was entrusted with the pious exercises and ceremonies. The monks in holy orders, for this expression is applicable to them, did not form part of a regular or general corporation, they were respected by the faithful, because they were thought to possess more knowledge and virtue than the common herd; but they did not exercise any official power. They appear to have been subject, in the rich convents and vihāras they inhabited, to a uniform discipline which dated from ancient times, but, numerous as they were, they were neither organized nor united under one common direction. Each vihāra or sanghārama kept apart and had its own administration, just as each province retained its own government. Religion had not overcome the spirit of division, and there was no more spiritual than political unity. The separate and unstable supremacies that sometimes existed with regard to the land, had never been attempted with respect to religion. The common faith rested on the identity of the writings which were universally venerated; it was maintained by its own power and by tradition; but it did not require that vast hierarchy which has proved indispensable to other nations. This singular fact is borne out by Hiouen-Thsang's testimony, and the evidence from a different point of view—contained in the Sūtras. Pious foundations were flourishing everywhere, from Kashmir down to the extreme point of the peninsula. Created by the munificence of kings and the piety of believers, they were kept up by them and existed by their beneficence; they were as opulent as they were numerous, but it would not seem that the monks ever thought of uniting under one rule all these scattered elements, in order to constitute a power which would probably have proved irresistible.

This usurpation took place in the neighbouring states, notably in Thibet, where the supremacy of the Grand Lama had established itself; but in India it was not even attempted, and the idea never seems to have occurred to any one.

Hiouen-Thsang gives us very few details about the attitude of Brahmanism in the presence of its rival, which seems in general to have enjoyed an easy triumph.

The Brahmans with whom Siddhārtha formerly discussed discuss no longer, they are called heretics; the Vedas are classed amongst secular books, and they are henceforth so little feared, that they are studied in the convents on the same footing as philosophy, grammar, logic and medicine. This was doubtless a painful position for the old Brahmanic orthodoxy, but no symptom of revolt or persecution can be traced. History does not precisely state when Buddhism began; but, thanks to the evidence of the Chinese pilgrim, it may be considered certain that towards the middle of the seventh century Buddhism still enjoyed complete tranquillity in India.

It considered itself very superior to the ancient faith; in its eyes Brahmanism was but the gross worship of spirits and Devas. The Brahmanic Pantheon was completely discredited, and a belief in those strange and impotent divinities was regarded as a kind of shame. The Brahmans did not know how to create an ideal accessible to the masses, and their metaphysical speculations, which were perhaps excellent for ascetics and men of learning, were not addressed to the vulgar herd, and could not appeal to them. The ideal that Buddhism created was, on the contrary, intensely human; and if the virtue of the Tathāgata was infinitely superior to that of other men, it nevertheless served as a pattern and guide for them. This is shown by the example of Hiouen-Thsang and many others; he takes the Buddha as his model, and the recollection of his heroic and saintly life assists him to become, in a certain measure, a hero and a saint. From this point of view Buddhism might well disdain Brahmanism, which was less moral and above all less practical; and it is evident that it loses no opportunity of manifesting a contempt, which its adversaries seem often to accept. The missionary saw Brahmans filling the meanest functions in the Buddhist temples.

Thus the religion of the Buddha does not appear to have been on its decline in India, when the pious Hiouen-Thsang went thither to seek the enlightenment which was fading in China. He found tradition alive everywhere, religious establishments flourishing and spread all over the country, which liberally maintained them; the most studious and learned teachers, a throng of disciples who diligently follow their lessons, in order to perpetuate them; in one word, a prosperous condition that seemed likely to continue for many centuries.

And what more particularly proves the power which at this epoch animated Buddhism, were the energetic controversies in which it was constantly engaged, both against its adversaries and in its own circle.

Buddhism was divided into two sects: that of the Great Vehicle, and that of the Little Vehicle, both of which could be traced back to the earliest days. Two hundred and twenty years before Hiouen-Thsang's journey, Fa-Hian had found them in the same situation. What differences separated them? And in what did their discussions exactly consist? This is a difficult question to solve; and hitherto it has remained obscure, although the Buddhist documents we possess quote at each instant the names of these two sects.

In the first place, the Great and Little Vehicle (*Mahāyāna* and *Hīnayāna*) were exactly alike in the boundless faith they had in the worship of the Buddha. They had only a different manner of honouring the Tathāgata according as they studied his merits and doctrines in different works; but in reality they both believed only in him, and both sects possess the same fervour.

From a Chinese catalogue quoted by Stanislas Julien,[1] it appears that the two Vehicles did not hold the same books as canonical and orthodox. The Great Vehicle had five series of sacred writings, while the Little Vehicle had nine.

The result of a comparison of these two lists of works is that the doctrine of the Little Vehicle is much less elevated than that of the Great Vehicle, as its name implies. And indeed Chinese authors generally admit, that the partisans of the Little Vehicle cannot attain Nirvāna, and are still subject to transmigration. They do not attain true metaphysics, but are content with the code of morals and discipline, to which they add the legends. This is evidently an inferiority which adherents of the Little Vehicle strive in vain to hide.

Moreover we see with what contempt Hiouen-Thsang—who belonged to the Great Vehicle—like nearly all the

[1] *San-tchang-ching*, in some unpublished documents that Stanislas Julien communicated to the author.

Chinese Buddhists, spoke of them. How often he extols the sublime precepts of the Great Vehicle, comparing them with scornful complacency to the narrow, mean views of the Little Vehicle, which to him seem incapable of ensuring eternal salvation. He purposely relates the legends that depreciate it, and never loses an opportunity of quoting any facts that may be prejudicial to it.

Notwithstanding this apparent inferiority of the Little Vehicle, that sect was as numerous as its rival in the peninsula in the days of Hiouen-Thsang. It existed in the kingdoms of Bamian and Kapisa in the north; in that of Kapilavastu, and even at Benāres; in the kingdoms of Hiranyaparvata and Champā in the east; in the kingdom of Malwah, which was considered the most enlightened after Magadha; in that of Vallabhi in the south; at Vaiṣāli in Central India; in Gurjara (Guzerāt) in the west, in Sindh and in many other places. It is true that the Great Vehicle generally predominated, and had in its favour number of its adherents as well as the purity of its doctrines. But this does not make it less tolerant; and in many kingdoms the two sects co-exist without excluding one or the other, and even without any great contest. Thus in Ṣilāditya's dominions at Kanyākubja, the partisans of the Little Vehicle exercise their form of worship in complete liberty, as indeed the contest in which the Chinese pilgrim was triumphant would prove. And it was the same in the kingdoms of Pundravarddhana, Kongkanapura, Mahāraṭṭha (the country of the Mahrattas), Atali, Ayodhyā (Oudh), Mathurā, Udjdjayana (Udjein), &c. In all these countries the Little Vehicle is followed as much as the Great, and Hiouen-Thsang does not quote a single act of violence inspired by fanaticism.

The most learned and pious monks mutually refuted one another with unwearying zeal; but their animosity did not extend beyond their arguments, and when the dialectic tournament was ended, the two sects resumed their good understanding, which lasted till the next contest, where self-love was alone at stake. Nevertheless, as the two Vehicles have their own particular convents the sects do not mix in ordinary life, and do not willingly avail themselves of each other's hospitality. When Hiouen-Thsang reached the capital of the kingdom of Kapisa, one of his companions, who belonged to the Little Vehicle, showed a certain repugnance at staying in a convent of the Great Vehicle. The Master of the Law yielded to this susceptibility, by going himself to reside in a convent of the Little Vehicle, which had in former days been the residence of the son of a Chinese emperor, retained there as a hostage. The fact was that the two Vehicles had different rules with regard to the food of the monks. The Little Vehicle only permitted three kinds of food, which were called the *three pure foods*; and it forbade all other. The prohibition might, however, under certain circumstances be disregarded; and the monks of the kingdom of *A-ki-ni* (Agni), who were renowned for the severity and purity of their lives and their submission to the laws of discipline, added some ordinary foods to the *three pure foods*. This excessive sobriety of the Little Vehicle was considered an error, perhaps because it recalled the dangerous austerities prohibited by the Buddha; and Hiouen-Thsang boasted to the king of Kutch, who received him in his palace, that he ate indiscriminately of every kind of food, leaving to the Gradual Doctrine, that is to say, the Little Vehicle, a practice which seemed to him both puerile and culpable. As the Little Vehicle was less esteemed, it frequently happened that it was abandoned for the superior doctrine; Hiouen-Thsang gives several such examples. It was thus that the famous Vasubandhu of Gandhara, imitating his master Asamgha, had passed from the schools of the Little Vehicle to those of the Great Vehicle, where he had become one of the greatest authorities. A whole convent in Magadha had been converted by the miraculous gift of a wild goose, which fell from the skies at the feet of the bursar, who on that day had found himself in great difficulties to provide for the monks' repast, as they could only eat the three pure foods.

Sometimes the change was made in the opposite direction; and as it was possible to be very learned although a partisan of the Little Vehicle, the Great Vehicle was abandoned, on account of its somewhat obscure theories, which appealed less vividly to the imagination. At the gates of the capital of the kingdom of Matipura, Hiouen-Thsang saw a stūpa consecrated to the memory of Gunaprabha, the author of numerous works, who, after having studied the Great Vehicle had left it and joined the Little Vehicle. It is probable, however, that such cases were rare. No disgrace was, however, attached to the practice of the Little Vehicle, for those who prided themselves on possessing thorough knowledge, while giving the preference to the Great Vehicle, studied indiscriminately both of them.

Not far from the learned convent of Nālanda, Hiouen-Thsang found on a mountain, called the Forest of Staffs, an ascetic renowned for his learning, whose teaching he diligently followed for two years. He was a Kshatriya who in his youth had displayed a great taste for study, and who, renouncing his caste, had become a Buddhist. He possessed a thorough knowledge of secular works, or books from outside as they were called; of the four Vedas, of works on astronomy, geography, medicine, magic, and arithmetic: but besides these he knew the Great and Little Vehicles, although he was a disciple of Sīlabhadra, the venerable superior of the Convent of Nālanda.

Hiouen-Thsang himself, in a letter of thanks which he wrote to the king of Kao-Tch'ang, after obtaining his release, boasts that he is acquainted with the two Vehicles, and expresses himself in the following manner: 'Hiouen-Thsang, thanks to his happy destiny, entered at an early date through the Black Gate (into a convent), and followed the master's teachings till he was about twenty years of age. All the illustrious sages and friends of a superior merit were consulted and interrogated by him. He studied thoroughly the precepts of the Great and Little Vehicle.' Later, when Hiouen-Thsang, who had written a treatise expressly to refute the errors of the Little Vehicle, returned to China, laden with the sacred treasures he had gone to seek in India, he took back with him the works of the Little Vehicle, which, although less precious, were almost as numerous as those of the Great Vehicle; and in his long retreat he translated both of them with equal care, if not with equal respect. During all his sojourn in India he had impartially studied the two Vehicles, under the guidance of the most authorized masters.

It would not seem, however, that the ancient doctrines of Brahmanic philosophy were quite extinct at the time when the Chinese pilgrim travelled through India. As he had an utter contempt for Brahmanism, he hardly notices it, nevertheless he was acquainted with it, and, when duty required it, he was able to refute it. It was thus that, before the great conflict with the partisans of the Little Vehicle at Kanyākubja, he engaged in a regular discussion with a Brahman upon different systems, and among others on that of the Sānkhya and the Vaiṣeshika. He analyzed them in order to demonstrate their absurdity. The arguments by which he thinks to overcome them may not appear very conclusive, but they at least prove that he had studied these theories, and that they were sufficiently prevalent for Buddhism to have to contend against them, even if it had no cause to fear them. The ancient philosophy therefore was not dead, and the Brahmans still cultivated it, although it possessed little life or influence.

Buddhism, on the contrary, was full of activity and energy. It would be difficult without the ample details furnished by Hiouen-Thsang, to have an idea of the important mental movement and enormous labour of which it continued to be the object. The monks, in all the vihāras and samghāramas, zealously applied themselves to the writing of books, when they possessed sufficient talent and authority to speak in their own name, or else they applied themselves to the study of the works sanctioned by orthodoxy. Throughout all India, Hiouen-Thsang, learned as he was, found personages worthy to discuss with him on the most delicate points of the Law, and even capable of enlightening him. These personages were deeply venerated for their intelligence by all who came near them, from the kings who aspired to converse with them, down to the people who worshipped them as saints. They gloried in the number of books they had read; and the professors of the Law who could quote and comment on the largest number were considered the most illustrious and were the most revered. They mutually questioned each other on the meaning of obscure passages, and woe to him who could not answer; false science was unmasked, and vanity pitilessly punished by richly deserved humiliation. Not only did the monks in their studious retreats distinguish themselves by these pious labours, but whole populations kept up and honoured the culture of letters, as for instance in Magadha and Malwah.

The Buddhist mind, which had no other food than the sacred writings, was exclusively given up to studying and explaining them; and these serious occupations sufficed to satisfy all the cravings of the heart and imagination. Sometimes indeed they might indulge in some momentary relaxation by the study of logic, astronomy, medicine, arithmetic or magic; but those profane pursuits were soon laid aside for the sole research needful, that of eternal salvation, which could only be acquired by meditating the Law of the Buddha and its boundless perfections.

In Hiouen-Thsang's time, that is about twelve hundred years after the death of the Buddha, the fervour of religious study and discussions had not slackened. The neighbouring countries, particularly those in the north, sought from India, the revered birthplace of the Buddha, the instruction it could alone impart, and which it liberally gave them. Hiouen-Thsang mentions over forty monks of his day whom he met, and whose teachings he followed or refuted in all the countries he travelled through.

Another course of studies about which Hiouen-Thsang also gives some curious and most precise information, are the translations of the Buddhists' writings made in China, by monks who came from India. Under the reign of Fou-Kien, prince of Thsin from the year 358 to 383 of the Christian era, a certain Sramaṅa called Dharmanandi translated the sacred books, and one of the Emperor's chamberlain's held the brush. From 397 to 415, another Indian Buddhiṣt naṃed Kumārajīva was the translator; and under the Second Wei dynasty, from 471 to 477, the translator was Bodhiruchi. Shortly before Hiouen-Thsang, in 627, an Indian professor, Prabhāratna, was entrusted with the translations, which one of the Emperor's ministers revised in order to ensure their lucidity and elegance. Thus, during many centuries, did China apply to Buddhistic India for its interpreters of the Law, and India was always able to furnish them.

Hiouen-Thsang not only gives these details as to individuals, but he also furnishes details upon the works themselves.

Besides the Sūtras, he mentions a quantity of Ṣāstras, Kārikās and Tīkas, all secondary books, but still very important, as they develop, complete, and comment on the original documents of the faith. If we were not afraid of wearying our readers, we could name fully one hundred. Such was the learned and devout society amid which Hiouen-Thsang lived during sixteen consecutive years, in order to acquire the orthodox knowledge that he was desirous of carrying back to his own less enlightened country. We may indeed smile at the ingenuousness of the missionary, who took so much trouble to collect absurd legends and extravagant beliefs, but this does not diminish his merit. We must, however, admit that our astonishment surpasses our contempt, for we had no idea that, in the seventh century of the Christian era, India possessed convents as numerous as those of our Middle Ages; schools and monks as learned and as laborious as our own; vivid religious preoccupations, and a complete collection of sacred writings; documents of all descriptions, which attest and keep up the dogmas of its faith; and princes and nations so pious and at the same time so tolerant. We do not seek to compare the fertile chaos of our Western Continent—at that period—with Indian Buddhism such as Hiouen-Thsang reveals it to us; but we may well doubt whether any intelligent and courageous missionary, who might have come from distant countries to our own, would have received so cordial a reception, and, more especially, if he would have been able to make such an abundant harvest. He would have been strangely puzzled to find on the Christian religion the 657 works the Chinese pilgrim was able to collect on the Buddhist faith; and when we see how small was the literary store in our most renowned schools, we may well consider that the Buddhist world studied its religion better than the Christian world did its own. It is true that it had already accumulated the labours of twelve hundred years, and that it had the whole Brahmanic system behind it; but western civilization had had equal advantages, which it had neglected. Later, its destinies were to be much higher; but at that moment the Christian world was in a state of inferiority which its pride little suspected; and which even now it is reluctant to admit. However, in face of precise and undeniable documents like those of Hiouen-Thsang's travels, our civilization must recognize that if it has no rivals it has had at least equals, which deserve all its consideration and even sympathy, notwithstanding their deficiencies and mistakes. Buddhism has, like our own civilization, stirred up the greatest problems that the human intelligence can evoke. It has not, it is true, found the solution, but it is no small honour to have made the attempt, and this noble effort, sterile as it was, it well calculated to disarm severity and compensate for many faults.

PART III

BUDDHISM AT THE PRESENT TIME IN CEYLON.

CHAPTER I.

Lord Torrington, Governor of Ceylon and the Buddhist priests in 1848. *Sources of the history of Ceylon; Burnouf's notes on the ancient names in that Island. The Rāmāyana. Greek and Roman accounts of Taprobane. Fa-Hian's journey to Ceylon; traditions collected by Hiouen-Thsang; Sinhalese annals. Turnour's Mahāvansa. Sir Alexander Johnston's undertaking in* 1826. *Deception practised by Sinhalese priests. Upham's publication. The sacred and historical Pāli books of Ceylon. Conversion of Ceylon to Buddhism. Analysis of the Mahāvansa. Supposed journey of the Buddha to Ceylon. The three Councils. Relations of Dharmaṣoka, king of India with Devānam-Pīya-Tissa king of Ceylon; interchange of ambassadors. Mahinda, Buddhist apostle, and his sister go to Ceylon. Branch of the Bodhi tree. Some important events in the history of Ceylon. The Buddha's tooth. Divers translations of the Canonical books and their Commentaries by Buddhaghosa in the fifth century of the Christian era.*

When in 1848 Lord Torrington, Governor of Ceylon, established a highway tax, the Buddhist priests protested, and demanded to be exempted from the tax. By this law, every inhabitant, without exception, was bound either to perform six days' labour on the highways, or in default to pay a certain sum of money. The Buddhist priests presented to the Governor a humble but at the same time dignified petition, in which they set forth how impossible it was for them to submit to this general rule; and the motives they gave were very forcible.

They represented that during four months of the year their

subsistence depended entirely on the alms given by the population, from whom they received their daily food, without even being permitted to ask for it; that, during the other eight months, when their subsistence was no less precarious, they were constantly travelling about; that they could neither work nor even take off their clothes for a moment without forfeiting their title and ceasing to be priests; and therefore they could not personally contribute to the construction of the roads. Moreover, that as they fasted, according to rule, eighteen hours out of every twenty-four, and never ate except between six o'clock in the morning and noon, they were incapable of executing any manual labour without falling ill; on the other hand, they could not replace an impossible labour by a pecuniary compensation, for according to their rules they could possess neither money nor property in any shape whatever; and that they could no more exact money from the faithful, than they could bread.

They added that, since the establishment of Buddhism in Ceylon, 316 years before the Christian era, they had never been compelled either to work or to pay any tax; that the convention of 1815, by which the inhabitants of Ceylon had freely surrendered to the English crown, stipulated, amongst other guarantees, the maintenance and independence of the Buddhist religion; and finally, that by compelling them to work, they would be violating their most sacred duties in this world and forfeit all hopes of a world to come. In consequence, they petitioned that the tax, in both its alternatives, should not be applied to them.

The Governor listened to this just claim, and acceded to their request, but this was not done, however, without a good deal of trouble. The Buddhist priests' protestation was followed by others. The Bishop of Colombo protested and alleged that it would give Pagan Buddhism an immense advantage over Christianity if their request was granted. If the Buddhist priests were exempted, why should not all other priests be also exempted? Would not Sinhalese fanaticism take advantage of this preference? Might it not be feared that it would raise a fresh obstacle to the progress of Christianity among the natives? On the other hand, the fiscal administration protested like the clergy, and while ready to recognize that the Buddhist priests could not be compelled either to perform the labour themselves or to pay the tax in money, it suggested a rather ingenious expedient, and proposed that they should be obliged to find substitutes.

Lord Torrington deserves great credit for having discerned what was just and right in such a conflict of different pretensions. By a special privilege he exempted the Buddhist priests, not, however, by virtue of their priesthood, but as mendicants. The facts stated by the petitioners were but too true: their vows, their traditional rules, their daily habits, their style of life, and their beliefs were all insurmountable obstacles; and the statesman recognized the force of a protest so well justified, and gave them full satisfaction [1].

The tolerance of the English administation was the more

[1] This petition can be seen in the *Blue Book* published in 1849 under the heading of Papers Relative to the Affairs of Ceylon. This document, which consists of 300 pages in folio, relates all the facts about the insurrection which occurred in 1848, and which, although unimportant, lasted several months. Lord Torrington's energetic measures soon suppressed it; the highway tax and other administrative measures had been the pretext, but in reality the Kandyans rose in 1848 as they had risen in 1818, 1827, 1834, and 1843, and as they may possibly again rise in rebellion. They resented a foreign yoke, and were always striving for the restoration of an Indian monarchy. The Kandyans must not be confused with the remainder of the Sinhalese population; they are more restless and warlike. They are of a different race, being generally descendants of the Tamils. Lord Torrington's administration was attacked by one of his successors, Sir H. G. Ward, but the former easily refuted these undeserved criticisms, and his reply, dated January 17, 1857, was published in the parliamentary reports. From the time of Lord Torrington's administration (May, 1847–November, 1850) dates the prosperity of Ceylon. Thanks to the impulsion he gave to all great works of public utility, the island already possessed, in 1851, 1800 miles of admirable roads, besides a large number of other financial ameliorations.

praiseworthy that it was perfectly aware of the bad influence exercised on the people by the Buddhist priests. They had aided and abetted all the insurrections which had broken out since 1815, as indeed they again did in that of 1848, which was caused by the false rumour spread throughout the island that France and England were at war, and that French troops were about to land in the port of Trincomalee. In the trial after the insurrection, when the principal offenders were punished, a Buddhist priest was implicated, found guilty, and condemned to death by court-martial, with eighteen other insurgents, and was executed in his priestly vestments and all the insignia of his office. This example, which had only had one precedent, was considered necessary in order to deter future imitators. The Sinhalese are extremely fanatical; if they fancy their relics run any danger, more especially the Buddha's famous tooth, which endows its proprietor with sovereign rights, they are at once roused and ready to take up arms, if only they can find a leader [1].

Throughout the whole country, and particularly in the northern and central provinces, there are a large number of temples, assiduously frequented and richly endowed by the magnificence of the faithful. The most important—to which convents are attached—are found in the Dombera district, north-west of Kandy; and in 1841 the pretender, Gongala-godda Banda, had himself crowned in the Temple of Dombula, one of the most venerated and ancient temples, said to have been built one century before Christ.

These facts would in themselves prove the power that Buddhism still possesses in Ceylon, and it is an interesting

[1] See the *Blue Book* already quoted: Papers Relative, &c., &c., p. 171. In 1818 the removal of the Buddha's tooth, transferred from one city to another, had been the signal for rebellion. In 1848 the English Resident at Kandy deemed it advisable to lock up the precious relic, in order to prevent its falling into the hands of the rebels. Later, when all danger was over, he restored it to the priests for the worship of the faithful.

study to see what its actual condition is after a rule of more than two thousand years. This work has been performed by Turnour in a masterly manner; he has brought to our knowledge one of the most important documents of Pāli-Sinhalese literature, and the *Mahāvansa*, in the form he has given it to us, is certainly one of the most valuable sources for researches into the ancient history of Ceylon. We shall refer to it later, but we will first rapidly pass in review what is known of Buddhism in Ceylon within historical times.

Eugène Burnouf had intended, at the outset of his studies in Pāli, to compose a special work on this subject. The *Journal Asiatique* of Paris gave an important fragment of his work on the ancient names in the island of Ceylon[1] Burnouf's studies would have chiefly been directed to the ancient geography of the island in its relations to history; but he was deterred from this undertaking by Hodgson's important discovery, and he therefore preferred to keep to the original Sanskrit works of Nepaul rather than the Sinhalese traditions and documents. Moreover, he intended taking up southern Buddhism later, after having thoroughly investigated northern Buddhism, and the appendixes of the *Lotus de la bonne Loi* show how far he had already carried his laborious researches.

One of the principal sources, and certainly the oldest, of the history of Ceylon is the *Rāmāyana*. Rāma undertook the conquest of the island in order to recover the beautiful Sītā, who had been carried off to Lankā (the ancient name for Ceylon) by the traitor Rāvana. But the well-known confusedness of this strange poem makes it difficult to extricate any reliable facts from the mass of extravagant fictions, in which monkeys and

[1] *Journal Asiatique* of Paris, January, 1851, p. 1 and following. Burnouf's memoranda had been read—we are told by a notice of M. Mohl, member of the Institute and Secretary of the French Asiatic Society—at two sittings of the Academie des Inscriptions et Belles-lettres, in March, 1834.

genii take a much more important place than heroes and men. It would, however, be a mistake to set the *Rāmāyana* aside, for it is almost the only evidence that can furnish us with some account of the state of the island before the introduction of Buddhism. The Hindus, as the *Rāmāyana* itself shows, had the strangest ideas about this country, although it was so near the peninsula, and the obscurity of their legends betrays little acquaintance with it [1].

With the introduction of Buddhism into Ceylon, this ignorance began to give way. But the evidence that attests this important fact is of a much later date than the fact itself, and the Buddha's religion had been established for six hundred years or more when the historians, if the author of the *Mahāvansa* and his successors can be so called, thought of recording traditions which were about to disappear.

The Greeks first knew Ceylon under the name of Taprobane [2] in the days of Onesicritus and Megasthenes, shortly after Alexander's expedition. But the Greeks never knew what religion the inhabitants of Taprobane professed, and moreover cared little for this kind of information. In their opinion Taprobane was only famous for its wealth, its pearls, and the cinnamon it produced. Later they knew more, without really knowing much, and the famous embassy of the King of Taprobane to the Emperor of China furnished a few more precise details, which Pliny has recorded. However, the Roman naturalist simply says, in mentioning the religion of Taprobane, that Hercules was worshipped there. It is certainly a very unexpected similitude if under the features of Hercules we are to recognize the Buddha.

The Chinese pilgrim Fa-Hian (395–416 A. D.) is the

[1] *Rāmāyana*, Canto I, chap. iv. ṣlokas 55, 77, 102, 103, and Cantos V and VI.

[2] Burnouf has shown the identity of the word *Taprobâne* with the Sanskrit *Tāmraparna*, one of the names by which the Indians designated the island of Ceylon, where the leaves of certain trees are copper colour.

first personal witness we have about Ceylon. It cannot be averred that he was a very exact or very intelligible historian; but as he speaks of what he has seen, his narrative deserves particular attention. After sojourning two years in the kingdom of Tāmralipti, south-west of the Ganges, he embarked on board a merchant ship going to Sinhala, or the kingdom of the Lion. The voyage lasted fourteen days before the small islands on the coast of Sinhala were reached; these, Fa-Hian tells us, numbered a hundred[1]. He found the Buddhist religion in full prosperity, and practised with more fervour than in any country he had visited in India. Fa-Hian accepts without hesitation the statement that Fo the Buddha had been to Sinhala, and left two imprints of his saintly feet, one to the north of the royal city, and the other on a high mountain (the famous Adam's Peak, which is the highest in the island, and over 7,000 feet high). Fa-Hian also heard the Sinhalese traditions about the branch of the Bodhi or Bo-tree miraculously conveyed from India to Sinhala, as well as the legend about the Buddha's tooth. This inestimable relic was publicly exhibited every year for the adoration of the inhabitants. The solemn procession took place at the time of the third noon. A herald announced it throughout the country several days before, and the people thronged to the ceremony. During the procession, pictures representing the five hundred different births or manifestations of the Buddha were exhibited, to revive the pious recollection of his merits and his miracles.

To perform the services of this flourishing religion, the kingdom of the Lion, Sinhala, possessed a numerous and wealthy clergy. Fa-Hian found five thousand monks at the Convent of the Fearless Mountain (Abhayagiri). In another convent, called the Great Convent, there were

[1] The islands of the Straits of Manaar.

three thousand, and at the chapel of the Bodhi there were two thousand. In the capital, which was very magnificent, but of which Fa-Hian forgets to give the name, the king alone fed five to six thousand. The Chinese pilgrim estimates from what he saw that the whole island must contain from fifty to sixty thousand monks; at least this was the approximate figure that the people of the country gave him. All these monks were individually as poor as the law of Fo demanded; every morning they went out with their alms-bowl in their hands, and silently waited till charity or the commiseration of the laity had filled it. If, however, the individuals were so completely destitute, the temples were extremely wealthy; the kings took pleasure in making them splendid donations; these had accumulated for centuries past, and the communities therefore ended by possessing an enormous amount of property[1].

The people were no less pious than the kings, and the four castes assembled regularly three times a month—the eight, fourteenth, and eighteenth day of each moon—to listen to the sacred preaching. These sermons were delivered from a pulpit, from which a monk appointed for the purpose addressed himself to the attentive multitude. Fa-Hian assisted at several of these salutary instructions, and in one, amongst others, he heard the whole narrative of the admirable story of the Buddha's vase. The devout pilgrim would have wished very much to retain this adorable legend, but unfortunately it had never been written down. However, as the clergy were very well informed, Fa-Hian was able to make an ample provision of works and books written in the *Fan* language (or language of the Brahmans, Sanskrit, or Pāli).

[1] The donations to the convents are still very considerable, and as they are generally free from all legal duties and all dues, they give rise to rather serious difficulties for the English administration.

All this information, given by Fa-Hian, is of great value, and shows Buddhism in all its splendour and power in the fifth century of our era, and more deeply rooted in Ceylon than in India, although it had been transmitted from India. Doubtless Fa-Hian, after sojourning there two years, might —if the object of his journey had been less special and his mind less preoccupied—have related much more about the curious country he was visiting. Although the Chinese people had not very frequent intercourse with the kingdom of the Lion (*Sse-tseu-Koue*), it is certain that commerce had attracted them thither long before Fa-Hian went there, indeed Pliny gives irrefutable proof of this. All that Fa-Hian tells us independently of religious matters is that the capital of the country was very fine, a fact that tallies with the account given by the Chinese ambassadors, and that the kingdom enjoyed perpetual peace. This probably means that peace was not disturbed during the whole time the Chinese pilgrim lived there; for this tranquillity hardly agrees with what is known of the character and history of the inhabitants of the island, from Rāvana, the fabulous ravisher of Rāma's spouse, down to the insurrection of our own time. With Fa-Hian's narrative the uninterrupted series of authentic documents begin, although it must be added that these native documents are neither as exact nor intelligible as could be desired. The *Mahāvansa* was composed, at least its first part, some years after Fa-Hian's journey.

As for Hịouen-Thsang, he had not the privilege of visiting Ceylon as he had intended. When he reached the kingdom of Dravida in southern India, and arrived at its capital, Kānchīpura, which was a seaport, he purposed crossing over to the island of Sinhala, which was only three days' distant by sea. But he was dissuaded from this voyage by two monks, who had precipitately left that country, and urged him not to go there. The king had just died, and the whole island was a prey to civil war as well as famine. This terrible news was confirmed by other fugitives, and Hiouen-Thsang prudently decided not to attempt such a dangerous, and probably useless, journey. But he gathered as much information as he could about the country which he regretted not having seen, as the learning of its monks was in high renown, and the Master of the Law had intended to study, with their assistance, certain canonical works that he had not yet sufficiently fathomed.

He learnt, however, that the kingdom of Sinhala, formerly called the Island of Precious Things, the Pearl Isle (*Ratnadvīpa*), was a vast country of about 7,000 *li* in circumference (1,740 miles)[1]. The capital, which was large, was forty *li* in circumference (nine miles). It was densely populated, but the land was exceedingly fertile. The inhabitants were of a dark complexion, generally short of stature, and violent and fierce in their habits. The worship of the Buddha, which had been introduced there one hundred years after the Nirvāna, was held in great honour. There were no less than a thousand convents or saṅghāramas, and ten thousand monks in the island; these were men of great learning and piety, but instead of wearing the yellow robe of the Indian Sramanas they were robed in black. They belonged for the most part to the sect of the Great Vehicle, and more especially that of the Sarvāstivādas. The vihāra of the Buddha's tooth was situated near the king's palace[2].

Hiouen-Thsang then relates two legends on the origin

[1] This estimation is about 450 miles above the mark.

[2] This is in perfect conformity with the present belief of the Sinhalese. It has been seen above that the Buddha's tooth always played a great part in the popular disturbances, because it was supposed that whoever possessed it had sovereign rights. The mention Hiouen-Thsang makes of the violent and ferocious character of the inhabitants of Sinhala applies to that part of the population which have remained almost savages even to our day, and which lie concealed in the most central and thickly wooded parts of the country; they are called Ueddas, and, as the Chinese pilgrim stated, are wild and ferocious in their habits.

of the name of Sinhala, the kingdom of the Lion. One of these legends is absurd; for it says that a lion, uniting with the daughter of a king, was the progenitor of the inhabitants of the island. The son of the Lion, having killed his father, was cast adrift on the seas as the punishment of his parricide, and the wind drove his ship on to the coasts of the island of Precious Things. His sister, who, it appears, was as culpable as her brother, was also sent to sea on a vessel that was cast on the Persian (*Po-la-sse*) shores, which since that time was called the kingdom of the Western Daughters. The sister peopled Persia by uniting herself with demons, and the brother peopled Ratnadvīpa, thanks to the women brought there by merchants, from whom he abducted them[1]. The second legend is much simpler: the son of an Indian merchant called Sinhala is said to have taken possession of the island on landing and given it his name.

It is regrettable that Hiouen-Thsang was not able to go to Ceylon as he had intended. Exact and observant as he was, he would have left much more valuable information than is contained in the meagre narrative of Fa-Hian.

But these more or less reliable testimonies given by the *Rāmāyana*, the Greeks, or the Chinese pilgrims, all emanate from strangers, and must be thrown into the shade by indigenous evidence, which is far more authentic and voluminous. By a rare and unique privilege in the Indian world, the island of Ceylon possesses exact and incontestable annals, which date back to at least the fourth century of our era, and even, it is almost certain, to a much earlier period. These annals have been kept and recorded from century to century down to our own time, and are preserved with such care as to

[1] The first legend is repeated under every form in all the Indian and Chinese books, and has been readily accepted; while the second, which is much more probable, had passed unnoticed. In the East the imagination of the people requires supernatural stories.

endow them with a kind of official character. The style of writing may appear very strange, and shock all our western habits of thought, for it is very different to any of our methods, from the Greek down to our own historians; but these annals, singular as they may seem, have nevertheless recorded the principal facts which make up the history of Ceylon.

Turnour has given in the *Mahāvansa* an exact idea of what these annals were, whether written in Pāli or in Sinhalese, under the direct authority of the kings who in succession governed the island. The following is a list of the principal works which still exist in Ceylon, and which it is to be hoped European philology will be able to publish at some early period.

First, the *Mahāvansa,* written in Pāli between the years 459 and 477 of our era, by Mahānāma, the uncle of King Dāsenkellīya. Mahānāma states that he drew the principal elements of his work from the Sinhalese documents existing in his time. He composed it at Anurādhapura, at that time the capital of Ceylon, and of which a considerable amount of ruins can still be seen. The *Mahāvansa* comprises the history of Ceylon from the Buddha's Nirvāna, 543 years B.C., down to the year 301 of our era; the author, in order to give clearness to his narrative, adds a commentary called the *Mahāvansa tīka,*[1] and Turnour was able to obtain a copy of this very scarce commentary, taken from the one kept by the priests in the vihāra of Mulgirigalla.

The *Mahāvansa* properly so called, or rather the personal work of Mahānāma, stops at the end of chapter xxxvii, that is to say at the end of Mahāsena's reign in 301. The continuation of the *Mahāvansa,* known under the name of

[1] Pāli, even in Mahānāma's time, was only known by the priests. It is therefore possible that Mahānāma brought the history of his country down to the moment when he was writing his work; but, as his commentary stops at the year 301, Turnour believes that the author also stopped writing the *Mahāvansa* at that date.

Suluvansa, giving an account from the year 301 to the year 1266, was composed by Dharmakirti at Dambedeniya, under the reign of Prākrama Bahu; and from 1266 to 1758 by Tibottuvena, under the reign of Kirti Srī, who reigned from 1747 to 1781 in the city of Kandy. The *Mahāvansa*, including the *Suluvansa*, is composed of a hundred chapters, and a little over nine thousand ṣlokas of sixteen syllables, or eighteen thousand verses.

The other annals of Ceylon, less famous than the *Mahāvansa*, are written in Sinhalese; these are the *Pudjavalli*, composed by Mairupāda, under the reign of Prākrama Bahu; the *Nikāya-Samgraha*, by Daivarakshita Djaya Bahu, under the reign of Bhuvaneka in 1347; the *Rajaratnākari*, composed towards the close of the fifteenth century by Abhaya-rāja; and lastly the *Rājavalli*, written by several different individuals at different periods, and of which certain portions are probably more ancient even than the *Mahāvansa*. All these annals begin their narrations at the time of the Buddha's birth, and even at an earlier date.

Such is the historical wealth possessed by the island of Ceylon.

The discovery of such treasures in any part of the Indian world was a most fortunate occurrence, and these were all the more valuable that they are exceedingly scarce in India. The attention of the English Resident was therefore drawn to these curious documents, and in 1826 Sir Alexander Johnston, Chief Justice and President of the Royal Council of Ceylon, took measures to have them published. He had lived a long time in the island, and by his functions as well as his literary tastes, had been in relation with the most learned priests and the most distinguished natives. In a praiseworthy desire to give the colony a code of laws better suited to its customs and religious beliefs and all its past history, he resolved to have a translation made of the principal works on the Buddhist faith, in order to enlighten the English administration and further its object. The Sinhalese population was no less interested in this judicious enterprise than was the English government itself.

At Sir Alexander Johnston's request the Buddhist priests furnished authentic, or rather what they alleged were authentic, copies of the *Mahāvansa*, *Rājavalli*, and the *Rajaratnākari*. 'These formed, according to what they told the Chief Justice, the most complete summary that existed of the origin of the Buddhist religion, its doctrines, its introduction into Ceylon, and the moral and political influence that these doctrines had exercised from the most remote epochs on the conduct of the national government and the customs of the natives.' Sir Alexander Johnston therefore accepted these valuable copies, which the Buddhist priests guaranteed as being authentic and scrupulously exact. In order to be more certain, he ordered that they should be compared, by two of the most learned priests, with the other copies that were kept in the temples. Having taken all these precautions, he handed the books to the official translators, and they worked under the supervision of a native functionary, who was supposed to be the best-informed man in both the Pāli and the Sinhalese languages. This translation, made with so much care, was revised by the Rev. M. Fox, a Wesleyan missionary, who had resided a long time in the island, and was afterwards confided to Mr. Edward Upham for publication.

Sir Alexander Johnston has himself given all these details in a letter in which he asked the officers of the East India Company to take under their patronage an enterprise which was likely to prove so useful, and had been inspired by such generous sentiments. After seven more years of labour, the translation appeared in 1833 in London, and King William graciously accepted its dedication.

Unfortunately the Buddhist priests had deceived Sir Alexander Johnston, and, either through ignorance or purposely, had given him incomplete or falsified copies of their books. As Turnour remarked with good reason, either the priests were incompetent for the task they had undertaken—that is, of translating the Pāli *Mahāvansa* into Sinhalese—or they had completely misunderstood what was demanded of them. Instead of translating the Pāli into Sinhalese so that the official translator might translate the Sinhalese version into English, they had made a work of their own, either by lengthening out the original works with extracts from the commentaries, or by shortening them in the most unintelligent manner.

When Upham's translation appeared in Europe the unfortunate omissions it revealed were soon noticed; and, without being aware of the peculiarities that we have just mentioned, Burnouf immediately drew attention to the serious differences that existed between the manuscripts he possessed of the Ceylon books and the new version made under the auspices of Sir Alexander Johnston by the Sinhalese priests. Later, Turnour divulged the mistake, not to say fraud, and showed that amongst all those who had co-operated at this work, from the priests who had recommended and revised the copies down to the official translators and the Rev. M. Fox, not one possessed sufficient knowledge to accomplish it. The work had therefore all to be done over again, and the learned societies were obliged to admit that, far from being acquainted with the sacred and historical books of Ceylon, they had only obtained a very imperfect knowledge of the contents of the Sinhalese chronicles. Notwithstanding the discredit this vexatious incident cast upon these studies, they were not to be discouraged; and as the documents really existed, and were accessible in their original form, it was to be hoped that, with a little more circumspection and criticism, other painstaking and skilful students would resume the undertaking and retrieve this first disappointment.

This Turnour did, with a talent that has classed him among the most distinguished Orientalists, and twenty years ago he published the first volume of the *Mahāvansa*.[1] Turnour, who began his labours long before Upham's publication, had suspended them on hearing of the approaching translation of the works he had been studying. But this publication was not calculated to damp his ardour, and while he continued to fill the public office assigned to him, he went on with his work which he had laid aside for a moment, but which he now resumed with more zeal than before. Turnour felt himself under the obligation of rehabilitating Sinhalese literature after the undeserved and involuntary check it had received. If such was his object he has fully attained it, for his *Mahāvansa* has shown, even incomplete as it is, what an abundance of information the Sinhalese chronicles contain, and the true nature of this information. In presence of the original text, doubt is no longer possible, and the translation which accompanies it reveals all its importance as well as its thorough authenticity.

This fortunate experiment shows, therefore, that the Sinhalese annals are worthy of notice and of publication. Although Buddhism was not a growth of Ceylon, as has been thought and is still sometimes asserted, it is certain that it was transplanted there at an early date, with an edition of the sacred writings in Pāli. This was unquestionably the greatest event in the history of the kingdom of the Lion, and, taking the *Mahāvansa* for our guide, we will now turn our attention to it.

It will be seen from the above the valuable information that is to be derived from this document, and also from similar ones. The date generally given as that of the

[1] We must remind our readers that Barthélemy St. Hilaire's book was published in 1860.

Buddha's death is entirely of Sinhalese origin; but all the Chinese, Tibetan, Burmese, &c. works agree in demonstrating that the date of the year 543 before the Christian era is almost a certitude, and till now no serious objection has been raised on this point. Moreover, it must not be forgotten that this chronology, so essential to the history of India, and even all Asia, is due to the Sinhalese annals. It will be shown how it is set forth in the *Mahāvansa*, and further study only confirms this.

The *Mahāvansa* also relates some of the events subsequent to the Buddha's death, entering into many important details, amongst others it mentions the three Councils which settled the Buddhist canonical writings. They were all three held at different periods, according to the necessities of the new faith, in that part of India which is watered by the Ganges. The Sinhalese can therefore have only known them through tradition; but the tradition they have retained is one that deserves thorough confidence, for it followed immediately the facts it recorded. Mahānāma, the author of the *Mahāvansa*, works upon indigenous materials, collected and prepared by the historians and annalists who preceded him. These annalists go back by degrees to the period when Buddhism came from Magadha and reached Sinhala, and their statements, which we only know by Mahānāma's work, were almost contemporary narratives of the events they relate.

After the Nirvāna of the Tathāgata and the history of the Councils, the *Mahāvansa* continues, century by century and year by year, to give an account of events, which it brings down to the end of the eighteenth century. The interest offered by this part of the *Mahāvansa* cannot be denied, but we do not intend to consider it at the present moment.

It must not be lost sight of that Ceylon, besides these instructive local chronicles, holds an important place in Buddhism by the particular collection of orthodox works it received at the time of the conversion of the island, and which it has carefully treasured up till now. It is well known that there are two editions of the canonical books of Ṣākya-muni's religion—one in Sanskrit, discovered by Hodgson in the Nepalese monasteries; and the other in Pāli or Magadhi, in the possession of the Sinhalese priests. These two collections, although written in somewhat different languages, since Pāli is the popular and Sanskrit the cultivated and even sacred dialect, thoroughly agree as to the substance. The doctrine and legends are identical, the works are often exactly alike, the language alone differs. Which therefore of these two collections must be considered the original? Which of them is only a copy? This is indeed an important question, that can only be solved by a comparative examination of the two collections, and which, to be thoroughly cleared up, would demand more labour than philologists have yet been able to bestow upon it. But whatever may be the solution in the future, it is to Sinhalese Buddhism that we must turn to get the works of the Pāli collection; for it is only in Ceylon that the intelligence and piety of the faithful have known how to keep this pledge of their faith unsullied, and they only have cultivated the language in which it is revealed. It is probable that the Pāli collection, brought from Magadha to Sinhala, was at a later period taken from Sinhala to Burmah and the countries east of India. At the present day, on the contrary, Ceylon receives from Burmah its religious inspirations and its chief priests; but there was a time when, in an inverse ratio, the island propagated and communicated the new faith to the neighbouring countries.

It is therefore clear that Ceylon played an immense part in the history of Indian Buddhism. The primitive language is still understood there, and the island is in possession of the most reliable annals. For these two reasons the *Mahāvansa* can be thoroughly trusted.

The author of the *Mahâvansa* first points out in a few words the object of his work. The compositions of his predecessors are either too concise or too diffuse; they are full of repetitions: 'he wishes to avoid these faults, by a work which shall be easy to comprehend and remember, and which will give the reader pleasure or pain, according to the nature of the deeds it relates.'

After this preamble, which only takes up two ṣlokas, Mahānāma immediately enters into his subject.

Following the example of the twenty-four preceding Buddhas, and more especially that of Dipankara, Gautama Buddha resolves to redeem the world and save it from evil. He undergoes all the requisite ordeals: and 'Our Conqueror,' as the pious Sinhalese says, 'attains the state of supreme and perfect Buddha, under the Bodhi tree at Uruvela,' in the kingdom of Magadha. It was at the full moon, in the month of Vaisākha. After remaining seven times seven days under the Bodhi-tree, he went to Benāres, and there made his first converts. He then sent abroad his sixty disciples, bidding them promulgate his doctrines throughout the world; and nine months after the Bodhi, he himself goes to Lankā, to sanctify it by his admirable teaching. The island was at that time a prey to the evil genii, the Yakshas. The Yakshas were gathered together in the centre of Lankā, on the banks of a charming river, in the gardens of Mahānāga, and the leaders were holding counsel, when suddenly the Buddha, coming through space into the midst of the assembly, struck them with terror by the rain, tempest and darkness that accompanied his appearance. Then hearkening to the entreaties of the Yakshas he had recourse to gentler measures, and preached a sermon which touched their hearts, and thousands of beings received the words of salvation. Eight years after this first visit, the Buddha returned to Lankā, doubtless to complete his mission of mercy: he again returned thither a third time, and since this memorable epoch 'Lankā, now made holy, has been revered by all good men, and has become a fit dwelling for mankind.'

Wherever the Buddha had sojourned in the island, his memory had been consecrated by a quantity of monuments, which had been successively raised and adorned by the pious monarchs who ruled over the country.

It will be seen, by this first chapter of the *Mahāvansa*, that if the author is, according to his promise, more concise than his predecessors, he is no less superstitious. Indeed, he would not be a Buddhist if he had not an imperturbable belief in all these legends, which he never criticizes, and which at the time he relates them date from a thousand years back. He even deserves thanks for having made such a moderate use of them. He leaves most of these traditions to the canonical books they are recorded in, and which may be perused by the faithful; and he only admits them into his narration with the most praiseworthy reserve. Mahānāma seems in reality only to mention the Tathāgata's visits to Ceylon in order to conform with popular opinion, and he does not give them more importance than they deserve, for later he relates with much more ample and exact details the real conversion of the island to Buddhism, about two centuries after the death of the Buddha.

However, he is not satisfied with the slight mention he made of the '*Conqueror*,' and in the second chapter he reverts to his family and genealogy. He makes him descend in direct line from the illustrious Mahāsammata, and mentions all the kings, successors of this prince, who had reigned at Kausāvatti, Rājagriha, Mīthilā, down to the great race of the Ṣākyas of Kapilavastu. At the age of nineteen the young Bodhisatwa left the world in order to fulfil his mission; he remained six years in solitude, meditation, and penance, and was thirty-five years of age when he again met the king

Bimbisāra, the friend of his childhood, whom he converted to the new faith. After forty-five years of preaching throughout Jambudvīpa, the Buddha died at Kusinārā, under the shade of two sāla trees. This was in the eighth year of the cruel Ajātaṣatru's reign, who had murdered his father Bimbisāra and usurped the throne.

The *Mahāvansa* does not reveal anything fresh, as all these events were already well known, but it is an important fact that it should so clearly and exactly confirm them. Its testimony is added to that of Nepaul and of the Pāli books, and to that of Fa-Hian and Hiouen-Thsang. The concordance of these proofs is as strong evidence as history can demand.

However, when the *Mahāvansa* treats of the three Buddhist Councils it is still more interesting; for nowhere do we find an account given so consecutively and with such details, nor, to all appearance, with such truth. Mahānāma has deemed it necessary to devote a whole chapter to each of these *Assemblies of the Law*, as he calls them (in Pāli, *Dhamma Sangīti*).

He gives the following account of the first Council. Seven days had scarcely elapsed since the Buddha had entered Nirvāna, when the great Kāṣyapa (*Mahā Kassapas*) summoned five hundred monks, whom he had chosen from amongst the most virtuous and learned. They met at Rājagriha, in the month Asala, in the first quarter of the moon. At the request of the monks, Ajātaṣatru, who had amended his ways and been converted, had had a large hall built for them at the opening of the Sattapaṇṇi cave, which still exists in the Vaihara hill, and the Order at once began their deliberations. On a throne placed to the north, and looking south, the president sat to direct the proceedings. A pulpit, placed in the centre of the hall facing the east, was prepared for the orators whom the president interrogated. The remainder of the Arahats, without having any particular seats, took their places on benches prepared for that purpose, according to their seniority. The first discussion was held on the second day of the second month of the Varsha (in Pāli, *vassa*, rainy season). The best beloved and most eminent disciples of the Buddha were there. Ānanda, his cousin, and inseparable companion for so many years, and Upāli, one of his most illustrious adherents, first entered the pulpit. Upāli was then interrogated by the high priest Kāṣyapa on the discipline or the *Vinaya*. The Sthaviras, that is the Elders (*Theros* in Pāli), chanted together Upāli's replies, and thus they learnt by heart the *Vinaya*. After Upāli, Ānanda, directed in the same way by the president, explained the *Dharma* or the Law. The assembly again chanted the words of Ānanda, and the *Dharma* was learned in the same way as the *Vinaya*.

These pious exercises lasted no less than seven months; and at the end of that time, *these benefactors of humanity* separated, persuaded that they had ensured for a period of five thousand years the power and splendour of the Buddhist faith. The first *Assembly of the Law* (Pathāma Dhamma Sangīti) was called the Assembly of the Sthaviras (*Therīya* in Pāli), because it had been exclusively composed of Arahats, and that the 'earth, rejoicing at having received such wonderful enlightenment swung itself six times,' says Mahānāma, 'over the deepest abysses of the Ocean.'

The fourth chapter of the *Mahāvansa* is devoted to the second Council. This one was held at Vaiṣali, in the tenth year of Kālāṣoka's reign, a hundred years after the Nirvāna. A heresy had sprung up at Waji (Odjein) and from there had spread over a great part of the northern provinces. The conventual rules had become relaxed, and discipline had lost much of its severity. The heretics had gained the king Kālāṣoka over to their side, and were on the point of carrying the day, when three monks, Yasa, Sambhūtta and Revata, united to contest their evil doctrines. Through the mediation of the priestess Anandi, Kālāṣoka's sister, they succeeded in changing the king's resolution, and he consented to declare himself in favour of the true faith before the Assembly at Vaiṣali. Revata, who would seem to have played in this new Council the same part that Kāṣyapa did in the first, skilfully confided the debates to eight monks whom he had himself chosen; four from the province of Pāchina and four from the province of Patheya. They retired to the Vālukarama Vihāra, where they prepared the decisions of the assembly which met at the neighbouring Vihāra of Mahāvana. On their propositions it consolidated the unsettled rules of discipline, and ten thousand priests, who had lent a willing ear to the heresy, were degraded. Revata was the soul of this reforming assembly, which numbered seven hundred members, and its labours, which were conducted on the same plan as the former one, lasted eight months. Among the eight principal personages, were several who had heard Ānanda, and who had learned from him how the first Council had carried on its pious work.

Mahānāma's narrative is much less clear upon the third Council than upon the two others; and he falls into the same error with which he reproached the former historians, namely diffuseness. He enters into lengthy and useless details about the reign of the famous Aṣoka, who had become sovereign ruler of all Jambudvīpa, two hundred and eighteen years after the death of the Buddha (B.C. 325).

The *Mahāvansa* gives the exact date. There had been only one schism in the first century, that of the Mahā-Sanghikas, but in the succeeding century there were no less than eighteen, which Mahānāma carefully enumerates. The faith, mutilated by these internal divisions and neglected by the people, in the midst of their civil wars, ran great risk of perishing. The lower castes had even gone so far as to have usurped the yellow robe of the monks; all public worship had been abandoned for the last seven years; it was therefore urgent that something should be done, to remedy these serious evils.

The powerful monarch, who had reached the throne by murdering all his brothers, numbering about one hundred, had been converted to Buddhism. His ostentatious piety was displayed in the most splendid monuments. In honour of each of the Precepts of the Law, eighty-four thousand edifices of all kinds were erected under his reign, in the space of three years; built either by himself, or by his vassals, the Rājas. The alms he bestowed on the monks were inexhaustible; and after he had embraced the Buddha's faith, and repudiated that of the Brahmans, he called himself Dharmāṣoka, that is Aṣoka, the Protector of the Faith. Touched by the complaints of the orthodox Buddhists, he appointed one of his ministers to root out the schism; but the incompetent minister failed to carry out his master's commands. His blind cruelty made many victims, but the discord still continued. At last the king himself was obliged to undertake the suppression of the heresy. He summoned to Pātaliputra (Patna) an assembly of priests called by his orders from all parts of Jambudvīpa, and a monk called Tissa presided with the same authority as Kāṣyapa and Yasa, aided by Revata, had exercised at the first and second Councils. Sixty thousand priests were degraded throughout India, and the ceremonies of the orthodox worship were everywhere re-established. This third Assembly of the Law, composed of a thousand monks, lasted nine months. This important event took place in the seventeenth year of Dharmāṣoka's reign.[1]

[1] The *Mahāvansa* states that the three Councils lasted seven, eight, and nine months. The regularity of this increasing length of the Councils seems somewhat suspicious; it may be due to chance, or it may be factitious. The result is that the third Council was held in the year B. C. 308. The Northern traditions, more reliable on this point than the Singalese, place it at an earlier date, to 400 years after the Nirvāna. This divergence has not yet been explained.

Mahānāma says very little, it will be noticed, about the third Council; but Dharmāṣoka's rule opened a new era for the island of Ceylon, and it was due to the sovereign monarch of India that Lankā was definitively converted. It would appear that the miraculous visits of the Buddha had not sufficed, for two centuries after the Nirvāna his teaching seems forgotten; and if the traces of his divine footsteps were still imprinted on the mountains of Sinhala, his doctrines were obliterated from men's hearts.

However, before relating with all proper details such a decisive event, Mahānāma thinks it necessary to revert to an earlier period; and he relates the legend of the union of the lion and a princess of Magadha. Vijaya, grandson of the lion, was banished from India on account of his crimes, and put on board a ship with his seven hundred accomplices; he landed in Lankā, in the province of Tambapanni (Tāmraparna), the very day that the Tathāgata entered into Nirvāna, after having saved the world. Mahānāma, oblivious of the fact that he had previously asserted that the Buddha himself had destroyed the Yakshas, represents them as being still all-powerful in Lankā when Vijaya reaches the island.[1] But Vijaya soon conquers them; he subjugates the petty princes who rule over the country, and to strengthen his power, he marries the daughter of a king of Madhura (Madras). After thirty-eight years of a prosperous reign, he dies at Tambapanni, a city he had founded on the spot where he had landed.

After an interregnum of one year, Pandurāsadeva, Vijaya's nephew, whom his uncle had summoned from Magadha, inherited the throne and settled at Upatissa, where he resided

[1] Here, Mahānāma explains the origin of the names Tambapanni (Tāmraparna, Taprobane) and Sinhala, given to Lankā. See Burnouf's notes on the ancient names of Ceylon. *Journal Asiatique de Paris*, January 1857, pages 54 and following.

thirty years. The whole island of Lankā obeyed his commands, but he had divided it amongst several subordinate chieftains, one of whom was Anurādha, the founder of the celebrated city that bears his name, which was for a long time the capital of Ceylon, and was situated north-west of Kandy, the present native capital. After Pandurāsadeva, with long intervals of civil war and anarchy, four other princes reigned in succession, till the great reign of Devānam-Pīya-Tissa, under whom the Tathāgata's religion was introduced and definitively established in Lankā.

Devānam-Pīya-Tissa, the most illustrious of the kings of Ceylon, was the second son of Mutasīva, his predecessor. Renowned for his piety and wisdom, even before he became king, he reigned peacefully forty years, from 307 to 267 before the Christian era, and from 236 to 276 of the Buddha's era; and he devoted himself during the whole of his reign to the development of the Tathāgata's law among his subjects. The most marvellous phenomena, reward of his rare virtue, had marked his coronation. On that propitious day, precious gems and rich metals sprang spontaneously from the soil and were scattered on the surface. Pearls and treasures buried in the depths of the sea came forth and lay in adundance on the shores of the island, happy at possessing such a master. A bamboo tree threw out three miraculous branches, one of silver, another laden with the most wonderful and choice flowers, and the third covered with paintings of the rarest animals and birds. The king, who was too modest to accept all these treasures for himself, determined to offer them to the great king Dharmāṣoka, whose fame had reached him. He therefore confided these magnificent gifts to four ambassadors, at whose head he placed his own nephew, and a Brahman known for his science. The ambassadors, accompanied by a numerous retinue, embarked at Jambūkola. They sailed seven days before reaching the

Indian coast, and took seven more days to get to Pātaliputra, the capital of the great Aṣoka. The Indian monarch received the marvellous gifts with the greatest joy, and not choosing that his gratitude should be less than his ally's generosity, he sent Devānam-Pīya-Tissa a profusion of regal ornaments for his new coronation[1]; and after detaining the ambassadors five months, he sent them back to Lankā, with the following message to their king: 'I have found refuge in the Buddha, the Law, and the Order; I have piously devoted myself to the religion of the son of the Ṣākyas. Thou, O master of men, recognize also in thy heart these incomparable refuges, and ask sincerely of them thy salvation.' The Sinhalese ambassadors, overwhelmed with honours and charged with this noble message, embarked at Tāmralipti (in Pāli, Tāmalettiya), and after navigating ten days, landed at Jambūkola, whence they had started six months previously. They transmitted to Devānam-Pīya-Tissa the pious exhortation of Dharmāṣoka; but it appears that this exhortation was not sufficiently powerful, for the heart of the Sinhalese king remained unmoved.

However, after the third Council, the great Aṣoka, Protector of the faith, determined to ensure the triumph of the Buddhic faith by sending numerous emissaries to the neighbouring countries. Proselytism had spread from the north of the peninsula, from Kashmir and Gandhāra, down to the Central Provinces, into the inaccessible country of the Mahrattas (Mahāraṭṭha) and to the foreign countries of Yonaloka and Aparantaka. Dharmāṣoka sent his own son Mahinda, who had been admitted into the Order twelve

[1] Although Mahānāma's national pride strives to hide the truth, it seems probable that at this epoch the king of Ceylon was a tributary of the Indian monarch, who was master of all Jambudvīpa. This is still more probable, from the fact that Aṣoka recommends the Sinhalese ambassadors to have their king crowned again; this was evidently a kind of investiture.

years before, with his sister Sanghamittā, to carry the word of the Tathāgata to the fortunate island of Lankā. Mahā Mahinda joyfully obeyed his father's commands, and started with four other monks, whose names deserve to be recorded with his own: these were Iṭṭhiya, Uttiya, Sambala, and Bhaddasāla. When he arrived in Lankā with his companions, Mahinda presented himself at once to the king Devānam-Pīya-Tissa, as the son and envoy of his powerful ally Dharmāṣoka. Devānam-Pīya-Tissa then remembered the pious advice his ambassadors had brought him, and lending a favourable ear to the discourse of the Buddhist apostle he was soon converted. As he set an example of profound veneration for the foreign monks, and personally waited upon them in the presence of his whole court during their meagre repast, the public enthusiasm rapidly increased. The king's step-sister, the princess Anūla, was converted, with five hundred women. The population of the capital thronged to the king's palace, where Mahinda was residing, to hear his teaching, and each day thousands were converted. Mahinda spoke the language of the country, and as the Mahāvansa says, 'thus he became the torch that lighted up all the island of Lankā.'

The number of monks rapidly increased, and vihāras were soon built for them, among others the Mahā-Vihāra, the most ancient and largest of all. These magnificent buildings, where the monks took up their abode during the rainy season, did not suffice. The king, in his munificence, added large donations, and in offering the Mahāmegha to Mahinda, he poured the consecrating water on the hands of the apostle, who gave him the plans for the construction of thirty-two stūpas. On another occasion, the king himself traced with his own hands the furrow that was to enclose a vast territory given to a convent. He himself drove the two royal elephants that drew the golden plough through the consecrated soil[1]. A crowd of buildings rose on all sides; and stūpas were erected wherever popular superstition fancied it found traces of the Tathāgata or of any former Buddhas.

The stūpas however required relics, for without these they would not be sufficiently holy; so Devānam-Pīya-Tissa, having begged his pious ally to give him some, Dharmāṣoka sent him one of the Buddha's collar-bones. The author of the *Mahāvansa* describes the public ceremonies with which the holy relic was received. It was deposited on the top of the Missaka hill, which henceforth took the name of Chetiya, and on this occasion the king's youngest brother, Mattābhaya, received holy orders, at the same time as several thousand persons.

All these ceremonies, however magnificent they might be, were, however, nothing in comparison to those which greeted the sacred branch of the Bodhi tree, under which the Tathāgata had become the supreme and perfect Buddha. The king Dharmāṣoka insisted on cutting it with his own hand at Bodhimanda; he himself placed it on the ship that was to take it down the Ganges, and he accompanied it as far as the place of embarkation at Tāmralipti. He shed copious tears on parting with it, and confided it to the care of his daughter Sanghamittā, who was going to Sinhala with eleven nuns; for though Mahinda could ordain priests, the law only permitted a woman to ordain priestesses or nuns.

Mahānāma, in relating the miraculous voyage of the branch of the Bodhidruma, changes the usually simple style of his narrative and becomes almost lyric.

'The vessel on which the branch of the Bodhi was shipped, rapidly cleft the billows, and at the distance of

[1] The author of the *Mahāvansa* indicates with the greatest precision, as a man well acquainted with the country, all the different places through which the royal furrow passed. These details, as well as many others given by Mahānāma, are very valuable with regard to the ancient geography of Ceylon. Burnouf intended making use of them.

a yojana, the waves of the great Ocean smoothed down before it. Flowers of five different colours blossomed around it, and the sweetest strains of music filled the air with melody. Innumerable offerings were brought by innumerable deities, while the Nāgas in vain had recourse to their magic power, to steal the divine tree.'

Sanghamittā, the High Priestess, frustrated their evil designs by the power of her sanctity, and the ship bearing this incomparable relic soon arrived at Jambūkola. Everything had been got ready on the shores to receive it with all the veneration it deserved. When the vessel came in sight, the king dashed into the sea, and, advancing till the water was up to his neck, he began a joyful and pious chant in honour of the Buddha. He then had the case in which the tree was put carried by sixteen persons of sixteen different castes, who deposited it in a magnificent hall prepared for it. He invested the sacred branch with the sovereignty of Lankā, and himself, for three days and three nights, stood as sentinel at the door of the hall offering it rich presents.

Imagination can follow the triumphal march of the branch from the Vihāra of Pāchina, where it had first been handed over to the priests, to Anurādhapura the capital, where it only arrived on the fourteenth day; 'at the hour when the shadows are longest.' At sunrise, it was carried in by the northern gates of the city, through which it was borne in procession, and it was taken out by the southern gate to be conveyed to the beautiful garden of Mahāmegha, where it was to be planted. Sixteen princes clad in the most brilliant garments stood ready to receive it; but the branch, breaking loose from the hands of men, suddenly rose in the air, where it remained before the astonished gaze of the crowd, lighted up by a halo of six luminous rays. It came down again at sunset, and planted itself in the soil, and for seven days a protecting cloud shaded it and watered it with salutary rain. Fruit grew on it in an instant, and the king was able to propagate throughout the island the marvellous tree, the Bodhi, the promise of eternal salvation.

Mahānāma, relates all these miracles and many others besides, without the slightest hesitation or criticism, and he gives them as occurring in the eighteenth year of Dharmāṣoka's reign.

What is more real is the piety of Devānam-Pīya-Tissa, which is shown by the vast and numerous monuments which he erected in all the parts of the island which were under his rule, and like him converted to the true faith. Mahānāma mentions these edifices one after the other; and it is probable that if researches were made, traces would still be found, for this historian's indications are sufficiently precise to ensure a favourable result. The Sinhalese monarch began these constructions with his reign, and for forty years he unceasingly continued them.

As this king died without children, one of his younger brothers, called Uttiya, succeeded him. The great Mahinda lived eight years under the new reign, and was able to consolidate the work of conversion he had so auspiciously undertaken. Living in retreat on the Hill of the relics (*Chetiya pabbata*), he was the spiritual governor of the kingdom, 'ruling over numerous disciples, directing the Church he had founded, fortifying the people by his teaching, which was similar to that of the Tathāgata himself, and delivering Lankā from the ignorance of sin.' At his death, he was given a splendid funeral; the king, overcome with grief, went himself to fetch the body, and bringing it back in the midst of the lamentations of the people, deposited it in the Mahā-Vihāra, consecrating there a chapel to his memory which was henceforth called Ambamālaka. After seven days of mourning and offerings, the body was burned; and the relics of the High Priest were divided, some of them being placed in a stūpa raised on the very spot, and the remainder being sent to the principal convents of Sinhala. As for the High Priestess Sanghamittā, she only survived her brother Mahinda one year, and at her death she received the same honours as had been bestowed on him. Such is, according to the *Mahāvansa*, the account of the conversion of Ceylon to Buddhism. Putting aside the fables created by superstition, there is nothing in this narrative that cannot be accepted. Whatever may have been the relations between Buddhic India and Sinhala before the reign of Devānam-Pīya-Tissa, it is evident that before that epoch Buddhism was not established in the island. It was the great Aṣoka, Protector of the faith, the powerful monarch who ruled over the whole of India, who converted Ceylon to the new faith. He introduced it by the peaceful means of preaching, and it was from Magadha that the apostles from whom Lankā received the Word had come. Relics of the Buddha were sent to Sinhala; and the ambassadors who conveyed them were at the same time propagators of the faith. These important events took place, according to the native chronology, about the year 300 B.C.

The introduction of Buddhism into Sinhala, did not however ensure peace, for during the reigns that followed that of Uttiya, the country was a constant prey to the invasions of the Tamils who came from the neighbouring coasts of India, or to civil wars among the different parties who contended for supremacy. One of the most celebrated kings of that time was Dushṭa-Gāmini, who reigned from the year 161 to the year 137 before Christ. He drove out the Tamils, with the help of five hundred priests who were incorporated in his army, and restored to the worship of the Buddha the same magnificence as in the days of Devānam-Pīya-Tissa and Uttiya. He built the Mahā-Stūpa, the largest of all the stūpas in Ceylon, as its name indicates. It was an enormous brick building, the ruins of which can still be seen near Anurādhapura; and at the solemn inauguration that took plàce in the year 157 B.C., admirable paintings were exhibited to the public gaze on which the Jatakas or successive births of the Buddha were represented. The Mahā-Stūpa was only finished under the reign of Saddhā-Tissa, a brother of Dushṭa-Gāmini; his own son, Sāli, having preferred to renounce his rights to the throne, sooner than give up a Chandali woman, whom he had made his wife.

Besides external and intestine wars, there were at times religious dissensions. The Mahā-Vihāra of Anurādhapura, which should have been the centre of orthodoxy, had seen its authority weakened by many schisms; and the convent of Abhayāgiri became almost its equal. A monarch of the name of Waṭṭa-Gāmini protected the schismatics, and it was to them he entrusted all the alms he distributed to his people. Under this prince's reign, in the year 89 B.C. the sacred texts of the *Pitakāttaya* (Pāli, the three Baskets), which till then had been orally preserved by the priests, as well as the orthodox commentary on the *Atthakathā*, were for the first time put into writing. This precaution appeared indispensable, in order that false doctrines should not, by the perversity of the people, stifle the true religion. Nevertheless, heresies continued to harass the faith, just as the invasions of the Tamils devastated the country, and three centuries elapsed before a king reigned who restored peace in Sinhala. This was the king Tissa, surnamed Vohārakarajā, because to him belongs the honour of abolishing torture, which cruel practice had existed in Ceylon from time immemorial. Full of generosity towards the priests, he paid off the debts due by the convents, which were heavily involved; he even did more, for he actively supported the orthodoxy of the Mahā-Vihāra, against the Vetulliya heresy professed in the convent of Abhayāgiri.

Under the reign of one of his successors, called Mahāsena, from 275 to 302 of the Christian era, it was, on the contrary, heresy that prevailed, and the monks of Abhayāgiri, gaining the king to their cause, had the Mahā-Vihāra, the home of their adversaries, destroyed. The cast out priests took refuge at Malaya, in the province of Rohana, and remained there in banishment for nine years. The Mahā-Vihāra was completely destroyed, and its most valuable contents taken to Abhayāgiri, which seemed to have gained a definitive victory. However, one of the king's ministers rose up in favour of the exiles, and the principal agent of the persecution, Sanghamittā, having been assassinated by a woman, the priests of the Mahā-Vihāra were recalled; their convent was rebuilt, and although they were not certain of enjoying lasting protection, they were able to re-establish religious worship according to their own rules. Moreover, Mahāsena, notwithstanding the mobility of his religious sentiments, seems to have been an enlightened and benevolent king; history has kept a record of his great works of public utility: sixteen fountains and a great canal called Pabbata which he had opened.

With Mahāsena's reign, the year 302 of the Christian era, the *Mahāvansa* ends. The work was continued, as we have already mentioned, under the name of *Suluvansa*, down to the middle of the last century. The son of Mahāsena, Sirimeghavarma, strove to retrieve his father's impiety, and in the ninth year of his reign (310 B.C.) the famous tooth of the Buddha (*Dāthādhātu*), hitherto kept at Dantapura, was brought to Ceylon by a Brahman princess. The relic was deposited in the temple of Dhammachakka, and soon became the object of popular enthusiasm and veneration.[1]

[1] The history of the Buddha's tooth is certainly one of the most curious among all the Buddhist superstitions. It has been the subject of a special work, the *Dāthādhātvansa*, which still exists, and which, written

It is not necessary to allude further to the history of Ceylon, nevertheless we must just mention, to the honour of the Buddhist faith, the reign of Buddhadasa, from the year 339 to 368 of the Christian era, who was also a great doctor, and who wrote in the Sanskrit language books that are still referred to at the present day. This benevolent king also founded a number of hospitals, and established a doctor for each district of ten villages. To this period must be attributed the translation of the Pāli Sūtras into Sinhalese.

Finally, it must be remembered that in the year 420 the Sinhalese *Atthakathā* was retranslated into Pāli by the celebrated Brahman Buddhaghosa. The *Atthakathā*, or commentary on the sacred books, had been translated from Pāli into Sinhalese by Mahinda; but in course of time the original Pāli had disappeared, and the unity of the orthodox texts suffered from this serious omission. Buddhaghosa was appointed to repair it. But the priests of the Mahā-Vihāra of Anurādhapura, to whom he applied, took the wisest precautions to be assured against any deception on his part. They first gave him to translate, as a test, two Gāthās, of which they had the authentic text in Pāli, and which Buddhaghosa was to translate from Sinhalese into Pāli. This translation was examined three times by the college of priests, and as Buddhaghosa honourably sustained this minute scrutiny, the priests no longer hesitated to confide to him the *Pitakattaya* and the *Atthakathā*. He thereupon retired to the vihāra of Ganthākara at Anurādhapura, and translated the whole of the Sinhalese *Atthakathā* into Pāli, 'according to the grammatical rules of the Magadha language, the root of all languages.' Buddhaghosa's version is still in use at the

century after century, was continued down to the middle of the last century. The tooth, after many peregrinations, was deposited in the Temple of Māligāwa at Kandy, and in 1847 Turnour had it in his own keeping as representative of the English government.

present time. As for him, after having finished this difficult work to the great satisfaction of the priests, he returned to Magadha, whence he had come, and lived there to a very advanced age.

It will be seen that the Buddhist priests of the fifth century were more fortunate, or rather more prudent, than Sir Alexander Johnston was in our day.

Such is the series of events related in the first volume of the *Mahāvansa*, which has been given to us by Turnour. The end of the work would be, in other respects, no less interesting; but although twenty years have elapsed since the first volume was published, it has not yet made its appearance. The style of this singular history is what might be expected: extremely simple, devoid of affectation, and generally sufficiently clear. The use of verse is not surprising in annals that aim at preserving an edifying recollection of the past. The verses of the *Mahāvansa* are more like rhymed prose than what is generally considered poetry. The Pāli language is as supple as Sanskrit, and in these flexible idioms everything can be written in verse, from grammars and dictionaries down to philosophical systems. The metre, with its precise and strict rules, is but a means of assisting the memory and ensuring the authentic preservation of the texts.

As to the talent of the historian, properly called, it may be judged by the preceding analysis. Mahānāma was an annalist, and nothing more. History, exact, austere, and searching, such as we understand it, did not suit these races; and the *Mahāvansa*, important as it is—although a masterpiece of Indian talent—is no exception to the rule. Sometimes the author tries to rise above his subject and draw some nobler lessons from the facts he relates. But the trivial and uniform reflexions on the instability of human things and the imperturbable power of the faith that recur at the end of each chapter, do not endow Mahānāma with the characteristics of a true historian. They merely show most excellent intentions; but he does not succeed in making his history a teaching, whatever pains he may have taken to do so. It is a recapitulation of absurd legends which he never criticizes, and an injudicious compendium of real events which are neither sufficiently understood nor sufficiently explained.

The extensive chronology contained in the *Mahāvansa* imparts to it its special value. Chronology is valuable everywhere, but infinitely more in India than elsewhere, as it is most scarce in that country. Mahānāma's system was very simple. He begins from the death of the Buddha, just as we begin from the birth of Christ. Nothing could be clearer than this mode of reckoning; and as the *Mahāvansa*, through subsequent writings, is continued and carried on till the middle of the last century, it is easy, with all the indications that are to be found in it, to trace back the course of time, and to attain, for the history of Ceylon, a preciseness that the history of India has never had. In this manner Turnour was able to re-establish, from the date of the Nirvāna and the landing of Vijaya at Tambapanni, the whole chronology of the Sinhalese kings down to the year 1798, when the last native king, Sri Vikrama Rājasingh, was dethroned by the English and died in captivity. Turnour was able to write this most useful work by referring entirely to reliable documents, without admitting conjectures; he had only consulted the native annals, and had found all the necessary materials in abundance.

CHAPTER II.

Actual condition of the Buddhist clergy in Ceylon, as described by the Rev. Spence Hardy, Wesleyan missionary. The novitiate; the ordination; letter from the Burmese high priest. Wealth of the Sinhalese clergy. Individual poverty of the priests; their austerity. The Canonical sacred writings in Ceylon. Public reading of the Bana (the Word). Festival at Pantura in 1839. The Upāsakas; the Pirit or ceremony of exorcism. The Bhāvanā or meditation; supernatural powers conferred by it. Meritorious acts (Sachakiriyas) and their miraculous influence. Nirvāna according to Sinhalese priests; their ardent faith; their spirit of tolerance; care bestowed on the education of children. Medical knowledge of the clergy; subordination of the clergy to the ruling powers. Division of Sinhalese clergy into sects. Relations of Sinhalese Buddhism with Christianity. Progress of Catholicism and education under the English rule. Statistics of Ceylon.

WE will now leave the past in order to study the actual condition of Buddhism in Ceylon, and we shall take our information more particularly from the writings of the Rev. Spence Hardy, aided by a few details gathered from other sources. Spence Hardy resided twenty years in Ceylon as a Wesleyan missionary (1825–1845). In the exercise of his sacred ministry he was thrown into constant intercourse with the natives, whom he strove to instruct and console. Full of zeal for his calling, he fulfilled his duties with a fervour that is testified by the two works he has published on Buddhism. As soon as he reached Ceylon he began the study of the language, in order to acquaint himself thoroughly with a religion which it was his ambition to supplant by a better one, and he never ceased the pursuing of the studies he had so energetically begun. He wished more particularly to be of use to the missionaries who should succeed him, and it was with this practical object in view that he wrote his two books, *Eastern Monachism* and *The Manual of Buddhism*.

The English missionaries must decide if Spence Hardy succeeded in carrying out his purpose, and if these two works have really assisted them in their struggle against the deplorable superstitions which they are striving to replace by the Christian faith. But it would perhaps have been preferable had Spence Hardy confined his labours to the present condition of Buddhism in Ceylon, and not undertaken such a very extensive work.

The history of Eastern Monachism is an extensive subject, and we have not at present sufficient materials to treat it properly. Spence Hardy only saw the monks, or rather Buddhist priests, in Ceylon. Buddhism, however, has spread to many other countries; it extends from Kashmir to the eastern frontiers of China, and from Ceylon to the north of Tibet. What a variety of countries, races, climates, languages, and beliefs! And who can pertinently say, in the present state of information, what Buddhism really consists in for each of these people? It is not granted to every one to reside twenty years in Ceylon, and Spence Hardy might have seized the opportunity of giving a monography, every detail of which would have been valuable, because each one would have been unimpeachably exact. A study limited to Sinhalese Buddhism in its present condition would have been of the greatest value and utility; for southern Buddhism has been concentrated in Ceylon, just as northern Buddhism was concentrated in Nepaul.

It is all the more to be regretted that Spence Hardy did not adopt this method, inasmuch that he seems to have thought of it himself, and to have been aware of the great value such a work would have possessed; for he says in his preface that in the present state of our knowledge on Buddhism, the authentic translations drawn from contemporary dialects may be very useful, as they reveal the sentiments and habits of the priests of the present time. He adds that the writings of the Sinhalese authors abound in Pāli quotations, of which language they possessed a thorough knowledge; and as in their eyes the books they translated or paraphrased are sacred writings, it may be supposed that their works give an exact idea of the original ones.

It appears that in Ceylon the novitiate of the priests is more strict than in other Buddhist countries. The novices, who in Sinhalese are called *Ganinnanses* or associates, are compelled to reside in the convent in which they receive their instruction. In other countries the rule is less exacting, and the novice may remain with his family, provided he goes as often as possible to receive the lessons of his spiritual teacher. In Ceylon, on the contrary, residence in the convent is an imperative condition, for the novice is considered a priest, and as such is subject to the same rules. Nevertheless the novice is free to choose the monastery or vihāra he desires to be attached to, and Sinhalese books have been expressly written to guide the young priest in his choice.

When he has decided, after long and minute self-examination, he states his intentions to a priest, taking with him a robe, which he must receive back from his hands, in order to begin his novitiate under this new garb. He then humbly asks his superior to pronounce over him the threefold Buddhist formulas (*tunsarana*), that is the threefold Refuges: 'I go for refuge to the Buddha, I go for refuge to the Law; I go for refuge to the Order,' the novice repeating the sacred formula after the priest; he then recites the *Dasa-sil* or Ten Precepts, which may be called the Novice's Decalogue:

'I take the vow not to destroy life; I take the vow not to steal; I take the vow to abstain from impurity; I take the vow not to lie; I take the vow to abstain from intoxicating drinks, which hinder progress and virtue; I take the vow not to eat at forbidden times; I take the vow to abstain from dancing, singing, music, and stage plays; I take the vow not to use garlands, scents, unguents or ornaments; I take the vow not to use a high or broad bed; I take the vow not to receive gold or silver.'

After pronouncing these vows, the novice enters the convent and daily fulfils his humble and laborious tasks. A manual, called the *Dina chariyāwa*, Daily Occupations of the Priest, minutely establishes the rules, from which he must not deviate. He must rise before daylight and wash (his first duty is to wash his teeth); then sweep the yard of the vihāra and round the Bo-tree; fetch the drinking water for the day, filter it, and place it ready for use. These first duties fulfilled, he is to retire to a solitary place and meditate for an hour on the rules he has obeyed and those that are to follow.

When the vihāra bell rings to announce the moment of the sacrifice, he must approach the stūpa in which the relics are enshrined, or the Bo-tree, and offer whatever flowers he has been able to procure, as though the Buddha were present in person. He must especially meditate on the great virtues of the Tathāgata, and beg the holy relics to absolve him of all the negligences and faults he may have committed. He must remain some moments prostrate worshipping, with his forehead, knees, and elbows touching the ground. He will consult his *Lita* or calendar, in order to know by the length of the shadows what hour it is, the age of the moon, and the number of years elapsed since the death of the Buddha. He must again meditate for a short time on the beneficial results of obedience to the regulations, and the unappreciable advantages of wearing the yellow robe. Soon after, taking the begging-bowl he must follow his superior in his daily round for food, taking care to remain at a proper distance from him, and hand him the bowl when they approach a village. On reaching it, the novice must cast down his eyes with the greatest care so as to avoid the sight of women, men, elephants, horses, chariots and soldiers. When the alms-bowl has been filled by the charity of the faithful, the novice takes back the bowl from his superior, who hands him also his upper garment, and both return to the vihāra.

The young man must then offer a seat to his master, wash his feet, and place the food before him; he can only partake of it himself after him, and must repeat certain sacramental stanzas before and after eating. He must then wash the alms-bowl and place it in the sun to dry before putting it away. After the meal is over he washes his face, and putting on his robe, silently worships the Buddha and his superior. He may then retire to a solitary place and again search his heart and give himself up to the exercise of the *Metta-bhāvanā*, or the Meditation on Kindness and Affection. About an hour afterwards he is to begin his studies from the sacred books, or copy one of them, asking his superior's assistance for any passages he does not understand. He then lights a fire and a lamp, and prepares everything for the reading of the *Bana*, or the Canon; he calls the priest who is to recite it, washes his feet, and sits down in the attitude prescribed for listening to the sacred readings, which finish by a recitation of the *Pirit* or exorcism used by priests. If after all these duties he still has a few moments' leisure before sunset, the novice is again to sweep the sacred places as he did in the early morning.

Such are the vows and regular occupations of the Sinhalese novices.

The layman who wishes for entrance to the Order must be at least eight years old before obtaining the novitiate, and at least twenty before receiving full initiation (ordination, *upasampadā*). The novitiate lasts about ten years; the parents' consent is absolutely necessary; and it would not seem that the spirit of proselytism leads the Ceylon priest to infringe this rule. The vocation declares itself in the schools which are kept by priests, and at a very early age the children who will be disposed to take orders show their inclination. Moreover, the vows are not irrevocable; and abjuration, although rare, is not impossible, nor is it considered a dishonour. It is simply regarded as a confession of weakness, which in its sincerity is creditable. The holy life is renounced because the monk feels himself incapable of loyally fulfilling its severe regulations. But in the majority of cases the novice steadfastly believes in the advantages of a religious life, and does not think of deserting it. He is taught that it delivers him from many evils, and ensures him the following benefits: he is delivered from the desire for riches and pleasure (*vastukama, klesakama*); he is sure of having food; he learns to be satisfied with whatever he is given; he fears neither the oppression of the wicked nor of kings; he is saved from all the anxiety entailed by the possession of land, horses, cattle, &c.; he need not fear robbers nor officials; he need not even rise at their approach; in one word, he is delivered from every sort of fear.

Doubtless these benefits are of a negative kind, but they are sufficient, with the hope of Nirvāna, to attract novices; and hitherto the Buddhist clergy of Ceylon has been easily recruited, although it is at present less numerous than in former days, when Hiouen-Thsang states the number of monks to have been six thousand. Discipline, moreover, is vigilantly maintained, and we will quote a document that proves how well the Ceylon priests understand the importance of the novitiate; this is a letter from the Burmese high priest (*Sangharāja*) in answer to the appeal of the Sinhalese priests for advice. It is dated in the year 1802.

'As it is erroneously believed,' the high priest writes, 'that certain regulations were not made for novices, and were only obligatory for priests who have received ordination, I will recall to you the following passage of the Commentary on the *Mahā-Vagga*, in order to show you what little ground there is for such an opinion. "As long as a monk," says this Commentary, "is ignorant of the details of the discipline he should follow, as long as he does not know how to put on his robes, or present the alms-bowl, or when to stand and when to sit down, or how to eat or drink according to the prescribed rules, he must not be sent into the houses where food is indiscriminately given to the priests, nor to places where it is distributed each day to some chosen priests. He must not either be sent into the forest or to any public assembly. But he must remain with some older priests, who shall instruct him like a child; he must be carefully taught what is and what is not permitted; each day he must be shown how to arrange his robe and wear it; and he should have explained to him all the parts of the discipline that he must observe." '

This instruction (*sandeṣa*) given by the Burmese high priest proves that the discipline of the novices in Ceylon had been relaxed at the beginning of this century, and that the need to re-establish it had been felt.

When the novice is sufficiently instructed, and he has attained the proper age, he then receives the ordination which is to make him a priest for the remainder of his life. The rules of ordination are very simple, and are contained in a little work called *Kammavacham*, which has been translated into Sinhalese; the following are the chief points. On the day appointed a chapter (*sangha*) is held of not less than four priests. The candidate is introduced, and is asked if the special things pertaining to a monk—the alms-bowl, robes, &c., which have been placed before the assembly—are his. On his reply in the affirmative he is shown the place where he must stand during his examination. He is first asked if he is free from any of the disqualifying diseases—leprosy, epilepsy, &c. Secondly, if he is a human being, a man, and a free man—a slave not being able to take orders without the consent of his master; if he has any debts; if he is exempt from the king's service; if he has the consent of his parents; if he is twenty years of age;—in one word, if he has all the conditions requisite for priesthood.

When these points have been settled, the president bids the novice advance in front of the assembled monks, and the novice, coming forward, says three times in a respectful voice, 'I ask the chapter for ordination' (*upasampadā*). The president declares that the novice is free from all that might hinder his admission, that he possesses all that a priest should possess, and that he asks for *upasampadā*. Then he repeats three times, 'Let those who are of opinion to grant this request remain silent, and he who opposes it declare so at once.' If the chapter silently consents to the candidate's admission, the president reminds the novice of some of the rules that he will henceforth have to submit to till the end of his life, such as the food he may receive, the clothes he may wear, the medicines he is permitted to use in case of illness, and the crimes which would cause his exclusion from the community. After this consecration, the newly-elected member declares that he submits to this law, without however taking a vow of obedience or making any kind of promise. From this moment the novice becomes a priest, and the Buddhist confraternity counts another member.

It often happens that a novice, presenting himself before the chapter for his examination, puts off the robes and resumes a layman's clothes, in order to put on with more solemnity the new robe, which shows the people his sacred calling. Sometimes he is accompanied to the place of ordination by his family, his friends, and by a crowd who carry banners in honour of the festivity. Sometimes, indeed, kings have mingled with the procession through the streets of Kandy, when the candidate was deemed worthy of such honour, either by his parentage or his virtues. At the present day the ordinations are only made in the capital by the hands of the Mahā-Nāyaka or the Anu-Nāyaka, that is the Director-General or the Assistant Director. But it appears that this is an innovation, and Spence Hardy remarks that this is a change similar to that which formerly transferred from the clerical community to the bishops alone the right of ordination.

Although the *upasampadā* does not confer an indelible character, it is extremely rare in Ceylon that the yellow robe is abandoned for a return to the world. This is sure evidence of the ardour of the Sinhalese faith. There are, however, Buddhist countries in which it is almost a sport to take or leave holy orders. In those countries there is hardly a single person who has not, at least once in his life, been a monk for a longer or shorter period; it is like a pious retreat taken on trial, but in which there is no wish to remain permanently. In Siam it is the custom every year, in the month of Asārha, for the king to cast aside his royal garments, shave his head, and assume the yellow robe of the novice, in order to do penance, with his whole court, in one of the most celebrated vihāras. The most devout monarchs carry their piety even a step further, for they bring in their retinue slaves they are supposed to have converted, whom they cause to be shaved and ordained as priests. It appears that in the kingdom of Ava the same practices are allowed. Doubtless they fancy they are performing an act of sincere piety, but at the same time they lower the respect which ought to be felt for the clerical character; and in Burmah it is a frequent thing for married people who wish to be divorced to become priests for a few months, in order afterwards to be able to marry again.

In Ceylon, ordination is a solemn act, and no one takes orders unless he has the firm intention of remaining faithful to them. This fact is an honour to Sinhalese piety, and Spence Hardy ascertained that such was really the case.

Another point which was easy to verify, and on which the author was able to obtain thorough information, is the great wealth possessed by the Sinhalese clergy. The vow of poverty is generally strictly observed, and, like in the first centuries of Buddhism, the monks only possess the eight following articles : three robes of different shapes, a girdle for the loins, an alms-bowl in clay or iron (*patāra*), a razor—complete tonsure being obligatory—a needle to mend their clothes, and a water-strainer through which they have to strain all they drink (*perahankada*). No individual monk is permitted to possess anything beyond these indispensable articles. But the community may be wealthy without disobeying the law, and in Ceylon they are extremely rich. In an inscription engraved on a rock at Mihintale, near Anurādhapura, which dates from the year 262 of our era, it is specified that the lands given to the vihāra are to remain the undivided property of the priests; that regular accounts are to be kept by special officers of the revenues of the temple, and that these accounts are to be made up at the end of every month, and must at the end of each year be presented to a chapter of priests appointed to verify and audit them, &c., &c.

It has always been held a principle in Ceylon, as well as in India, that the whole territory belongs to the monarch; but in practice this principle has had very numerous exceptions, and from the earliest times the temples and even individuals have possessed land. It is very probable that at first the royal donations were the reward of signal services rendered to the person of the king or to the state, and that in course of time these properties, which had become hereditary, were given to the vihāras to avoid taxation, and held on leases by the former landlords. When the kings made these generous donations to the temples, they were careful to impose on the cultivators of the soil certain obligations towards the priests.

A multitude of inscriptions attest this, besides the one at Mihintale. The lands thus granted ceased to be liable for any service to the king, and the services originally due to him were transferred to the temple. The Sinhalese clergy had thus become extremely wealthy, and as the personal maintenance of the monks, reduced to the strict limits above mentioned, cost very little, the community was benefited by all the favours and all the savings.

'When I passed,' Spence Hardy says, 'in travelling through the interior of Ceylon, before landscapes that would justify the legend which makes out this island to be the earthly paradise, and I noticed lands that were exceptionally fertile, I almost always found on inquiry that they were the property of the priests.'

Robert Knox, in the interesting narrative of his long captivity in Ceylon, made the same remark.[1] The enormous extent of the sacerdotal lands and the wealth of the convents had also struck him. The farmers of the vihāras were the most prosperous in the island; the priests demanded moderate rentals, and their estates were admirably cultivated by men who made good profits. The revenues were used to keep up the vihāras, temples, and stūpas, as well as to provide for the expenses of the worship and the pay of the numerous officials attached to each community.

In an official report made by Lieutenant-Colonel Colebrooke, one of the commissioners appointed in 1831, we find the following passage: 'The estates belonging to the temples consist of the largest tracts of cultivated land in the provinces of Kandy. In several of the temples and colleges, registers are kept of the land that belongs to them; but as these registers have not been examined, it has not been possible

[1] Robert Knox's curious narrative has been republished several times, and shows the internal condition of Ceylon in the last half of the seventeenth century; he was a prisoner there from 1659 to 1680.

to ascertain exactly what they contain. At my request the registers of the principal temples of Kandy have been translated, and it has been proved that the tenants and possessors of what are called the temple estates are in many provinces subject to different kinds of servitudes and contributions, whenever they may be demanded by the priests. These stipulations are minutely detailed in the registers, and the tenant farmer of each allotment has either a particular duty to fulfil, or he is bound to pay a particular tax, either for the repairs of the temple, or the maintenance of the chiefs and the priests and their officials, or for the great festivals of the year.'

It may with good reason be thought that there is a vast difference between the wealth and prosperity of these temples and the primitive institution of the Buddha, so simple and so scrupulously attached to poverty.

Nevertheless, the Sinhalese priesthood has remained faithful to its vows of poverty, and observed all the rules, precise even to puerility, with a perseverance which for twenty centuries has never been relaxed. The Buddhist priest absolutely declines to be fed except by the alms he receives. He goes from house to house in the neighbouring town or village to present his alms-bowl. He may not utter a word to express a wish, or point out any food he may by chance have seen; and he must always keep his eyes downcast, gazing fixedly before him 'at the distance of a yoke.'

The canonical books prescribe with the greatest care all the details regarding mendicity, the *Vinyapti*. The monk on approaching a house, begging-bowl in hand, must not make any sign or sound that might warn the inhabitants of his presence. If he is not seen, or if nothing is given him, he must pass on in silence without a gesture or word of reproach, otherwise he would commit a grievous sin. Some houses, where his virtue or reputation might be endangered, the priest is ordered to avoid; but he is on no account to pass by any on the pretext of its poverty. He must not remain a long time before a house so as to become importunate, nor must he present himself more than three times in a place where nothing has been given him. When the bowl is full, the monk retires home and eats in solitude the food he has been given, whatever it may be.

According to Spence Hardy, the Sinhalese monks still observe all these practices, which have lost none of their severity; the only difference they make is that they avoid begging at the houses and in the districts of the poorer castes, such as the washermen and the mat-makers.

It cannot be denied that the founder of Buddhism showed great wisdom in imposing upon his monks absolute silence and perfect resignation during the collection of the alms, which he made their only source of supply, for he thereby ensured a long existence to this singular institution. Other founders of mendicant orders have not had the same foresight, or perhaps had less ascendency over their adepts, and the result has been that society soon became weary of the intolerable importunity of the monks. Moreover, the Buddha made alms-giving one of the principal virtues he commended to the faithful, and none other holds such a place in the Buddhist legends, by the self-denial it demands, and especially by the incomparable results it produced on those who practised it. Alms, when taken from personal gains, are particularly meritorious, and it is related that a devout king of Ceylon used to work in the fields, like a common labourer, in order to give the portion of rice he received as salary to a venerable priest. It is even added that he remained three consecutive years on a sugar-cane plantation so as to offer to the priests all the sugar he received as wages. He thus gave alms by the sweat of his brow instead of simply drawing it from his royal treasury. It is also related that the parents of the famous king Dushṭa-Gāmini had made him take an oath in his childhood, that he would never eat a repast without first putting aside, from his own food, a share for the priests. The king faithfully kept his word, but in a moment of absent-mindedness, having neglected this duty, he performed penance, and built a stūpa and a vihāra, in expiation of his involuntary fault.

If by some unfortunate misadventure the priest received no food at all, what was he to do? Was he bound to die of hunger? This question has not been laid down in such precise terms by Buddhic law, but everything goes to prove that it would unhesitatingly enforce this extreme measure. On no pretext must the mendicant speak; on no pretext must he break the rule which enjoins on him to live solely on what is given him. If death be the consequence of this submission to the Law, it matters not, and Buddhism generally fears death too little to be stopped by such a consideration, which in such a case would only be regarded as a merit[1]. The minutiæ of the discipline as regards diet are as strict as on any other point, and when so many precautions are taken in order that food may not become the occasion of sin, it is tantamount to a prohibition of all food that does not exactly conform with the unchangeable prescriptions of the Law.

These prescriptions are no less numerous or imperative as regards the monks' clothing. The monk has three robes, formed of two undergarments—the *antāra-vāsaka* and the *sanghāṭi*—and one loose robe which covers the whole of his body, except the right shoulder, called the *uttarāsanga*. He

[1] The legends quote a good many examples calculated to stimulate the piety of the monks. One of the Buddha's disciples refuses a remedy that will cure him, because the medicine had been prepared from directions he had given with another intention, and that he might have seemed to have asked for. Another monk, sooner than eat fruit fallen from a tree, which the proprietor had not given him, runs the risk of dying of hunger. During a famine, the Buddha's disciples are reduced to feeding on horses' oats, and the Tathāgata does not allow them to use their supernatural powers to procure more suitable food.

can never dispose of them, and if in any pressing circumstance—a danger for instance—he has been obliged to leave one of his robes in the village, it must not be left there more than six days, unless by special permission. When a robe has been lost or stolen, or is worn out, the monk has not the right to demand another. If the king or any high personage gives money to buy a robe, the priest cannot take the money, which must be handed over to a third person for the purchase of the robe. If the intermediate agent is dishonest, and does not give the robe, the priest must not exact it; all he can do is to warn the pious giver who has advanced the money. The proper time for offering new robes is at the end of the rainy season, and the monk cannot accept them earlier than ten days before the end of the Varsha (the retreat in the vihāras during the rainy season). If, by chance, a monk should have received a robe outside of the prescribed time, he must bring it back to the chapter, who dispose of it in favour of another priest. The robes must be of common cotton cloth, for nothing can be too simple for the mendicant; if the garments are new, they must be soiled with mud and dust before being worn; the more strict monks only wear rags picked up in the graveyards.

In Ceylon, the month that follows the Varsha, or rainy season, is called the robing month (*Chīvaramasa*). At this epoch the faithful offer the priests pieces of cotton cloth called *katina*. The chapter receive the gifts; and a robe is granted to the monk who seems to have the most urgent need of it, or rather to the priest who, during the Varsha, has read and commented on the canonical books to his brethren. The chapter, assisted by a few laymen, sew the robe together, and dye it a dull orange colour; these preparations must be done in a day, or sixty hours, according to the way the natives reckon time.

On certain occasions, the cotton material is itself woven under the eyes of the chapter. The hall in which the *Bana* has been read is filled with women seated on the floor, who bring cotton, just as they have taken it from the tree; other women draw it from its capsules, and prepare it for the spinners, who convert it into thread. The thread is given to weavers, who await out of doors with their hand-looms, and who hurriedly weave a cloth. The same evening, the priests receive it, and sew it into a robe, which they dye the desired colour; this is always a dull orange colour. However, in spite of this uniformity, there are still slight differences, according to the taste of the monks; and Spence Hardy knew an old priest who wore, with a certain degree of pride, a handsome silk robe that had been sent him by a Siamese king. Moreover the monks never change their robes for any ceremonial; they are taken off only when they leave the community; and this was the reason why a priest, who in 1818 was executed as a rebel, underwent his sentence clothed in his sacerdotal garments. He could only be deprived of them if he had demanded it, otherwise it would have been a dreadful outrage which foreigners had no right to inflict on him; they could kill him, but not degrade him.

Although the law of the Buddha did not make it an absolute rule for monks to live in solitude, or, as is said, 'in the forest,' yet there are many priests who build themselves a shelter far from towns and villages, in which they habitually reside. In Ceylon, the vihāra, which was at first intended to receive the monks during the rainy seasons, became by degrees a regular temple, and ceased to be a convent. Generally the huts of the Sinhalese priests are made of light partitions, filled in with mud, the roofs being thatched with straw or coconut leaves. There are rules describing the dimensions of these pitiable shelters, the length of which must not exceed twelve empans, and the width seven. The anchorite may only take possession of it when the chapter has ascertained if the hut is not larger than is deemed necessary. The priest has, however, been free to choose the spot; and if he has chosen well, he will have little cause to fear either insects, or serpents, or wild beasts. If he wishes strictly to observe the rule he will never leave the forest, except to beg his food from some neighbouring town, from which his hut must be distant at least 500 bows, or within range of a stone thrown by a strong arm. The priest who is a less rigid observer of the Law, resides during the four months of the Varsha in a village; some still less strict spend the four hot months as well as the Varsha in a town. Moreover there are as minute directions, in the Buddhic code of discipline, about the residence of the monks, as there are about mendicity and clothing. Certain priests live only in graveyards, or rather they spend their nights there, and only leave them before sunrise to go and beg their daily bread. In Ceylon, these austerities do not, it would seem, add to their reputation; Spence Hardy saw in 1835, near Nigombo, a priest who professed never to have inhabited a house, and who lived exclusively on fruit. His singular appearance and mysterious existence made him a terror to children, and sensible people looked upon him as a madman.

The Sinhalese priests are never seen without an alms-bowl or a fan in their hands; this latter they hold before their eyes, to avoid seeing anything that might offend their sight. They are generally followed by a servant, who, in the language of the country, is called *abittaya.*

At the present day there are no priestesses in Ceylon, as there are in Burmah, Siam, in the kingdom of Arrakan, and even in China. The Buddha had most reluctantly consented to ordain nuns; and this institution, of which in his prudence he had foreseen all the objections, had never prospered. In

Ceylon, Sanghamittā's and Anulā's example had not been followed; and it is probable that, from the earliest period, the Sinhalese women gave up all idea of becoming nuns. Robert Knox mentions a custom that existed in his day, and which has since fallen into disuse: at certain times of the year, the women went out to beg for the Buddha, and on these occasions they carried in their hands his image covered by a white veil. They were given one of the three following articles: oil for the Buddha's lamp, rice for a sacrifice to him, or cloth to make him a robe; money, it seems, was also given. This begging was an act of piety, and when the higher class of women did not go, they had themselves represented by their maids, whom they sent in their place. At the present day this custom, of which Robert Knox was an eye-witness, no longer exists.

The Canonical sacred books of Ceylon, like those of all the Buddhist races, comprise three classes and forms, which are called in liturgic style 'The Three Baskets' (*Pitakatayam* in Pāli, *Tun-Pitaka* in Sinhalese). Turnour has already given a complete list of the Canonical books of Ceylon. Spence Hardy confirms this list, and adds some interesting details worthy of notice.

The Sinhalese Three Baskets comprise, as usual, the *Vinaya*, the *Sūtras*, and the *Abhidharma*, that is, the books on discipline, on the legends, and on metaphysics. We place the Three Baskets in the same order as Spence Hardy, who probably followed the indications of the Sinhalese priests. Generally the *Sūtras* are placed in the first rank, secondly the *Vinaya*, and then the *Abhidharma*; but their order of classification is of little consequence, the number, titles, and size of the books remaining the same.

The Sinhalese *Vinaya* is composed of five works. The first two are a kind of criminal code; the next two a religious and civil code. The fifth is only a commentary and an explanation of the other four, in the shape of a catechism, which facilitates their study. The whole *Vinaya* is, for the convenience of the faithful, divided into 169 lectures (*banavaras*), each consisting of 250 stanzas, a stanza being composed of 4 *pādas* of 8 syllables, or 32 syllables in all. There are thus 42,250 stanzas in the whole of the *Vinaya*, without reckoning the *Samantapāsādikā*, which has 27,000.

The 'Basket' of *Sūtras*, or discourses of the Buddha, forms the most considerable part of the *Tun-Piṭaka*. The *Sutta-Piṭaka* also comprises five works; of which the last is divided into several others. The *Sūtras*, if we are to rely on the *Saddharmālankāre*, contain no less than 200,000 stanzas independently of the commentary, which has even more.

The *Abhidharma*, or Metaphysics, is composed of seven works; and the texts comprise 96,250 stanzas, while the commentaries contain only a third at the most.

If we are to believe tradition, Mahinda brought these works when he came, under the reign of the great Aṣoka and by his orders, to convert Sinhala to Buddhism. These works were accompanied by a commentary, the *Atthakathā*, which was held in almost the same veneration as the text itself, and which was translated by Mahinda, from the original Pāli, brought from Magadha, into Sinhalese. The Sinhalese translation of the *Atthakathā* sufficed for many centuries, and gradually replaced the authentic and primitive text, which fell into disuse and was lost. Hence, in the year 430 of the Christian era, the famous work of the Brahman Buddhaghosa, who, as we have already mentioned, re-translated into Pāli Mahinda's Sinhalese translation. The Pāli version of the *Atthakathā* made by Buddhaghosa is the only one that exists at the present time, and the priests know no other. But it would seem that this commentary has for some time lost most of its authority with the priests, who, having carefully compared it with the text, have discovered that it misrepresented it, by the addition of absurd stories; and in disgust they have returned to the original *Sūtras*, though these are often not more reasonable than the *Atthakathā*.

It is needless to insist on the extreme importance of all these works, which to this day are understood by the most intelligent among the native priests. Spence Hardy states that he saw a complete and correct collection of them in the possession of the Rev. D. J. Gogerly, head of the Wesleyan missions in Ceylon. Gogerly was residing at Pondra in 1835, and had become acquainted with the most enlightened priests in the maritime provinces of the island; in the space of a few years, he had been able to collect all the sacred works, which formed no less than seven or eight of our ordinary 8vos. Turnour, who possessed a no less valuable collection, had intended making a general analysis of the Sinhalese *Tripitaka*, with the aid of the priests, whom he enjoyed gathering round him; but he had to renounce this lengthy undertaking, finding that he had not sufficient leisure. Spence Hardy, probably for similar reasons, had equally to give up this work, although he admitted its utility. 'As long as an exact analysis of the *Pitakas* has not been made,' he writes, 'and that the most interesting parts have not been translated at full length, we cannot flatter ourselves that we possess a complete and thoroughly authentic statement of the Buddhist doctrines. This work would not exceed the powers of any single individual; but, to be carried out to perfection, it would demand a thorough knowledge of the languages, literature, and metaphysics; unwearying perseverance, easy and constant intercourse with the most learned of the native priests, besides a longer residence in the country than can be generally made by those who devote themselves to these studies.'

These observations are very sensible, but they only augment our regrets. Spence Hardy possessed most of the requisite conditions, and it is a pity that, during his long residence in Ceylon, he was not able to collect the materials for the work he so well describes, and of which he felt the need was so great. He did, however, undertake drawing up a list of all the native works actually in use in the island. He counted 465 of these, half of them in Pāli, 80 in Sanskrit, and 150 in Sinhalese or in Elu, the ancient form of the Sinhalese language. As the author took the trouble to make these researches, he ought at least to have given us the nomenclature of these 465 works; for the titles alone would have taught us a good deal about the present state of literature in Ceylon.

However that may be, such are the sacred books studied by the Buddhist priests of the island, which they use for the instruction of the people. At certain periods of the year the people are called together, to listen to the reading of the *Sūtras* or the *Bana*. These edifying lectures mostly take place in the rainy season; at other times, the priests are generally scattered about, and it would be more difficult for them to address the throng of the faithful. The place where the lecture is held, *banamaduva*, is usually a raised stand of several steps in the shape of a stūpa. These temporary edifices are built in the enclosures of the vihāras, but they may be constructed elsewhere, the choice of the place being left to the person who undertakes the expense of this meritorious action. At the summit of the stand is a platform, on which the priest who officiates stands; and the people listen to him, seated on mats scattered about on the ground. The stand is covered with bright cloths—so that the stones and woodwork are hidden—and decked out with flowers, moss, and fresh boughs of trees. As these readings generally take place at night, the enclosure is lighted up by lamps and lanterns suspended to the wall, or held in the hands or even fastened on to the heads of the most pious of the believers. Banners, flags, shawls, flutter in the air; the women are dressed in their best clothes, with their hair carefully drawn back from the forehead, and twisted into a knot, held up by silver pins and little metal combs tastefully arranged. The men are dressed in cotton garments of dazzling whiteness. From time to time, the loud beat of the tamtam, or music, or even rounds of musketry are heard; it is, in fact, as much a festivity as a religious ceremony. Sometimes trunks of trees covered with silver paper, with boughs laden with artificial gems or leaflets of the books to be read on that holy occasion, are distributed among the crowd. According to popular belief, these trees ensured to those who touched them the fulfilment of all their wishes; meanwhile they are used to distribute the text of the prayer that the priest is about to recite. In the most conspicuous place a large copper bowl is placed, in which the people deposit alms for the maintenance of the worship.

At a reading of the *Bana* which was held at Pantura in 1839, Spence Hardy saw a hundred priests gathered together to officiate at it. The pulpit from which the reading was delivered turned on a pivot, doubtless in order that each listener might in turn hear the *Bana* without changing his place. In the night-time fireworks were let off; and a kind of representation, half dramatic, half mystic, was performed, in which a personage acting the part of a messenger from the world of the gods appeared, splendidly robed, and escorted by two personages dressed as kings, with crowns on their heads and swords in their hand. Other allegorical personages went about the enclosure, riding elephants or horses. Fifty native soldiers, dressed in English uniforms, unceasingly fired off their guns, while the priests marshalled round the pulpit continued to chant the Pāli verses. The state swords of eight of the principal chiefs of the island (*Adikars*) were hung round the pulpit.

The festival at Pantura was an extraordinary one, and on less solemn occasions things were done more simply. The platform of the stand is often occupied by several priests, who read in turn passages from the sacred books, from copies written in big letters on magnificent palm-leaves. The officiating priest reads the text in a kind of intoning voice, something between chanting and reading. Generally the Pāli text is alone recited, and then the people do not understand a word; sometimes, however, after the Pāli text has been recited, a priest gives an interpretation in Sinhalese, for the benefit of the people. Each time that, in the course of reading, the name of the Buddha is pronounced, the whole crowd unanimously responds '*Sādhu*,' a Sanskrit word equivalent to our 'Amen, So be it.' The tone in which the reading is done is very calm and very monotonous, the voice never being raised and no emphasis ever indulged in. However, some priests by the softness of their tone of voice or the lucidity of their explanations become favourites with the masses, as is the case with our own preachers.

Every month there are four periods in which the *Bana* is regularly read; these are at the four changes of the moon—the day of the new moon, the eighth day after it, the fifteenth day of the moon, or the day of the full moon, and the eighth day after the full moon. These days, chosen by Buddhism for the religious exercises, are precisely those prohibited by Brahmanic law. Manu recommends, very clearly, that the *Vedas* shall not be read on the days when the moon is about to change[1]. It seems probable that the natural antagonism of the two religions influenced the Buddhists in their choice, in order to distinguish themselves from their adversaries. Perhaps even this easy way of reckoning tempted them, nothing being easier than to observe and follow the changes of the moon.

[1] *Laws of Manu*, Book IV. ṣloka 114: 'The day of the new moon kills the master; the fourteenth lunar day kills the disciple; the eighth day and that of the full moon destroy the recollection of the sacred writings. It is therefore necessary to abstain from all readings during those days.'

On the eve of each of the four sacramental days, which are called *poyas* or changing, the devout layman concentrates his thoughts; he must think of what he will do on the morrow, and meditate on his firm resolution to remain faithful to the precepts given by the Buddha to the laity. On the morning of the *poya* day, he eats the frugal repast he has prepared on the preceding evening, and goes at an early hour to a priest, or even simply a devout man (*upāsaka*) like himself, well versed in the knowledge of the *Bana*. He respectfully approaches this person, and says to him, 'It is my intention to keep the precepts.' Then he recites the formula for the Threefold Refuge, 'I go for refuge to the Buddha, &c.,' adding the principal precepts of the Law. If the believer has no eminent person to whom he can address this act of faith he may recite it to himself, without anybody's assistance. Having thus prepared himself, he goes to the priest, to receive from him the instruction of the *Bana*. During the whole of the *poya* day he must carefully avoid doing anything that can harm others, nor must he incite any one to commit any such act. It is better even to avoid all business transactions, and all the calculations that business entails. These mundane interests would distract and sully the mind, which must be kept perfectly pure, as well as the clothes that are worn. If the devotee should happen to be sick unto death, and could not personally attend the *Bana*, he can request the priest to come to him to read the sacred books; the book is then brought in great pomp, the priest reads it with unction, and he continues reading till the sick person has given up his spirit or feels relieved.

All these practices are very praiseworthy, and can only be commended, as they encourage piety, disinterestedness, benevolence, and virtue. Superstition has, however, claimed its share, and turned to its own ends the reading of the *Bana*. Extracts have been made of certain passages in the sacred writings which are specially read at the ceremony called the

Pirit, and these form a kind of manual of exorcisms. The Sinhalese, who are as credulous as the Indians, the Chinese, and most of the Asiatic races, fancy that all the ills that befall humanity proceed from the maliciousness of the demons, the *Yakshas*. Means must therefore be found to combat their hostility or appease their wrath. The perusal of the *Pirit* can destroy their power, and the Buddha himself pointed out this marvellous and beneficial secret to mankind. Spence Hardy was present in 1828 at a reading of the *Pirit*, and, aided by the recollection of a few other persons who, like him, witnessed the ceremony, he gives the following description of it:

'At sunset, numerous groups of believers arrived from all sides; the women, who were the majority, brought with them coconuts and oil as offerings. When it grew dark the coconuts were placed in niches, expressly arranged in the walls of the court of the vihāra, and by the aid of cotton wicks lamps were soon provided. The wall that surrounded the Bo-tree was lighted up in the same way, and, as many of the people had also brought torches made of cotton and resin, the whole enclosure was in a moment bathed in light. The gaiety and manners of all the groups moving about showed full well that, if the object of the gathering was a religious one, it was also looked upon as a time of festivity and rest. Another reason why these assemblies were so popular and so much the fashion, is that they were the only occasions on which the young people of both sexes could see and be seen by each other, without being obliged to maintain the reserve and constraint which were the rule of everyday life.

'The service lasted seven days, and the first evening was in a way only preparatory. The building where the people met was the one in which the habitual reading of the *Bana* took place. A relic of the Buddha, enshrined in a casket, was placed on a platform designed for that special purpose; and the presence of this relic was supposed to lend to this ceremony all the efficacy that it would have possessed if the Buddha himself had performed it. The priests were assembled on another platform. At the close of the preliminary service a consecrated rope, called *Pirit nūla*, was fastened to the interior walls of the edifice, reaching from the priests' platform to that of the relic; and as the priests in chorus intoned the religious chants, they each took hold of the cord, establishing in this manner a communication between each of the officiating priests, the relic, and the interior walls of the building.

'From the morning of the second day till the evening of the seventh, the platform on which the reading took place was unceasingly filled with priests, both by day and night. When two priests had to be replaced by two others, one remained seated reading, while the other gave his seat to his substitute, and the second priest only made his exchange when the first substitute had begun reading. Thus for the whole of the six days, the reading of the *Pirit* was continued without a moment's interruption. There were never less than twelve priests in attendance, generally indeed there were twenty-four, and two were always officiating. As they were relieved every two hours, each priest officiated two hours out of twenty-four. In addition, all the priests who took part in the ceremony met together three times a day, at sunrise, at noon, and at sunset, to chant together the three principal passages of the *Pirit*, called *mangala*, *ratana*, *karanīya*, which were accompanied by some verses drawn from other sources. Then the reading of the *Pirit* was resumed, and the same formulas were gone through till the seventh day, when a new series had to be started.

'On the morning of the seventh day, a large procession was organized, in which the armed and unarmed men were marshalled. A special personage represented the *Devadūtaya*, or Messenger of the Gods. The procession, headed by priests, went to certain places where the gods were supposed to reside, and solemnly invited them to attend the service before it was finished, in order to share its benefits. Until the messenger and those who followed him had returned, the priests who had remained on the platform stopped reading and remained seated.

'At the festival I witnessed,' adds Spence Hardy, 'the messenger was introduced in great pomp, and to make his apparition appear more supernatural, sulphur was burnt before him. One of the priests having proclaimed in a loud voice the names of the different gods and demons who were invited to the ceremony, the messenger replied that he was sent by those very divinities, and, repeating their names, he declared that they would come to the service. The formula of the Threefold Refuge, which formed part of the recitation, was then chanted by all the persons present. In the midst of all these superstitious and absurd ideas, much excellent advice was given; but, as it was all in a language that the people did not understand, the ceremony could hardly be expected to produce any really useful results.'

We are not told what became of the crowd of believers during those seven days and nights. It is probable that they relieved each other like the priests did, although doubtless with less regularity.

It would moreover appear that the Sinhalese priests, by limiting their public ministrations to reading the *Banà*, and to the somewhat unintelligible explanations they give of it, take little heed of maintaining their authority. They have become estranged from the people, and a class of devout laymen has arisen, which has by degrees replaced and supplanted them. These benevolent and pious substitutes go from house to house to read the sacred writings in the Sinhalese language, and condescend to impart the most homely instructions. Spence Hardy found many of these lay-priests working with great success in several districts, especially in the neighbourhood of Matura.

Besides the regular worship and authorized superstitions, there were a quantity of individual superstitions, which had their own particular rules and code. The Buddhists had inherited from the Brahmans the deplorable idea that science and virtue conferred supernatural powers on men. There does not exist in India a single school of philosophy which has not held out to its adepts these absurd and deceptive promises. Buddhism would have made a most excellent reform had it been able to eradicate these insensate ideas; unfortunately, however, it adopted all the Brahmanic follies, and only strengthened them by doing so. No miracle seemed too great for the Buddha to perform, and any one of his disciples, by following his example, was deemed capable of attaining the same power.

Spence Hardy has drawn from several Sinhalese works very curious and novel details upon meditation, and the supernatural power it confers on those who practise it according to the prescribed rules. There are five different kinds of meditation, or *Bhāvanā:* first, the meditation on love, in which the monk thinks of all beings—including his enemies—and longs for happiness for each; the second meditation is on pity, in which the mendicant is to think of all beings in distress; the third meditation is on joy, in which he is to think of the gladness and prosperity of others, and to rejoice in their joy; the fourth meditation is on impurity, in which the mendicant thinks of the vileness of the body, and the horrors of disease and corruption; and, lastly, the fifth meditation is on serenity, the source of unalterable tranquillity. The ascetic is minutely instructed in all the different processes his mind must follow in order that each meditation may be concentrated on the special object it has in view. Amid these strictly psychological rules, we often find the highest and most elevated sentiments. The forgiveness of injuries, and contempt for the body, are in truth excellent and useful recommendations, and it is good for man to meditate on the instability of earthly things, so that he may not attach more importance to them than they deserve. But the Buddhist *Bhāvanā* is not satisfied with this, and aims at a very different result; it is only so carefully practised in order to obtain supernatural powers. We will not dwell further on this paltry side of devotion and asceticism, but we recommend to our readers the chapter in which Spence Hardy treats of the ten kinds of *Kasina*, without, however, informing us if these practices—which are intended to throw the mind into a state of ecstasy—are still in force among the Sinhalese priests, or whether they have remained a dead letter, in the obscure works which describe them.

All these follies, so much admired by the vulgar, are the special prerogative of the monks. The laity may also, however, aspire to supernatural powers, and to obtain these a kindly thought is often as efficient as prolonged meditation. A meritorious action performed in this life, or even in a former one, endows the being who has performed it with miraculous power. This special power receives the name of *Sachakiriya* (meritorious action), and is acquired not only in virtue of the deed itself, but also by the mere recollection of this deed. The following two examples are taken from the *Visuddhimargga Sanne* :—

The mother of a Sinhalese devotee having falling dangerously ill, the doctor ordered her to eat some hare. Her son thereupon goes out and snares a hare; but as the animal cries out, the young man reflects, and says to himself: 'How can a life be saved by the destruction of another life?' And he sets the poor animal free. When on his return home he relates what he has done, his father and his family only jeer at him; but he goes up to his mother, and says to her: 'From infancy down to the present day, I have never to my knowledge destroyed life in any creature. By the power of this meritorious action (*Sachakiriya*), may you be cured.' And the illness immediately ceased.

The mother of a priest called Mahāmitta fell ill of an ulcer. She begged him through his sister to tell her of a remedy. The priest answered: 'I ignore the healing properties of plants; but I possess a much greater power. Since I have taken holy orders, I have never violated any of the precepts of the law; and by virtue of this *Sachakiriya* let my mother be healed.' And the ulcer instantly dried up and disappeared.

Spence Hardy quotes two other legends, showing the magic effect of the *Sachakiriya*, taken from the life of the Buddha himself. These two legends are recorded in the *Cariyā-Pitaka*, the last book of the *Sutta-Pitaka*; but they do not present much interest. In one of these, the Buddha, who at that time lived under the form of a king, bestows his eyes upon a poor blind Brahman; in the other, he saves the lives of the fishes in a dried up pond. By the virtue of a *Sachakiriya*, he recovers his eyes, and rain falls into the lake where the fish were dying for lack of water. These miracles, performed by the Buddha, are not surprising; but that the least of the faithful should be able to produce them by a single act of faith was a fact well calculated to excite the fervour of all Buddhists; and to credulous minds it furnishes a very powerful though fallacious stimulant to faith. It is also the cause of the most deplorable superstitions, which are as frequent in orthodox Brahmanism, as in Buddhic heresy.

On the most essential point of doctrine, the Nirvāna, Spence Hardy fails to give us the precise information we should have desired.

In the innumerable passages concerning Nirvāna, the doctrine of the Buddhists leaves us in impenetrable obscurity; it is never clearly defined, for the Buddhist authors only tell us what Nirvāna is not, but never exactly what it is. They define it by comparisons and epithets, but are not concerned to make it well understood nor indeed to understand it themselves. It is impossible to pierce the veil in which they purposely envelop it; and we can only obtain the vaguest glimpses of light on the subject.

We have therefore drawn the conclusion that Nirvāna was annihilation, and we have not feared to maintain this opinion, however extraordinary it may appear.

This is also Spence Hardy's opinion; and his long intercourse with the Sinhalese Buddhists, whom he endeavoured to convert, lends great weight to his judgment. He expresses his opinion in the following manner:—

'Nirvāna is the destruction of all the elements of existence . . . when the principles of existence are annihilated; this annihilation is Nirvāna. . . . The Buddhist who does not believe in the substantial existence of human personality, nor in the existence of a supreme Being, does not look for absorption, but only absolute annihilation. This system is perfectly logical, for materialism, atheism, and complete cessation of all existence, are ideas which hold together, and likewise disappear together; if the first two ideas are proved, the third follows as a natural consequence.'

Spence Hardy ends his chapter on Nirvāna, as follows: 'Thus Nirvāna is neither a state of sensual enjoyment nor a state of intellectual enjoyment; it is neither a state of the body, nor a state of consciousness. It is neither consciousness nor absence of consciousness. Nirvāna must therefore be annihilation, and the being who enters into it must cease to exist.'

We believe, for our part, that this is the true interpretation of

Nirvāna, and it is also that of the majority of those who have studied Buddhism[1]. All the texts hitherto known, notwithstanding a few trifling contradictions, seem to point to the same conclusion; whereas the objections, being mostly of a general character, are for this reason of little value. In the history of the human mind, nothing is more surprising and depressing than the belief in annihilation; but if it is an averred fact, affirmed by the Buddhist writings themselves, we must perforce accept though we deplore it.

This is why we should have wished that the Wesleyan missionary had questioned the Sinhalese priests on this capital point of doctrine, and had sought to obtain a clear understanding of what it really was in their mind. He represents himself as 'having spent thousands of hours during the twenty years he resided in Ceylon, palm-leaf in hand and a converted Buddhist priest at his side, ready to assist him in any difficulties of the text they perused together.' These were very favourable circumstances for the study of the impressions left in the minds of his neophytes by the Buddhic doctrine; for it was more particularly the Christian belief in immortality which he endeavoured to teach them. Spence Hardy would surely have had more than one opportunity of discovering the real meaning of Nirvāna from these newly converted Buddhists; and though he does not explicitly say that he had attempted this delicate investigation, yet we may conclude that he had done so, and that his conviction as to the meaning of Nirvāna was drawn from the knowledge he thus obtained. If the Buddhist priests of Ceylon had indeed held the views on immortality which are gratuitously attributed to them, he would evidently have been aware of it,

[1] Amongst others, Burnouf, who had thoroughly studied this question, never varied in his opinion. His authority on such a subject is all the greater from the fact that he was as deeply versed in philosophy as in philology, two studies which rarely go together.

for it would have greatly facilitated his task as a missionary. Moreover, his opinion of the Sinhalese priests amongst whom he lived was in general a favourable one, for he renders justice to their qualities, while pointing out their faults. He finds them faithfully fulfilling the irksome duties imposed upon them by the law of the Buddha which, though so ancient, had lost none of its authority over them; and they have remained to this day very nearly what their predecessors were twenty centuries ago. They go the same rounds through the native villages with their alms-bowls; they walk silently along the roads with measured steps and downcast eyes, head uncovered and naked feet, their alms-bowl hung round their neck and hidden under their robe when not in use. They generally hold a fan, which they keep before their faces to avoid the sight of women, lest impure thoughts should be awakened in their minds; this constraint and the austerities they practice are doubtless the cause of the singular appearance of these priests who, with few exceptions, seem less intelligent than the common people; for the expression of their countenance is unhappy, though they often bear the impress of the serenity and sweetness peculiar to the Buddhist doctrine.

In his intercourse with them, Spence Hardy always found them benevolent and hospitable, and, when treated with courtesy, they sought the society of Europeans. In his frequent excursions into the interior of the island, the Wesleyan missionary had often occasion to appeal to their hospitality, either for a shelter at night, or from the excessive heat of the day; and it was hardly ever refused. The anchorite would often bring him the remains of his own meal, and would choose what was best in his alms bowl to offer to his guest. He would even provide him with tobacco or some other delicacy to show his pleasure at the visit he was receiving; but his pleasure was mingled with curiosity, for all that belonged to his visitor was examined with interest, from his Bible down to his watch. It is true that Spence Hardy spoke the native language, and this doubtlessly greatly facilitated his access to these holy men.

Moreover, it does not appear that the Buddhist priests ever betrayed any rivality or intolerance towards the apostle of a different faith. Spence Hardy attributes this disposition to their indolence and indifference, as well as to their unmoveable belief in the truth of their own system. These different motives doubtless exist; but we must also add that the habit of tolerance is common to all Sinhalese priests. Spence Hardy notices that by the side of most of the Buddhist vihāras, there exist devālas, in which Sanskrit prayers are recited in honour of the Brahmanic divinities. As the Sinhalese priests sanction the close proximity of a worship they reprobate, and may have good reason to fear, it is quite natural that they should not display any fanaticism against the Christian faith. In the early days of Wesleyan Missions in Ceylon, the Buddhist priests asked the missionaries to lend them their school rooms for the reading of the *Bana*; and it was difficult to make them understand the motives of their refusal. They never felt any such scruples, and it is probable that they would willingly have lent their vihāra for the celebration of Christian worship.

It has been already remarked, to the credit of Buddhism, that it has always retained a most sincere and unvarying spirit of tolerance. The Buddha never used any other weapons than persuasion and gentleness; he never had recourse to violence, and his adepts have remained faithful to his noble and rare example. Buddhism had at divers epochs and in divers countries undergone violent persecution; but it never seems to have thought of retaliation. Even the divisions of the Great and Little Vehicles did not entail persecution.

A school is attached to every hermitage, and a Buddhist monk teaches the children reading and writing. In return the children assist him in his daily work, carry water to the vihāra, or sweep the yard in their leisure hours. The discipline of the schools is extremely lenient, although the tasks are difficult, for the alphabet contains no less than fifty letters [1]. The masters devote much time and labour on their scholars, who on their side are dutifully submissive to their teaching. The instruction of children is therefore one of the chief occupations of the Sinhalese priests, who accomplish this duty with much self-abnegation, and, in rendering this service to society, partially compensate for what they cease to contribute to it by their celibate and apparently useless lives.

Moreover there are priests who study and practice medicine with more or less success; and their medical skill is all the more appreciated by the people that it is gratuitously bestowed. It merely consists in astrological observations and exorcisms. Their remedies are generally composed of a quantity of ingredients, and, as they sometimes happen to cure, they enjoy, as doctors, great authority and reputation. In 1827 a priest who, at Matura, was appointed Mahā-nāyaka, or

[1] Spence Hardy gives some curious details about the books used in the Sinhalese schools and the instruction given to the children. The Sinhalese alphabet is copied from the Devanāgari alphabet; the number of letters and their classification are similar, but their form is different. Although this alphabet has twice as many letters as ours, it is not as difficult to learn, as Spence Hardy seems to think. The regular and symmetrical disposition of the vowels and consonants is a great help, and it is easy to pass from single letters to letters united into syllables. The Sinhalese children soon learn to repeat their alphabet by writing the letters on the sand with their finger. The whole course of instruction in a Sinhalese school is comprised in fourteen works, written in the four languages: Modern Sinhalese, Ancient Sinhalese or Elu, Pāli and Sanskrit. Spence Hardy gives the titles and a short analysis of each of these fourteen works. The last is Amara-Singh's Sanskrit Dictionary, the *Amara-Kosha*, which has been reprinted several times. Spence Hardy remarks that the Sinhalese children are precocious and intelligent, but that their development is arrested at the age of puberty. This phenomenon is not peculiar to the Sinhalese race; it exists in almost every Oriental country, particularly in Egypt.

director-general of the district, owed his nomination to this office entirely to his fame as a doctor [1].

Other priests spend their time in copying books, but their zeal in this respect is not very great; their collections of books are very incomplete; and when perchance they are more numerous they generally consist of works that have been handed down from earlier times. In the present day, literary work is neglected, and the Sinhalese priests are the more to be blamed, that they have at hand all the necessary materials for their work; as they have only to gather a few palm-leaves to make up the necessary volume [2].

As a corporation the priests are held in little respect by the people; the state of mendicity to which they are condemned is doubtless the cause. They are in too dependent a position to obtain due consideration; this was evidently a danger for the Buddhist institution, and was only averted by the solitude enforced on the priests during the greater part of the year. In Ceylon the priests seem to have observed the difficult rule of continence with an austerity which rehabilitates them. Spence Hardy had heard their avidity often criticized, but never their licentiousness; and this is all the more meritorious that the native population is extremely licentious, not respecting even the most sacred family ties [3].

It would seem that at a certain period and under certain more devout or weaker princes, the Sinhalese priests obtained

[1] We have already mentioned a king of Ceylon, Buddhadāsa (A. D. 339-368) who was a great doctor, and whose works still exist. It is probable that the study of medicine in Ceylon owes its origin to Sanskrit works on this subject.

[2] Doubtless this material facility has greatly contributed to preserve these kind of intellectual documents in India, where they have been so much better preserved than in the days of antiquity or our middle ages. In these climates the paper taken from the trees was never lacking for those who wished to make use of it.

[3] Spence Hardy nevertheless quotes a case of which he was witness, when an incontinent priest was pursued by the women and expelled from the village, for having tried to seduce a young girl who had brought him cakes as an offering to the Buddha.

many privileges, and among others, that of impunity. The yellow robe protected the culprits; and more than one criminal became a monk in order to escape the punishment he deserved. Under Udaga III, towards the end of the tenth century, a rebellion having broken out, the chief rebels assumed the priestly garb to elude the vengeance of the king; but notwithstanding their sacred robes, the king had them seized and beheaded. It is true that the popular fanaticism was aroused by this sacrilege, and the populace, rising again, inflicted the same punishment on many of the king's courtiers. Alarmed at this exorbitant power, which the priests too often abused, the king resolved to restrict it, and under the reign of Rāja Singh, about two centuries and a half ago, the privilege of the personal inviolability of the priests was abolished. We have already mentioned that the English rulers have been obliged to execute several priests who, during the last forty years, have been the instigators or leaders in various rebellions.

In the last century, the authority of the kings was so well established that they were able to regulate at their will the monastical institutions. The King Kirtisri, who reigned from 1747 to 1781, decreed that ordination could only be conferred on the agricultural class, the *Govi* caste, the most numerous and powerful in the island. This was an important innovation, as it was distinctly opposed to the primitive law of the Buddha, who admitted no distinction of caste, and through Nirvāna called all men equally to eternal salvation. Kirtisri, by another provision of his decree, commanded that, in future, ordination should only be conferred in Kandy, the residence of the kings; and he divided all the monks into two communities, under the rule of the two great convents of Malvata and Asgiri. The heads of these communities were always to reside in Kandy, near the king, and were granted equal authority. The doctrine of the two communities was essentially the same; the only difference between them was, that the corporation of Malvata possessed a larger number of vihāras, and ruled over the southern part of the island; while the corporation of Asgiri ruled over the temples of the north. All the priests of Ceylon belong to either one or the other of these two corporations.

The exact motives that influenced King Kirtisri are not known, but it seems probable that, in dividing the monks into two bodies, he aimed at diminishing their power by breaking up their unity. This was a clever stroke of policy, but the reform met with great difficulties. The castes excluded from holy orders, and more particularly the lower castes, were extremely dissatisfied. One of them indeed, that of the Chaliyas, resolved to escape from the consequences of the king's decree still in force after his death. The Chaliyas assert themselves to be the original inhabitants of the island, and are as a rule more intelligent and active than the other natives. From the earliest period they had special charge of the cultivation and sale of cinnamon, and had realized large profits from this business, which they have always carried on to the satisfaction of the various governments who employed them.

The Chaliyas were not only rich and powerful, but they were also remarkable for their religious fervour. Towards the close of the last century they sent a member of their caste, called Ambagahapitya, with five others, as novices to the countries in which the Buddhist faith had retained its greatest purity. Ambagahapitya was to be solemnly ordained there, in order to be able to ordain the people of his caste on his return to Ceylon. After a long journey he settled in Burmah, the faith seeming purer there than elsewhere. He was graciously received by the king and the priests, and remained there the necessary time to receive holy orders; and in 1802 he returned to Ceylon with five Burmese priests and the novices who had accompanied him and had, like him, been ordained. It was on this occasion that the Burmese high priest wrote the letter or monitory we have already quoted.

As soon as the mission reached Ceylon, it eagerly made use of the powers it had received, and ordained several priests; and a third community was soon formed in opposition to those of Malvata and Asgiri. At first it was recruited exclusively among the Chaliyas, but its influence gradually spread, and monks from other castes were admitted. This was a return to the spirit and letter of primitive Buddhism. The new corporation was called the corporation of Amarapura, the name of a Burmese city, in order to recall its origin; and it became the rival of the two others, who seem to have united against the common enemy. A native writer, the descendant of an old Portuguese family, gave, some ten years ago, the following description of this rivalry.

'The two parties,' said Adam de Silva, 'indulge in ardent controversies, and mutually deny each other the right to Nirvāna. Their reciprocal animosity equals that of the most bigoted sects of any other religion; it is so violent that they absolutely refuse to bow to one another when they happen to meet. They mutually gratify each other with such epithets as "impure monk" (*duksīlaya*). The object of the Amarapura corporation is to bring back Buddhism to its primitive purity by freeing it from polytheism, caste prejudice, and all the corrupt practices which in course of time have sullied it. However difficult the task, the priests of Amarapura seem to have succeeded, for they made numerous proselytes in different provinces, especially in that of Saffragan, which may now be considered the centre of reform.'

The differences of doctrines between the Amarapura and Siamese sect, as the other corporations were called, are in reality somewhat important; the following are the principal points of dissension.

The Amarapura sect openly preaches against the superstitions brought from India, and never invoke the Hindu Gods during the recitation of the *Pirit*. It confers holy orders on all castes, without distinction, as the Buddha did. It reprobates the mundane occupations of the Siamese priests, who practise medicine and astrology, and prohibits, under pain of excommunication, these deviations from the primitive rule. It refuses to recognize the authority of the royal decrees in respect of religion, particularly with regard to the privileges conferred by Kirtisri on the Malvata and Asgiri establishments. Ordination, it declares, can be conferred anywhere, and always possesses the same value, provided it is conducted according to the prescribed rules. The Amarapura sect does not admit the precepts of former Buddhas, unless they have been sanctioned by Gautama Buddha. It does not therefore allow a blessing to be recited, or thanks to be uttered when food or any other gift is received. It does not either permit the use of two seats, or the presence of two priests at the reading of the *Bana*. It also forbids that this reading should be done in a tremulous voice. And what is much more important: the reforming sect expounds and preaches the Vināya to the laity, whereas the Siamese priests only read it to the monks, and that with closed doors. It only allows confirmation several years after ordination, whereas the opposite sect unreservedly permit it immediately after. It celebrates the feast of lamps, without preaching or reading, whereas the Siamese read the *Bana* all through the night. Finally the Amarapuras differ from the Siamese in their costume, or rather in the manner in which they wear their robes; both shoulders are covered by a fold that reaches from under one arm to the other. They refrain from shaving their eyebrows as is the custom of the Siamese. The Amarapuras study Pāli literature with great assiduity in order to find arguments against the errors and corruptions of their adversaries. And, as Spence Hardy remarks, it is certain that these studies and discussions only increased and widened the distance which already separated the two sects.

In 1835 a new sect arose against which the Amarapuras and the Siamese were for a time united. The subject of contention was the precise time of the year at which the Varsha retreat should begin. The priest who raised this controversy was more learned in astronomy than his adversaries, but he had few partisans, and the motive of the heresy was not serious enough for it to assume much importance. It died out in the course of a few years, and never spread beyond the Bentoste district where it had arisen. The priest who promoted it was called Attadassa, and may still be living.

All these facts tend to prove that the Buddhist faith has remained deeply rooted in the hearts of the natives of Ceylon, for heresies are proof of life; indifference alone shows decay.

Buddhism, however, is in a different position now that Christianity has made its way in Ceylon; more especially since the watchful and powerful administration of the English Government has introduced a higher order of civilization. It may be said that, judging by all that has taken place in the last fifty years, Christianity is likely to supplant Buddhism. This is a question no less interesting to study than those we have already treated; and we will try to complete all we have said about the past and the present condition of Sinhalese Buddhism by a few words as to the future [1].

Spence Hardy says that there are only 2,500 Buddhist priests at the present day in Ceylon. If we compare these figures not only with those given by Fa-Hian, but also with those mentioned by Hiouen-Thsang, we find that they are

[1] We have taken most of our information from the official documents published by Parliament: The Report we have already mentioned on the insurrection in 1848; the Report in 1852; and Viscount Torrington's Correspondence, 11th of May, 1857.

singularly diminished. In the official reports of 1856 the total population of the island is set down as 1,691,924 inhabitants [1]; but the priests have not been numbered apart, and we must therefore rely on Spence Hardy's estimation.

The influence of Buddhism is gradually decreasing with the increasing success of Christianity. The English Government bestows a grant upon three Protestant sects: the Anglican, the Scotch Presbyterian, and Dutch Presbyterian Churches. This grant, of which the Anglican Church receives four-fifths, attains an annual sum of £13,000; but in 1850 it was proposed to reduce it, and to leave the maintenance of the worship to the fervour and generosity of the faithful. The Catholic Church has no grant; and this anomaly is explained, not by a rivalry of sects, but by the wealth of that Church which requires no assistance, and to which moreover full liberty is accorded [2].

[1] The following official estimates are contained in the Report made by the financial committee of the Executive Council of Ceylon published on the 1st of July, 1852, by order of the House of Commons: folio, 268 pages. It was upon this report, drawn up by Lord Torrington, December 13, 1849, that the whole administration of the island was reorganized. The condition of the population in the different provinces may be found at page 55, appendix B. The Western province contained 499,678 inhabitants; the Southern 265,289; the Eastern 114,274, the Northern 255,415, and the Central 323,043. Total 1,458,359. In 1832 the population did not exceed a million of souls; but, as the administration improved, it rapidly increased. It must now number at least 1,800,000 souls. The census of 1850 gave 1,572,743 inhabitants, and that of 1856, 1,691,924.

[2] In this respect the Executive Council of 1849 displayed the most liberal and judicious feeling. It expressed surprise at the establishment of an Anglican Bishopric at Colombo, as there were in Ceylon so few members of the English Church; and it recalled the fact that, in 1844, there had only been an Archdeacon under the jurisdiction of the Bishop of Madras. The Council did not explicitly propose to abolish the Bishopric of Colombo; but it pointed this out as a desirable reform. The Council maintained the small grant allotted to the Dutch Presbyterian Church out of respect for its past history, as that Church had long been the only one available for the Christian population of the maritime provinces. Finally, the Council pointed out that the official neglect of the Catholic Church was a cause of jealousy and discord which it would be good policy to avoid. It is evident that the

The Anglican faith meets with little success among the native population of Ceylon, and in 1852 an intelligent observer[1] stated that it did not number more than 1,500 adherents. The Wesleyan has spread a great deal more, although not protected by the Colonial government; and a return made in 1851 states that it had, at that time, 4,792 proselytes.

All these Protestant sects, however, sink into insignificance by the side of Catholicism, which daily increases in power. The monopoly of Catholicism belongs to the Portuguese, who first introduced Christianity into the island at the beginning of the sixteenth century[2]. At the present time there are two Catholic vicarages; one at Colombo, under the authority of the Bishop of Cochin and Goa; the other at Jafna, created in 1836 by pope Gregory XVI under the direct sway of the Roman See. The Mission for the propagation of the faith is composed of fifty priests, mostly Spaniards, Portuguese, and Italians. In 1852, six French priests resided at Kandy, where a Church had been built and was maintained by the native converts.

At the beginning of the eighteenth century Catholicism had only 70,000 adherents. In 100 years this number has more than doubled; in 1848 it counted 113,000, and in 1852 155,000 members. This marvellous increase is easily explained. Every year, especially since 1840, a very large immigration of Hindus takes place, and it is more especially among this Hindu-Sinhalese population that Catholicism succeeds. These Hindus, Parsees, and Malabars, are more

Council would have suppressed all the subventions had it been free to do so.

[1] The traveller to whom we allude, and to whom we are indebted for part of this information is Mr. Anthony Rey, Chancellor of the French Consulate in the Mauritius.

[2] In 1836 the tomb of Don Juan Monteiro de Setnelo, Portuguese Bishop of the island, who died in 1530, was discovered at Colombo. Catholicism in Ceylon thus dates back to more than three centuries ago.

docile and laborious than the natives. They come over twice a year for the coffee harvest, crossing the Straits in *donies*, small boats of about fifty tons; and many of them remain and settle in the island. In 1852, the number of this floating population amounted to 40,000. Hence the increase of the inhabitants of Ceylon, and at the same time that of the Catholic neophytes. By a secret but strong affinity, the Hindus are more inclined to accept Catholicism than any other Christian form of worship. The Sinhalese, especially the Kandyans, remain faithful to Buddhism, just as they remain, like their ancestors, labourers and warriors.

By the side of the Christian propaganda of the churches is that of the schools, which is perhaps more powerful and penetrates deeper. In 1841 a central committee of the schools for the instruction of the Sinhalese population was established, and it unremittingly continues its functions. With a creditable spirit of tolerance the committee admitted Anglicans, Wesleyans and Catholics on the board, and their united efforts were directed, without distinction of sects, to the enlightenment and instruction of all the children received in the schools; from the academy at Colombo, and the native normal school, down to the mixed schools in which English and Sinhalese are taught, and even to the ordinary Sinhalese schools. In 1850 there were no less than 128 schools of all kinds for boys and girls, most of them under the supervision of Portuguese masters. The grant given them by government was about the same as that accorded to the clergy.[1]

[1] The Report of the committee on the reforming of the schools throughout the island is dated 9th August, 1848. The committee divided all the educational establishments into five classes: (1) the Academy of Colombo, and the normal school for the instruction of native masters; (2) the Central schools in Colombo and Kandy; (3) the elementary schools, where instruction was exclusively given in English;

Such are the forces of Christian propaganda against which Sinhalese Buddhism has to defend itself, besides those of civilization which do not cease to extend. Ceylon is one of the most beautiful colonies, if not one of the most powerful of England, and for the last ten years its prosperity has marvellously increased. The native religion must therefore necessarily lose ground in the face of a religion which brings with it such great advantages and welfare.[1]

We are far from saying that Sinhalese Buddhism is bound to destruction or even to decay; but it is certain that Christianity, particularly under the Catholic form, has already made great progress. The Buddhist clergy does not seem to prepare itself for the struggle by renewed zeal; at the most does the fanaticism of certain priests endeavour at times to rouse the population to rebellion, thereby only betraying their weakness. It is only by serious study and a return to the purity of the primitive faith that the Buddhist

(4) the mixed schools, in which the teaching was carried on partly in English and partly in Sinhalese: (5) the schools that were exclusively indigenous, in which the native language only was used. In all these schools the scholars paid for their schooling; from twelve pounds at Colombo down to three shillings a year in the Sinhalese schools. In 1849 the Government grant amounted to £10,868 sterling. In 1856 the schools contained 23,348 children.

[1] In Lord Torrington's defence of his administration against the attacks of one of his successors, Sir H. G. Ward, he furnished on this point some important and exact information. In his letter of 17th January, 1857, to the Right Hon. Mr. Labouchere, he stated that the imports, which in 1846 only reached the sum of £998,859 sterling, had successively increased, and in 1855 had attained £1,457,770. The exports had increased in a still greater proportion from £407,809 to £1,350,410 sterling. The revenues had risen from £416,407 to £476,273, while the expenditure had diminished from £498,205 to £405,609 sterling. In 1856 the revenues were £504,175, and the expenditure £457,137 sterling. The imports had risen to £2,714,565 and the exports to £1,663,612 sterling. Labour was paid at the rate of £2 to £3 a month. Cattle was represented by 840,000 animals. In the island 771,170 acres were in cultivation, 345,932 in pasture land, and 5,037,303 acres were uncultivated. In all there were 560,025 agriculturists; 49,367 workmen in the factories, and 70,886 employed in trade.

clergy would have some chance of saving their religion. But we doubt that their vitality would be equal to the effort; nor indeed is it to be desired, for although it cannot be denied that the law of the Buddha has rendered great services to these races, yet it could not be regretted if, in the natural course of things, and through a pacific and beneficent propaganda, it should be replaced by Christianity.

That day is doubtless still far off, but as it may even now be foreseen, philologists should lose no time in collecting and publishing the documents of Sinhalese history and religion, thus following in the steps of George Turnour, who has so admirably succeeded in revealing the *Mahāvansa*.

APPENDIX.

I.

FESTIVAL OF THE BUDDHA'S TOOTH IN 1858.

THE following letter, published by the *Presse*, December 6, 1858, gives some interesting information concerning the worship of the Buddha's tooth in Ceylon in the present day.

KANDY, Oct. 12, 1858.

The somewhat monotonous calm of our delightful country has been broken by one of the great festivities that Ceylon offers to the public once or twice in the course of a century: the solemn exhibition of the Buddha's tooth. The vast and beautiful pagoda of Mahiyangana, where this relic is preserved with the greatest veneration, is one of the most famous sanctuaries of the Buddhist world, and is the resort of considerable numbers of devotees, who go there every year as a pilgrimage, on the occasion of certain religious solemnities. The Buddha's tooth is seldom taken out of the mysterious kind of tabernacle in which it is enshrined in nine concentrical gold boxes, set with diamonds, rubies, and pearls; and the bonzes consent to display the relic only on such occasions as the visit of some great personage, come from afar for the express purpose of a pilgrimage to Mahiyangana.

This circumstance presented itself on the ninth of this month, when two Burmese high priests brought special letters of recommendation to the English Governor, without whose authorization, the bonzes cannot open the tabernacle. We must not forget that at the beginning of the occupation, the English Government had taken the precious tooth into its own keeping, lest, on the pretext of a public exhibition, the Sinhalese should gather together with a view to rebellion. Within the last few years it has been restored to the Temple of Mahiyangana, but on the express condition that it should not be shown without the permission of the Governor of Kandy.

The motive which determined the visit of the two illustrious pilgrims is curious enough to be worth relating. Buddhism in Ceylon has two sects of bonzes : the Siamese and the Burmese sect of Amarapura. The first one is the most numerous and the most wealthy; it possesses the finest pagodas and the largest convents in the island, and magnificently entertains the Siamese faithful who come there in pilgrimage. In its turn it sends its novices to Siam, to perfect themselves in the study of the Pāli language, and the mysterious transformations of the Buddha; hence the intercourse between the bonzes of the two countries is frequent.

The second sect has, on the contrary, few adepts; but they are remarkable for an austerity of behaviour and a fervour of devotion, which inspire the deepest respect.

These latter seldom return to their fountain-head, having no means of travelling. Nevertheless, two of them visited Burmah a few years ago, and during their stay in Ava, where the emperor received them with great honour, they learned, to their extreme surprise, that a tooth of the Buddha, eight inches long, was preserved in that city, and was the object of the greatest veneration on the part of the Burmese Buddhists.

The two pilgrims having conceived doubts as to the authenticity of this relic, declared them to their host; and the emperor thereupon commanded that all the bonzes of the capital and the neighbourhood should assemble in council to discuss this grave question, in the presence of the strangers who had raised it.

The principal argument used by the Sinhalese before the council, was founded on the inordinate length of the Burmese tooth, which was more than double that of Ceylon, the latter being recognized as undeniably authentic by all true Buddhists. They declared that not one of the sacred books contained the smallest proof that the Buddha had predestined one of his teeth to be preserved in Burmah, and they ended their demonstration by quoting a passage from the sacred book *Dāthāvansa*, in which it is positively asserted that Gautama Buddha had left no other relic on earth but the one in Dalada, now in Kandy.

In the presence of a fact so serious for the orthodoxy of the worship, the Burmese emperor decided that two of the most learned among the bonzes should go to Ceylon to examine the rival relic, and make a report on its authentic characteristics.

It was to settle this vexed question that the Burmese bonzes had come to Ceylon, and as they were furnished with credentials from their sovereign, the English Government could not refuse to allow them to examine the relic.

Sir John Braybrooke appointed the 9th of October as the day for the exhibition. When the news spread throughout the island, the enraptured population rose *en masse*, and flocked to Kandy like a swarm of locusts, cooking their food in the fields and sleeping in the open air while the ceremony was pending.

The English police had taken all the necessary precautions to guard against disorder, and although the crowd was enormous, not a single untoward incident occurred.

Externally, the Mahiyangana pagoda was decked out with flags, banners, streamers, garlands, and inscriptions, which on the dark green background of the banian trees produced a magnificent effect of colour. Internally, the temple was hung with draperies of the seven colours of the rainbow, bordered with gold braid and fringe; hundreds of lamps and chandeliers shed floods of light over the scene, although it was midday; and, lastly, on a platform, raised in the centre of the building, rose an altar, resplendent with gold and precious gems, and surmounted by a wide canopy, which was adorned with waving plumes.

At twelve o'clock the Governor, accompanied by the two Burmese pilgrims, his retinue, and a certain number of English ladies attracted by curiosity, entered the pagoda and seated himself on a platform near the altar. The preliminary ceremonies, however, took up no less than two hours, and excited a general feeling of impatience.

At last the shrill sound of a trumpet was heard, the door of the sanctuary opened and a long procession of bonzes issued forth, slowly followed by the high priest of Mahiyangana bearing the tooth of the Buddha in a crystal casket, resting on a water-lily of massive gold.

At this sight loud acclamations of *Sadhu! Sadhu!* burst from the enthusiastic throng, who fell prostrate on the ground, while the tamtams, trumpets, and flutes filled the immense dome of the pagoda with a medley of indescribable sounds.

The relic was placed on the altar under the daïs, and the Burmese were then permitted to examine it at leisure. After them the crowd passed in the greatest order round the platform till nightfall, and, thanks to the excellent measures taken by the police, the whole population was enabled to satisfy their curiosity without a single accident taking place.

The piece of ivory which is supposed to have graced the Buddha's jaw is about the size of the little finger; it is of a fine tawny yellow colour, slightly curved in the middle and thicker at one end. In the centre of the big end, which is supposed to be the crown of the tooth, is a small hole, about the size of a pin's-head; at the opposite extremity, which would answer to the root of the tooth, an irregular mark seems to indicate that a fragment of the relic has been taken off.

On looking at the transversal veining of the ivory, it is easy to see that it is only a piece of a tooth, and not a complete one; but it would not be advisable in this country to throw a doubt on the perfect authenticity of an object held in such veneration, and even regarded as miraculous.

It is doubtful whether the Burmese envoys were convinced by their examination of the relic, or that it is likely to dethrone the tooth worshipped in Ava. But if we may judge from the paltry sum they offered to the temple, two hundred rupees, we should hardly fancy so. However, their visit will doubtless attract other visits, and when the Government has ascertained by repeated experience that it can, without inconvenience or danger, allow a more frequent public exhibition of the divine tooth, the prestige attached to this worship will gradually disappear, and the Buddhists will at last be convinced *de visu* of the foolishness of their belief.

Mahāvansa, Chap. XXXVII, page 241; *Turnour's edition.*

'In the ninth year of the reign of Sirimeghavanna (A. D. 310), a certain Brahman princess brought the Dathādhātu, or tooth relic of the Buddha, hither from Kalinga, under the circumstances set forth in the Dathādhātuwansa. The monarch receiving charge of it himself, and rendering thereto, in the most reverential manner, the highest honours, deposited it in a casket of great purity. made of "phalika "stone, and lodged it in the edifice, called the Dhammachakko, built by Devanam-Piya-Tissa.

'In the first place, the rāja, expending a lac, in the height of his felicity, celebrated a Dathādhātu festival, and then he ordained that a similar festival should be annually celebrated, transferring the relic in procession to the Abhayagiri wihāra.'

II.

THE THREE COUNCILS.

The First Council.

Mahāvansa, Chap. III, page 11, Turnour's edition.

'The supreme incomparable, the vanquisher of the five deadly sins, who was gifted with five means of perception, having sojourned for forty-five years (as Buddha), and fulfilled in the utmost perfection every object of his mission to this world, in the city of Kusinārā, in the sacred arbour formed by two "Sal" trees, on the full-moon day of the month of *wesakha*, this luminary of the world was extinguished. On that spot innumerable priests, princes, Brahmans, traders, and suddras, as well as devas, assembled. There were also seven hundred thousand priests, of whom the thēra[1] Mahā-Kāṣyapa was at that time the chief.

'This high priest, having performed the funeral obsequies over the body and sacred relics of the divine Teacher, and being desirous of perpetuating his doctrines for ever, on the seventh day after the Lord of the Universe, gifted with the ten powers, had demised; recollecting the silly declaration of the priest Subadda, who had been ordained in his dotage, and moreover recollecting the footing of equality on which he had been placed by the divine Sage, by conferring on him his own sacred robes, as well as the injunctions given by him for the propagation of his doctrines; this all-accomplished disciple of the Buddha, for the purpose of holding a convocation on religion, convened five hundred priests, who had overcome the dominion of the passions, of great celebrity, versed in the nine departments of doctrinal knowledge, and perfect in every religious attribute. On account of a disqualification (however) attending the thēra Ananda, there was one deficient of that number. Subsequently the thēra Ananda, also having been entreated by the other priests to take part in the convocation, was likewise included. That convocation could not have taken place without him.

'These Universe-compassionating (disciples) having passed half

[1] Thēra, elder. Thēravāda, doctrines of the Elders, believed by orthodox Buddhists to be identical with the Three Pitakas as now existing in Ceylon; see Rhys Davids.

a month—in celebrating the funeral obsequies seven days, and in the festival of relics seven days—and knowing what was proper to be done, thus resolved: "Keeping *wassa* in the city of Rājagriha, let us there hold the convocation on religion; it cannot be permitted to other (priests) to be present."

'These disciples making their pilgrimage over Jambudīpa as mendicants, administering consolation in their affliction (at the demise of the Buddha) to the vast population spread over the various portions thereof in the month of *asala*, during the increase of the moon, being the appropriate bright season, these supports of the people in their faith reached Rājagriha, a city perfect in every sacerdotal requisite. These thēras, with Kāṣyapa for their chief, steadfast in their design, and perfect masters of the doctrines of the Supreme Buddha, having arrived at the place aforesaid to hold their *wassa*, caused, by an application to King Ajātaṣatru, repairs to be made to all the sacred buildings during the first month of *wassa*. On the completion of the repairs of the sacred edifices they thus addressed the monarch: "Now we will hold the convocation on religion." To him (the king) who inquired "What is requisite?" they replied, "A session hall." The monarch inquiring "Where?" in the place named by them—by the side of the Webhara mountain, at the entrance of the Sattapani cave—he speedily caused to be built a splendid hall, like unto that of the devas. Having in all respects perfected this hall, he had invaluable carpets spread there, corresponding with the number of the priests. In order that, being seated on the north side, the south might be faced, the inestimable, pre-eminent throne of the high priest was placed there. In the centre of that hall, facing the east, the exalted preaching pulpit, fit for the deity himself of felicitous advent, was erected.

'The king thus reported to the thēras: "Our task is performed." Those thēras then addressed Ananda, the delight (of an audience): "Ananda, to-morrow is the convocation; on account of thy being still under the dominion of human passions, thy presence there is inadmissible; exert thyself without intermission, and attain the requisite qualifications." The thēra, who had been thus enjoined, having exerted a supernatural effort and extricated himself from the dominion of human passions, attained the sanctification of *arahat*.

'On the second day of the second month of *wassa,* those disciples assembled in that splendid hall.

'Reserving for the thēra Ananda the seat appropriate to him alone, the (other) sanctified priests took their places according to their seniority. While some among them were in the act of inquiring "Where is the thēra Ananda?" in order that he might manifest to the (assembled) disciples that he had attained the sanctification of *arahat,* (at that instant) the said thēra made his appearance—emerging from the earth, and passing through the air (without touching the floor)—and took his seat in the pulpit specially reserved for him.

'All these thēras, accomplished supporters of the faith, allotted to the thēra Upāli (the elucidation of the) *Vinaya,* and to the thēra Ananda the whole of the other branches of *Dhamma.* The high priest reserved to himself (the part) of interrogating on *Vinaya;* and the ascetic thēra Upāli that of discoursing thereon. The one, seated in the high priest's pulpit, interrogated him on *Vinaya,* the other, seated in the preaching pulpit, expatiated thereon. From the manner in which the *Vinaya* was propounded by this master of that branch of religion, all these thēras, by repeating (the discourse) in chants, became perfect masters in the knowledge of *Vinaya.*

'The said high priest (Mahā-Kāṣyapa), imposing on himself (that task), interrogated on *Dhamma* him (Ananda) who, from among those who had been his auditors, was the selected guardian of the doctrines of the Supreme Ruler. In the same manner the thēra Ananda, allotting to himself that (task), exalted in the preaching pulpit, expatiated without the slightest omission on *Dhamma.* From the manner in which that sage (Ananda), accomplished in the Wēdēha, propounded the *Dhamma,* all these priests, repeating his discourse in chants, became perfect in *Dhamma.*

'Thus this convocation, held by these benefactors of mankind for the benefit of the whole world, was brought to a close in seven months, and the religion of the deity of felicitous advent was rendered effective for enduring five thousand years by the high priest Mahā-Kāṣyapa. At the close of this convocation, in the excess of its exultation, the self-balanced great earth quaked six times from the lowest abyss of the ocean.

'By various means in this world divers miracles have been performed. Because this convocation was held exclusively by the thēras, (it is called) from generation to generation the *thērīya convocation.* Having held this first convocation, and having conferred many benefits on the world, and lived the full measure of human existence (of that period), all these disciples (in due course of nature) died. In dispelling the darkness of the world these disciples became, by their supernatural gifts, the luminaries who overcame that darkness. By (the ravages of) death, like unto the desolation of a tempest, these great luminaries were extinguished. From this example, therefore, by a piously wise man, (the desire for) this life should be overcome.

'The third chapter in the *Mahāvansa*, entitled 'The First Convocation on Religion, composed equally to delight and afflict righteous men.'

The Second Council.

Mahāvansa, Chap. IV, page 15, Turnour's edition.

'Udāyibhaddaka, the perfidiously impious son of Ajātaṣatru, having put (his parent) to death, reigned sixteen years. Anūruddhaka, the son of Udāyibhaddaka, having put him to death; and the son of Anūruddhaka, named Munda, having put him to death; these perfidious, unwise (princes in succession) ruled. In the reigns of these two (monarchs) eight years elapsed. The impious Nāgadāsaka, son of Munda, having put his father to death, reigned twenty-four years. The populace of the capital, infuriated (at such conduct), designating this "a parricidal race," assembled and formally deposed Nāgadāsaka; and desirous of gratifying the whole nation, they unanimously installed in the sovereignty the eminently wise minister bearing the (historically) distinguished appellation of Susunāga. He reigned eighteen years. His son Kālāṣoka reigned twenty years. Thus in the tenth year of the reign of King Kālāṣoka a century had elapsed from the death of the Buddha.

'At that time a numerous community of priests, resident in the city of Vaiṣāli, natives of Wajji—shameless ministers of religion—pronounced the (following) ten indulgences to be allowable (to the priesthood): viz. "salt meats," "two inches," "also in villages," "fraternity," "proxy," "example," "milk whey," "beverage," "covers of seats," gold and other coined metals [1]. The thēra Yasa, having heard of this heresy, proceeded on a pilgrimage over the Wajji country. This Yasa, son of Kākandaka, the Brahman versed in the six branches of doctrinal knowledge, and powerful in his calling, repaired to that place (Vaiṣāli), devoting himself at the Mahāvansa Wihāra to the suppression of this heresy. They (the schismatic priests), having placed a golden dish filled with water in the apartment in which the *uposatha* ceremony was performed, said (to the attendant congregation of laymen), "Devotees, bestow on the priesthood at least a Kahapanan." The thēra forbade (the proceeding), exclaiming "Bestow it not; it is not allowable." They awarded to the thēra Yasa (for this interference) the sentence of *palesāraniyan*. Having by entreaty procured (from them) a messenger, he proceeded with him to the capital, and propounded to the inhabitants of the city the tenets of his own faith. The (schismatic) priests, having learned these circumstances from the messenger, proceeded thither to award to the thēra the penalty of *ukkipētan*, and took up their station surrounding his dwelling. The thēra (however) raising himself aloft, proceeded through the air to the city of Kosambiyā; from thence, speedily dispatching messengers to the priests resident in Pathēya and Avanti, and himself repairing to the Ahōgangā mountain (mountain beyond the Ganges), reported all these particulars to the thēra Sambhūta of Sāna.

'Sixty priests of Pathēya and eighty of Avanti, all sanctified characters who had overcome the dominion of sin, descended at Ahōgangā. The whole number of priests who had assembled there from various quarters amounted to ninety thousand. These sanctified personages having deliberated together, and acknowledged that the thēra Revata of Soreya, in profundity of knowledge and sanctity of character, was at that period the most illustrious, they departed thither for the purpose of appearing before him. The said thēra having attended to their statement and, being desirous (on account of his great age) of performing the journey by easy stages, departed at that instant from thence for the purpose of repairing to Vaiṣāli. On account of the importance of that mission, departing each morning at dawn, on reaching the places adapted for their accommodation, they met together again (for consultation) in the evenings. At a place (where they had so

[1] These are the opening words of the sentences descriptive of the ten new indulgences attempted to be introduced into the discipline of the Buddhistical priesthood, an explanation of which would lead to details inconvenient in this place.

assembled) the thēra Yasa, under the directions of the chief priest Sambhūta, at the close of a sermon, addressing himself to the celebrated thēra Revata, inquired what the ten (unorthodox) indulgences were. Having examined those rules, the thēra pronounced them inadmissible, and said, "Let us suppress this (schism)."

'These sinners, with the view to seducing the renowned thēra Revata to their party, collecting a vast quantity of priestly offerings, and quickly embarking in a vessel, arrived at the place where the principal priests were assembled, and at the hour of refection set forth the chant of refection. The thēra Sālhā, who was resident at that selected place, and had overcome the dominion of sin, reflecting whether the doctrine of the Pathēya priests was orthodox, it appeared to him to be so. The Mahā-Brāhma (of the world, Sudhāwasā), descending unto him (Sālhā), addressed him thus: "Adhere to that doctrine." He replied that his adherence to that faith would be steadfast. Those who had brought the priestly offerings presented themselves to the eminent thēra Revata. The thēra declined accepting the offerings, and dismissed the pupil of the sinful fraternity (who presented them).

'These shameful characters, departing thence for Vaiṣāli, and from thence repairing to the capital, Pupphāpura, thus addressed their sovereign Kālāṣoka: "We, the guardians of the dwelling of our divine Instructor, reside there in the land of Wajji, in the Mahāvana Wihāra. The priests resident in the provincial villages are hastening hither, saying 'Let us take possession of the Wihāra!' O Maharāja, prevent them." They having (thus) deceived the king, returned to Vaiṣāli.

'In the (aforesaid) selected place where the (orthodox) priests had halted unto the thēra Revata, for the purpose of suppressing the schismatic indulgences, eleven hundred and ninety thousand priests congregated. He had decided (however) not to suppress the heresy at any place but that at which it had originated. Consequently the thēras and all these priests repaired to Vaiṣāli. The deluded monarch despatched his ministers thither. Misguided, however, by the interposition of the gods, they proceeded in a different direction. The sovereign having (thus) deputed these ministers (to the priesthood) in the night, by a dream he saw that his soul was cast into the Lōkakumbiyā hell. The king was in the greatest consternation. To allay that (terror) his younger sister, the priestess Anandi, a sanctified character, who had overcome the dominion of sin, arrived, travelling through the air: "The act thou hast committed is of the most weighty import; make atonement to the orthodox ministers of the faith; uniting thyself with their cause, uphold true religion. By adopting this course peace of mind will be restored unto thee." Having thus addressed him she departed. At the very dawn of day the monarch departed to Vaiṣāli. Having reached the Mahavana Wiharā he assembled the priesthood, and having examined the controversy by listening to both parties, he decided in favour of the cause of true religion. The sovereign having made atonement to all the ministers of true religion, and having avowed his adherence to its cause, he said, "Do ye according to your judgment, provide for the due maintenance of religion;" and having extended his protection to them he departed for his capital (Pupphāpura).

'Thereupon the priesthood assembled to inquire into these indulgences; there in that convocation (however) endless and frivolous discussions arose. The thēra Revata himself then advancing into the midst of the assembly, and causing to be proclaimed the *Ubbāhikāya* rules, he made the requisite arrangements for the purpose of suppressing this heresy. By the *Ubbāhikāya* rules he selected for the suppression of the sacerdotal heresy four priests of Pāchīna and four of Pathēya. These were the four Pāchīna priests: Sabbakāmi, Sālhā, Kujjasōbhita, and Wāsabhagāmika. These were the four Pathēya priests: Revata, Sambhūta of Sāna, Yasa the son of Kākandaka, and Sumana. For the purpose of examining into these (controverted) indulgences, these eight sanctified personages repaired to Wālukarāma Wihāra, a situation so secluded (that not even the note of a bird was heard), and free from the strife of men. The high priest Revata, the chief of the interrogating party, questioned the thēra Sabbakāmi in due order on these indulgences one by one. The principal thēra Sabbakāmi, who had been thus interrogated by him (Revata), declared, "By the orthodox ordinances, all these indulgences are inadmissible."

'There (at the Wālukārama Wihāra) having in due form rejected this heresy, in the same manner in the midst of the convocation at Mahāvana Wihāra, (to which they returned), they again went through the interrogations and replies. To the ten thousand sinful priests who had put forth the ten indulgences, these principal orthodox priests awarded the penalty of degradation. Sabbakāmi was at that time high priest of the world, and had already attained a standing of 120 years in the ordination of *upasampāda.* Sabbakāmi, Sālhā, Revata, Kujjasōbhita, Yasa the son of Kākandaka, and Sambhuta a native of Sāna—these six thēras were the disciples of the thēra Ananda. Wasābhagāmika and Sumana, these two thēras were the disciples of the thēra Anurudha. These eight pious priests in aforetimes had seen the deity who was the successor of the former Buddhas.

'The priests who had assembled were twelve hundred thousand; of all these priests, the thēra Revata was at that time a leader. Thereupon, for the purpose of securing the permanency of the true faith, this Revata thēra, the leader of these priests, selected from those who were gifted with the qualifications for sanctification, and were the depositaries of the doctrines contained in the Three (Pitakas), seven hundred sanctified disciples (of the Buddha, for the purpose of holding the convocation on religion). All these thēras, having Revata for their chief, protected by King Kālāṣoka, held the convocation on religion at the Wālukārama Wihāra. According to the form observed in interrogation and illustration on the former occasion, conducting this meeting precisely in the same manner, it was terminated in eight months. Thus these thēras, who were indefatigable in their calling, and absolved from all human afflictions, having held the second convocation on religion, in due course attained *Nibbuti* (Nirvāna).

'Hence bearing in mind the subjection to death of the disciples of the Saviour of the Universe, who were endowed with the sanctification of *arahat*—who had attained the state of ultimate beatitude—and had conferred blessings on the beings of the three *bhawas*, recollecting also the liability of the rest of mankind to an interminable transmigration, let (the reader) steadfastly devote himself (to a life of righteousness).

'The fourth chapter in the *Mahāvansa*, entitled The Second Convocation on Religion, composed to delight and afflict righteous men.'

The Third Council.

Mahāvansa, Chap. V, page 41, Turnour's edition.

The *Mahāvansa* first relates at great length some of the principal events of the reign of Aṣoka, the grandson of Chandragupta (the *Sandracottus* of the Greeks); then it proceeds to relate the conversion of this king, who, after he had embraced Buddhism, took the surname of Dharmāṣoka, that is Aṣoka, Protector of the Faith. Finally, it mentions the third Council, convened to put down a number of heresies; and the *Mahāvansa* continues as follows:—

'The king within seven days, having sent two yakkhos, caused all the priests in Jambudīpa to be assembled. On the seventh day, going to the splendid temple built by himself, he directed the whole priesthood, without any omission, to assemble. Seated together with the thēra within the curtain, and calling up to him one by one the heretic priests, "Lord," inquired the sovereign, "of what religion was the deity of felicitous advent?" Each, according to his own faith, propounded the *Sassata* and other creeds (as the religion of the Buddha). The king caused all those heretic priests to be expelled from the priesthood. The whole of the priests thus degraded was sixty thousand. He then asked the orthodox priests, "Of what religion is the deity of happy advent?" They replied, "The religion of investigated (truth)." The sovereign then addressed the thēra: "Lord, is the Supreme Buddha himself of that *vibhajja* faith?" The thēra having replied "Yes," and the king having heard that answer, overjoyed, "Lord," he exclaimed, "if by any act the priesthood can recover their own purity, by that act let the priesthood (now) perform the *upōsatha*."

'Having thus addressed the thēra, and conferring the royal protection on the priesthood, he re-entered the celebrated capital. The priesthood, restored to unanimity of communion, then held the *upōsatha*.

'But the thēra from many asankya of priests selected a thousand priests of sanctified character—possessing the six perfections of religious knowledge, and versed in the *Tripitika* and perfect in the four sacerdotal qualifications—for the purpose of holding a convocation. By them the convocation on religion was held; according as the thēras Mahā-Kāṣyapa and Yasa had performed the convocations (in their time), in like manner the thēra Tissa (performed) this one. In that hall of convocation the thēra Tissa preached a discourse illustrative of the means of suppressing doubts on points of faith.

'Thus, under the auspices of King Aṣoka, this convocation on religion was brought to a close in nine months by these priests. In the seventh year of the reign of this king, this all-perfect minister of religion, aged seventy years, conducted in the utmost perfection this great convocation on religion and the *pavaranan.* At the conclusion of the convocation, on account of the re-establishment of religion, the great earth, as if shouting its *Sādhu*, quaked.

'The instrument of this mission having left his supreme residence in the Brāhma-loka world, and descended to this impure human world, for the advancement of religion;—who, capable of advancing the cause of religion, would demur?

'The fifth chapter in the *Mahāvansa*, entitled The Third Convocation on Religion, composed alike to delight and afflict religious men.'

The *Atthakathā*, a Sinhalese work much older than the *Mahāvansa*, and which is a very extensive commentary on the *Pitakattaya*, the Three Baskets of the Buddhist writings in Ceylon, has also preserved the history of the Three Councils, as far as regards the parts relating to the Vinaya, the Samantapāsādikā. The *Atthakathā* returns to the subject a second time in another of its articles called Sumangala Vilāsini, a commentary on the *Digha-nikāya*, one of the five works which compose the Sūtra-Pitāka of Ceylon. George Turnour has translated from the Sumangala Vilāsini all that treats of the first Council (*Journal of the Bengal Asiatic Society*, vol. vi, part ii, page 510 and following). We do not reproduce the lengthy details of the Sumangala Vilāsini, because they would not add anything to what we already know. This account had moreover a special purpose, and was evidently written to prove the authenticity of the Sinhalese *Pitakattaya* and the *Atthakathā*, which it asserts was written at the time of the first Council, directly after the death of the Buddha. This origin is highly improbable. It seems more likely that the *Tripitaka* and the *Atthakathā* were brought by Mahinda, son of Dharmāṣoka, when he came to convert Sinhala to the Tathāgata's faith. The *Atthakathā* in its present form was translated from Sinhalese into Pāli by Buddhaghosa from the year 410 to 432 of the Christian era.

THE END.

SIR JOHN LUBBOCK'S

HUNDRED BOOKS

ARRANGED

ACCORDING TO PRICES AND ACCORDING TO SUBJECTS.

GEORGE ROUTLEDGE & SONS, LIMITED,

LONDON, MANCHESTER, AND NEW YORK.

JUNE, 1895.

LETTER FROM SIR JOHN LUBBOCK.

May 12th, 1895.

MY DEAR SIRS,

You have indeed carried out the issue of the "Hundred Books" with great energy and success.

I did not think that you would have been able to manage it in so short a time as four years.

On all accounts I cordially hope that the result may come up to your just expectations.

I am, my Dear Sirs,

Yours sincerely,

JOHN LUBBOCK.

Messrs. GEORGE ROUTLEDGE & SONS, Limited.

A CLASSIFIED LIST OF

SIR JOHN LUBBOCK'S HUNDRED BOOKS.

ARRANGED ACCORDING TO PRICES.

Price 15s.

86 Humboldt's Travels. 3 vols.

Price 10s. 6d.

71 Hume's History of England. 3 vols.

Price 8s. 6d.

90 Green's Short History of the English People

Price 7s.

33 Gibbon's Decline and Fall of the Roman Empire. 2 vols.

Price 6s. each.

8 Smiles's Self Help
80 Œuvres de Molière
88 Darwin's Origin of Species

(3)

Price 5s. each.

26 Pendennis. By W. M. THACKERAY
49 Malory's Mort d'Arthure
78 Xenophon's Anabasis and Memorabilia
81 Sakoontala; or, The Lost Ring. Translated by Sir MONIER MONIER-WILLIAMS
83 & 84 Livy, Books I. to V.; Tacitus's Germania and Agricola
91 Spinoza's Tractatus Theologico —Politicus, etc.
—94 St. Hilaire's Buddha ←
98 & 99 The Ramayana and the Mahabharata

(8)

Price 3s. 6d. each.

1 Herodotus. Translated from the Text of Baehr, by HENRY CARY, M.A.
6 Mills' Political Economy
7 Carlyle's French Revolution
9 White's Natural History of Selborne

Price 3s. 6d. each—*continued.*

10 The Pickwick Papers By CHARLES DICKENS
11 The Shi King. Translated from the Chinese by WILLIAM JENNINGS, M.A.
12 Pope's Homer's Iliad and Odyssey
14 Montaigne's Essays
15 Mills' System of Logic
16 Lewes's Biographical History of Philosophy
17 Thackeray's Vanity Fair
18 The Shah Nameh, the Persian Poet, of Firdausi
19 Captain Cook's Three Voyages Round the World
22 Sale's Koran
23 Charles Knight's Shakspere
24 Boswell's Life of Dr. Johnson
25 Scott's Ivanhoe. With Steel Plates
27 Thucydides. Translated by W. SMITH, D.D.
28 David Copperfield By CHARLES DICKENS
31 Adam Smith's Wealth of Nations
32 Chaucer's Canterbury Tales
35 Don Quixote. With Illus.
37 Robinson Crusoe. Illustrated by J. D. WATSON
38 Dryden's Poetical Works
39 Langhorne's Plutarch
40 The Last Days of Pompeii. By Lord LYTTON
41 Bunyan's Pilgrim's Progress. Illustrated by J. D. WATSON
43 Aristotle's Ethics
44 Wake's Apostolical Fathers
47 Pascal's Thoughts on Religion
50 Emerson's Essays
51 The Nibelungen Lied
52 Selections from Burke
53 Spenser's Faerie Queene
56 Scott's Poetical Works
57 The Arabian Nights' Entertainments
62 Milton's Poetical Works

GEORGE ROUTLEDGE AND SONS, LIMITED.

CLASSIFIED LIST OF

SIR JOHN LUBBOCK'S HUNDRED BOOKS.

ARRANGED ACCORDING TO PRICES.

Price 15s.

86 Humboldt's Travels. 3 vols.

Price 10s. 6d.

71 Hume's History of England 3 vols.

Price 8s. 6d.

90 Green's Short History of the English People

Price 7s.

33 Gibbon's Decline and Fall of the Roman Empire. 2 vols.

Price 6s. each.

8 Smiles's Self Help
80 Œuvres de Molière
88 Darwin's Origin of Species

(3)

Price 5s. each.

26 Pendennis. By W. M. THACKERAY
49 Malory's Mort d'Arthure
78 Xenophon's Anabasis and Memorabilia
81 Sakoontala; or, The Lost Ring. Translated by Sir MONIER MONIER-WILLIAMS
83 & 84 Livy, Books I. to V.; Tacitus's Germania and Agricola
91 Spinoza's Tractatus Theologico—Politicus, etc.
94 St. Hilaire's Buddha
98 & 99 The Ramayana and the Mahabharata

(8)

Price 3s. 6d. each.

1 Herodotus. Translated from the Text of Baehr, by HENRY CARY, M.A.
6 Mills' Political Economy
7 Carlyle's French Revolution
9 White's Natural History of Selborne

Price 3s. 6d. each—*continued.*

10 The Pickwick Papers By CHARLES DICKENS
11 The Shi King. Translated from the Chinese by WILLIAM JENNINGS, M.A.
12 Pope's Homer's Iliad and Odyssey
14 Montaigne's Essays
15 Mills'. System of Logic
16 Lewes's Biographical History of Philosophy
17 Thackeray's Vanity Fair
18 The Shah Nameh, the Persian Poet, of Firdausi
19 Captain Cook's Three Voyages Round the World
22 Sale's Koran
23 Charles Knight's Shakspere
24 Boswell's Life of Dr. Johnson
25 Scott's Ivanhoe. With Steel Plates
27 Thucydides. Translated by W. SMITH, D.D.
28 David Copperfield By CHARLES DICKENS
31 Adam Smith's Wealth of Nations
32 Chaucer's Canterbury Tales
35 Don Quixote. With Illus.
37 Robinson Crusoe. Illustrated by J. D. WATSON
38 Dryden's Poetical Works
39 Langhorne's Plutarch
40 The Last Days of Pompeii. By Lord LYTTON
41 Bunyan's Pilgrim's Progress. Illustrated by J. D. WATSON
43 Aristotle's Ethics
44 Wake's Apostolical Fathers
47 Pascal's Thoughts on Religion
50 Emerson's Essays
51 The Nibelungen Lied
52 Selections from Burke
53 Spenser's Faerie Queene
56 Scott's Poetical Works
57 The Arabian Nights' Entertainments
62 Milton's Poetical Works

A CLASSIFIED LIST OF

SIR JOHN LUBBOCK'S HUNDRED BOOKS.

ARRANGED ACCORDING TO PRICES.

Price 3s. 6d. each—*continued.*

64 Keble's Christian Year
65 Macaulay's Essays and Lays of Ancient Rome
68 Wordsworth's Poetical Works. Illustrated
69, 95 & 96 Plays of Aristophanes, Sophocles, and Euripides, in one volume
72 Locke on the Human Understanding
73 Addison's Essays
75 Hume's Essays
76 Cicero — Offices, Friendship and Old Age
85 The Antiquary. By Sir WALTER SCOTT
89 Westward Ho! By CHARLES KINGSLEY
92 Adam Bede. By GEORGE ELIOT
100 The Bible

(49)

Price 2s. 6d. each.

2 Darwin's Voyage of a Naturalist
45 Bacon's Novum Organum
46 Demosthenes on the Crown. Lord BROUGHAM
48 Berkeley's Human Knowledge
54 Gulliver's Travels
58 Burns's Poetical Works
60 Longfellow's Dante
63 Goethe's Faust
74 Taylor's Holy Living and Dying

(9)

Price 2s. each.

29 Byron's Childe Harold
30 The Plays of Æschylus. Translated by R. POTTER
34 Dialogues of Plato. HENRY CARY, M.A.
36 Sheridan's Plays
42 Carlyle's Past and Present

Price 2s. each—*continued.*

59 The Imitation of Christ. THOMAS A KEMPIS
61 Plays from Molière. By ENGLISH DRAMATISTS
66 Butler's Analogy of Religion
67 Lord Lytton's Horace
70 & 97 Gray's Poetical Works, Pope's Essays on Man, etc.
77 Hesiod
93 The Analects of Confucius. Translated by WILLIAM JENNINGS, M.A.

(12)

Price 1s. 6d. each.

3 The Meditations of Marcus Aurelius
4 The Teaching of Epictetus
5 Bacon's Essays
13 Dryden's Virgil's Æneid
20 Goldsmith's Vicar of Wakefield
21 Schiller's William Tell
55 Aristotle's Politics
79 Voltaire—Zadig et Micromegas
82 Descartes — Discours de la Méthode
87 Confessions of St. Augustine

(10)

Price of the 100 *Books in* 100 *Vols.*

	£	s.	d.
1 at 15s.	0	15	0
1 at 10s. 6d. ...	0	10	6
1 at 8s. 6d. ...	0	8	6
1 at 7s.	0	7	0
3 at 6s.	0	18	0
8 at 5s.	2	0	0
49 at 3s. 6d. ...	8	11	6
9 at 2s. 6d. ...	1	2	6
12 at 2s.	1	4	0
10 at 1s. 6d. ...	0	15	0
	£16	12	0

A CLASSIFIED LIST OF

SIR JOHN LUBBOCK'S HUNDRED BOOKS.

ARRANGED ACCORDING TO SUBJECTS.

Essays, Letters, & Speeches.

		s.	d.
5	Bacon's Essays	1	6
8	Smiles's Self Help	6	0
14	Montaigne's Essays	3	6
42	Carlyle's Past and Present	2	0
50	Emerson's Essays	3	6
52	Selections from Burke	3	6
65	Macaulay's Essays	3	6
73	Addison's Essays	3	6
75	Hume's Essays	3	6
76	Cicero—Offices, Friendship, and Old Age	3	6

(10)

Fiction.

10	The Pickwick Papers. By CHARLES DICKENS	3	6
17	Vanity Fair. By W. M. THACKERAY	3	6
20	Goldsmith's Vicar of Wakefield	1	6
25	Ivanhoe. By Sir WALTER SCOTT	3	6
26	Pendennis. By W. M. THACKERAY	5	0
28	David Copperfield. By CHARLES DICKENS	3	6
35	Don Quixote	3	6
37	Robinson Crusoe	3	6
40	The Last Days of Pompeii. By LORD LYTTON	3	6
54	Gulliver's Travels	2	6
57	The Arabian Nights Entertainments	3	6
79	Voltaire—Zadig et Micromegas	1	6
85	The Antiquary. By Sir WALTER SCOTT	3	6
89	Westward Ho! By CHARLES KINGSLEY	3	6
92	Adam Bede. By GEORGE ELIOT	3	6

(15)

History and Biography.

		s.	d.
1	Herodotus	3	6
7	Carlyle's French Revolution	3	6
24	Boswell's Life of Johnson	3	6
27	Thucydides	3	6
33	Gibbon's Decline and Fall of the Roman Empire, 2 vols.	7	0
39	Plutarch's Lives	3	6
46	Demosthenes on the Crown	2	6
71	Hume's History of England, 3 vols.	10	6
78	Xenophon's Anabasis and Memorabilia	5	0
83 & 84	Livy—Books I. to V., Tacitus's Germania and Agricola	5	0
90	Green's Short History of the English People	8	6

(12)

Legendary.

18	The Shah Nameh of the Persian Poet Firdausi	3	6
49	Malory's Mort d'Arthure	5	0
51	The Nibelungen Lied	3	6
98, 99	The Ramayana, The Mahabharata } 1 vol.	5	0

(5)

Philosophy.

16	Lewes's Biographical History of Philosophy	3	6
45	Bacon's Novum Organum	2	6
48	Berkeley's Human Knowledge	2	6
55	Aristotle's Politics	1	6
72	Locke on the Human Understanding	3	6
82	Descarte's Discours de la Methode	1	6

(6)

GEORGE ROUTLEDGE AND SONS, LIMITED.

A CLASSIFIED LIST OF

SIR JOHN LUBBOCK'S HUNDRED BOOKS.

ARRANGED ACCORDING TO SUBJECTS.

Poetry and the Drama.

		s.	d.
11	The Shi-King—The Old "Poetry Classic" of the Chinese	3	6
12	Homer's Iliad and Odyssey	3	6
13	Virgil's Æneid	1	6
21	Schiller's William Tell	1	6
23	Shakspere's Plays and Poems	3	6
29	Byron's Childe Harold	2	0
30	The Plays of Æschylus	2	0
32	Chaucer's Canterbury Tales	3	6
36	Sheridan's Plays	2	0
38	Dryden's Poetical Works	3	6
53	Spenser's Faerie Queene	3	6
56	Scott's Poetical Works	3	6
58	Burns's Poetical Works	2	6
60	Longfellow's Dante	2	6
61	Plays from Molière by English Dramatists	2	0
62	Milton's Poetical Works	3	6
63	Goethe's Faust	2	6
67	Lord Lytton's Horace	2	0
68	Wordsworth's Poetical Works	3	6
69	Plays of Aristophanes }		
95 & 96	Plays of Sophocles and Euripides }	3	6
70 & 97	Gray's Poetical Works & Pope's Essay on Man, &c. }	2	0
77	Hesiod	2	0
80	Œuvres de Molière	6	0
81	Sakoontala, or the Lost Ring Translated by Sir MONIER MONIER-WILLIAMS	5	0

(27)

Religion and Morals.

		s.	d.
3	The Meditations of Marcus Aurelius	1	6
4	The Teaching of Epictetus	1	6
22	The Koran	3	6
34	Dialogues of Plato	2	0
41	Bunyan's Pilgrim's Progress	3	6
43	Aristotle's Ethics	3	6
44	Wake's Apostolical Fathers	3	6

Religion and Morals—continued.

		s.	d.
47	Pascal's Thoughts on Religion	3	6
59	Thomas à Kempis—The Imitation of Christ	2	0
64	Keble's Christian Year	3	6
66	Butler's Analogy of Religion	2	0
74	Taylor's Holy Living and Dying	2	6
87	St. Augustine's Confessions	1	6
91	Spinoza's Tractatus Theologico-Politicus	5	0
93	The Analects of Confucius	2	0
94	St. Hilaire's Buddha	5	0
100	The Bible	3	6

(17)

Science.

		s.	d.
6	Mill's Political Economy	3	6
9	White's Natural History of Selborne	3	6
15	Mill's System of Logic	3	6
31	Adam Smith's Wealth of Nations	3	6
88	Darwin's Origin of Species	6	0

(5)

Voyage and Travel.

		s.	d.
2	Darwin's Voyage of a Naturalist	2	6
19	Captain Cook's Three Voyages	3	6
86	Humboldt's Travels, 3 vols.	15	0

(3)

Summary.

Essays, Letters, and Speeches	10
Fiction	15
History and Biography	12
Legendary	5
Philosophy	6
Poetry and the Drama	27
Religion and Morals	17
Science	5
Voyage and Travel	3
	100

GEORGE ROUTLEDGE AND SONS, LIMITED.